Global Sport Marketing

This book is not an official publication of the IOC or USOC.

D1451860

Titles in the Sport Management Library

— • —

Case Studies in Sport Marketing

— • —

Developing Successful Social Media Plans in Sport Organizations

— • —

Developing Successful Sport Marketing Plans, 4th Edition

— • —

Developing Successful Sport Sponsorship Plans, 4th Edition

— • —

Economics of Sport, 2nd Edition

— • —

Foundations of Sport Management, 3rd Edition

— • —

Fundamentals of Sport Marketing, 4th Edition

— • —

Law in Sport: Concepts and Cases, 4th Edition

— • —

Media Relations in Sport, 4th Edition

— • —

Sponsorship for Sport Managers

— • —

Sport Facility Management:
Organizing Events and Mitigating Risks, 2nd Edition

— • —

Sport Governance in the Global Community

— • —

Ticket Operations and Sales Management in Sport

For an updated list of Sport Management Library titles please visit

www.fitpublishing.com

Global Sport Marketing:

Sponsorship, Ambush Marketing, and the Olympic Games

Norm O'Reilly, PhD
Ohio University

Richard W. Pound, Esq
Stikeman Elliot LLP

Rick Burton, MBA
Syracuse University

Benoît Séguin, PhD
University of Ottawa

Michelle K. Brunette, PhD Candidate
Nipissing University

FiT
PUBLISHING

A Division of the International Center
for Performance Excellence
West Virginia University
375 Birch Street, WVU-CPASS
PO Box 6116
Morgantown, WV 26506-6116
www.fitpublishing.com

Library of Congress Card Catalog Number: 2015933050

ISBN: 978-1-935412-43-4

Cover Design: Bellerophon Productions

Front Cover Photo: Danny Birrell Photography.

Back Cover Photos, from left to right: International Law and Order Photo © Tomloel | Dreamstime.com; Soccer Globe Photo © Sextoacto | Dreamstime.com; The Gold Coast Commonwealth Games 2018 Photo © Lucidwaters | Dreamstime.com; and Mobile Payment Concept Photo © Choneschones | Dreamstime.com.

Production Editor: Nita Shippy

Copyeditor: Mark Slider

Proofreader: Geoffrey Fuller

Indexer: Geoffrey Fuller

Typesetter: Bellerophon Productions

Printed by: Sheridan Books, Inc.

10 9 8 7 6 5 4 3 2 1

FiT Publishing
A Division of the International Center for Performance Excellence
West Virginia University
375 Birch Street, WVU-CPASS
PO Box 6116
Morgantown, WV 26506-6116
800.477.4348 (toll free)
304.293.6888 (phone)
304.293.6658 (fax)
Email: fitcustomerservice@mail.wvu.edu
Website: www.fitpublishing.com

Contents

Contents

Acknowledgments

A book of this scope and specificity—even with five authors—does not come to fruition without the help and support of many personal and professional contacts.

As a group, we called on colleagues, former students and current students to help us along the way and to provide us with content area expertise at key points in the book. We'd like to acknowledge here those chapter co-authors and case study co-authors who provided impactful content to the book. A sincere thank you from us to Khanh Be (Chapter 1 Case Study), Lia Taha Cheng (Chapter 2 Case Study), Francois Robert (Chapter 2 Case Study), Lane MacAdam (Chapter 3), Patrick Ryan (Chapter 9), Amanda Fowler (Chapter 8), Teddi Firmi (Chapter 14), and Dana Ellis (Chapters 12 and 13). The work of Margie Chetney, research assistant, is also noted.

A passion for the Olympic Games and global sport marketing usually means weeks, if not months, away from family while participating, administering, managing, or volunteering at global sport. Thus, we issue our sincere thanks and love to our respective support networks of family and friends, who put up with late nights and absenteeism. Specifically, we'd like to thank Nadege, Emma, Kian, Thomas, Leland, Barb, Chantal, Genevieve, Marc-Andre, Alexandre, Nellie, Malin, Jamie, and Claude.

The authors would also like to thank Thomas Bach of the International Olympic Committee, Emilio Collins of the National Basketball Association, and Ricardo Fort of Visa Inc. for their time and support in writing forewords to the book. Finally, the authors recognize the photography excellence of Andrew Burton and thank him for his contributions to the book.

Foreword

Lausanne, July 2015

Commercial support for the Olympic Games can be traced all the way back to the very first modern Games in Athens, Greece, in 1896. The IOC remains a privately funded, independent organization, and as such, the support of the business community for the IOC, the Olympic Games, and the Olympic Movement is essential.

The Olympic Games have grown over the decades to become more popular than ever, and this is in large part due to the financial, technical, and promotional support of our broadcast partners and our global sponsors. In the last two editions of the Olympic Games, London 2012 and Sochi 2014, we witnessed record global audiences of 3.6 billion and 2.1 billion respectively, with more hours of Olympic sports coverage made available to more people in more countries than ever before.

With 93 percent global brand recognition, the appeal and awareness of the Olympic Games remain amongst the highest for any event or brand in the world.

Thanks to the financial support of our partners, the IOC enjoys commercial success. We are on course to deliver record revenues for the benefit of the whole Olympic Movement, which includes future organizers of the Games; National Olympic Committees, their teams and their athletes; and International Sports Federations.

The IOC redistributes more than 90 per cent of its revenues to sport and to the athletes. This means that the IOC invests the equivalent of more than three million dollars a day—every single day of the year?to support worldwide sport at all levels.

In this book, the authors tell the story of Olympic marketing, sponsorship, and ambush marketing within the broad context of global sport marketing. The Olympic Games have come to the forefront of sports marketing over recent decades. Key concepts of sports marketing, for example global sponsorship and innovative sponsorship activation, grew to prominence in and around the Olympic Games and have many of their roots linked to the activities of Olympic sponsors of the Games.

The fact that the book is written by a group of authors that includes Dick Pound, International Olympic Committee Member and past Vice-President of the IOC, and Rick Burton, past Chief Marketing Officer of the United States Olympic Committee, provides deep insight into the workings of marketing in this context.

This book is an important part of the literature on Olympic marketing. I hope it will be used widely to continue to grow the effective and appropriate promotion of sports marketing strategies globally.

—Thomas Bach
President
International Olympic Committee

Foreword

Next year, the National Basketball Association (NBA) will celebrate its 70th season, and our league has never had more of a global footprint than we do today. With more than a dozen offices around the world, games broadcast in over 200 countries and territories, and nearly 100 current NBA players of international origin, basketball continues to be one of the most popular sports in the world. Our global ascendance hit a turning point at the 1992 Barcelona Olympics, where for the first time in history NBA players competed on the Olympic stage, with the legendary Dream Team easily winning gold.

Global expansion of the NBA continues to this day, with targeted marketing initiatives and countless basketball participation programs staged around the world. My colleagues and I coordinate global marketing partnerships and help the league align with some of the most well respected corporate brands to amplify league marketing, engage fans, and celebrate the game. Sponsorship is a critically important aspect of our global growth and requires a deep understanding of the tenets of global sports marketing, including sales, activation, media, and rapidly evolving consumer behaviors.

Professor Norm O'Reilly of Ohio University—my alma mater—grasps these concepts in a deeply meaningful way. So when he asked me to write a foreword for this book, I was excited to participate. He and his team of highly accomplished authors have put together an insightful and comprehensive book on the global sport marketplace. In the pages that follow, you will find a solid mix of critical fundamentals, case studies, and expert insight into marketing and sponsorship. I hope you not only enjoy it but are also able to apply its lessons to your own role in the sports marketing industry.

—Emilio Collins
Executive Vice President, Global Marketing Partnerships
National Basketball Association

Foreword

As a fellow student of sport business, it is my pleasure to write this foreword to this much needed work that takes a global approach to looking at sport marketing. The team of authors represent a group of experts, who bring a variety of perspectives—necessary to truly provide a reference guide to marketing in such a complex space. Here at Visa, our link to global sport marketing is through our sponsorship of the Olympic Games, which we activate all over the world.

Sponsorships—and in particular Olympic sponsorships—can drive consumer passion and business growth. If activated in the right way, at the right time, they have the power to translate affinity for the sport to brand loyalty and product adoption. This is what makes the investments pay off for Visa and its clients.

Since 1986, we have been a proud worldwide sponsor of the Olympic Games. We are the exclusive payment services partner of the International Olympic Committee and the only card accepted at the Olympic Games. Visa believes in the values of the Olympic movement and its unique ability to engage the world in a way that is positive and inspirational. The Olympic Games provide the world with an opportunity to celebrate the athletes' achievements, a great metaphor for every human being.

Thanks to our association with the Olympics, our brand is more recognized, trusted, and appreciated by people around the world. When they realize Visa supports the Games, they like us better and use our products more often. Sponsoring major global sport properties like the Olympic Games makes good business sense for Visa and our clients.

Our story at Visa is inspired by acceptance and access. Through our sponsorship, we help facilitate the development and advancement of the payments in host countries. The universality of our brand message and product portfolio—providing the best way to pay, and be paid, for everyone, everywhere—is a story we can continue to tell for years to come through our partnership with the Olympic Games.

In today's world, where brand and trust mean so much, the marketing of the Olympic Games and other global sport properties requires skilled, informed, and talented business experts trained in our discipline. This book provides deep insight and background into many of these and should be read closely by those seeking to enter into our field.

Enjoy the read.

All the Best,

—Ricardo Fort

Senior Vice President, Global Brand, Product and Sponsorship Marketing

Visa Inc.

1

Introduction and Introductory Case Study

HISTORY OF THE BOOK

Although it is uncommon, but not unheard of, to have a team of five main authors on a book, we believe that the team who came together to pen this work provides a necessary combination of experience, youth, knowledge, passion, and study. It brings a blend of athletic, academic, professional, and executive experiences along with a variety of backgrounds to a global topic that demands such. Within the group, we have PhDs, a law degree, an IOC member, an MBA, two accountants, and a variety of fields of study. We have written numerous books, manuscripts, industry reports, and theses. Professionally, we have experience working for international and national sport organizations, national Olympic committees, international federations, and provincial/state sport organizations, marketing agencies, and sponsors of sport. Athletically, we have an Olympian, an Ironman, two Commonwealth Games participants, and experience as high performance athletes in swimming, diving, ringette, Nordic skiing, cycling, and distance running. As a group, we have attended more than 40 Olympic and Paralympic Games and countless professional, national, and domestic sport events in almost every imaginable capacity.

When the five of us came together on this book and topic, we felt we could share knowledge and insights into the quickly globalizing sport marketing industry, with particular emphasis on three core elements that are highly relevant to our industry: (i) Olympic marketing, (ii) sport sponsorship, and (iii) ambush marketing. Although these elements are far from mutually exclusive, each does have its own body of literature and domain of practice. Some elements (e.g., marketing) are well-established academically and practically, while others (e.g., ambush marketing) are still characterized by a high degree of uncertainty. So, under the umbrella of global sport marketing, we decided to write this book based on our mix of academic knowledge, practical experience, case examples, and executive insights. It is intended to provide useful direction to scholars and practitioners alike, and ends with a roadmap of our suggested path for the future of these subfields.

The book is written with two specific target readers in mind. First, for those who seek to work in global sport (i.e., an aspiring international sports professional), the book is written to provide you with tools, knowledge, inside information, and practical examples to help you succeed. Second, for those already working in global sport, the cases, research, concepts, and executive contributions are designed to help you continue to further your career. In addition, we hope that others outside of these two groups, such as fans of Olympic sport and those with an interest in marketing, generally, may also find the book to be informative.

STRUCTURE OF THE BOOK

In order to share the content relating to the important issues inherent in global sport marketing, the Olympic Games, and ambush marketing, the book is laid out in three parts, each with its own theme and each building on the previous one. The first section lays the core foundation for the following two, which delve more deeply into sponsorship and, then, ambush marketing. A final chapter summarizes the previous chapters and presents a roadmap for sponsors, ambushers, and the Olympic Movement by which to best navigate the future.

Following the introductory chapter—which presents an overview and illustrative case of global marketing—the first part of the book provides the underlying foundations and core concepts for the later parts and summary roadmap. Part I includes specific chapters to provide in-depth content on the marketing, sport, legal, and Olympic concepts that are necessary to explore sponsorship and ambush marketing in Parts II and III. Chapter 2 kicks off Part I by outlining the key principles and concepts of global sport marketing. Chapters 3 to 5 outline the landscape and market of global sport, while Chapters 6 and 7 support the importance of effective leadership in the Olympic Games and National Olympic Committees. Chapters 8 and 9 introduce international sport law, Olympic marketing, and the convergence of the two areas.

Part II explores the marketing tactic of sponsorship, a core aspect of the book and one of increasing use and effectiveness in practice. Part II begins with Chapter 10, which positions sponsorship within the promotional mix available to marketers, followed by a deeper exploration of the sponsorship mix and the challenges facing organizations where sponsorship is prevalent. In Chapter 11, we present a tangible, grounded view of sponsorship, called 'Olympic Sport Sponsorship Sales: An NOC Perspective, focused on the practical reality and day-to-day challenges that face marketers working on sponsorships, be they sponsor, property, or agency. Part II finishes with Chapters 11 and 12 to explore lessons we can draw from the history of Olympic sponsorship from 1896 to present.

In a manner similar to Part II, Part III explores a key threat to sponsorship—ambush marketing—in detail. Part III includes five specific chapters. The first two introduce ambush marketing and provide a deep assessment of it (Chapters 14 and 15). Chapter 16 explores how sponsors and properties should respond to ambush marketing, followed by cases of ambushes at the Olympic Games (Chapter 17). Part III ends with a deeper exploration of ambush marketing to provide clear illustrations of various aspects and situations in which ambush can occur (Chapter 18). Finally, Chapter 19 draws a summary from Parts I, II, and III in order to provide recommendations to lead the field into the future.

DEFINING GLOBAL SPORT MARKETING

© Andrew Burton

Global Sport Marketing, as written, includes three individual words, each with its own contextual meaning. First, *global* refers to international or multinational or the ability to transcend borders. As a practical matter, it refers to a lens that is outside of a particular country, which although it sounds intuitive, has dramatic implications for any organization on a number of levels such as language, border crossing, tax implications, culture, citizenship, and more. For the best understanding of this book, readers must think beyond their own home countries.

Second, though we recognize that scholars have struggled to find consensus for descriptions that distinguish between sport, physical activity, recreation, and play, in this book, we use the term *sport* when our focus is on physical (and sometimes mental) activity that is organized and structured, usually with specific rules of play and competition. Our view is part of a growing understanding that sport is a physical and competitive pursuit in which a "winner" is determined. More easily operationalized, the term *Olympic sport* is used to include all of the sports on the programs of the Olympic Summer Games and the Olympic Winter Games. In the 2013–2016 Olympic quadrennial, 35 sports were considered official Olympic Sports, with IOC-recognized international federations (IF) that were responsible for development of each sport, as listed in Table 1.

The Olympic Sports and International Federations listed in Table 1 include many of the most influential sport organizations on the planet. Conceptually, an IF is a not-for-profit organization, which acts as the global steward for the health, development, growth and high-performance elements of its sport throughout the world. Its members are the National Sport Organizations (NSOs) of that sport (e.g., Athletics Canada or Korean Baseball Organization) and it is the rights holder in respect of any world championship event in that sport. Readers should note that the 35 Olympic sports listed in Table 1 may be subject to changes soon, as the IOC under the presidency of Thomas Bach, is

Table 1.1. List of Recognized International Federations		
Official Olympic Sport	**International Federation**	**Initial**
Aquatics	Fédération Internationale de Natation	FINA
Archery	World Archery Federation	WA
Athletics	International Association of Athletics Federations	IAAF
Badminton	Badminton World Federation	BWF
Basketball	International Basketball Federation	FIBA
Biathlon	International Biathlon Union	IBU
Bobsleigh	Fédération Internationale de Bobsleigh et de Tobogganing	FIBT
Boxing	International Boxing Association	AIBA
Canoe/Kayak	International Canoe Federation	ICF
Curling	World Curling Federation	WCF
Cycling	International Cycling Union	ICU
Equestrian	Fédération Équestre Internationale	FEI
Fencing	Fédération Internationale d'Escrime	FIE
Football	Fédération Internationale de Football Association	FIFA
Golf	International Golf Federation	IGF
Gymnastics	International Gymnastics Federation	FIG
Handball	International Handball Federation	IHF
Hockey	International Hockey Federation	FIH
Ice Hockey	International Ice Hockey Federation	IIHF
Judo	International Judo Federation	IJF
Luge	International Luge Federation	FIL
Modern Pentathlon	Union Internationale de Pentathlon Moderne	UIPM
Rowing	International Rowing Federation	FISA
Rugby	International Rugby Board	IRB
Sailing	International Sailing Federation	ISAF
Shooting	International Shooting Sport Federation	ISSF
Skating	International Skating Union	ISU
Skiing	International Ski Federation	FIS
Table Tennis	International Table Tennis Federation	ITTF
Taekwondo	World Taekwondo Federation	WTF
Tennis	International Tennis Federation	ITF
Triathlon	International Triathlon Union	ITU
Volleyball	International Volleyball Federation	FIVB
Weightlifting	International Weightlifting Federation	IWF
Wrestling	International Federation of Associated Wrestling Styles	FILA

considering the introduction of new sports on the Olympic program, with ideas including rock climbing, skateboarding, and others currently being discussed. Thus, it is possible that new IFs will be created and added in coming years, while others may be removed from the list.

The third and final word in global sport marketing is, of course, *marketing*. Marketing has been well established as one of the key disciplines of business. Defined by the American Marketing Association (1985) as "the process of planning and executing the conception, pricing, promotion, and distribution of ideas, goods, and services to create exchanges that satisfy individual and organizational objectives," it is known to be an activity that involves an exchange or a relationship between two parties that, in principle, provides a win-win benefit for both. For example, Visa is a long-time partner of the IOC. It is safe to assume, therefore, that the partnership has been a win for Visa (e.g., increased sales, increased use of the card, branding, return-on-investment, etc.) and a win for the IOC (e.g., revenue generation, co-promotional efforts, etc.). Visa's co-promotional effort with Samsung (another Olympic sponsor) to promote a mobile phone contactless-payment system at the London 2012 Games is an example of network-based relationship marketing.

To understand global sport marketing, it is important to grasp the meaning, as well as the interrelationships between each of the three individual words, as described above. Based on the definitions of each of the three terms, global, sport, and marketing, global sport marketing is characterized as an activity that reaches consumers in at least two countries that is either

- the exchange of value between two entities where at least one of the entities receives a sport product (e.g., tennis racquet), sport service (e.g., coaching), or changes/maintains a sport-related behavior (e.g., participation, doping); or
- the exchange of value between two entities where neither entity receives a sport product or service, but sport is used indirectly as the promotional vehicle (e.g., sponsorship, ambush marketing, branding) to market a nonsport product (e.g., automobile, beverage, insurance, etc.).

In both of the two scenarios, the exchange between the two parties involves a process of building a marketing mix comprised of the strategic elements of product, price, promotion, and place, or the famous 4 Ps of marketing efforts (Kotler & Keller, 2011) that is global in nature and involves some sport aspect, as identified in the two scenarios described above.

THE GLOBAL SPORT MARKET

At the global level, sport is unique in offering a live, unscripted event that can draw audiences from around the world, which may feel emotionally tied to athletes and teams (especially national teams). Global sport presents an opportunity for marketers to capitalize on fans' attachments, loyalty, and passions, as they convey their brands' goals and messages. Respected global consultancy PWC forecasted the 2015 global sports market, which comprises sport sponsorship, gate revenues, media rights fees (TV, radio, internet, etc.), and merchandise (PWC, 2011), to be a growing (3.7% annually) market that is estimated to exceed US $145 billion by 2015, of which US $45 billion will be sponsorship, or about 29% of the total global sport market.

Previous researchers (AT Kearney, 2009) report that football (soccer) is the dominant single sport globally, and that multisport events (e.g., the Olympic Games, Asian Games, etc.) represent about 8% of the overall market. Regardless of the sport or the industry in which the marketer is using sport as a promotional vehicle, sport has often demonstrated the ability to provide marketing benefits beyond that of other properties. Besides the pure physical and mental benefits of sport participation (e.g., reduction of heart disease, stroke, cancer, osteoporosis, diabetes, depression, anxiety, and stress; improvement of self-esteem and self-image), taking part in sport can bring a range of social benefits, such as generating a sense of belonging, social inclusion, language learning, bonding, community identity, and integration (Bailey, 2005; Brunette et al., 2010). This emotional attachment to sport, and through sport, along with sport's ability to transcend national and international borders, brings massive appeal for sport as a marketing tool. Further, the global nature of sport is enhanced by the fact that written (e.g., scores and statistics) and linguistic (e.g., referee signals) elements are minimized for sport in comparison with other fields of human exchanges.

Global sport marketing involves many different marketing strategies and tactics related to sport products or nonsport products through sport, including sponsorship, sampling, public relations, celebrities, event, advertising, contests, hosting, and hospitality. A key element is that these sponsorship programs are multicountry in their application, such that planning must be done with a global perspective that seeks exchanges in multiple countries, while still recognizing and accommodating particular local differences. For example, in the beverage category, for Olympic sponsor Coca-Cola's Coke product, a lighter-colored version is sold in Brazil than in the United States and Canada to account for local preferences.

MARKETING THEORY ELEMENTS
AND GLOBAL SPORT MARKETING

The American Marketing Association's 1985 definition of marketing (see above) focused on exchanges. More recently, its definition of marketing has evolved to focus on long-term, multiple exchanges (i.e., relationships) as opposed to one-time transactions (a.k.a., single exchanges). The current definition is "Marketing is the activity, set of institutions, and processes for creating, communicating, delivering, and exchanging offerings that have value for customers, clients, partners, and society at large" (AMA, 2013). Taken in a global context, this definition suggests that global marketing is marketing that occurs in two or more countries, as a set of processes that allows for the building of relationships between an organization and its internal (e.g., employees, consultants) or external (e.g., suppliers, customers) stakeholders. An important element in the 2004 AMA definition is the idea of delivering value through the relationship, such that both parties see value/benefit from the relationship.

Whether it is global or local in its focus, sport marketing is based on the underlying idea that marketing programs seek to meet the needs and/or wants of consumers in certain target markets. Indeed, at the most basic level of sport marketing, the satisfaction of consumer needs and wants ranges from very basic elements like recovery drinks after exercise to very sophisticated elements such as self-actualization through being a season ticket holder supporting the local professional sports club. For global sport marketing, note that the needs and wants of target markets vary considerably country by country and region by region. For example, some people in the world live in poverty while others live in free enterprise societies where most have personal technology, disposable income, and leisure time, leading to wants that often involve entertainment, health benefits, and social gratification, all of which can involve sport, either as direct products or as a promotional platform for nonsport products.

An element of marketing theory that is of enhanced importance in the global context is the idea of *relationship-marketing*, a key element of modern marketing as presented in the 2004 AMA definition of marketing set out earlier. Enabled by expanding modern technologies over the past decade or so, relationship-marketing ability increases continually as a means to enable sport marketers to reach every consumer engaged in such technologies in a personalized and customized way. Examples of these 'modern' relationship-marketing efforts include global fan clubs, custom sport equipment, and custom merchandise offerings. For example, many Premier League football clubs in Europe have large and expansive fan clubs in Africa, and a golfer can now go online and order a custom-made club tailored to his or her abilities and attributes. English Premier League soccer (football) club Manchester United may be the best example of global marketing in sport. According to a 2012 survey by Kantar, the club has a global fan base of 659 million fans, 50% of whom live in the Asia-Pacific region of the world, and commercial partners in 72 countries, from all over the globe.

The segmentation, targeting, and positioning (STP) concept that allows marketers to reduce the total population of interest into reachable, manageable market segments is another important marketing concept that is highly relevant to global sport marketing. To ensure that the marketing message reaches the most appropriate audience in any particular circumstance, a basic STP review must be completed. This is especially salient in a complicated global context, in which a blanket promotional statement is highly unlikely to result in the intended uptake among the various target groups the marketers want to reach. Regarded as the bridge to marketing strategy (i.e., the link between the background market research and the strategy to implement), utilizing STP allows marketers to use what has been learned through external analysis, an examination of political, economic, social, and technological (PEST) factors and other research, and apply it to execute the most efficient and effective marketing implementation. By understanding which particular segments (e.g., active females with children, 30–49 years of age) out of the masses should be targeted, and how that global sport product should be positioned, the most ideal marketing mix can be employed (O'Reilly & Séguin, 2011).

As described in the summary of TOP sponsors and host country of the Olympic Games (see sidebar), global sports marketing requires thorough market segmentation, even if the location of the event may not be a major concern for a global sponsor. Notably, the TOP sponsors tell us that they activate (i.e., implement) differently in each of the 206 marketing territories of the Olympic Games. Clearly, an international approach to sport marketing entails considering each potential consumer in the world who might purchase the product or service, and establishing a categorization of that total market that results in various segments of individuals or groups with similar needs and wants (O'Reilly & Séguin, 2011). The various attributes (or bases) by which to segment a global market may or may not include country/region and certainly will include other

© Lucian Milasan | Dreamstime.com

THE SPONSOR-GLOBAL EVENT MARKETING RELATIONSHIP

Summary of article published in the *Journal of Sport and Tourism* by Norm O'Reilly, Louise Heslop & John Nadeau in 2011 (Volume 16, Number 3, Pages 231–257).

This research was based on a review of marketing studies and, primarily, an expert interview with the leadership of Coca-Cola's Global Olympic Marketing. The study provides important insights into marketing at this level, much of which is relevant here. Notably, the research found that global sponsors should (i) carefully consider such partnerships strategically with a long-term focus on benefits, (ii) plan and invest heavily in activation at the local level based on where the event is held to maximize local impacts regardless of where the event is held, (iii) work with the partner to prevent ambush marketing, and (iv) dedicate resources to building a strong relationship with the partner. An important reminder from the Coca-Cola executives is that the host location (country/city/region) of the mega-event is not a major concern as long as it provides the requisite global reach; it is the related content and country by country activation. Indeed, the executives emphasize that the specific event should be viewed as separate from the marketing content. That is, the event (e.g., the Olympic Games) is the platform from which the content for activation is created at a localized level to reach potential consumers in that specific region.

variables (e.g., gender, age, income, profession), but it is likely that country/region is important given a few of the key bases of segmentation related to country (i.e., culture, race, language). In this regard, a global market in which many rich cultures, languages, sporting trends, and interested demographics exist does not necessarily mean that target markets are simply defined by country borders. A soccer fan of the Portuguese national football (soccer) team may very well live, work, and experience the local cultures and traditions in Brazil, while hockey fans in Canada and Russia may respond to beer sponsors in an identical manner. Therefore, more thought has to be put into the specific needs and wants of the global sport consumer/segments, based on understanding the relevant environment(s).

Tactically, once the various segments of the global market have been identified, the marketer must then determine those that should be pursued, given available resources. With such unique attributes, global target markets usually require multisegment or differentiated strategies for the target markets identified in the segmentation process. This entails distinct marketing mixes customized to each target market (O'Reilly & Séguin, 2011). For example, one sponsor of the 2018 Winter Olympic Games in Korea may have specific and distinct marketing plans for Korea, Europe, and North America (multisegment strategy), while another is using the platform of the 2018 Games to communicate globally how it differs from its main competitors on certain attributes (e.g., price) with activation plans that may differ by target/country (differentiated strategy). IEG (2014) reports that Omega, the official timekeeper of the Olympic Games and a TOP sponsor, activates digitally, socially, and on-site to target three primary markets (China, Russia, and Europe) with its sponsorship of the Olympic Games. This differentiation speaks to the positioning aspect of STP, whereby marketers shape (or re-shape) the perception of their products in the minds of consumers based on factors such as price, quality, novelty, and more.

Case Study 1.1

The Impact of Fan Motivation on Global Sports Marketing of Women's Mega Sport Events: The Case of the FIFA Women's World Cup Canada 2015 in Ottawa, Ontario[1]

This chapter introduces global sport marketing, often from the perspective of the mega-events that characterize the Olympic movement and the 9-figure details that characterize the related media, sponsorship, and marketing relationships around these events. However, there is much more to global sport marketing, as there are tens of thousands of events or games each year throughout the world that involve global audiences or participants from more than one country or media/social media attention from multiple nations. Athletes are marketing themselves outside of their home countries. NSOs are seeking partnerships and revenue to help them send teams to events around the world. Thus, global sport marketing is vast, even though it is often not as high profile as one might think. The places where highly skilled marketers are needed are often not with the Olympic Games or similar mega-events. Indeed, the chal-lenges in the global sport marketing process are apparent in events, sponsorships, agencies, athletes, and organizations of all sizes, popularity, and country-of-origin. In an effort to demonstrate this reality early in the book, included is a case study on the smaller-scale, yet still global, the 2015 FIFA Women's World Cup to be held in Canada.

Last hosted in Germany in 2011, the 2015 edition in Canada will welcome 24 international teams in six host cities. Given its scale, the marketing challenges associated with the event are significant, as reach is lower, resources less, and impact not as clear. This renders the efforts of marketing, such as the segmentation process, more challenging and more important. Indeed, with segmentation, the marketing team for FIFA 2015 and, to be successful, the teams in each of the six host cities need to consider all elements of marketing, including STP.

Case Study Context

It was a late May 2014 afternoon in Ottawa, Ontario, one of the six host cities for the up-coming FIFA Women's World Cup Canada 2015 (FWWC2015). Like Vancouver, Edmonton, Winnipeg, Montreal, and Moncton, Canada's capital city was getting ready to contend with a series of games that make up the most prestigious female sporting event in the world. With the first match kicking off on June 6, 2015, FWWC2015 was now just over a year away. The key issue for management was ticket sales. For Ottawa, this meant a goal of selling out nine matches at a newly renovated Frank Clair Stadium, equipped with 24,000 seats (Edmonds, 2013).

Valerie Hughes, Venue General Manager (VGM) for the Ottawa venue, was on the phone as she sat in her Bank Street office, finishing her weekly marketing conference call with the five other VGMs and members of the National Organizing Committee (NOC), the group responsible for overall co-ordination of FIFA 2015 in Canada. Each VGM shared updates on the implementation of their current marketing plans, but all expressed that they were patiently waiting on the "Official Draw" in December 2014, when the match schedule would be filled with the names of the FWWC2015 qualifying countries. Until they knew those names, streamlining their marketing and promo-

(Continued on next page)

Case Study 1.1 *(continued)*

tional tactics to the countries that would play in their specific venue was not yet possible. Imagine the challenge they all faced, having to market games for which the participant countries were not yet certain! Yet preparation, they all agreed, was essential, as reaching, if not surpassing, an event-wide $1.5 million revenue goal would be impossible without it (Hughes, personal communication, August 15, 2013). Notably, the VGMs, like Valerie, were well aware that Team Canada would not likely play in their venue and knew it would be difficult to motivate fans to attend games not featuring the home country favorites. Team Canada has garnered much attention and admiration since its unbelievable Olympic run to a bronze medal at the London 2012 Olympic Games (Arthur, 2009).

"How do we entice fans to buy tickets to watch teams they may have no emotional connection with, featuring athletes that Canadians, both native and immigrant, don't feel represent them? What factors would motivate them to come out to our games, and how can we cater our marketing to these factors? On the other hand, how do we reach target markets that do have inherent interests in countries like Colombia or Iceland, for example?" Valerie posed these questions to the VGMs and her team almost daily, knowing that everyone had been trying to find the answers since Day One. With 24 teams set to play in the FWWC2015, she felt that 24 multi-segment or differentiated target marketing would be required.

If this was not difficult enough, general promotion and marketing for FWWC2015 would be challenged by the innumerable other events and sporting properties in the local Ottawa marketplace. With one year left to go, Valerie knew she was up against stiff competition in vying for the attention of potential ticket buyers. Logistical issues such as during-the-day kick-off times for several of Ottawa's match schedule would further complicate her marketing plans in motivating fans to purchase tickets.

Nearing the end of the conversation, Valerie offered one more piece of insight for the group. "We also have to remember that with the FIFA Men's World Cup and FIFA U-20 Women's World Cup taking place in the next two months, a lot of opportunity exists for crosspromotion. This can be a great basis for stirring fan motivation and interest for FIFA events. Let's also not forget that many of our venues are situated in the center of huge grassroots soccer networks and geographic areas with rich multi-ethnic and immigrant populations. Both these factors should be a definite focus of our marketing strategies."

Once the call finished, Valerie reflected on her recommendations and realized that listening to her own advice would be key in ensuring a sold-out Frank Clair Stadium for the entire Ottawa match schedule. The wheels were now spinning, and Valerie and her team were ready to generate feasible, unique, resourceful, and effective marketing solutions.

Background Concepts

Similar to other major multivenue events, the FWWC counts on ticketing revenue as a key source of revenue, where potential buyers on a local, national, and even international scale must be considered. Thus, having a sound understanding of what motivates sport fans to partake in major international sport events is a crucial step in the marketing of any global event, such as the FWWC2015.

Fan Motivation for Women's Sport Events

Brokaw (2000) identified that *true fans* are sport fans who are concerned with the enjoyment of the game or event itself, and whose attendance intentions are not easily impacted by the outcome of the game, the venue, financial considerations, social dimensions, or entertainment. This group offers the most loyalty to sport marketers, but is often not the target group for sport marketers, such as Valerie and the FWWC2015. Instead, it is the casual fans that provide the majority of attendance revenue at sport events (Hall et al., 2010), and thus the vital work of the event marketers is to position their event (in this case the FWWC2015) as a superior option among many entertainment alternatives (Robertson & Pope, 1999).

The actual *experience* (or perceptions of what the actual experience will be) at the event is also a major consideration for potential ticket buyers. Kahle and Riley (2004) explain that fans or event attendees are more concerned with the overall quality of the entertainment experience, and less so with the sport event and its outcome. This is an important consideration for Valerie and her team, as planning for a positive event day experience surrounding the games themselves and, equally important, conveying this value to potential ticket buyers, will be keys to a successful marketing effort. Additional research (see Hall et al., 2010) supports this view and suggests that a focus on the emotion construct of fan motivation is important, which consists of the arousal of a spectator's emotions by variables such as whether the sport event is considered to be stimulating, satisfying, or stirring. Hall et al. (2010) note, specifically that

> The emotion construct has a strong relationship with intention to attend a sporting event. The build-up of an event, the desirability of attending the event, and the level of satisfaction and stimulation with the event all contribute to the emotion construct. If spectators perceive that the event will be fun, challenging, stimulating and satisfying, then they are much more likely to want to attend an event in the future. (p. 333)

This implies—for event marketers like Valerie—that resources need to be allocated towards building this sense of anticipation and excitement about the event, and that efforts and activities need to be undertaken to create a sense of fun and excitement should an individual decide to purchase a ticket to attend the event. Indeed, formulating a social atmosphere and sense of escapism is vital. Strong emotional ties come naturally for fans who are able to purchase tickets for games featuring teams and athletes that represent them. For fans in the Ottawa marketplace who are not afforded such representation on the field, properly repositioning the sport product will be essential in triggering ticket purchases, since that attachment is missing if Team Canada is not playing.

The work of Funk et al. (2001) and subsequent revisions (Funk et al., 2002; 2004) were one of the initial attempts to examine consumer interest, specifically in women's sporting events. Surveying 1,321 attendees at opening-round matches at the FIFA Women's World Cup 1999 (FWWC1999), Funk et al. drew attention to the particular sport product, the games themselves, and the unique event motives that attracted spectators to the event. Their findings indicate that interest in the sport of soccer, interest in the team, excitement in the matches, supporting women's opportunities in sport, and the aesthetics and vicarious achievement explained 35% of the variance in respondents' interest in purchasing tickets to attend the FWWC1999 (Funk et al., 2001). Funk et al. (2002) supplemented these results with the inclusion of the importance of role models for young females as added motivators in attending women's professional soccer events. Ferreira and Armstrong (2004) also cited similar results, indicating that the opportunity to see a role model, supporting women's sport leagues, receiving entertainment value, and lower costs as being motivators for attending women's sport events. Further, the prestige of an international championship such as the FWWC2015 is an additional asset for global sport marketers, as is awareness of the factors that motivate ticket purchase. This, in turn, allows sport marketers to tailor the advertising message of an event to the specific object of attachment for the potential fans, and thus sell more tickets (Funk et al., 2002).

Identifying Fans Who Seek Sport Tourism to Celebrate Subculture

While fans' interest in a particular sport is a significant motivator for ticket purchase, marketers must also consider that the sporting event (and all its ancillary events) is an opportunity for fans to identify with an associated subculture. In the case of the FWWC2015, this is the global soccer culture. Considered to be the set of identifiable beliefs, values, and means of symbolic expression, a subculture is based on experiences that are highly visible, easily accessible, and especially relevant in the environment of that particular sport (Green, 2001). Further, the act of attending or participating in a certain sport event expresses an attachment to the this set of related subculture meanings for the attendee (Green, 2001), which is no less important than the sporting activities themselves. For example, consider the 2015 World Ringette Championships slated for Helsinki, Finland, in December of 2015. Although relatively small in size, the sport of ringette, a game that resembles ice hockey, played largely by female participants on ice, has a passionate following in two countries (Canada and Finland) where current and past players have a strong devotion to the sport and its subculture. Thus, organizers of the 2015 Championships would be wise to target both Canadians and Finnish with an experience that celebrates both the championships and the culture of the sport.

Sport marketing researchers have validated this claim that for participants of a given sport whose choice is to travel to sport destinations, the reason for this choice is "the opportunity to come together to share revelry in the instantiation of their identity" (Green & Chalip, 1998, p. 286). Thus, for fans engaging in sport tourism merely to watch the sport, event organizers and marketers must remember to augment the sport product through a variety of add-on activities and services in order to highlight the subculture of the event (Green, 2001). The purpose of this augmentation is to enhance and broaden the event's appeal, enticing more people with the means to attend the event to actually purchase a ticket and attend. In the case example of the FWWC2015, for area residents to consider attending games in Ottawa and to commit to purchasing tickets, observing an offering that will allow them to be part of a subculture should help Valerie, and her team, reach their revenue goals.

Event Tourism

Another benefit of attending a global sporting event is the opportunity to immerse one-self in sport tourism and, for some, discovering a new city or even nation. This can occur directly through visiting another country or indirectly via attending a global sporting event in one's own country. For the FWWC2015, most marketing efforts will be concentrated regionally in the Ottawa area. However, Valerie and her team must also consider fans who may intend to travel to Ottawa because it is the closest venue or due to a particular interest in visiting the city.

Tourism management research acknowledges that several push and pull factors exist in attracting sport tourists. *Pull factors* include the attractions that are associated with the destination and thus incite potential tourists to book directly or ask a travel agent about visiting that particular destination. Conversely, *push factors* are associated pre-dominantly with intangibles having to do with the motives, needs and interests of the traveler, often via marketing efforts to a third party travel agent or travel site. As with many marketing products today, the push and pull factors are thought to work together to determine travel intentions and destination choice (Kim & Chalip, 2003) (i.e., travel decisions are typically made based on a combination of push and pull factors).

As sport marketers for the Ottawa venue, Valerie and her team must consider what the City of Ottawa itself has to offer to attract out-of-town fans with the means to travel and interest to attend. As Canada's capital city, Ottawa is home to a number of low cost/no costs attractions and events, such as Canada Day festivities, and the daily 'changing of the guard' on Parliament Hill. In summary, the challenge for event mar-keters is to recognize how to capitalize on the motives and backgrounds of potential ticket buyers in order to optimize event interest, while mitigating the perception of con-straints, such as cost, to drive purchase and attendance at the event.

© Coco77 | Dreamstime.com—Parliament Of Canada Photo

Local Marketing Challenges One Year Prior to an Event

Although a major event—such as the FWWC2015—is a special occasion for a host city, it often faces competition from other events—both special and regular—in that city. For Ottawa and the FWWC2015, this is no different as the city is no stranger to high-caliber sport events, which makes the promotion of the FWWC2015 more difficult among a city population already bombarded with sports and entertainment options.

As of 2011, the Ottawa-Gatineau census metropolitan area (CMA) had a population of 1,236,324, of which 51.4% were women, and 48.6% men. In the CMA, 56.6% of the total population aged 15 and over were either married (45.0%) or living with a common-law partner (11.6%), and of these couples, 49% have children in their household (Statistics Canada, 2012). Of particular interest to sports marketers is the fact that this CMA boasts one of the highest median household incomes in Canada, with the Ottawa component of the CMA earning $94,700 and the Gatineau component earning $81,040 in 2010 (Statistics Canada, 2013). This capacity for higher discretionary spending among the Ottawa-Gatineau population is appealing to marketers.

Although events related to FWWC2015 are going on throughout the summer of 2015, with the Canadian Football League (CFL) Ottawa RedBlacks preparing to return to play for their inaugural season in the fall of 2014, much of the hype surrounding sport in Ottawa will be directed towards football. The RedBlacks are owned by the Ottawa Sports and Entertainment Group (OSEG), who oversee the operations of the Ottawa Fury soccer club (National Soccer League) and the Ottawa 67's hockey team (Canadian Hockey League) as well. OSEG has entered into a public-private partnership with the City of Ottawa, to transform the current stadium—the "New Lansdowne"—into a revitalized urban park centered around Frank Clair Stadium (OSEG, 2013). In addition to the return of the CFL, Ottawa is home to two CIS (Canadian Interuniversity Sport) universities also offering year-round sport (University of Ottawa, Carleton University), the National Basketball League's (NBL) Ottawa Skyhawks and the National Hockey League's (NHL) Ottawa Senators. Each of these organizations will be contending for its share of the sport entertainment marketplace including ticket buyers' dollars in 2015. From a competitive perspective, the FWWC2015 group has a challenging undertaking. In addition, the city of Ottawa also hosts numerous concerts, festivals, annual events, and is home to museums and many additional entertainment options, and certain other special events to happen in 2015, including 100th anniversary celebrations related to Canada's participation in World War I. Valerie knew that positioning FWWC2015 versus these offerings was important.

Promotion of Daytime Games

The FWWC2015 schedule is shared amongst six cities. With Montreal and Edmonton each playing host to a semi-final game, and Edmonton and Vancouver hosting the bronze and gold matches respectively, Ottawa's ticketing mandate is to sell out six round-robin games, two rounds of 16 games, and one quarter-final match. Ottawa's match schedule includes both Thursday, June 11, and Wednesday, June 17, as doubleheaders, with one game falling in primetime evening hours, and the other within working day hours (FIFAa, 2013). With potential audiences at work or even school, filling 24,000 seats for the daytime games will be a difficult ticketing sales challenge.

The 2015 match schedule is presented on the facing page.

In Germany for the FWWC2011, average attendance for round robin games without the home country varied significantly between the afternoon and evening games, as evenings typically drew about 5,000 more people than afternoon games. This will challenge the Ottawa FWWC2015 staff to develop ticketing programs or offers that cater to and incentivize daytime crowds.

Not All Teams are Created Equal

Additional factors that could also complicate ticket sales strategies include the nature of the teams drawn to play in the Ottawa venue. Though all six venues are guaranteed to have one top six team play two of their round robin games in their respective stadiums, marketing plans have to consider the fact that most games will consist of two fairly low-profile (for Canadian audiences) international teams. Since the names of those countries will not be revealed until the official draw, and the chances of Canada playing in Ottawa are slim, Valerie and her marketing team need to come up with a plan that focuses on drawing crowds to low-profile, but high-action and high-caliber games. This will be especially challenging in light of FIFA's strict no free-ticket policy (i.e., every ticket must be purchased).

As of the time of this case study (May 2014), what *is* known of the match schedule are the slots allotted to each FIFA-associated confederation. With Canada, as hosts, automatically entered to play, the remaining 23 spots are given to (FIFAb, 2013):

- The top five Asian Football Confederation (AFC) teams,
- The top three Confederation of African Football (CAF) teams,
- The top eight Union of European Football Associations (UEFA) teams,
- The top three Confederation of North, Central American, and Caribbean Association Football (CONCACAF) teams, with the fourth-place finishers facing a playoff against the third-ranked team from CONMEBOL,
- The top two South American Football Confederation (CONMEBOL) teams, with the third-place finishers facing a playoff against the fourth-ranked team from CONCACAF, and
- The top Oceania Football Confederation (OFC) team.

One of the top six women's soccer teams in the world will be guaranteed to play two round-robin matches in Ottawa, ensuring at least one relatively well-known team in women's soccer will grace the field at Frank Clair Stadium.

Grassroots Marketing

The Canadian Soccer Association (CSA) played a leadership role in securing the right to host the FWWC2015 and will help promote the event to its vast grassroots network of clubs, coaches, officials, and players. As of 2014, the CSA had an extensive participa-

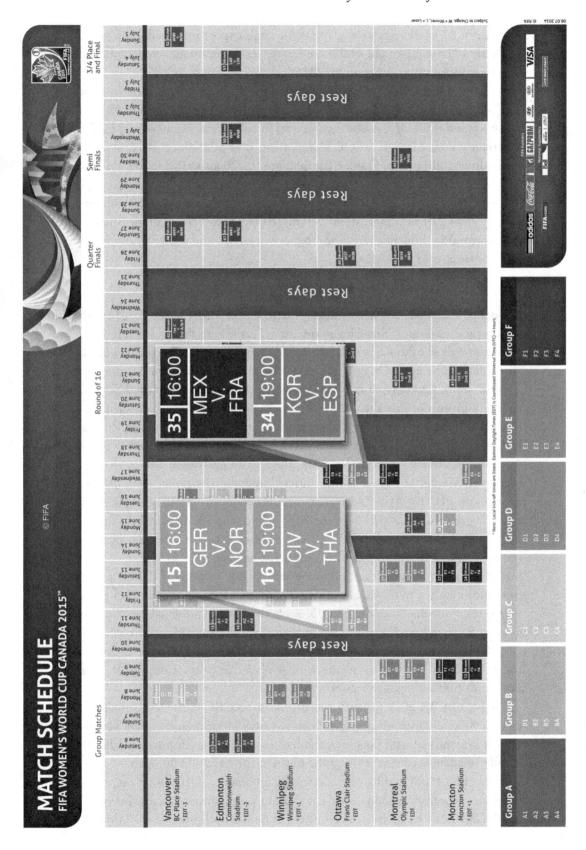

tion base of 824,181 registered players (the largest sport in Canada), of which over 81.3% are 18 or younger and 41.2% are females, both important demographics for this event (Canadian Soccer Association, 2014).

In Ottawa, leveraging the provincial grassroots influence the CSA has with the Ontario Soccer Association (OSA), and regionally with the Eastern Ontario District Soccer Association (EODSA), is a key action item to sell tickets. The OSA and EODSA are important stakeholders. The EODSA represents over 50,000 registered players, most within driving distance of Frank Clair Stadium. Its 70 associated soccer clubs around the Eastern Ontario area service youth, senior, house league, and indoor soccer players. And with 32 of the EODSA clubs offering youth programs, a ticket sales opportunity for the FWWC2015 exists (Eastern Ontario District Soccer Association, 2013). Valerie needs to consider how this target group can be reached and what will motivate them and their families to buy tickets.

FIFA Men's World Cup and FIFA U-20 Women's World Cup

As Valerie looked outside her window, dozens of cars drove along Bank Street with country car flags proudly fluttering in the wind. People with their colorful international jerseys also walked by as the craze of the FIFA Men's World Cup Brazil 2014 had clearly started descending upon Ottawa. She knew that the current buzz surrounding international soccer in Canada had to be leveraged for the promotion of the FWWC2015, especially given the fact that the FIFA U-20 Women's World Cup Canada 2014 (FU20WWC) was kicking off in Edmonton, Toronto, Montreal, and Moncton later in the summer of 2014. FIFA soccer was the theme of this summer, and thus the perfect backdrop for creating awareness around the FWWC2015 and setting the stage for ticket sales. Though the 2014 World Cup will undoubtedly garner more media attention than the FU20WWC2014, the latter would certainly be a strategic opportunity for promoting the FWWC2015. With the 2014 World Cup taking place between June 12 and July 13, 2014 and the FU20WWC2014 between August 5 and 24, 2014, a large window of opportunity lay ahead for Valerie and her staff.

In 2010, when South Africa hosted the World Cup, millions of Canadians watched the month-long action on CBC and Radio-Canada. Opening-round matches drew an average television audience of 956,000, while the World Cup Final drew in a record-breaking 5.816 million Canadians across both channels. Scott Moore, Executive Director of CBC Sports at the time, was reported to believe that with the times zones in Brazil, key 2014 World Cup games will be played at prime time and thus lead to another 30–50 % increase in viewership (Kelly, 2010).

The FU20WWC2012 in Japan was broadcast on CBC to modest audiences. With the time zones of Japan making it difficult to watch live games, television audiences in Canada averaged 11,100 people (Canadian Broadcasting Corporation, 2010). The overall Canadian audience reach of the tournament was 200,000, with a peak match audience of 28,450 (Canadian Broadcasting Corporation, 2010). With more favorable time zones in both Brazil and Canada, and the assumed greater inherent interest for the FU20WWC2014 being hosted right here at home, both the 2014 World Cup and

FU20WWC2014 are expected to experience higher television audiences than their most recent counterparts.

CHAPTER SUMMARY

This chapter aimed to provide the foundations for the chapters that follow by defining global sport marketing and the global sport market, and pointing out essential elements of marketing theory.

Key Chapter Questions: Case Challenge

The FWWC2015 case study can be summarized into a list of questions about this specific situation and the national and local challenges it encompasses. In the context of global sport marketers, however, these questions could be typical for any international event of this level being held anywhere in the world. Thus, readers are encouraged to extrapolate what they learn from this case to other situations.

1. Without knowing the specific international teams that will play at Frank Clair Stadium in June of 2015, what marketing and promotional tools should Valerie and her team utilize to ensure maximum awareness of the FWWC2015 taking place in Ottawa? What local stakeholders can be engaged to make sure people know that the event is coming to their city?

2. With Match #15 and Match #35 both taking place during the day on June 11th and June 17th respectively, what marketing tactics can be utilized to ensure a full stadium? Are there specific community groups that can be approached, or certain ticketing programs that could be implemented? If so, what would they be?

3. Operating with a very strict no-free ticket policy, how can Valerie and her staff ensure that seats are bought, not simply given away or "comped," so that Frank Clair Stadium will look full and vibrant when games are broadcast on national television?

4. What can be done in a capital city, home to many international embassies, ambassadors, and organizations, to sell out games with lesser-known countries playing?

5. Operating in close tandem with the CSA and its vast grassroots network, how can these assets be used to the advantage of FWWC2015 event marketing, especially in the Ottawa and Eastern Ontario area? What are the advantages of pinpointing this market for potential ticket sales?

6. With FIFA action happening throughout the summer of 2014, how can Valerie and her marketing team leverage the popularity of other international sport properties such as the 2014 World Cup and the FU20WWC2014, to supplement their efforts?

7. One element that Valerie and her team could consider would be to develop a tagline for the Ottawa event. One idea would be a montage of the guards at Parliament Hill and an action photo of women's football and the tagline, "This is not the only changing of the Guard in Ottawa!" Does this make sense? What other suggestions do you have?

Part I

Core Foundations

2

Principles of Global Sport Marketing

For many companies, the prospect of going global is as appealing as it is daunting. Moving from a national (or even regional) to an international focus brings with it the challenges of understanding and reaching new and very different target markets, and determining how to appeal to these global markets, often against competitors from that country. A global marketing plan is needed, but it must be one that enables the organization to differentiate itself from other global or national players for purposes of influencing the choices of consumers, fans, and participants. The table below provides context and examples of national and international organizations and their targets.

Table 2.1.				
Focus	**Example**	**Consumer Target**	**Fan Applications**	**Participants**
International	Coca-Cola	Entire beverage market in every country of the world	Association with Olympic Games, FIFA World Cup, Professional Sport, NASCAR, etc.	Target events with hydration beverages (water, Powerade, etc.)
	Sony	Targets all different types of people all over the world. The range of products includes televisions, computers, stereos, video game systems, cameras, etc.	Association with FIFA World Cup, UEFA's Champions League, action sports (X Games, Team Action Cam), Major League Baseball, etc.	Target events for its PlayStation product, cameras, TVs, etc.
National	CIBC (Canada)	Canadians	2015 Pan American Games	CIBC Run for the Cure
	Canadian Tire	Canadians	Canadian Olympic Committee, Canadian Paralympic Committee, Canadian National Hockey League Teams, Canadian NSOs	Jumpstart (corporate foundation)

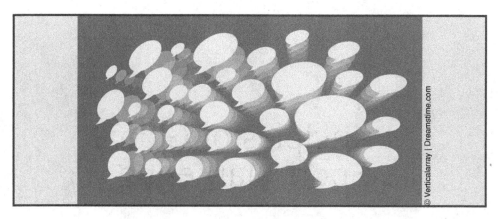

At both the global and national levels, effective segmentation and targeting is required, given the increased cultural, trade, consumption, and other dimensions that are inherent in working in multiple countries. This is then reflected in the resulting marketing strategy.

Similar to any area of business, the use of social media is an increasingly important element of any modern marketing mix and is an element that allows for more facilitated global efforts, since communications and messaging can go global in real time, with resulting potential global benefits (or possible repercussions) depending on the content, quality, and sensitivity of the messages. A classic example is the social marketing battle between Powerade and Gatorade following what has been dubbed "Crampgate" during Game 1 of the 2014 National Basketball Association (NBA) finals when star player LeBron James suffered from major cramps due a very hot playing environment (due to air-conditioning failure). Powerade, a sponsor of James since 2003, was very active in tweeting about their support of James up until Game 1 but went quiet post game. Gatorade, the nonsponsor and market leader in Powerade's category, reacted quickly to the opportunity. One tweet read "we [Gatorade] were waiting on the sidelines, but he prefers to drink something else," while another—"with a game this hot, we're right at home"—referenced the fact that James appeared to be drinking Gatorade (from a bottle with the label removed) during the game. This imitation was later dubbed "#LeBroning" on Twitter. Gatorade later apologized, then deleted, these tweets but the message was conveyed. In the apology note, Gatorade emphasized their long-time partnership with the Miami Heat, James's team at the time, which they sponsor. Gatorade is also a long-time NBA sponsor. James, however, is sponsored individually by Powerade.

GLOBAL MARKETING FUNDAMENTALS

The fundamentals of global marketing are no different than the fundamentals of marketing in general—they are just expanded to an internal context/focus/market where global marketing involves devising one or more strategies to communicate the value of a company's products and services to appeal to a global target market (i.e., target markets in multiple countries). The basic marketing elements include the 4Ps of marketing strategy to meet the needs of global consumers by offering a *product*, at a certain *price*, through a distribution *place* where consumers can learn about it through a series or unique offering of *promotional* strategies. In the case of global marketing, marketers adjust their 4Ps based on the way their new country target markets may be similar to or different from the company's local or traditional markets.

Organizations must also consider their own goals and objectives as they globalize. If the organization is a brand seeking to grow its business, it needs to embrace local cultures and tastes while concurrently maintaining the consistency of their product offerings across global borders. For example, consider the marketing strategies of international food chains McDonald's and Boston Pizza. McDonald's operates in more than 100 countries of the world, with common (e.g., Big Mac) items across countries offered in a standard format, but also provides a variety of regional selections, including taro pie in Tokyo, poutine in Ottawa, beer in Paris, and McAloo tikki burger in Delhi (Authors'

note: this burger was ordered via a separate entrance for vegetarian clients, which was physically divided from the beef-serving side of the store). Boston Pizza, on the other hand, markets items that vary only slightly by location, with a marketing strategy that attempts to provide customers with a uniform experience whether at the first franchise location in British Columbia or at one of their many global locations. If the organization is a sports property seeking to expand its series of events (e.g., Ironman Corporation) or grow its sport [e.g., International Ice Hockey Federation (IIHF)], the challenge differs because, as a sports body, the new entrant must work with local clubs, local community sport organizations, and government bodies. For example, when the Ironman Corporation seeks to launch a new event in a new country (e.g., Ironman Barcelona first held in October 2014), it needs to do so with knowledge of the triathlon federation in that country, current races, and rules/regulations that may already be in place for the sport. Similarly, if the IIHF develops a plan to grow hockey in Denmark, it must work with its member national sport organization in Denmark.

GLOBAL MARKETING STRATEGY

As outlined in the fundamentals, global marketing is nevertheless still marketing, but applied to a global context. Therefore, global marketing strategy is based on the 4Ps, developed via market research and a segmentation process that seeks to assess and determine prospective target markets that the corporation and its products or services can reach through global or local (or a mix) promotional campaigns. Importantly, in any marketing initiative, companies need to differentiate themselves from other competitors, as they identify markets to target, and build grassroots strategies that may support their marketing plan. Research shows that global marketers often find that sport can offer a unique, or at least effective, communication tool to help generate awareness about the brand and associated products and services at the global and local levels. This is reflected in sponsorship estimates that show that sport attracts more than half of what is spent annually on sponsorship rights fees globally (IEG, 2014).

The following subsections outline some key steps in the marketing strategy process including differentiation, segmentation, targeting, and positioning. An example of a global marketing effort is the "Heineken House," an Olympic Games-based marketing strategy that began at the 1992 Olympic Games and continues today. The Heineken House (see http://www.hollandheinekenhouse.nl)—a partnership between Heineken and the Dutch Olympic Committee/Dutch Sports Federation—is a temporary venue set up on site at each Olympic Games that serves as a meeting place, an event host, a dance bar, offices, and a hosting place for athlete recognition/medal ceremonies. It has become a fixture for Olympic Games spectators and athletes (post-competition) with marketing benefit for Heineken.

DIFFERENTIATION

In the global marketing mix, it is argued that a competitive advantage in the form of a differentiated product offering is more important than in domestic marketing. The rationale for this distinction is based on the fact that a global offering must overcome possible consumer interest to support local providers (i.e., the global offering must be better than, not just equal to, the local offering). Forms of differentiation include a good external communications strategy to encourage diverse markets to buy into the value of the brand (e.g., Nike) or a clearly superior product on some attributes (e.g., Apple). In the case of differentiation via external communications, such communications need to place the brand in the spotlight in a manner that enables the products and services to be seen as valuable to the public or increase the demand for related offerings from local partners (Vail, 2007).

Practically, with the increased global competition and ever-growing access of consumers to products and services, businesses need to develop ways to help consumers differentiate their brand(s) and product(s) from their competition, particularly local competitors and substitutes. Strategically, some organizations seek to build relationships with a cause or high-profile issue in the target communities having an affinity for that cause or issue, in order to generate support and increased perceived value related to their product, as a way to differentiate it from the competition. For example, the Homeless World Cup is an event that attaches itself to homelessness as a cause, which initially attracted the interest of Nike as a founding partner and supporter. As a published case study (see Foster & O'Reilly, 2011) details, Nike was attracted to the event due to the mix of its attachment to an important and relevant cause, as well as its ability to provide positive marketing outcomes for Nike.

In summary, differentiation—in its many forms—is effective and marketers are encouraged to identify niche market segments as they target and position their brands in the global marketplace. Differentiating in a global context must be undertaken in a way that provides the new target market with a product that meets their expectations. A well-known illustration is the foray of the National Football League (NFL) into Europe via its failed venture NFL Europe. Although the NFL is enormously successful in North American and attracts global audiences to its games (all 32 clubs are based in the United States), many claim that by not providing an offering that fit with the NFL brand (i.e., the new market had limited interest in a lower-quality version of the NFL product), failure resulted. A similar argument has been brought forward around the multiple failures of professional soccer in North America (pre-MLS) when the level of play was viewed to be inferior to play in Europe.

GLOBAL STP: SEGMENTATION, TARGETING, AND POSITIONING IN AN INTERNATIONAL SETTING

Although differentiation, as well as other strategies, can allow organizations and their products/brands to find success in new global markets, this normally only happens when a thorough strategic exercise is undertaken, that includes the processes of *segmentation*, *targeting*, and *positioning* (STP). Included in almost every sport marketing textbook and course, STP is the logical process of defining which aspects of a larger market will be pursued, and how. The first step is segmentation, which involves identifying a meaningful population of potential customers, and dividing, or segmenting, that population into prospective buying groups, based on a profile of their needs. Once segmented, targeting is the process whereby marketers evaluate the value of the prospective target segments to help prioritize certain segments over others for purposes of deciding which they will pursue. The targeting decision often involves considerations such as size of the market, its potential profitability, and how accessible/reachable it may be through marketing efforts. The final phase, positioning, involves identifying the differential feature(s) that might be attractive versus the competition in each selected target market group and building a specific marketing strategy for each group. For example, the marketing vice-president of the Kontinental Hockey League (KHL) club in Sochi, Russia, in the 2014–2015 season might identify three target markets (e.g., tourists for single game tickets, local hockey fans for season tickets, and local business for suite sales), each of which would then have its own position and marketing strategy (4Ps) specific to that target market. The marketing vice-president of the Australian Football League (AFL) building a series of marketing strategies to increase fan club membership in each of the 18 clubs who play in markets of differing sizes and competition levels would be another example. Thus, STP helps to determine the focus (target and differentiation) of the effort and, in turn, drives the integrated marketing strategy and the product, price, place, and promotions (the 4Ps) to enter the global market.

Some marketers suggest that STP is the most important tactical aspect of any marketing strategy process, as it allows the marketer to be efficient, determine specifically who its offering(s) should reach and how. A good marketer realizes that people have vastly differing needs, wants, interests, and passions. Indeed, everyone grew up with their own experiences, backgrounds, parents or guardians, interests, homes, etc. These various experiences result in differing views and interests, which translate to varying needs and wants, the core of marketing direction and thinking. Quite simply, human beings are unique, but often similar in many respects, thereby allowing us to group up, or segment, people by commonalities. This is supported by the Law of Large Numbers, which states that the more times you repeat an experiment (or research), the more likely you are to get to the true expected value. Thus, by undertaking ongoing market research to track the success of target marketing plans and altering these plans based on the resulting feedback, the process of reaching these targeted segments improves over time.

So, why learn STP? Why does it matter? Why do marketers everywhere stress its importance, even if the concepts have been around for years? The answer is actually quite simple: STP is linked to the bottom line since the proper use of the STP tools can lead to profitability via reduced costs/improved efficiency. STP drives efficiency, as it enables the marketer to uncover specific unsatisfied needs and wants (i.e., product/service demand) in particular markets and, in turn, to develop a product and/or service supply (or offering) to meet such demand. Such an approach saves the marketer from expenses related to trying to promote the product/service to customers who are not part of the target markets (i.e., those who otherwise may have been targeted if no STP process had of been undertaken). Third, STP can be viewed as the pathway to marketing strategy, since no strategy should be drafted unless an STP process has been undertaken to enable the marketer to eliminate alternatives with low likelihood of success.

STP can be referred to as the "bridge" to marketing strategy, and this is certainly the case in Olympic marketing and ambush marketing. The rationale for this acronym lies in the fact that a well-implemented STP process allows the marketer to learn from the background market research it has done, to develop the marketing strategy and tactics more efficiently, with a particular focus on who it is targeting and how it can position the product(s)/service(s) in the minds of those target consumers versus competitive offerings. Thus, STP links market research to marketing strategy.

Segmentation

Although a number of the global Olympic sponsors (and global sponsors of other mega-events such as the FIFA World Cup) do target the mass market population (i.e., "everyone"), the vast majority of organizations are not able to afford or to manage these types of promotions. In addition, these organizations typically offer products and/or services that are not used by the entire population. This combination led marketers—seeking improved efficiency—to the concept of segmentation, in which they seek to break down the total market into "reachable chunks" for which they can build specific targeted marketing programs. Often called *target markets* or *market segments*, these groups of customers are then analyzed, based on the segmentation research, to determine which ones can be most profitable (or beneficial in the case of not-for-profit organizations), which is the process known as targeting, or the "T" in STP!

Segmentation is not a new concept in marketing. It has been commonplace for many years. It is, however, taking on newfound importance in the Olympic Games of the 21st century, where certain segments are targeted by certain media distribution channels (e.g., packaged primetime television, live sport network television, online streaming, social media) and by certain sports (e.g., snowboarding, mountain biking, equestrian, sailing), all of which attract certain determinable markets. In turn, the ability to reach these segments may be of interest to particular sponsors and marketers for a variety of reasons. For example, the live streaming of a half-pipe event might be of high interest to youth-focused brands, but of limited interest to adult-focused brands. Thus, particularly in today's markets, the identification, selection, and pursuit of market segments is an important, if not vital, aspect of any global marketing plan. Even a global Olympic sponsor seeking to target the majority of the mass market (e.g., Coca-Cola, Visa), needs to segment by sport and by medium and by messaging to reach, among others, youth, moms, men 24–39, as they seek to break down their market into a series of statistically similar, reachable groups.

Practically, there are a number of tools available to marketers to help them segment their markets. A simple, data-driven process is recommended that allows a marketer to become efficient in the identification of segments. First, the marketer must select the relevant variables or bases of segmentation by which to divide the overall market. These bases should be those factors that are relevant to the particular product and market (e.g., gender, age, hard core fan or passive fan, income, job, activity level). There are thousands of bases of segmentation to consider. The key, of course, is to undertake research to identify those that are *truly* measures that divide a market into relevant segments for the product/service of interest. For example, in the case of a sport drink manufacturer, activity level would be a relevant basis of segmentation, but race would not. Once selected, these bases are then used to slice the market into segments. The more bases used, the more complex and more specific the segmentation is. In more complex scenarios, it is useful to use a spreadsheet to undertake such a process. Second, once the profile is complete, research is undertaken to learn more about each identified segment (i.e., who are they, what do they want, why do they buy, when do they buy, how do they buy, etc.). Once this profiling is complete, the targeting phase of STP can be undertaken.

An example of a basic segmentation grid from the point of view of the National Hockey League (NHL) seeking to grow its sale of merchandise in Sweden is presented on the following page. This example, although simple, outlines a segmentation undertaken with two bases (level of fandom and income) of the Swedish market of ice hockey fans. Although some of the boxes in the grid are the same/similar, there are differences for each of the four segments.

Targeting

Once a profile of differentiated, yet similar, segments has been created, the next phase of the STP process is targeting, which—quite simply—answers the question of which of these segments should be pursued. More specifically, this is the decision-making process of selecting where to invest marketing resources and how to do so. It is not a decision that should be taken lightly, since failing to pursue highly profitable segments or implementing a marketing plan for a segment that is not sufficient can have devastating impacts on the organization.

Table 2.2.				
Base #1	**Hard Core Ice Hockey Fan**		**Passive Ice Hockey Fan**	
Base #2	High Income	Low Income	High Income	Low Income
Who?	Former player, childhood fan	Ice hockey fan, fan of Swedish national team	Socialite, business professional	Sport fan, fan of Swedish national teams
What?	Customized jerseys, high-quality clothes	Team jersey, hat, T-shirt, others	Customized jerseys, high-quality clothes	Team jersey, hat, T-shirt, others
Where?	Online, high-end mall or store, arena location/ kiosk	Online, at game, sales at retail, giveaways	Online, high-end mall or store, arena location/ kiosk	Online, at game, sales at retail, giveaways
Why?	Link to NHL star or retiree, gift for kid	Expression of being of fan	Association to sport, team, player	Bandwagon jumper or commemoration
When?	Around high interest times: Olympics, NHL playoffs, IIHF World Champs	Anytime, when merchandise is on sale	High-interest times: Olympics, major NHL games, Hall of Fame induction	High-interest times: Olympics, major NHL games, Hall of Fame induction
How?	Cash or credit	Cash or credit	Cash or credit	Cash or credit

There are normally three targeting approaches from which to select. The first is an undifferentiated target, where the sponsor is seeking to go after all consumers, such as Coca-Cola via the Olympic Games. Second, differentiated targeting is the pursuit of two or more different segments with a different and distinct marketing approach for each. An example would be the Dairy Farmers of Canada marketing chocolate milk by targeting both athletes replacing elements as a result of physical effort and kids for a fun treat. Third, focused marketing or the commitment to one specific target market segment is a strategy used to target a specific niche, such as Cervelo bicycles targeting time trial cyclists and Adidas, which built its early brand by building high-performance, technical, shoes specifically with no initial interest in the "soft" products and fashion aspect of broader sport. Interestingly, missing the jogger market and the fashionable sport clothing booms led to the effective forced sale of Adidas by the Dassler family.

So, how does a marketer make this decision? The clear recommendation is to consider each of the identified segments (resulting from the segmentation process) on four particular aspects: extent, reach, ROI, and evaluation. Extent refers to the size of the particular market whether in terms of numbers or the purchasing capacity (or wealth) of that segment. Reach is the ability to communicate with that segment. Do channels exist to which they will respond? Does the marketer have, or have access to, the technologies in place to do so in an efficient manner? ROI asks whether that segment can be profitable once the marketing platform is put in place. Is the segment sufficient? Can

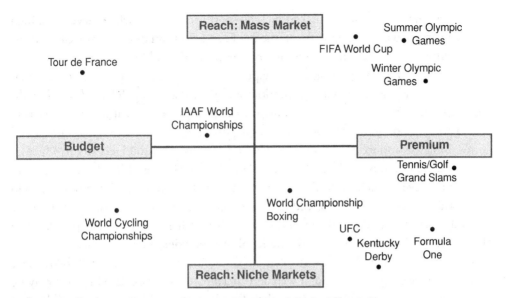

Figure 2.1. Perceptual Map of a Sample of Global Sport Events.

the market be reached efficiently enough to leave a satisfactory post-sale margin? Finally, evaluation asks whether metrics and measures exists for this segment whereby success and ability to penetrate this segment can be tracked.

Positioning

The final stage of STP is perhaps the most important. This is the phase of the process when the segments to target have been analyzed and target markets identified and the marketer is ready to build a strategy. In order to be successful, however, prior to building out the 4Ps of that strategy, the positioning of the offering (in the minds of the target market) versus the competition, specific to that target market (or markets) must be articulated. In particular, the question of how selected target(s) should perceive the offering, versus the offerings of competitors, must be answered. Is it based on price, or luxury, or quality, or brand, or a particular association? Is it Red Bull, which differentiates on premium, brand, and edge? Or, Volvo and safety? Omega and precision timing?

Practically, positioning is the process of seeking a particular niche or differentiated "angle" where the offering is different from the competition set, namely, that it has some unique (or perceived to be unique) difference. For example, a perceptual map based on author opinion only of global sporting events is presented above to show where each may be positioned based on the variables of reach (global versus niche) and access to spectate (premium versus budget).

SPORT AS A GLOBAL MARKETING TOOL

The use of sport as a global marketing tool is well documented. Pegoraro et al. (2010) noted that "sport as a corporate marketing tool provides increased flexibility, broad reach, and high levels of brand and corporate exposure" (p. 1454). In the integrated marketing mix, sport marketing can include sport sponsorship, which develops a high level of perceived association between the brand and the team or event, as well as advertising through the media that bring the sport event to the public.

Major international sporting events happen only with the help of funding from major national and international organizations and their marketing dollars. Indeed, without support from the private sector, organized sport as we know it today—especially international sport—would not exist. Mega-sporting-events draw global attention and offer immense opportunity for global marketers to use their budgets to introduce or reinforce their brands on the global stage. The Olympic Games, FIFA World Cup, and other mega-events such as the Asian Games and the Commonwealth Games, can help companies reach new markets and gain the opportunity to create lasting legacies for their associated brands, products, and services. It is well established that sport fans are highly devoted to their teams at the national (e.g., national hockey teams) or international level (e.g., Team USA at the Olympic Games). Loyal sports fans will follow their teams in televised games through web and social media, so associated brands may be viewed by the fans as a way to support their favorite teams or players. For example, Bud Light's ongoing social media efforts to associate with the National Football League and its Super Bowl drive fans of the NFL to consider Bud Light for beer purchase. Similarly, if a sponsor can build a strong association to a player, it may limit benefits accrued to a competitor who sponsors that player's team. For example, Nike may sponsor the Argentina national team (football) at the World Cup but the club's star player Lionel Messi uses Adidas.

THE IMPORTANCE OF REACH

As described under STP, the manner by which marketers differentiate their products and find niche market segments in a global context often involves, or relates to, the concept of *reach*. Here, reach refers to the audience in multiple countries who have access to or may possibly receive a given marketing message. The reach of a marketing message may exceed the targeted audience (e.g., an automobile advertisement at the

Youth Olympic Games may be seen by a large television viewing audience, but only a small percentage of that group are of driving age, hold a valid driver's license, have the needed means, and are planning to purchase a vehicle in the next year).

Thus, the challenge inherent with reach lies in actually reaching—or touching—those people in the target market(s) in a meaningful way. The president of a leading web-based group-buying site, Gary Lipovetsky, listed ten effective and cost-effective ways to reach target consumers (adapted from Lipovetsky, 2011):

- **Understand audience:** Marketers need to be clear on the target market demographic and location.
- **Use a performance-based marketing model:** Ads should always be strategically tied to revenue potential and evaluated for return on investment.
- **Do not underestimate word-of-mouth:** Encourage strategies that allow customers to be the company's marketing voice and consider incentives for referrals.
- **Plan and set clear goals:** Have a comprehensive business and marketing plan, and a vision of what is needed to succeed.
- **Pace your advertising and marketing goals with your cash flow:** Move at a pace that the company infrastructure and finances can support.
- **Premium partnerships:** To save financial resources, find a reliable partner to help spread marketing messages and share resources.
- **Social networking strategies:** Online social network sites are a key to attracting and communication with new customers. Facebook, Twitter, and YouTube are cost-effective marketing tools.
- **Building blocks:** Build on existing assets (e.g., develop interactive capabilities on your website and use cross-promotion strategies).
- **Value customer service:** Respect customer feedback and loyalty, and provide a reason to return and share the message with others in your target audience.
- **Use incentives:** Use strategic incentives (e.g., discounts, referral rewards, and loyalty incentives) in your marketing strategy to build awareness about the brand.

Reaching audiences is an important part of any global marketing strategy as companies aim to influence the choices of current and prospective consumers.

INFLUENCING CHOICE IN A GLOBAL SETTING

Marketing is the art of influencing decisions and behaviors of individuals. Global marketing is concerned with influencing decisions and behaviors of individuals in more than one country, who speak different languages, have considerable cultural variations, and who live life differently on numerous levels. On the practitioner side, global marketers know that people increasingly have access to more choices with regard to both their time and their discretionary income. This is good for some businesses since, for example, certain global businesses can use their immense buying power to offer lower priced products to customers in locations all around the world (e.g., Wal-Mart). On the other hand, the increased availability of choice may also mean increased global competition for consumer dollars in that global product category (e.g., airline travel).

Drawing on a model developed by the Canadian Institutes of Health Research in the marketing of their partnership with Kellogg for the "Canada on the Move Program," as reported by Craig et al. (2007), there are six variables that help change consumer behavior in such a context. First, the marketing message needs to *expose* audiences to the marketing message, and second, to generate a sense of *awareness* about the message. Once consumers are aware, then, third, they may pay more attention to related messages and develop a deeper *knowledge* about the brand or product. With that knowledge, fourth, consumers might develop an *intention* in relation to the marketing message (in essence deciding to buy into the message or not). If the intention is positive toward the brand, then the final goal may be achieved: the consumer's choice is influenced to make a *behavioral change* (or make a purchase).

SOCIAL MEDIA IN GLOBAL MARKETING

In today's world of global marketing, perhaps nothing influences the choices of individuals like social media. Using social media in global marketing implies that companies are willing to listen immediately to the needs and wants of consumers around the world, and rapidly develop and modify products and marketing messages accordingly. Indeed, users look to social media to compare and rate products, publically, with both positive and negative impacts. In these situations, social media can help deliver marketing messages to target audiences and help consumers feel more connected to the brand, but also offer an unfiltered message directly from consumers about negative perceptions about a company's quality, service, and values. In turn, the organization can learn and adapt its marketing and products efficiently, based on the feedback.

The brand messages generated through social media can be in a constant state of change and be shaped by the public rather than those inside the organizations. The rise in social media has made the general public an important part of a social marketing campaign—important, yet unpredictable. For example, as reported in August 2014, Red Bull paid out more than US $13 million to customers in a settlement around false advertising to reportedly avoid the potential negative reputational damage that could result via social media (BEVNET, 2014). This is one of many recent examples in which a company was litigating in relation to the matter of a product or service with a customer(s), where the matter went (or could have gone) viral on social media and the resulting reputational damage was (or would have been) so great that the company withdrew the proceedings and settled with the customer(s). Thus, as marketers collect global social media input to learn from, they can create programs, products, and marketing messages that are shaped based on the analysis of input (via market research, STP, and other marketing tools).

In marketing with social media, companies are looking to global crowd-sourcing and other market research techniques as they seek to inform the creation and adaption of products for future marketing campaigns that will showcase products and product attributes that people actually want. For example, Houpt (2011) noted that Fiat Brazil and its marketing team at AgênciaClick Isobar collected input from 17,000 people in 160 countries as they created the Fiat Miao car. In Fiat's case, global marketing research started before the product was even ready to launch. This early market research via crowd-sourcing both helps companies create/revise products that meet consumer demands, but also helps build excitement about new products where people (in the target market) feel like they have influenced the creation.

In British Columbia, Canada, 'BC on the Move' is an organization that uses social media marketing campaigns aimed to encourage citizens to become more active. BC on the Move (2011) identified four ways to best leverage social media in the marketing messages. First, companies should learn how their target communities obtain and consume information (e.g., Facebook, Twitter, blogs). Second, companies need to be clear about their program goals relevant to their social media presence (e.g., does running a social media contest help draw new users to the website or help learn what inspires consumers, or help engage with local media?). Third, organizations need to consider ways by which to engage the target audience (e.g., blogs, group pages on Facebook). Finally, the fourth tip is to be patient in creating an online community: loyal brand followers do not happen overnight. While messages can go global in real-time, responses take time, but the genuine responses to become community members are worth the wait.

Social media as a marketing strategy through sport can help attract new users to services, help promote products and programs, raise satisfaction levels of product users, enhance fan experiences, and boost the outreach of the marketing plan (see Bryant et al., 2001; Dharod et al., 2011; Grier & Bryant, 2005). Marketing through social networking sites encourages users to generate content related to the brand, product, or services, while social news sharing and business blogs and podcasts help support marketing messages through meaningful integration of users. As consumers are increasingly seeking brands and products that meet ethical standards or support charitable causes, social media can be implemented within marketing to help promote the brand's commitment to corporate social responsibility. The impact of social media in global marketing can, however, be difficult to measure in terms of return on investment (ROI). This lack of clarity around ROI refers to the challenge in measuring it, much of which has to do with attributing changes back to a particular marketing effort. For example, if Visa sees a spike in its Facebook likes or Twitter followers after a promotion related to its Olympic Sponsorship, it may be difficult to measure whether those spikes lead to increased credit card use or changes from MasterCard or American Express to Visa.

GLOBAL GRASSROOTS MARKETING

A modern approach to marketing is grassroots marketing, in which strategies aim to influence the choice of consumers by targeting small groups of consumers in community settings in the hope that the message will spread from the ground up. For example, a coffee chain may sponsor a kids' sports league or a number of youth clubs to show its support at the community (a.k.a., grassroots) level. The strategy can often cost less than traditional top-down strategies, as target groups are smaller and major media buys are normally not part of the activation. The idea of a global grassroots marketing strategy brings to mind the work of Malcolm Gladwell (2002) in his book, the *Tipping Point: How Little Things Can Make a Big Difference*. In this book, Gladwell observed that *word-of-mouth* epidemics are spread from the bottom-up helping to re-energize brands into international trends, including the sudden rise of Hush Puppies suede shoes after years of stagnation. In these cases, when small groups of people start to change their behaviors, trends start to tip and sometimes a snowball-effect results, creating a marketing windfall.

CULTURE AND INTERNATIONAL MARKETING

As global brands cross borders and expand their exposure in many countries of the world, companies need to consider how their marketing strategies need to be revised for each of the diverse regional, linguistic, and cultural groups they may now be targeting. An important aspect of such an effort is cultural diversity, which recognizes that groups of people vary in the way they use language, embrace technology, politics, religion, and education, and the distinct group values and social norms. Marketing research can help to develop an understanding of the needs of diverse cultures, but having a cultural insider is a preferable, if not expected, practice in the global marketing context in order to avoid making a cultural *faux pas*. For example, the Kenneth Cole fashion company learned this lesson as it attempted to promote its clothing line by making light of the political turmoil in Cairo (Egypt), as its tweet "Millions are in uproar in #Cairo. Rumor is they heard our new spring collection is now available . . ."

As Sibley (2012) described, negative feedback resulted immediately as the campaign reportedly offended millions, and prompted Kenneth Cole to make a formal statement of apology. Language translation is also tricky without knowing the cultural context and can lead to problems for organizations pursuing global marketing efforts. For example, when Pepsi entered the Chinese market, its photo of a hand reaching out of the grave holding a Pepsi can, its original English caption "Pepsi brings you back to life" was not as well received by the Chinese public when the translation changed the meaning to "Pepsi brings your ancestors back from the grave" (Sibley, 2012).

NEUROMARKETING IN THE GLOBAL SETTING

Neuromarketing is arguably the hottest new area of marketing, as science is helping shape a new way of studying consumers' brain responses. Using MRIs, EEGs, and heart monitors while consumers are exposed to advertisements is helping marketing researchers to understand what stimulates consumers and what helps make emotional connections to their brands and products. These findings are also informing what drives our decisions and our behaviors.

Belgian neurosurgeon, Dr. Patrick George, provides six guidelines to utilize neuro-marketing in marketing strategy (Valtat, 2013):

1. Be irresistible. Sell to the sense of the client. Appeal to her eyes, his ears, their hands.
2. Be inescapable. Sell to his hormones through pleasure, sex, and drugs.
3. Be emotional. Stress and joy. Sell to the emotions of the customer.
4. Be unforgettable. Sell to the memory of the client. Tell him stories. Make her laugh.
5. Be incredible. Sell to the subconscious of the client. Appeal to his basic leadership instincts.
6. Be irreproachable. Sell to their intelligence and aptitude. Help them make the right decision.

Opportunities for neural marketing in global sport are extensive as technologies continue to become more available for measurement and tracking.

CHAPTER SUMMARY

A global marketing campaign is unique to individual organizations, each with its own global and national goals, visions, and objectives. An integrated global marketing plan uses different strategies to attract, retain, and renew consumers. The way companies differentiate their brands and products at the worldwide level, and the way they segment target markets, may call for different strategies in the promotional mix. Marketers are embracing newer marketing techniques that were undervalued or not previously available only 10 and 20 years ago: STP, social media marketing, and grassroots marketing are now part of the norm in marketing plans, while marketers are paying an ever greater attention to the role of culture in their marketing messages. New trends, such as neuro-marketing, will continue to develop and evolve, with the ability to change the very nature and meaning of marketing in the not-so-distant future.

Chapter Questions and Activities

1. How does global marketing differ from domestic or local marketing? Give three examples of each to illustrate.
2. What differentiates global sport marketing from sport marketing?
3. Name three important marketing concepts and apply them specifically to sport.
4. Pick a country of your choice that is outside of the G20 (i.e., the group of 20 highly developed countries who meet regularly on issues of common interest, including the United States, Canada, England, France, Japan, and others). Next, pick a current Olympic Top Sponsor. Now develop a segmentation grid, a targeting plan, and a perceptual map to enter that country with one of the sponsor's products or services.

5. The perceptual map in the chapter positions a number of global sport events. Re-do the perceptual map with your view on those events and add at least five additional sport events to the map.

6. If you were teaching a class on global marketing, what advice would you give to students on (i) diversity and (ii) sensitivity?

7. Social media, as outlined, has many pros and cons ranging from the ability to reach many people quickly to the loss of control of your brand. If you were put in charge of social marketing for the IOC, what three activities would you put in place in your first month on the job?

8. Neuromarketing has very exciting prospects for any marketer. Select a global sport event of your choice and assume you are the VP of marketing for that event. Outline five ways by which neuromarketing could potentially help you.

3

Applications of Global Sport Marketing

This chapter is intended to build upon Chapter 2, which presented and outlined a variety of key concepts and elements of global sport marketing, much of which was *internationalizing* accepted marketing principles such as differentiation, segmentation, positioning, social media marketing, and neuromarketing. This chapter is an introductory case study with the objective of applying various concepts of global marketing, as well as introducing sponsorship, mega-events, and the Olympic/Paralympic movement, all of which are important aspects of the balance of the book.

The case presented here outlines the Canadian Paralympic Committee's (CPC) sponsorship activation challenges. It provides background information on the history of the Paralympic Movement, the International Paralympic Committee (IPC), and various sporting events for Paralympian athletes. It discusses sponsorship, sponsorship activation, and the increase in promotional efforts surrounding the Paralympic Movement, as well as contextual information on the CPC and its current partners, and provides examples of successful sponsorship activations by similar properties.

IN-DEPTH INTRODUCTORY CASE STUDY: CANADIAN PARALYMPIC COMMITTEE

Canadian Paralympic Committee Sponsorship Activation: Bringing Sponsorship to Life

As the sun beamed through the windows of his office in downtown Ottawa, Canada's capital city, François Robert, Executive Director of Partnerships at the CPC, smiled as he thought about the CPC's new partnership with Canadian Imperial Bank of Commerce (CIBC), a major Canadian bank. It was the fall of 2013 and, following weeks of meetings and negotiations, this partnership could not have come at a better time with the Sochi 2014 Winter Paralympic Games only months away. With CIBC's support of Canadian Paralympians, as well as the CPC's many other partnerships, François knew that he must now focus on leveraging these sponsorships through activation strategies. His biggest challenge would be facilitating the CPC's partners to activate going into

Sochi 2014. He felt that the CPC
had been effective in generating Paralympic awareness by building its
brand around the athletes' stories.
With the increase in coverage on the
national public network, the Canadian Broadcasting Corporation
(CBC), and national sports network
Rogers Sportsnet, François felt confident that the CPC was now a valuable property for sponsors. He knew

© Catthesun_Dreamstime.com_Momoko Dekijima (Japan) Competes On Winter Paralympic Games in Sochi Photo

that his partners would want to build their visibility and association with the CPC
while ensuring customer engagement and brand image enhancement.

HISTORY OF THE PARALYMPIC MOVEMENT

Individuals with impairments have been involved in sport since the 19th century when
sport clubs had been established for the deaf in 1888 in Berlin (International Paralympic Committee, 2013a). However, it became more recognized following World War
II, when Dr. Ludwig Guttmann, a German neurologist and neurosurgeon, was asked by
the British government to open a spinal cord injuries center in 1944. At the Stoke Mandeville Hospital in Great Britain, Dr. Guttmann used sport as a form of therapy and re-
habilitation for soldiers and civilians with impairments. This evolved further into a
competition, and the first Stoke Mandeville Games were held in 1948 to coincide with
the Olympic Games in London. In 1952, ex-servicemen from the Netherlands took
part in the competition, giving rise to the international Paralympic movement. The 9th
Annual International Stoke Mandeville Games became the first Paralympic Games. The
event featured 400 athletes from 23 countries and was held in 1960 in Rome, Italy. The
first Paralympic Winter Games were held in Örnsköldsvik, Sweden, in 1976. To date,
the Paralympic Games have taken place every four years, and since 1988, they have
been held in the same host cities as the Olympic Games. The word *Paralympic* origi-
nates from the Greek preposition 'para' meaning beside or alongside, and therefore represents a competition held in parallel to the Olympic Games (International Paralympic
Committee, 2013a).

THE INTERNATIONAL PARALYMPIC COMMITTEE

The IPC is a nonprofit organization and the global governing body of the Paralympic
Movement (International Paralympic Committee, 2013b). Originally known as the
International Coordinating Committee of World Sport Organizations for the Disabled
(ICC), the IPC organizes the summer and winter Paralympic games and serves as the
International Federation for nine sports and their respective World Championships.
The IPC's vision is "to enable Paralympic athletes to achieve sporting excellence and in-
spire and excite the world" (Appendix A). Its mission is to provide sport opportunities
for all individuals with a disability, and it ranges from initiation to the elite level. The

Paralympic values of courage, determination, inspiration, and equality are promoted by the 70 IPC team members at the IPC headquarters in Bonn, Germany (International Paralympic Committee, 2013h). They have a strong and positive relationship with the International Olympic Committee (IOC) and, since their agreement of "one bid, one city" in 2001, they have been able to collaborate and cooperate on financial, sponsorship, and marketing deals (Park, Yoh, Choi, & Olson, 2011). The IOC now makes awarding the Olympic Games to a city conditional upon that city agreeing to stage the Paralympic Games shortly after the Olympic Games have been completed. This has brought certainty to the regular celebration of the Paralympic Games and has greatly increased the ability of the IPC and its national organizations, such as the CPC, to attract sponsors and partners.

THE CANADIAN PARALYMPIC COMMITTEE

The CPC is the private, nonprofit organization that represents Canada in the Paralympic Movement (Canadian Paralympic Committee, 2013a). Its vision is "to be the world's leading Paralympic nation" (Canadian Paralympic Committee, 2013a, p. 1). Along with its 25 member and partner sport organizations (See Appendix B), the CPC's mission is "to lead the development of a sustainable Paralympic sport system in Canada to enable athletes to reach the podium at the Paralympic Games" (Canadian Paralympic Committee, 2013a, p. 1). The CPC develops programs and opportunities to increase parasport participation. Parasport has adapted equipment and rules designed to make sport accessible for individuals with a disability (Canadian Paralympic Committee, 2013b).

Canada's first appearance in the Paralympic Games was in 1968 in Tel Aviv, Israel, when the Canadian wheelchair team competed with teams from 29 other countries (Canadian Paralympic Committee, 2013c). As a result of the efforts of Toronto orthopedic surgeon Dr. Robert Jackson, the 5th Paralympic Games, originally known as the Torontolympiad, were hosted in Toronto in 1976. This initiated support from the Canadian government, which granted funds to assist in creating sport opportunities for individuals with a disability. In 1981, the Canadian Federation of Sport Organizations for the Disabled (CFSOD) was established, which later became the CPC in 1993. In the new millennium, Canada has achieved great success at the international level. At the 2004 Paralympic Summer Games in Athens, Greece, Canada finished third overall with 72 medals. This best-ever finish was repeated at the 2006 Paralympic Winter Games in Torino, Italy, with 13 medals and a sixth overall result. The success continued at the 2007 Parapan American Games in Rio de Janeiro, Brazil, where Canada finished second with 112 medals. Breaking its Winter Games record, Canadian athletes garnered 19 medals on home soil at the 2010 Vancouver Paralympic Winter Games (Canadian Paralympic Committee, 2013c).

PARALYMPIC GAMES

The Paralympic Games are held every two years, alternating between summer and winter Games. They include 28 sports, 6 winter and 22 summer (Canadian Paralympic

Committee, 2013d). People with a physical disability, visual disability, or an intellectual disability are eligible to compete at the Paralympic Games (Canadian Paralympic Committee, 2013e). However, following the 2000 Sydney Paralympics scandal, when Spain's intellectually disabled men's basketball team was found to have nondisabled athletes competing, the IPC temporarily removed this category from the Paralympic Games. The category was reincorporated at the London 2012 Paralympic Games in the sports of athletics, swimming, and table tennis. To create fair and equitable competition, athletes are grouped in classifications based on the degree of activity limitation as a result of their disability. This ensures that success in a competition is based on skill and training instead of the level of disability. The classification is also sport dependent; therefore, an athlete may be eligible in one sport but may not meet the criteria in another (Canadian Paralympic Committee, 2013e).

PARAPAN AMERICAN GAMES

The Parapan American Games are a summer multisport event available to nations of the Americas and are held every four years in the year before the Summer Paralympic Games as a regional qualifying event (TORONTO 2015 Pan American/Parapan American Games, 2013). Although the first Pan American Games were held in 1951, the first Parapan American Games did not take place until 1999 in Mexico City, where 1,000 athletes from 18 countries competed in four sports. For the first time in 2007 in Rio de Janeiro, the Parapan American Games were held in the same city as the corresponding Pan American Games. As a result of its increased popularity, TORONTO 2015 expects to host the largest Parapan American Games ever (TORONTO 2015 Pan American/ Parapan American Games, 2013).

COMMONWEALTH GAMES

The Commonwealth Games are a multisport event involving athletes from the Commonwealth nations and takes place every four years. The first edition of the games was held in Hamilton, Ontario, in 1930 (Commonwealth Games Federation, 2013). From 1962 to 1974, the Commonwealth Paraplegic Games were held on four occasions alongside the Commonwealth Games (DePauw & Gavron, 2005). It was not until the 1994 Commonwealth Games in Victoria, British Columbia, that athletes with a disa-

© Lucidwaters | Dreamstime.com—The Gold Coast Commonwealth Games 2018 PhotoCommonwealth Games 2018 Photo

bility were included in exhibition events. Two Games later, for the first time, athletes with a disability were included as complete members of their national teams and full medal participants. This made the 2002 Commonwealth Games in Manchester, England, the first fully inclusive international multisport event (DePauw & Gavron, 2005).

SPONSORSHIP ACTIVATION

The momentum of the Paralympic movement has provided an opportunity for the CPC to leverage their brand as an attractive property for potential sponsors to reach corporate objectives. With the increase of the number of Paralympic athletes and participating countries (Appendix C), as well as the growth in media coverage of the Paralympic Games (Appendix D), the Paralympics have become an attractive property for potential sponsors (Park et al., 2011).

Companies spend millions of dollars on sport sponsorships to differentiate themselves from competitors in a cluttered marketplace (Appendix E). Advertising alone is insufficient; therefore, companies use sponsorship to associate themselves with an organization, athlete, or event (O'Reilly & Séguin, 2013). The sponsor seeks to create a bond with consumers by connecting with the emotion that is attached to the sport property. Using this avenue of communication, sponsors are able to reach target and potential markets. In addition, they are able to meet corporate objectives including "increasing awareness, changing/enhancing corporate image, reaching specific market segments, generating media benefits, achieving sales, creating hospitality opportunities, and gaining competitive advantage through exclusivity" (O'Reilly & Séguin, 2013, p. 247).

A successful sponsorship requires an integrated approach, since it should be embedded into the marketing and promotional mix (O'Reilly & Séguin, 2013). The sponsee (event/property) and sponsor should collaborate to maximize the value of the sponsorship. This can be achieved through activating the sponsorship by investing additional funds, usually at least three times the initial investment, into activation activities. These supplemental marketing or promotional tactics can include sales promotion, hospitality events, point-of-purchase, packaging, pricing, advertising, media initiatives, and production of merchandise. A sponsee should create opportunities for its sponsors to activate their sponsorships, while protecting the sponsors' exclusivity from ambush marketing attempts.

The sponsee must present the tangible and intangible benefits of the sponsorship to the sponsor (O'Reilly & Séguin, 2013). As return on investment (ROI) is critical to sponsors, sponsees must provide additional tools and tactics to add value to the sponsorship. This begins with listening to the sponsors and understanding what they require. According to the International Event Group (IEG, 2011), value can be added to sponsorship offers by eight different methods.

1. Sponsees should offer sponsors additional reach by integrating them into their social media efforts.
2. Sponsees should create new sponsorship inventory (i.e., the list of assets that a sponsor could purchase) by allowing sponsors to use their different mediums in their promotional activities.

3. Providing sponsors with the chance to establish relationships with their stakeholders will generate beneficial business-building opportunities.

4. Sponsees should authenticate the sponsor's products and services through on-site product sampling and demonstrations.

5. The sponsee should support their partners' community outreach efforts through a co-branding program.

6. Providing additional benefits at no extra cost will enable the creation of a strong relationship between both parties.

7. Sharing unsold inventory will add value and demonstrate appreciation of their support.

8. Sponsees should deliver hospitality events and additional VIP benefits to over-deliver on their sponsorship.

Through this multidimensional approach, sponsees can create value for their sponsors and ensure a mutually beneficial relationship.

PROMOTIONAL EFFORTS OF THE PARALYMPIC MOVEMENT

Paralympic sport is captivating the world, and through bold marketing campaigns, Paralympic awareness has increased substantially. Companies have created advertisements and messages that seek to change the perception of disability. A heartwarming Guinness commercial that features a group of friends playing wheelchair basketball has gained over 4.5 million views on YouTube (Appendix F). The Paralympic brand seems to be well recognized and well positioned, with corporate sponsors seeing value in being associated with the Paralympics. Various organizations have created many marketing initiatives to enhance the Paralympics' image and create awareness about them. Samsung, official partner of the 2012 London Paralympic Games, created an inspirational commercial that promoted the "Sport doesn't care" message (Appendix G). This successful campaign attained over 5 million views on YouTube and will remain as a lasting emotional legacy of the 2012 London Paralympic Games.

Another effective promotion prior to the Games, was Channel 4's (England) bold campaign, "Meet the Superhumans" (Appendix H), which generated a sustained amount of excitement leading up to and during the 2012 London Paralympic Games. The CPC has also invested in initiatives to generate awareness and interest in Paralympic sport. Their "Super Athletes" campaign (Appendix I) includes powerful vignettes that demonstrate the highly competitive nature of the Paralympic Games. Through brave creativity and flawless execution, the CPC attempts to change viewers' perceptions of Paralympic athletes. These campaigns, along with CPC's "It's More than Sport" campaign (Appendix J) and Paraswimming commercial (Appendix K), Petro Canada's Vancouver Paralympics activation (Appendix L), and BMW's vignette for the London 2012 Paralympics (Appendix M), have been built around the athletes' stories.

CANADIAN PARALYMPIC COMMITTEE

The CPC relies on the support from its partners, which are its second largest revenue source (Appendix N). Due to the increase in media coverage and number of viewers of the Paralympic Games, the CPC has become a valuable property for sponsors. The 2012 London Paralympic Games were watched by 3.8 billion viewers, 2.8 million tickets to the event were sold, and there were 82.1 million views of the IPC's Facebook pages (Appendix O). Looking specifically at the CPC, from 2011 to 2012, it had more than 317 million media impressions in print, broadcast, and online (Appendix P), which is a 300% increase from the previous year's 75 million impressions (Canadian Paralympic Committee, 2012).

Research has begun to demonstrate that consumers hold relatively positive attitudes towards the Paralympic Games (Park, et al., 2011). A study by Park, Yoh, Choi, and Olson (2011) revealed that consumers had moderate-high purchase intentions toward corporate sponsors of the Paralympic Games. This finding has been consistent in other sports as well. One of the best examples is NASCAR and its fans' purchase intentions for sponsors' products (Mullin, Hardy, & Sutton, 2007). NASCAR fans have a high loyalty toward the sponsors of NASCAR, evidenced by their higher level of trust towards sponsors' products than that demonstrated by other sport fan groups. NASCAR fans frequently chose brands based on NASCAR sponsorships. Furthermore, more than 40% of NASCAR fans indicated that they have switched brands after a company became a sponsor (Mullin, Hardy, & Sutton, 2007). These findings provide evidence that sponsorships are valuable opportunities for companies to increase sales objectives and promote brand awareness.

With this support derived from marketing studies and literature, and the unique opportunity to position itself as both a sport and a cause, the CPC has successfully renewed many partnerships, as well as attracted new sponsors. CPC's current partners include CIBC, Pfizer Canada, Petro-Canada, Procter & Gamble (P&G), Air Canada, Bell Canada, Hudson's Bay Company (HBC), and Canadian Tire (Canadian Paralympic Committee, 2013f). CPC has been working with these partners to activate their

sponsorships and enhance the value of the association. The CPC and its sponsors realize that just using the CPC's trademark is insufficient; instead, they must utilize the equity of the brand to activate mutually beneficial partnerships.

P&G has successfully activated its sponsorship with the CPC and COC through its "Thank You, Mom" campaign. P&G wants to thank moms for all that they do to support their children and provide them with helpful products to make their lives easier (P&G, 2012). They created a series of videos about Canadian parasport athletes and their mothers. Canadian sledge hockey player Greg Westlake was the first Paralympic athlete to be highlighted in P&G's "Raising an Olympian" series. Not only does it allow P&G to attach itself to the emotion evoked from the video, it also enhances the visibility of a top Paralympic athlete resulting in a mutually beneficial sponsorship for all parties involved. Through the "Thank You, Mom" campaign and app, in addition to Games-themed P&G branded products, P&G demonstrates an effective example of sponsorship activation based on their interest in reaching moms, who are most likely to be the decision-makers regarding the purchase of P&G products, or those of its competitors.

The CPC forged several new sponsor partnerships for the Sochi 2014 Paralympic Games to increase recognition of the Canadian Paralympic Team and the Paralympic brand. The CPC has collaborated with HBC to create a custom Sochi 2014

Case Study 3.1

Coca Cola and London 2012

Coca-Cola has been associated with the Olympic Movement since 1928 (The Coca-Cola Company, 2010), resulting in a strong, long-term partnership. Its recent sponsorship of the 2012 London Olympics provided another opportunity for the worldwide brand to implement its creative activation techniques. It created 120 pieces of Olympic content, which included an anthem, a documentary, a television show, a custom mobile app, live events, and the Beatbox pavilion on-site (International Event Group, 2013). Its "Move to the Beat" campaign harnessed adolescents' passion for music to connect them to London 2012. (It is important to note that Coca-Cola has regularly featured unique music and songs as part of its marketing campaigns, including its famous "I'd like to teach the world to sing in perfect harmony" launched in the early 1970s). The "Move to the Beat" campaign embraced social media as more than four million consumers uploaded videos to Coke's Facebook page and it enhanced the event experience with digital extensions in its Beatbox pavilion at the Olympic Park (International Event Group, 2013). It gave 1,300 "Future Flames" the opportunity to take part in the Olympic Torch Relay, created the biggest vending machine in London and provided refreshments for approximately 4,000 athletes, 7,000 officials, 20,000 workers and volunteers and more than 6 million spectators (The Coca-Cola Company, 2013).

Coca-Cola effectively engaged its consumers in its multidimensional marketing mix by creating content and tapping into emotion. On a smaller scale, the NHL and Molson Canadian activated their sponsorship by producing the PrePlay online game to enhance the television viewing experience, increase social engagement, and strengthen sponsorship messaging (Appendix R).

© Jorisvo | Dreamstime.com—Piccadilly Circus London 2012 Photo

Paralympic Games t-shirt, setting a lucrative precedent for future games (Appendix Q). The CPC collaborated with the CIBC on community welcome home events for competing Paralympians. Additionally, Air Canada's awareness campaign and in-flight video promoted awareness among passengers (Canadian Paralympic Committee, 2014). CPC's partnerships with CIBC, HBC, and Air Canada are beneficial for both the sponsee and the sponsor due to productive and collaborative activations.

Case Study 3.2

CPC and Sponsorship

After reflecting upon the progress the CPC has made in the last few years, François knew there was still much work to be done. With the Sochi 2014 Winter Paralympic Games approaching, he knew that the CPC must collaborate with its sponsors in order to develop creative activation strategies. Keeping in mind that CPC's sponsors want to build their visibility and association with a valuable cause, François recognized that his marketing team must create opportunities for customer engagement and brand image enhancement. Partnering with the CPC's sponsors to create unique and creative campaigns would be his priority over the next few months. As the reality of his tight timeline became more evident, François created a list of questions on which he and his team would need to focus immediately.

Case Questions

1. How can the CPC leverage the power of its brand and market it as a valuable property in which sponsors can be induced to invest?

2. How can the CPC provide activation opportunities for its current sponsors? What can it do for its sponsors? What properties (events, athletes, programs, naming rights, etc.) can it offer? How can the success of sponsorship activation be measured?

3. What are good examples/best practices of effective sponsorship activations?

Case Study 3.3

Visa and the NFL

Visa successfully activated its sponsorship with the NFL through a sweepstakes campaign. Cardholders could enter the contest by using their Visa cards and one lucky fan would win tickets for him- or herself and ten friends to Super Bowl XLVI. Visa's platform, "fans enjoy watching football more when sharing it with others" (Visa, 2011, ¶1), as well as Visa's brand, were promoted through many different channels (e.g., YouTube, Facebook, advertisements, credit cards decorated with team logos, and financial literacy video games).

1. Digital advertisements that appeared on popular football websites such as NFL.com
2. National television commercials of Ned, the fictitious NFL fan who won the contest by simply swiping his Visa card
3. YouTube online webisodes of Ned's journey to Super Bowl XLVI
4. Weekly Twitter contests for regular season NFL tickets
5. Client and merchant activation
6. Point-of-sale branding at 15 NFL team stadiums
7. Financial Football initiative
8. Facebook promotions

This campaign, done in partnership with the NFL, was mutually beneficial for both parties and there were over 1.2 million views of Ned's journey on YouTube. Through activation and creativity, consumers will remember this successful sponsorship campaign.

Appendix A
International Paralympic Committee Vision and Mission

Vision and Mission

"To enable Paralympic athletes to achieve sporting excellence and inspire and excite the world."

- To guarantee and supervise the organization of successful Paralympic Games.

- To ensure the growth and strength of the Paralympic Movement through the development of National Paralympic committees (NPCs) in all countries and support to the activities of all IPC member organizations.

- To promote and contribute to the development of sport opportunities and competitions, from initiation to elite level, for Paralympic athletes as the foundation of Paralympic sport.

- To develop opportunities for female athletes and athletes with a severe impairment in sport at all levels and in all structures.

- To support and encourage educational, cultural, research and scientific activities contributing to the development and promotion of the Paralympic Movement.

- To seek the continuous global promotion and media coverage of the Paralympic Movement, its vision of inspiration and excitement through sport, its ideals and activities

- To promote the self-governance of each Paralympic sport either as an integral part of the international sport movement for able-bodied athletes, or as an independent sport organization, whilst at all times safeguarding and preserving its own identity.

- To ensure that in sport practiced within the Paralympic Movement the spirit of fair play prevails, violence is banned, the health risk of the athletes is managed, and fundamental ethical principles are upheld.

- To contribute to the creation of a drug-free sport environment for all Paralympic athletes in conjunction with the World Anti-Doping agency (WADW).

- To promote Paralympic sports without discrimination for political, religious, economic, impairment, gender, sexual orientation or race reasons.

- To ensure the means necessary to support future growth of the Paralympic Movement.

Source: International Paralympic Committee. (2012). International Paralympic Committee Annual Report 2012. Retrieved December 31, 2014, from http://www.paralympic.org/sites/default/files/document/130710121410906_WEB _IPC_13_AnnualReport_2012_final.pdf

Appendix B

Members of the Canadian Paralympic Committee

MEMBERS

The CPC would like to recognize the important role of the national sport and disability community in the success of the Paralympic Movement:

Source: Canadian Paralympic Committee. (2014). Canadian Paralympic Committee 2013–2014 annual report. Retrieved January 27, 2015, from http://paralympic.ca/sites/default/files/uploads/ContentImages /About/annual_repport_2013-2014-en-low-v2.pdf

Appendix C

Summer Paralympic Games Overview

Year	Location	Number of Countries	Number of Athletes	Shared Venue with Olympics
2012	London, Great Britain	150*	4200*	Yes
2008	Beijing, China	146	3951	Yes
2004	Athens, Greece	135	3808	Yes
2000	Sydney, Australia	122	3881	Yes
1996	Atlanta, USA	104	3259	Yes
1992	Barcelona, Spain	83	3001	Yes
1988	Seoul, Korea	61	3057	Yes
1984	Stoke Mandeville, Great Britain & New York, USA	41 (GBR) 45 (USA)	1100 (GBR) 1800 (USA)	No
1980	Arnhem, Netherlands	42	1973	No
1976	Toronto, Canada	38	1657	No
1972	Heidelberg, Germany	43	984	No
1968	Tel Aviv, Israel	29	750	No
1964	Tokyo, Japan	21	375	Yes
1960	Rome, Italy	23	400	Yes
1952	Stoke Mandeville, Great Britain	2	130	Yes
Note: *Expected number, Source: International Paralympic Committee (2011)				

Source: Park, M., Yoh, T., Choi, Y., & Olson, M. (2011). Consumer attitudes toward the Paralympic Games and purchase intentions toward corporate sponsors of the Paralympic Games: Market segmentation strategy. *Journal of Venue & Event Management, 3*, 1–15.

Appendix D

Media Coverage of Recent Paralympic Games

The Paralympic Games	Broadcasting Time	Cumulative Audience
Athens 2004 (Summer Games)	617 hours	1.86 billion
Torino 2006 (Winter Games)	285 hours	1.42 billion
Beijing 2008 (Summer Games)	1,810 hours	3.84 billion
Vancouver 2010 (Winter Games)	1,560 hours	1.59 billion
Note: Source: International Paralympic Committee (2011)		

Source: Park, M., Yoh, T., Choi, Y., & Olson, M. (2011). Consumer attitudes toward the Paralympic Games and purchase intentions toward corporate sponsors of the Paralympic Games: Market segmentation strategy. *Journal of Venue & Event Management, 3*, 1–15.

Appendix E

Appendix E is included to provide information about companies who invest significantly in sponsorship to inform thinking about potential sponsors for the CPC in the case studies and other global sport organizations.

Top US Sponsors—Companies Spending More Than $15 Million

Amount	Company	2010 Rank	2009 Rank
$335M–$340M	PepsiCo, Inc.	1	1
$245M–$250M	The Coca-Cola Co.	2	2
$220M–$225M	Anheuser-Busch Cos.	3	4
$210M–$215M	Nike, Inc.	4	3
$185M–$190M	General Motors Co.	5	5
$175M–$180M	AT&T, Inc.	6	6
$155M–$160M	MillerCoors LLC	7	7
$150M–$155M	Toyota Motor Sales U.S.A., Inc.	8	8
$135M–$140M	Ford Motor Co.	9	9
$130M–$135M	Adidas North America, Inc.	10	10
$105M–$110M	Verizon Communications, Inc.	11	17
$85M–$90M	Bank of America Corp.	12	12
$80M–$85M	The Procter & Gamble Co.	13	13
	Sprint Nextel Corp.	14	11
$60M–$65M	FedEx Corp.	15	15
$55M–$60M	Motorola, Inc.	16	19
$50M–$55M	The Home Depot, Inc.	17	14
$45M–$50M	State Farm Cos.	18	16
	Chrysler Group LLC	19	18
	Mars, Inc.	20	20
	Citigroup Inc.	21	22
	J. P. Morgan Chase & Co.	22	32
	United Parcel Service	23	25
$40M–$45M	Berkshire Hathaway, Inc.	24	38
	Bridgestone Americas, Inc.	25	28
	Shell Oil Co.	26	27
	Wells Fargo & Co.	27	23
	Target Corp.	28	26
	Mercedes-Benz USA, LLC	29	39
	Lowe's Cos.	30	21
$35M–$40M	Visa	31	29
	Diageo North America, Inc.	32	34
	Dr Pepper Snapple Group, Inc.	33	35
	McDonald's Corp.	34	30
	American Express Co.	35	43
	Sirius XM Radio Inc.	36	24
$30M–$35M	Canon U.S.A., Inc.	37	41
	Aflac Inc.	38	–
	General Mills, Inc.	39	46

(Continued on following page)

Appendix E *(continued)*

Top US Sponsors—Companies Spending More Than $15 Million

Amount	Company	2010 Rank	2009 Rank
	Time Warner Inc.	40	33
	Nationwide Financial Services, Inc.	41	37
	MasterCard Int'l, Inc.	42	40
	Yum! Brands, Inc.	43	45
	American Honda Motor Co.	44	42
$25M–$30M	Capital One Financial Corp.	45	–
	American Airlines	46	50
	Eastman Kodak Co.	47	52
	Exxon Mobil Corp.	48	44
	Dupont Co.	49	49
	Nestlé USA, Inc.	50	31
	Office Depot, Inc.	51	48
	Hewlett-Packard Co.	52	60
	The Allstate Corp.	53	36
$20M–$25M	3M Co.	54	–
	Under Armour, Inc.	55	–
	Chevron Corp.	56	51
	Microsoft Corp.	57	55
	Sunoco, Inc.	58	58
	Papa John's Int'l, Inc.	59	–
	Red Bull North America, Inc.	60	56
	BMW of North America, LLC	61	66
	IBM Corp.	62	59
	Best Buy Co.	63	61
	Sony Corp. of America	64	53
	Sears Holdings Corp.	65	47
$15M–$20M	Delta Air Lines, Inc.	66	–
	Kia Motors America, Inc.	67	–
	Kraft Foods Inc.	68	–
	Unilever United States, Inc.	69	57
	BP America, Inc.	70	64
	The Goodyear Tire & Rubber Co.	71	–
	Subway Restaurants	72	–
	Samsung Electronics America, Inc.	73	63
	The Hershey Co.	74	–
	Discover Financial Services, Inc.	75	–
	Cisco Systems, inc.	76	–
	The Sherwin-Williams Co.	77	–

Source: http://www.sponsorship.com/IEGSR/2011/05/16/Deep-Pockets--The-Biggest-Sponsorship -Spenders-of.aspx

Appendix F
Guinness Wheelchair Basketball Commercial

Guinness Wheelchair Basketball Advert | Round Up Your Mates | Ro...

GuinnessEurope · 38 videos

▶ Subscribe   3,050

4,680,602

👍 973   👎 63

👍 Like   🗨

About   Share   Add to   ılıl   🏳

Published on Sep 13, 2013
The choices we make reveal the true nature of our character.
Guinness has a simple belief; when people come together, the
extraordinary can happen. Our new ad celebrates spending
quality time with friends and in doing so a richer life results.
What will you choose? Round up your mates for Guinness 2013.

Category   Entertainment
License   Standard YouTube License

Source retrieved December 31, 2014, from http://www.youtube.com/watch?v=hbA6U3OeRRs

Appendix G

Samsung and London 2012 Paralympic Games Partnership

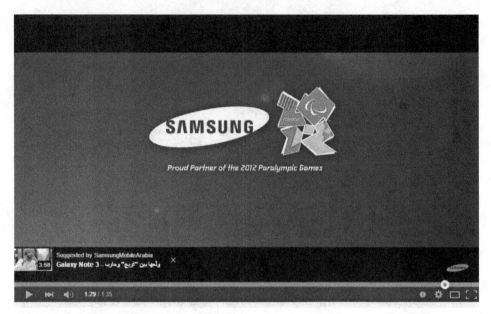

[Paralympics - London 2012] - Sport doesn't care who you are - Everyone can take part

Published on Sep 4, 2012
London 2012 Paralympics - Sport doesn't care where you're from, if you're a man or a woman, tall, thin, big or short. Sport doesn't care how you got here, how much money you make, what you believe in or not. It doesn't care if you have two legs, one leg or wheels. Sport only cares that you're here to take part and give your all to win.

Source retrieved December 31, 2014, from https://www.youtube.com/watch?v=dBcsyWIXgQY

Appendix H
Paralympics Channel 4 Advertisement

Left to right:
Claire Cashmore (swimming)
Steve Brown (WC rugby)
Jon-Allan Butterworth (cycling)
Jonnie Peacock (athletics)
Simon Munn (WC basketball)
Dave Clarke (5-a-side-football)
Hannah Cockroft (athletics)
Jody Cundy (cycling)
Ellie Simmonds (swimming)

1:25 / 1:31

Channel 4 Paralympics - Meet the Superhumans (Annotated Version)

C4Paralympics · 549 videos

Subscribe 4,346

1,145,272

8,944   91

Source retrieved December 31, 2014, from http://www.youtube.com/watch?v=kKTamH__xuQ

Appendix I

Canadian Paralympic Committee Super Athletes Campaign

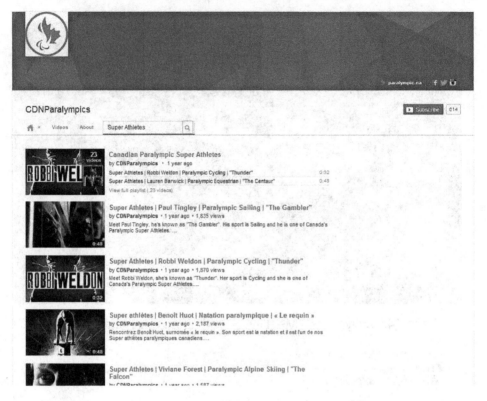

Source retrieved December 31, 2014, from https://www.youtube.com/user/CDNParalympics/search?query=Super+Athletes

Appendix J

Canadian Paralympic Committee—It's More Than Sport Campaign

It's more than sport (:60s): A Canadian Paralympic Committee commercial

CDNParalympics

Subscribe 1,028

180,316

+ Add to   Share   ••• More   143   3

Published on Aug 30, 2012
Some have been involved in parasport for years. Some have just begun their start. Whether participating for social reasons or because one day, they might want to go for Paralympic gold, these participants are feeling the rush of participation in parasport. It's more than sport. Get Involved. Watch our new ad and find out how to participate as a participant, coach or volunteer at www.paralympic.ca/get involved.

Source retrieved December 31, 2014, from http://www.youtube.com/watch?v=raA4HUv9kqA

Appendix K

Canadian Paralympic Committee and Stephanie Dixon Advertisement

Source retrieved December 31, 2014, from http://www.youtube.com/watch?v=MDgqMz37NfE

Appendix L

Petro-Canada and Vancouver 2010 Paralympic Games Partnership

Petro-Canada - Canada's Tyler Mosher Dreams Big

CDNParalympics

Subscribe 1,028

151 views

+ Add to   < Share   ••• More

👍 0   👎 0

Uploaded on Jul 22, 2011
Petro-Canada is one of the Canadian Paralympic Committee's Team Sponsors.

Vancouver 2010 Paralympic Winter Games

SHOW MORE

Source retrieved December 31, 2014, from http://www.youtube.com/watch?v=tzjJWMySs_k

Appendix M

BMW Vignette for London 2012 Paralympic Games—David Weir

The Ultimate Driving Machine

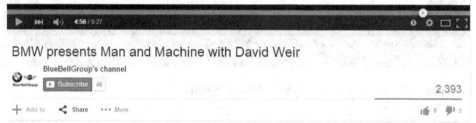

BMW presents Man and Machine with David Weir

BlueBellGroup's channel

Subscribe 48

2,393

Add to   Share   ••• More   8   0

Published on Mar 21, 2012
Man and Machine, a documentary by Yann Yannakis Jones on the Paralympian David Weir and his relationship with his wheel chair. It explores how David Weir needs to connect seamlessly with his chair to deliver his ultimate performance. At the same time it shows how the connection between the driver and the car is also central to BMW in delivering the ultimate driving experience. An official BMW video from BMW, shared with you by Blue Bell, BMW dealerships in Wilmslow and Crewe, Cheshire. Visit www.thebluebellgroup.co.uk for more info on the BMW range. BMW are a sponsor of the London 2012 Olympics Games.

Category   Autos & Vehicles
License   Standard YouTube License
Created using   YouTube Video Editor
Source videos   View attributions

Source retrieved December 31, 2014, from http://www.youtube.com/watch?v=x7NKsiBqZ1U

Appendix N

Canadian Paralympic Committee Revenue by Source

REVENUE BY SOURCE – 2011/12

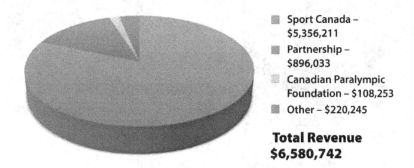

- Sport Canada – $5,356,211
- Partnership – $896,033
- Canadian Paralympic Foundation – $108,253
- Other – $220,245

Total Revenue $6,580,742

REVENUE BY SOURCE – 2015/16 (projected)

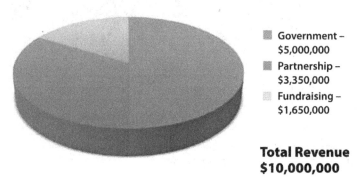

- Government – $5,000,000
- Partnership – $3,350,000
- Fundraising – $1,650,000

Total Revenue $10,000,000

Source retrieved December 31, 2014, from http://paralympic.ca/sites/default/files/uploads/Content Images/About/annual_repport_2011-2012-en-low-v2.pdf

Appendix O
Summer Paralympic Games—
Spectators, Viewers, and Media Coverage

Canada wins the bronze medal after defeating Norway in sledge hockey at the 2014 Paralympic Winter Games in Sochi, Russia. [Photo: Matthew Murnaghan/Canadian Paralympic Committee]

Source retrieved December 31, 2014, from http://paralympic.ca/sites/default/files/uploads/Content Images/About/annual_repport_2013-2014-en-low-v2.pdf

Appendix P

Media Reach—CPC Initiatives 2011–12

On Twitter, in March 2014 alone, CPC's impressions reached

76.3 million

with the hashtag *#WHATSTHERE* reaching an all-time high for CPC of

5,020

click-throughs.

The @CDNParalympics Twitter account also set a record in finishing the year with

12,697 followers, 212%

more than last year.

Caroline Bisson talks to Benoit Huot after Canada's Team Welcome Ceremony prior to the Sochi 2014 Paralympic Winter Games in Sochi, Russia. (Photo: Matthew Murnaghan/Canadian Paralympic Committee)

Source retrieved December 31, 2014, from http://paralympic.ca/sites/default/files/uploads/Content Images/About/annual_repport_2013-2014-en-low-v2.pdf

Appendix Q

Canadian Paralympic Committee and HBC Clothing Launch

Gearing up for Sochi 2014, the HBC clothing launch in October 2013 in Toronto featured Sochi hopefuls from both the Olympic and Paralympic teams.

Source retrieved February 10, 2015, from http://paralympic.ca/sites/default/files/uploads/Content Images/About/annual_repport_2013-2014-en-low-v2.pdf

Appendix R

Molson Canadian and NHL Sponsorship Activation

4/15/2015   Double Vision: Activating Through The Second Screen - IEG Sponsorship Report

THE LATEST ON SPORTS, ARTS, CAUSE AND
ENTERTAINMENT MARKETING

ACTIVATION | JUL 2, 2012

Double Vision: Activating Through The Second Screen

Properties can use the second screen to enhance the consumer
experience and add value to sponsorship packages.

The growing number of consumers using smart phones and tablet
computers to augment the TV viewing experience has created a new
activation platform for properties and sponsors: the second screen.

Pro sports leagues, teams and other types of properties are increasingly
using custom games, Twitter feeds and other digital platforms to engage
consumers as they watch live televised events.

That content includes up-to-the-minute statistics, exclusive content and
interactive games based on on-field action.

The NHL in April rolled out Molson Canadian NHL PrePlay, a
predicative online game. Fans that played the game while watching the
Stanley Cup finals could win points by correctly predicting the outcome
of on-the-ice action before it actually happened. Questions ranged from
who would win a face-off to the team that would win the game. Fans
accessed the game through Apple devices.

The league created NHL PrePlay to enhance the TV viewing experience by bringing fans closer to the sport.

"Unlike five years ago, no one is passively watching TV. We are using the second screen as a tool to deepen engagement," said Kyle McMann, the
NHL's vice president of partnership marketing.

While fan engagement is the primary driver behind NHL PrePlay, the online app provides another valuable benefit: A new consumer touchpoint for
Molson Canadian. Molson Coors Canada and MillerCoors, LLC last year inked a seven-year, nine-figure deal with the NHL, the largest in the
league's history.

"Molson Canadian is all about creating social engagement. Molson Canadian NHL PrePlay demonstrates the power of a brand to facilitate fun,
social interactions around hockey," said McMann.

Others also see value in the second screen.

"Sports rightsholders should consider the second screen as a means to creatively drive value for sponsors by amplifying their message and
connecting them to social activity unfolding around a TV broadcast," said Steve Cobb, founding partner of Active8Social, a social media agency that
specializes in fan engagement and activation platforms for sports brands.

"There is an expectation for enhanced viewing content. The second screen is a trend that is here to stay," said Tom Richardson, president and
founder of Convergence Sports & Media, a media and marketing consultancy.

In a nutshell, properties can use the second screen to accomplish the following:

- Prompt broadcast tune-ins
- Sustain TV viewership
- Engage fans
- Amplify sponsor messaging
- Access new sponsorship inventory

The popularity of the second screen is expected to grow as more consumers use mobile devices to gain a deeper connection with televised events.
Eighty-eight percent of tablet owners and 86 percent of smartphone owners used their device while watching TV at least once during a 30-day
period in late 2011, according to a recent Nielsen Co. report.

Forty-five percent of tablet owners used the device while watching TV on a daily basis, while 26 percent reported simultaneous TV and tablet use
several times a day. Smartphone owners showed similar dual usage of watching TV with their phones, with 41 percent saying they use their phone
at least once a day while tuned in.

The Many Forms Of The Second Screen

Second-screen content can reside on a myriad of platforms ranging from custom game apps to Facebook pages and Twitter feeds.

For example, Anheuser-Busch InBev in May supported its UEFA sponsorship with a multi-faceted social media platform around the FA Cup, while
NASCAR in June kicked off an integrated partnership with Twitter.

Below, *IEG SR* highlights two increasingly popular second-screen platforms.

Appendix R *(continued)*

Molson Canadian and NHL Sponsorship Activation

Custom apps. Rightsholders can choose from a growing number of app developers that offer products ranging from custom games to online platforms. Players include Shazam Entertainment, Pre Play Sports and Zeebox.

The NHL worked with Pre Play to develop Molson Canadian NHL PrePlay. The upstart created a similar game for Subway around the 2012 Super Bowl.

The NHL and Molson Coors worked closely with Pre Play to ensure the Molson Canadian brand was integrated into the game in an authentic, relevant manner, said McMann. The background of the game features the brand and the iconic image of the Canadian Rockies.

"It was more than ''Here is banner ad space where we can drop in Molson Canadian.' The product is designed to live as one entity."

The product was a success, with the average user session clocking in just shy of 25 minutes, said McMann. The league plans to expand the game to the Android platform for the 2012-2013 season, he added.

Some app developers position their products as an ambush marketing platform. For example, Kwarter is pitching its FanCake online game to both sponsors and non-sponsors. The company develops real-time predictive sports games despite a formal relationship with teams.

"A company may not have rights to the big screen, but maybe they can do something on the second screen," said Carlos Diaz, Kwarter co-founder and CEO.

A partnership with FanCake makes sense for smaller companies that might not have the budget for a full-fledged team sponsorship, he said.

Twitter. The micro-blogging site is aligning with sports leagues and TV networks to access content around live sporting events.

That includes Twitter's new partnership with NASCAR, around which it is offering curated content through Twitter.com/#NASCAR.

Like the NHL and NHL PrePlay, NASCAR aligned with Twitter to enhance the fan experience.

The two organizations kicked off the program at the June 10 Sprint Cup Series race at Pocono Raceway. The track added a hashtag to the name of the race: The Pocono 400 presented by #NASCAR. The dedicated Twitter site contains curated content ranging from driver tweets to sponsor promotional mentions.

NASCAR activated the tie with several on-site promotions. Those included a Tweet Hunt and Tweet Your Seat contest, the latter of which dangled the opportunity to wave the green flag at the start of the race.

Twitter also is striking deals with media partners. The company earlier this year announced a strategic partnership with ESPN, around which the two organizations are offering bundled advertising packages around major sports events. The two companies will promote the content across Twitter, the ESPN network, ABC and ESPN digital assets.

"Working together, ESPN and Twitter are giving marketers a clear and powerful way to link on-air and online social conversations around sports," said Joel Lunenfeld, Twitter's vice president of global brand strategy, in a statement.

Twitter and ESPN kicked off the partnership with a promotion during the NBA Finals. The #GameFace promo encouraged fans to tweet photos of their best game face, with *NBA Tonight* analysts revealing the best photos at the end of each game. ESPN displayed the images in a photo gallery on ESPN.com/NBA.

The two companies plan to run similar promotions around the Super Bowl, NCAA Men's Basketball Tournament and other major sports events.

Omid Ashtari, head of sports & entertainment, manages Twitter partnerships.

Sources
NHL, Tel: 212/789-2000
Activ8Social, Tel: 202/531-8943
Convergence Sports & Media, Tel: 203/216-0328
Kwarter Inc., Tel: 415/795-1455
Twitter, Inc., Tel: 415/222-9670

SIDEBAR
Two Examples Of Second Screen Activation

July 2, 2012:

A growing number of sponsors and rightsholders are using the second screen to enhance the TV viewing experience. Below, two examples:

Budweiser/FA Cup. InBev AB leveraged its sponsorship of the FA Cup with a second screen promotion during May 5 FA Cup Final TV broadcast. The beverage giant is in the first year of a three-year partnership with the soccer organization.

The integrated campaign featured exclusive content, interactive widgets and a social TV platform. That included a Twitter promotion that dangled an FA Cup 2013 VIP match experience, a link to the official Man of the Match voting platform on Budweiser's Facebook site, and an online game that allowed fans to share their most enthusiastic referee calls with friends and family.

The Be the Ref game resided on the Zeebox social media platform.

Target/GRAMMY Awards. The Recording Academy this year supported the GRAMMY Awards

Appendix R *(continued)*

Molson Canadian and NHL Sponsorship Activation

4/15/2015   Double Vision: Activating Through The Second Screen - IEG Sponsorship Report

with GRAMMY Live, a mobile app for the iPad, iPhone and iPod Touch.

The app featured tweets, blogs and live videos including content from the GRAMMY Awards red-carpet arrivals, the pre-telecast ceremony and the official GRAMMY Celebration after-party.

The app was sponsored by Target Corp., a GRAMMY Awards advertiser. The retailer used the program to promote CD sales: The app included a link to the retailer's web site and CDs by GRAMMY Award-nominated artists.

IEG Sponsorship Report

From IEG, leading the way in sponsorship consulting, valuation, measurement and strategy.

Visit sponsorship.com
About IEG
Contact IEG
Sponsorship Blogs
Sponsorship Jobs

Lesa Ukman, Chief Insights Officer
Jim Andrews, SVP / Content Director
William Chipps, Senior Editor
Kevin Thull, Digital Strategy
Eva Barriga, Senior Designer
Phillip Ushijima, IT Director
General Inquires
Contact An Editor
Submit A Story Idea
Submit News

IEG SR Home
Subscribe to IEG SR
Print IEG SR
Manage My Subscription
Login / Logout
View Cart

Follow IEG on Twitter
Terms of Use
Advertise
Privacy Policy

312/944-1727

Source retrieved December 31, 2014, from www.sponsorship.com/iegsr/2012/07/02Double-Vision--Activating-Through-The-Second-Seree.aspx

4

Introducing the
Global Sport System

Global sport is complex—very complex. It comprises a complicated and multi-faceted set of processes for unifying, governing, regulating, and enhancing. There are thousands of organizations and hundreds upon hundreds of millions of fans, participants, volunteers, and employees. It is huge. It exists, at one level or another, in every country or jurisdiction on Earth. Its appeal varies by country and by continent, as does its management and the marketing undertaken. It is changing, and quickly. New sports are created, old sports wane in popularity, the players and managers change and so do the rules. Trying to make sense of it is the objective of this chapter and the one that follows. In order to do this, the perspectives of sport as war, sport as the stock market, sport as passion, sport as a business, and sport as a lifestyle are presented as ways by which to view sport.

SPORT IS GOOD

An underlying assumption of this chapter is that sport is essentially good, or at the very least it provides some good things to societies and the myriad people who live in them. With hundreds of colleges and universities worldwide offering sport management, sports marketing, kinesiology, or sports MBA degrees, a student could possibly draw the conclusion that sport is, at least, relevant. This is not unlike the scene that opens the seminal college fraternity movie *Animal House* where two students are walking past a statue on the university's main campus and the plaque on the memorial reads "Knowledge is Good." It all seems so obvious.

But is sport good? Well, in some ways, yes. *Sports Illustrated* writer Michael Rosenberg wrote in the May 26, 2014 issue of that magazine that "spectator sports, at their best, reflect the society we wish we had. People [on teams] get along regardless of ethnic or economic background. They get what they earn, not what they are given. In real life, we look at growing economic inequality and wonder if anything can be done. Then we flip on the TV, see Miami trailing by 10 in the second quarter and think, 'Hey, there's a chance . . .'"

Perhaps that word *chance* is the key thing. Nike once made an in-house inspirational video for its employees that suggested that the reason Nike existed, the reason Nike made athletic shoes and competition apparel, was because they wanted to believe that the impossible could be made to happen in real life. There was a chance for athletes all over the world to "thrill us [Nike employees] once again." These concepts of superb performance, of courage, of altruism and sacrifice, of teamwork and unimaginable victories, give reason to believe that sport is indeed good.

On its best days, sport is better than war or politics, poverty or crime. It is ballet and opera, drama and comedy. It is almost always unscripted (not counting professional wrestling) and most close contests are riveting. An NHL Stanley Cup game in sudden death overtime is almost unbearable, as tension continues mounting. A big 4th and inches play in American football is fraught with torment. So is a penalty kick to advance in the World Cup. Ask any Englishman or Englishwoman.

Sport, in and of itself, does not solve problems, but it can make the world's collective residents look differently at the challenges of a daily grind or for just a few moments (or hours), take young minds and old minds alike off the many problems that each of us must solve. Indeed, if for no other reason than that, sport is better than good. It is, to borrow from the movie *Bill and Ted's Excellent Adventure*, "most excellent."

SPORT IS WAR

In its modern form, many argue that sport has replaced warfare as a means for countries to express their strength, culture, and values. Events such as the Olympic Games, FIFA World Cup, IAAF World Athletics Championships, Rugby World Cup, IIHF World Ice Hockey Championships, and many more, pitch athlete against athlete, country against country on a global stage in a much more progressive manner than military action. Legendary 1970s stories of Canada versus the Soviet Union in ice hockey or battles amongst Eastern Bloc countries in water polo provide powerful examples of how sport can take on a geopolitical as well as athletic or marketing role in the world. Other examples include dictator Adolf Hitler using the 1936 Berlin Olympic Games for political reasons or politicians from various countries boycotting the Olympic Games of 1976, 1980 and 1984.

As these examples emphasize, sport has often been a context for larger political issues and this phenomenon continues to today, as global events have become battlefields for country pride and competition. Just observing the long-term investments in high performance sport of host countries of Olympic Games as they lead up to hosting, with one of the primary objectives of winning medals, provides evidence of this proposition. This reality, in turn, has led to the increased importance of performance at these events, whether athletically, through the accumulation of medals, technically as a host country, or politically, as a member of a global sporting association. In a forum where the world is watching and a country's image is at stake, many are dubbing this as "the global sport arms race," a demonstration of the international power of sport, and its important role in global government relations.

Evidence of this importance can be found in the increasing interest of governments in investing in high-performance sport where the goal is Olympic medals. Notable examples include the Australian Institute for Sport leading up to the 2000 Sydney Games, the 'Own the Podium' program supported by the Canadian government launched in advance of the 2010 Vancouver Games, and UK Sport as the London 2012 Games approached. These efforts include a few common elements, including (i) a national mandate provided through statute or enabling legislation, (ii) a central authority with a mandate to deliver policies and programs, (iii) overarching policy objectives, (iv) measurable performance achievements, (v) coordinated delivery of programs and services, and (vi) ongoing measurement and evaluation.

THE POWER OF SPORT AND
THE GLOBAL SPORTING ARMS RACE

"SPORT HAS THE POWER TO CHANGE THE WORLD. IT HAS THE POWER TO INSPIRE. IT HAS THE POWER TO UNITE PEOPLE IN A WAY THAT LITTLE ELSE DOES. SPORT CAN AWAKEN HOPE WHERE THERE WAS PREVIOUSLY ONLY DESPAIR. SPORT SPEAKS TO PEOPLE IN A LANGUAGE THEY CAN UNDERSTAND."

—*Nelson Mandela*

This statement by the iconic antiapartheid leader, Nelson Mandela, former President of South Africa, speaks volumes as to the power that sport can transmit to society. Notably, sport as a force for good was recognized by the United Nations in 2005 when the world body declared the UN International Year of Sport and Physical Activity in recognition of the role that sport and physical education play at the "individual, community, national and global levels."

To illustrate further the global appeal of sport, consider that while the United Nations recognizes only 193 nations as member states, FIFA, the governing body of football (soccer), and the International Association of Athletics Federations (IAAF), which governs athletics, each boast 212 members. At the 2012 Olympic Games in London, England, a record 204 national delegations (NOCs) competed in the Games, demonstrating conclusively that sport does, indeed, bring the world together to play. The country versus nation versus jurisdiction comparison is interesting and supports the role sport plays globally. This discrepancy is due to differing criteria applicable to recognition for political and/or sport considerations. Thus, for example, Taiwan is a FIFA eligible team that is not fully recognized as an independent country by the UN. There are also historical remnants in sport that have led to separate recognition of former colonies or protectorates, now politically incorporated into states for governance purposes, but not for sport, such as Bermuda. Some sports recognize components of the United Kingdom, permitting "national" teams from England, Scotland and Northern Ireland.

For individual humans, sport can contribute to one's personal development, general health, and/or self-esteem. For communities—whether defined by geography, interests, or culture—sport can provide opportunities for community building, as well as for supporting particular social causes such as youth at risk, promoting volunteerism, or improving physical activity levels. At the national (or even state/provincial) level, sport has the ability to contribute to economic development and social capital, improved public health, and can create very special unifying moments of national pride. Finally, as noted, on a global scale (multicountry), sport can have a significant positive impact on development, public health, and peace.

In most developed countries, sport is incredibly pervasive in the lives of citizens. The sport pages are the most-read section of daily newspapers and online blogs, sport is a popular topic around the office water cooler, and sport venues are places where millions of families spend their weekends. Indeed, the local arenas or soccer pitches have often become a primary meeting point for many communities. In these countries, sport, more than any other social pursuit, may become a catalyst for national unity, such as winning an Olympic gold medal in a high-profile sport, capturing the World Cup, or hosting the world for a major mega-event. A powerful example is the gold medal men's ice hockey game at the 2010 Vancouver Winter Olympic Games, played between the United States and Canada. In Canada, the game was the most watched television broadcast (sport or non-sport) in Canadian history. Roughly half of the Canadian population tuned in (16.6 million viewers) with peak audiences attracting more than two-thirds of the country.

ILLUSTRATION OF A SPORT SYSTEM: THE EXAMPLE OF CANADA

In considering the international sportscape, it is vital that a sport marketer understand that, although there are certain similarities across all countries and jurisdictions, it is equally clear that each country also has its own organizational and structural differences. For example, some countries have very heavy government involvement (e.g., China, Canada, Norway, Australia) while others (e.g., USA) have no direct government support. Even within those benefitting from government support, there are vast differences. For example, much of Pakistan's support is via the military and the World Military Games are a priority for the country. In order to provide an example, a case study of the Canadian sport system is provided here to give an example of how one nation is structured from a sport perspective.

In Canada, the sport system is supported —in part—by multiple levels of government (implicit in a federal state having different levels of legislative jurisdiction) that provide both policy leadership and financial support to enable grassroots participation, development, and the pursuit of excellence at the national and international levels, for those who have the requisite skills and interests. Although there are exceptions, historically and generally, the federal government has been responsible for the high -performance side while provincial governments took on the participation and development aspects, a division of responsibilities consistent with the federal constitutional regime. Not-for-profit organizations and volunteer groups deliver programs to allow sport participation, coaching development, and the planning and staging of events. These include multi-sport organizations and national sport organizations, as well as provincial sport organizations, amongst others. Private corporations support government-provided resources via sponsorship, donations, and partnerships. Media organizations, each in their own manner, promote opportunities to participate and enjoy sport, including the broadcast or webcast of sporting competitions on television and via the web, by radio and through print. At times, various external public sectors such as health and education collaborate to promote the benefits of participation in sport and physical activity, in a reciprocal manner, to advance their own objectives (e.g., reduction of childhood obesity and sedentary lifestyles).

This Canadian framework is underpinned by the Canadian Sport Policy (updated in 2012), which has been endorsed by federal, provincial, and territorial governments and the sport community. This is the second generation of the Policy, the first having been endorsed in 2002. The Policy sets directions for governments and other organizations that are "committed to realizing the positive impacts of sport on individuals, communities and society" for the period 2012–2022. It addresses participation, development, high performance, and capacity considerations. The Policy's vision is to create a "dynamic and innovative culture that promotes and celebrates participation and excellence in sport." The implementation of the Policy is undertaken via a series of action plans carried out, depending on the scope of a particular plan, by the various stakeholders, individually, collectively, bilaterally, and multilaterally. The Policy also has a monitoring mechanism to measure progress towards the goals and objectives identified within the Policy. For example, on

© Sergeibach | Dreamstime.com—Canadian Photo

(Continued on next page)

the high-performance side, the Policy identifies the importance of high-performance sport for a modern nation and outlines roles and responsibilities of various players that "strives for Canadian athletes to consistently achieve podium level performances in sports at Olympic and Paralympic Games and their Senior World Championships." Via the *Own the Podium* program, results and potential future results are closely monitored, tracked, and evaluated.

SPORT EXCELLENCE STRATEGY

Since the Australian government instituted a plan for its athletes to perform at a very high level leading up to the 2000 Summer Olympic Games (held in Sydney), it has become commonplace for governments, especially in host countries, to implement sport excellence strategies to allocate resources, coaching, sport science expertise, facilities, and other supports to maximizing performance at the Olympic Games. In the case of Canada, that strategy identifies key objectives and actions in the areas of *Collaborative Leadership, High Performance Facility Access, System Development,* and *Knowledge Mobilization* in order to advance the goals of the strategy.

As noted previously, the UK, after initially scoffing at Own the Podium in Vancouver, quickly adopted its own version of that program for 2012, with considerable success. In some cases, governments create organizations to drive this process, such as the Australian Institute for Sport and UK Sport to drive the excellence agenda. The countries' National Olympic Committees (NOCs) and National Paralympic Committees (NPCs) are normally involved and sometimes contribute financial and other resources along with the government. Typical tactics adopted by these specialized excellence organizations include targeted investments in specific athletes, sport science, equipment, and coaching.

In order to better understand the factors that contribute to international sporting success, a group of researchers came together in 2002 and launched an initiative called Sports Policy Factors Leading to International Success (SPLISS), which included researchers from eight nations who prepared a study that compared sport structures, policy, and performances in six nations. The study (published in 2007) outlines a series of nine pillars that are suggested as the policy factors that lead to international sporting success, including

- financial support,
- integrated approach to policy development,
- participation in sport,
- talent identification and development system,
- athletic and post-career support,

- training facilities,
- coaching and coach development,
- international competition,
- scientific research.

A common element within many sport excellence strategies is the development and inclusion of a Long-term Athlete Development Model (LTAD).

While the research findings of the SPLISS report seem to suggest an increasingly homogenous elite sports development system, as observed in the sample nations studied, the report was unable to predict with any certainty the direct relationship between the common policy factors and sporting success, with the exception that financial support and coaching seemed to correlate to success and an effective system in the countries observed. While researchers continue to grapple with finding the keys to international sporting success, more nations are responding to the increasingly strong competition base for medals by increasing their investment in high-performance sport. This increased focus on high performance tends to lead to a decreased focus (not to mention less resources) on sport development and participation level sport. The proverbial *global sporting arms race* continues to be waged at many levels. Of the policy factors identified in the SPLISS report, international competition was identified as an important contributor to international success. Hosting these types of events (e.g., Olympic Games, Pan-American Games, Asian Games, European Games) leads to legacy in the form of built competition/training facilities, improved coaching/volunteer base, additional program funding for competition and training, and enhanced sport science and medicine services.

However, it is important to note that the competition inherent in this global sporting arms race also brings risks of threats to sport, via the risk and reward nature of such a dynamic. Potential risks include

- doping—athletes, teams, or political systems using illegal performance enhancements;
- match fixing—internal (coach, player) or external (referee, gambler) altering the outcome of a game;
- corruption—government or association members or employees acting in illegal ways for personal or performance benefit related to winning or the need to win;
- violence—player or spectator behaviors related to the all-consuming drive to win;
- other unethical behaviors guided by a disproportionate desire to win medals and to win the global race.

© Preckas | Dreamstime.com—Basketball Sports Violence Photo

SPORTACCORD

SportAccord[1] is an important boundary spanner in international sport. Global sport organizations and international federations (IFs) associate through SportAccord, which acts as an umbrella organization for all Olympic and non-Olympic IFs as well as organizers of multisports games and sport-related international associations (e.g., Right to Play). SportAccord is an international sport body with 91 full members (IOC recognized IFs, other IFs—all of which govern specific sports worldwide) and 16 associate members (organizations that conduct activities closely related to the IFs). One of SportAccord's mandates is to establish multisports games that group together similar sports to promote the members' interests and visibility (SportAccord, 2012). In addition to SportAccord members, a number of other international sport organizations—both IFs responsible for a sport globally and global multisport organizations that serve many sports—exist around the world of varying sizes and scopes. The members and associate members of SportAccord are presented in the following table, with a brief description of each, along with the IOC recognized IFs, IPC-recognized IFs, and other global sport organizations that act as IFs formally or informally.

INTERNATIONAL FEDERATIONS (IFs)
RECOGNIZED BY THE IOC

As presented earlier in the book (Table 1.1) and repeated within the Table 4.1 list of all global sport federations, the IOC recognizes a smaller group of IFs than exist, although many are small or niche or involved in activities that some may view more as leisure pursuits than sports. See Table 1.1 or Table 4.1 for the full list of IFs recognized by the IOC and who participate on the Olympic program. The IFs recognized by the IOC are divided into two associations, one for the summer Olympic sports and one for the winter Olympic sports. The IOC further recognizes a group of IFs whose sports are not on the Olympic program.

Table 4.1.			
Sport/Event	Member	Initial	Description
Akido	International Aikido Federation	IAF	Non-Olympic Sport IF
Airsoft	International Airsoft Practical Shooting	IAPS	Non-Olympic Sport IF
Air Sports	Fédération Aéronautique Internationale	FAI	Non-Olympic Sport IF
Aquatics	Fédération Internationale De Natation	FINA	Olympic Sport IF
Archery	World Archery Federation	WA	Olympic Sport IF
Athletics	International Association of Athletics Federations	IAAF	Olympic Sport IF
Aussie Rules	Australian Football League Commission	AFL	Non-Olympic Sport IF
Auto Racing	Fédération Internationale de l'Automobile	FIA	Non-Olympic Sport IF
Badminton	Badminton World Federation	BWF	Olympic Sport IF
Bandy	Federation of International Bandy	FIB	Non-Olympic Sport IF

(Continued on next page)

Sport/Event	Member	Initial	Description
	Table 4.1. *(Continued)*		
Baseball/Softball	World Baseball Softball Confederation	WBSC	Non-Olympic Sport IF
Basketball	International Basketball Federation	FIBA	Olympic Sport IF
Basque Pelota	Fédération Internationale de Pelota Vasca	FIPV	Non-Olympic Sport IF
Beach Soccer	Beach Soccer Worldwide	BSWW	Non-Olympic Sport IF
Biathlon	International Biathlon Union	IBU	Olympic Sport IF
Billiard Sports	World Confederation of Billiard Sports	WCBS	Non-Olympic Sport IF
Blind Sports	International Blind Sports Federation	IBSF	Global Multisport Org.
Bobsleigh	Fédération Internationale de Bobsleigh et de Tobogganing	FIBT	Olympic Sport IF
Boccia/Football 7's	Cerebral Palsy International Sports and Recreation Association	CPISRA	Non-Paralympic Sport IF
Bodybuilding	International Federation of Bodybuilding and Fitness	IFBB	Non-Olympic Sport IF
Boot Throwing	International Boot-Throwing Association	IBTA	Non-Olympic Sport IF
Boules Sports	Confédération Mondiale des Sports de Boules	CMSB	Non-Olympic Sport IF
Boxing	International Boxing Association	AIBA	Olympic Sport IF
Boxing	World Professional Boxing Federation	WBPF	Non-Olympic Sport IF
Bowling (Can 5 Pin)	Canadian 5 Pin Bowlers Association	C5PBA	Non-Olympic Sport IF
Bowling (10 Pin)	Fédération Internationale des Quilleurs	FIQ	Non-Olympic Sport IF
Bridge	World Bridge Federation	WBF	Non-Olympic Sport IF
Broomball	International Federation of Broomball Associations	IFBA	Non-Olympic Sport IF
Canoe/Kayak	International Canoe Federation	ICF	Olympic Sport IF
Casting	International Casting Sport Federation	ICSF	Non-Olympic Sport IF
Cerebral Palsy	Cerebral Palsy International Sport and Recreation Association	CPISRA	Global Multisport Org.
Chess	Fédération Internationale des Échecs	FIDE	Non-Olympic Sport IF
Commonwealth Games	Commonwealth Games Federation	CGF	Major Games
Cricket	International Cricket Council	ICC	Non-Olympic Sport IF
Croquet	World Croquet Federation	WCF	Non-Olympic Sport IF
Curling	World Curling Federation	WCF	Olympic Sport IF
Cycling	International Cycling Union	ICU	Olympic Sport IF
Dance Sport	International DanceSport Federation	IDSF	Non-Olympic Sport IF
Darts	World Darts Federation	WDF	Non-Olympic Sport IF
Deaf Sport	International Committee of Sports for the Deaf	ICSD	Global Multisport Org.
Dragon Boat	International Dragon Boat Federation	IDBF	Non-Olympic Sport IF
Draughts	World Draughts Federation	FMJD	Non-Olympic Sport IF
Equestrian	Fédération Équestre Internationale	FEI	Olympic Sport IF
Fencing	Fédération Internationale D'escrime	FIE	Olympic Sport IF
Fishing	International Confederation of Sports Fishing	CIPS	Non-Olympic Sport IF

(Continued on next page)

Table 4.1. (Continued)

Sport/Event	Member	Initial	Description
Fistball	International Fistball Association	IFA	Non-Olympic Sport IF
Fives	Rugby Fives Association	RFA	Non-Olympic Sport IF
Flying Disc	World Flying Disc Federation	WFDF	Non-Olympic Sport IF
Floorball	International Floorball Federation	IFF	Non-Olympic Sport IF
Foosball	International Table Soccer Federation	ITSF	Non-Olympic Sport IF
Football	Fédération Internationale de Football Association	FIFA	Olympic Sport IF
Football (Gaelic)	Gaelic Athletic Association	GAA	Non-Olympic Sport IF
Football (US)	International Federation of American Football	IFAF	Non-Olympic Sport IF
Go	International Go Federation	IGF	Non-Olympic Sport IF
Goalball/Judo/Football	International Blind Sports Federation	IBSA	Non-Paralympic Sport IF
Golf	International Golf Federation	IGF	Olympic Sport IF
Gymnastics	International Gymnastics Federation	FIG	Olympic Sport IF
Handball	International Handball Federation	IHF	Olympic Sport IF
Harness Horse Racing	Harness Horsemen International	HHI	Non-Olympic Sport IF
Hockey	International Hockey Federation	FIH	Olympic Sport IF
Horse Racing	International Racing Bureau	IRB	Non-Olympic Sport IF
Hurling	Gaelic Athletic Association	GAA	Non-Olympic Sport IF
Ice Hockey	International Ice Hockey Federation	IIHF	Olympic Sport IF
Intellectual Disability	International Sports Federation for Persons with Intellectual Disability	INAS	Global Multisport Org.
Intercrosse	Fédération Internationale d'Inter-Crosse	FIIC	Global Multisport Org.
Judo	International Judo Federation	IJF	Olympic Sport IF
Ju-jitsu	Ju-jitsu International Federation	JJIF	Non-Olympic Sport IF
Kabaddi	International Kabaddi Federation	IKF	Non-Olympic Sport IF
Karate	World Karate Federation	WKF	Non-Olympic Sport IF
Kendo	International Kendo Federation	IKF	Non-Olympic Sport IF
Kickboxing	World Association of Kickboxing Organizations	WAKO	Non-Olympic Sport IF
Kung Fu	International Kung Fu Federation	IKF	Non-Olympic Sport IF
Lacrosse	Federation of International Lacrosse	FIL	Non-Olympic Sport IF
Labour Sport	International Labour Sport Federation	CIST	Non-Olympic Sport IF
Life Saving	International Life Saving Federation	ILSF	Non-Olympic Sport IF
Luge	International Luge Federation	FIL	Olympic Sport IF
Mallakhamb	Mallakhamb Confederation of World	MCW	Non-Olympic Sport IF
Masters Games	International Masters Games Association	IMGA	Major Games
Military Sports	International Military Sports Council	CISM	Global Multisport Org.

(Continued on next page)

Table 4.1. *(Continued)*			
Sport/Event	**Member**	**Initial**	**Description**
Miniature Golf	World Minigolfsport Federation	WMF	Non-Olympic Sport IF
Mixed Martial Arts	United Fighting Challenge	UFC	Major Games
Mixed Martial Arts	International Sport Combat Federation	ISCF	Non-Olympic Sport IF
Modern Arnis	International Modern Arnis Federation	IMAF	Non-Olympic Sport IF
Modern Pentathlon	Union Internationale de Pentathlon Moderne	UIPM	Olympic Sport IF
Motorcycle Sport	Fédération Internationale de Motocyclisme	FIM	Non-Olympic Sport IF
Moutaineering	Union Internationale des Associations d'Alpinisme	UIAA	Non-Olympic Sport IF
Mountain Boarding	International Mountainboard Riders Association	IMRA	Non-Olympic Sport IF
Mountain Running	World Mountain Running Association	WMRA	Non-Olympic Sport IF
Muay Thai	International Federation of Muaythai Amateur	IFMA	Non-Olympic Sport IF
Netball	International Federation of Netball Associations	IFNA	Non-Olympic Sport IF
Orienteering	International Orienteering Federation	IOF	Non-Olympic Sport IF
Panathlon	Panathlon International	PI	Global Multisport Org.
Parabadminton	Parabadminton World Federation	PBWF	Paralympic Sport IF
Paralympic Games	International Paralympic Committee	IPC	Major Games
Parkour	World Freerunning Parkour Federation	WFPF	Non-Olympic Sport IF
Pitch and Putt	International Pitch and Putt Association	IPPA	Non-Olympic Sport IF
Practical Shooting	International Practical Shooting Confederation	IPSC	Non-Olympic Sport IF
Poker	International Federation of Poker	IFP	Non-Olympic Sport IF
Pole Sports	International Pole Sports Federation	IPSF	Non-Olympic Sport IF
Polo	Federation of International Polo	FIP	Non-Olympic Sport IF
Powerboating	Union Internationale Motonautique	UIM	Non-Olympic Sport IF
Powerlifting	International Powerlifting Federation	IPF	Non-Olympic Sport IF
Racketlon	International Racketlon Federation	FIR	Non-Olympic Sport IF
Raquetball	International Racquetball Federation	IRF	Non-Olympic Sport IF
Rafting	International Rafting Federation	IRF	Non-Olympic Sport IF
Rogaining	International Rogaining Federation	IRF	Non-Olympic Sport IF
Roller Sports	International Federation of Roller Sports	FIRS	Non-Olympic Sport IF
Rope Skipping	World Rope Skipping Confederation	WRSC	Non-Olympic Sport IF
Rope Skipping	International Rope Skipping Federation	IRSF	Non-Olympic Sport IF
Rowing	International Rowing Federation	FISA	Olympic Sport IF
Rubik's Cube	World Cube Association	WCA	Non-Olympic Sport IF
Rugby	International Rugby Board	IRB	Olympic Sport IF
Rugby League	Rugby League International Federation	RLIF	Non-Olympic Sport IF

(Continued on next page)

Sport/Event	Member	Initial	Description
Sailing	International Sailing Federation	ISAF	Olympic Sport IF
Sailing (disabled)	International Federation for Disabled Sailing	IFDS	Paralympic Sport IF
Sambo	Federation International of Amateur Sambo	FIAS	Non-Olympic Sport IF
School Sport	International School Sport Federation	ISF	Global Multisport Org.
Sepak Takraw	International Sepaktakraw Federation	ISTAF	Non-Olympic Sport IF
Shinty	Camanachd Association		Non-Olympic Sport IF
Shooting	International Shooting Sport Federation	ISSF	Olympic Sport IF
Shuttlecock	International Shuttlecock Federation	ISF	Non-Olympic Sport IF
Skating	International Skating Union	ISU	Olympic Sport IF
Skiing	International Ski Federation	FIS	Olympic Sport IF
Skibobbing	International Skibob Federation	FISB	Non-Olympic Sport IF
Ski Mountaineering	International Ski Mountaineering Federation	ISMF	Non-Olympic Sport IF
Sled Dog Racing	International Federation of Sleddog Sports	IFSS	Non-Olympic Sport IF
Soft Tennis	International Soft Tennis Federation	ISTF	Non-Olympic Sport IF
Special Olympics	Special Olympics		Major Games
Sports Climbing	International Federation of Sport Climbing	IFSC	Non-Olympic Sport IF
Sports Facilities	International Association for Sports and Leisure Facilities	IAKS	Global Multisport Org.
Sports Press	Association Internationale de la Presse Sportive	AIPS	Global Multisport Org.
Squash	World Squash Federation	WSF	Non-Olympic Sport IF
Sumo Wrestling	International Sumo Federation	ISF	Non-Olympic Sport IF
Surfing	International Surfing Association	ISA	Non-Olympic Sport IF
Table Hockey	International Table Hockey Federation	ITHF	Non-Olympic Sport IF
Table Soccer	International Table Soccer Federation	ITSF	Non-Olympic Sport IF
Table Tennis	The International Table Tennis Federation	ITTF	Olympic Sport IF
Taekwondo	World Taekwondo Federation	WTF	Olympic Sport IF
Tchoukball	Fédération Internationale de Tchoukball	FITB	Non-Olympic Sport IF
Tennis	International Tennis Federation	ITF	Olympic Sport IF
Timekeepers	Fédération Internationale des Chronométreurs	FIC	Global Multisport Org.
Throwball	International Throwball Federation	ITF	Non-Olympic Sport IF
Triathlon	International Triathlon Union	ITU	Olympic Sport IF
Tug-of-War	Tug-of-War International Federation	TWIF	Non-Olympic Sport IF
Underwater Sports	Confédération Mondiale des Activités Subaquatiques	CMAS	Non-Olympic Sport IF
University Sports	Federation Internationale du Sport Universitaire	FISU	Major Games
Volleyball	International Volleyball Federation	FIVB	Olympic Sport IF

Table 4.1. *(Continued)*

(Continued on next page)

Sport/Event	Member	Initial	Description
	Table 4.1. *(Continued)*		
Volleyball (disabled)	World Organization Volleyball for Disabled	WOVD	Paralympic Sport IF
Vovinam	International Vovinam Federation	IVF	Non-Olympic Sport IF
Vovinam	The Vovinam-VietVoDao World Federation	WVVF	Non-Olympic Sport IF
VX	Global VX (formerly: International Rock-It-Ball Federation		Non-Olympic Sport IF
Water Skiing	International Water Ski Federation	IWSF	Non-Olympic Sport IF
Weightlifting	International Weightlifting Federation	IWF	Olympic Sport IF
Wheelchair Basketball	International Wheelchair Basketball Federation	IWBF	Paralympic Sport IF
Wheelchair Fencing	International Wheelchair and Amputee Sports Federation	IWAS	Non-Paralympic Sport IF
Wheelchair Rugby	International Wheelchair Rugby Federation	IWRF	Paralympic Sport IF
Wheelchair Sport	International Wheelchair and Amputee Sports Federation	IWASF	Global Multisport Org.
World Games	International World Games Association	IWGA	Major Games
Wrestling	International Federation of Associated Wrestling Styles	FILA	Olympic Sport IF
Wushu	International Wushu Federation	IWUF	Non-Olympic Sport IF
Yoga	Yogasports Confederation of World	YCW	Non-Olympic Sport IF
*Note: Each federation listed above has a website with full details on the organization, easily viewed via any search engine.			

The summer sports combine under the Association of Summer Olympic International Federations (ASOIF), which includes many of the largest IFs in the world such as FIFA, FINA, FIBA, and IAAF, as well as some of the smallest ones like BWF, WA, FIE, and IWF. FIFA, for example, has a membership of 212 national associations, organizes dozens of global tournaments, and has a multibillion dollar budget. FIE (fencing), on the other hand, is a more typical IF, as it operates its World Championship and World Cup with a membership base of 145 NSOs. Many IFs include a number of sport disciplines under their responsibility, such as FIVB (volleyball and beach volleyball) and FIG whose responsibility includes sports aerobics, traditional gymnastics, rhythmic gymnastics, sports acrobatics, trampoline, and tumbling. Similarly, the ITU is responsible for triathlon as well as its sister sports of duathlon (run-bike-run) and aquathlon (swim-run).

The winter IFs on the Olympic program combine similarly under the umbrella of the Association of International Winter Olympic International Federations (AIOWF). This small group of IFs includes the IBU, WCF, FIBT (responsible for both bobsleigh and skeleton), IIHF, ISU (figure skating, speed skating, and short track speed skating), FIL, and FIS (alpine skiing, Nordic combined, cross country skiing, freestyle skiing, ski jumping, and snowboarding). Finally, as noted, another 33 IFs are recognized by the IOC as part of the Association of the IOC Recognized International Sports Federations (ARISF). These IFs are included in Table 4.1 as well and include a number of IFs that are groups of other IFs, such as FAI (aerobatics, air racing, ballooning, gliding, hang gliding, and parachuting/skydiving), WBSC (baseball and softball), WCBS (carom billiards, pocket billiards/pool, and snooker), CMSB (bocce, bowls, boule Lyonnais, and pétanque), FIRS (inline hockey, roller racing, rink hockey, and roller derby), and IWSF (water skiing and wake boarding).

FEDERATIONS RECOGNIZED BY THE INTERNATIONAL PARALYMPIC COMMITTE (IPC)

In a manner similar to that used by the IOC, the IPC also recognizes 12 IFs that are involved with Paralympic sport. The IPC itself serves as the international federation for another 8 IFs, including Alpine skiing, athletics, ice sledge hockey, Nordic skiing, powerlifting, shooting, swimming, and wheelchair dance sport. In each of these sports, the IPC assumes the role of the IF, since the sports are not yet developed enough or the resource base is too low for an effective independent IF to function effectively. For the 12 IFs that do oversee Paralympic sport, 7 are also the able-bodied sport IF and 5 are Paralympic sport-specific IFs (also included in Table 4.1). These IFs are listed here:

1. Archery: WA
2. Badminton: Parabadminton World Federation (PBWF)
3. Cycling: UCI
4. Equestrian: FEI
5. Rowing: FISA
6. Table Tennis: ITTF
7. Wheelchair curling: WCF
8. Wheelchair tennis: ITF
9. Sailing: International Federation for Disabled Sailing (IFDS)
10. Volleyball: World Organization Volleyball for Disabled (WOVD)
11. Wheelchair Basketball: International Wheelchair Basketball Federation (IWBF)
12. Wheelchair Rugby: International Wheelchair Rugby Federation (IWRF).

Outside of the Paralympics, there are a number of other disabled sports federations in operation at the international level for sports that are not on the program of the Paralympic Games. These include boccia and football *7-a-side*, which are both managed by the Cerebral Palsy International Sports and Recreation Association (CPISRA). There is football *5-a-side*, a different version of the sport, under the leadership of the International Blind Sports Federation (IBSA), which also oversees the disabled sports of goalball and judo. Finally, wheelchair fencing is under the jurisdiction of the International Wheelchair and Amputee Sports Federation (IWAS). CPISRA, IBSA, and IWAS are all included in Table 4.1.

CHAPTER SUMMARY

This chapter outlines the various organizations involved in global sport system organized under the IOC, the IPC, IFs, governments, and other related and typically not-for-profit organizations. The purpose of the chapter is to inform the reader of the vast number of organizations responsible for a large number of sports (and leisure pursuits) globally, as well as to outline the role that sport plays in large-scale global activities.

Key Chapter Questions

1. If you became president of an International Federation that is recognized by the IOC, but whose sport is not on the program of the Olympic Games, what considerations might you explore or what activities would you put in place if you sought to pursue getting on the program of the Olympic Games?
2. In the Paralympic Games, why—in your view—are some sports managed by the IFs of their able-bodied counterpart, others by IFs specific to Paralympic sport, and still others by the IPC itself? What would be the pros and cons of each of these three situations?
3. Consider the chapter outline "Global Sports Arms Race." What is your view on this? Should taxpayer dollars be allocated to high-performance sport? Is sport participation and health not a better use of dollars? Outline the arguments for and against.
4. Sport excellence has been shown to work in countries like Canada, the UK, and Australia when governments invest heavily. Should the United States, one of a few countries where no public dollars go to sport, reconsider?
5. Table 4.1 provides an extensive list of global sport federations. Select three from the list that manage a sport that you do not know much about and do web research to outline the global footprint of that sport (or discipline).
6. What is your view on the overall structure of IFs in sport. Are there too many? From a marketing perspective, would fewer organizations responsible for more sports each be more effective in obtaining resources?

5

The Market-Based Side of Global Sport

As introduced in Chapter 4, the global sport system is complex, international, diverse, vast, and contributes in a variety of ways to modern society. However, there is an aspect of the system—which was only lightly touched upon in Chapter 4—that is about open markets, private ownership, asset appreciation, and brand equity. The focus of this chapter is professional sport with its (largely) for-profit clubs, players' unions, and ever-growing franchise values. Although there are a number of subtle and minor differences (and certainly lots in common) between the world of IFs and the world of professional sport leagues, the key difference is that owners of professional sport clubs earn profits/losses each year and can sell the asset (often for an appreciated amount) if they so choose. This difference has profound impact on how professional sport is organized, managed, and administered *vis-à-vis* IFs and the similar global associations discussed in Chapter 4.

PROFESSIONAL SPORT

Professional sport includes leagues, teams/clubs, coaches, executives, and players whose value rises when things go well (e.g., on-the-field product is high quality, sport/club/player are attracting new fans, exciting star players with charisma/talent are showcased, media rights deals are significant, sponsorship is high, games are sold out). This value is captured in the resulting increased revenues via both ticket sales revenues and non-ticket revenues (such as television, online streaming, merchandise, sponsorship, etc.). In addition, assets (clubs, teams) can also increase in value long term based on these successes (i.e., franchise value, future sponsorship/naming rights revenue, and potential future contract/salary for a player/coach/executive). Given its structure, this for-profit nature, professional sport is viewed as a partnership of sovereign entities that agree on certain governance principles and procedures in the pursuit of their separate business interests and who control the entrance and exit of participants/athletes, clubs/teams, partners/sponsors, and certain suppliers of goods and services.

Although professional sport leagues and clubs are normally more geographically focused than IFs, many leagues and clubs have taken a very global view regarding their marketing efforts and growth. For example, the National Basketball Association (NBA) now has offices in more than 40 countries around the world with accompanying partnerships and marketing activities, although 29 of its clubs are located in the United States and 1 in Canada. At the club level within other sports, major clubs like the New York Yankees, Manchester United, Barca, the Montreal Canadiens, and San Antonio Spurs have significant followings outside of their home territories via global media coverage of games, fan clubs, or merchandising.

Structurally, professional sport is very hard to classify and describe in terms of its landscape, its organizations, and its scope. Its organizations consist of leagues, clubs, owners, players, players' associations/unions, and supporting agencies. These organizations are usually for profit at the club level, but leagues, associations, and unions are normally not-for-profits. For example, the NBA (league) and the NBA Players Association (union) are not-for-profit organizations while the Dallas Mavericks and Toronto Raptors, NBA clubs, are for-profit organizations. The scope, finances, fan interest, and marketability vary considerably sport-to-sport, country-to-country, league-to-league, and club-to-club, with some clubs valued at over US $2 billion and others worth less than 10% of that amount. In Major League Baseball (MLB), for example, *Forbes* magazine estimates the New York Yankees to be the highest valued club in the league (2013 data) at US $2.5 billion, while it reported the Columbus Blue Jackets to be the lowest valued club in the National Hockey League (NHL) at US $175 million. The effective global sports marketer needs, therefore, to be generally aware of the global landscape—both Olympic and professional sport—in which it operates. In today's sports industry, professional and Olympic sports often converge, including professional players participating in the Olympic Games, efforts relating to antidoping, and partnerships to grow a sport globally between leagues, clubs, and sport federations. For example, FIBA and the NBA have partnered on a number of initiatives to grow the game of basketball around the world, such as the Basketball without Borders sport development program.

As to the global structure of professional sport, the first basis on which to differentiate is team-sport (e.g., football) versus individual-sport (e.g., tennis). Within each of these broad groups, there are considerable differences in how the sports are organized. The landscape of professional sport is presented in two subsections, one devoted to the team sport leagues and one about the individual sport leagues.

PROFESSIONAL TEAM SPORT LEAGUES/ASSOCIATIONS

Team sport leagues include professional sports leagues consisting of clubs in which a group of athletes competes together against another group of athletes in a competitive event, or series of such events. A number of sports/leagues/associations are presented and classified in alphabetical order.

Baseball

The sport of baseball is popular in North America, Japan, Taiwan, Australia, Korea, Venezuela, Cuba, Italy, and the Dominican Republic. The most prominent league is

Major League Baseball (MLB), headquartered in New York with 30 member clubs (29 in the United States; 1 in Canada) that play in two designated leagues, the American League and the National League. Following a 162-game season, the top 10 teams contest a post-season with the final round being the best-of-7 game, the World Series (whose name could be viewed as ironic given that only two countries field teams in the MLB). Each MLB franchise has a number of farm teams or feeder teams where their develop-

ing talent plays. This is Minor League Baseball, which is contested at the (descending) AAA, AA, A, and lower levels. There are hundreds of Minor League Baseball Clubs across North America. There are also independent baseball leagues (i.e., no affiliation to MLB) that play in various regions around North America, including the American Association of Inde-

pendent Professional Baseball, the Atlantic League of Professional Baseball, the Canadian-American Association of Professional Baseball, the Frontier League, the North American League, and Pecos League. Although these leagues may occasionally be host to a future MLB player, this is very rare and they tend to be very locally focused. Outside of the United States and Canada, there are baseball leagues in 14 other countries of the world, including Columbia, the Dominican Republic, Mexico, Nicaragua, Panama, Puerto Rico, Venezuela, China, Taiwan, South Korea, Japan, Australia, Italy, and the Netherlands. Evidence of the importance of a global presence, the World Baseball Classic was started in 2006 (and repeated in 2009 and 2013) in order to grow the game globally. Japan won the first two Classic titles, with the Dominican Republic winning in 2013.

Basketball

The sport of basketball is arguably the most global of games after football (soccer). The leading organizations are the NBA, the professional league based in North America with offices in more than 40 countries, and FIBA—the IF based in Switzerland. The global footprint of the sport has grown considerably over the past quarter-century. In addition to the NBA, there are dozens of leagues in countries or multiple countries around the world. Clubs in these leagues can be found, for example, in Slovenia, Australia, Croatia, Spain, Bosnia, Herzegovina, Czech Republic, Serbia, Montenegro, Latvia, Lithuania, Estonia, Sweden, Germany, the United Kingdom, Belgium, Norway, Puerto Rico, China, Netherlands, Greece (multiple leagues), Iran, Korea, Finland, Italy, Israel, Argentina, France, Mexico, Brazil, New Zealand, Philippines, Russia, Poland, Taiwan, and Turkey. The United States is also home to one of the only professional women's sport leagues in the world, the WNBA (Women's National Basketball Association).

© Ecophoto | Dreamstime.com—Cricket Action Photo

Cricket

Unlike baseball and basketball, the sport of cricket is not popular in North America, but it does have an enormous following in England and a number of its former colonies, including India, West Indies, Australia, Sri Lanka, Bangladesh, New Zealand, and South Africa, where the sport flourishes and where leagues exist. The most notable league in cricket is the relatively new Indian Premier League (IPL), which has franchise values in the hundreds of millions of dollars and is unquestionably the most popular sporting league in India. The story of the IPL is highly relevant to this book as it has experienced rapid growth since being announced in 2007 by the Board of Control for Cricket in India. The IPL raised almost US $2 billion from franchise fees (with the eight initial clubs sold via auction for nearly US $800 million), media rights and sponsorship prior to its launch, and is now characterized by sold-out stadiums, star players, and a massive worldwide audience. The initial title sponsor paid US $50 million for a five-year deal.

Cycling

Cycling is a tremendous example of a professional team sport, where major global brands invest large sums to sponsor teams who compete in major multiday tours and one-day races around the world. Enormously popular in Europe, the professional side of the sport has grown in North America, South America, Australia, and Asia in recent decades. Although doping challenges have plagued the sport recently, its "Grand Tours" (Tour de France, Giro d'Italia, Vuelta a España) are global television and spectator events annually. The Tour de France is the most recognized of the Grand Tours. The event and its participating teams are heavily sponsored.

Hockey

Hockey is a sport whose nature differs globally. Some play on ice (ice hockey), others on grass (field hockey), and some on hard surfaces with inline skates (inline hockey). Each version of the game has its own leagues, although the version on the ice is, by a large margin, the most advanced professional sport. North America's National Hockey League (NHL) has 23 US-based and 7 Canadian teams. Minor league hockey, like baseball, is the feeder system to the NHL and includes a number of leagues in North America, including the American Hockey League (AHL), the East Coach Hockey League (ECHL), the Southern Professional Hockey League (SPHL), in the US only, the Ligue Nord-Americaine de Hockey, in Canada only, and the Federal Hockey League (FHL). At the amateur high-performance level, the Canadian-based Canadian Hockey League (CHL) is where most NHL players develop. The CHL comprises 3 leagues, organized geographically across the country: the Ontario Hockey League (OHL), the Quebec Major Junior Hockey League (QMJHL), and the Western Hockey League (WHL). Ice hockey leagues are also prominent and highly developed in Europe, with a number of single-country and multicountry leagues. The largest league in Europe is the Russian based Kontinental Hockey League (KHL) but high-level professional ice hockey leagues and clubs also exist in Germany, Sweden, Finland, Switzerland, Norway, Austria, Belgium, Italy, Belarus, and Czech Republic.

Women's ice hockey is also developing and leagues exist, including the Canadian Women's Hockey League, the Austrian Women's ice hockey Bundesliga, and the German women's ice hockey Bundesliga. The field hockey version is played in Europe, India, and Australia with leagues in India (World Series Hockey, Hockey India League), Europe (Euro Hockey League), England (England Hockey League), Spain (Division de Honor de Hockey Hierba), Australia (Australian Hockey League), and Malaysia (Malaysia Hockey League). Finally, the relatively new version of inline hockey, where players play on inline skates, has a single league in the United States (Major League Roller Hockey).

Football (Soccer)

In professional team sport, football (soccer in North America) is by far the most extensive with regard to the number of countries where elite professional sport is played. The elite professional leagues in the sport are among the most watched and influential professional leagues on the planet. These include Bundesliga (Germany), Premier League (England), La Liga (Spain), Serie A (Italy), Serie A (Brazil), Liga MX (Mexico), Major League Soccer (MLS) in North America, Eredivisie (Netherlands), Ligue 1 (France), Primera División (Argentina), J1 League (Japan), Primeira Liga (Portugal), Premier League (Russia), Super League (China), Pro League (Belgium), Super League (Turkey), Premier League (Ukraine), Allsvenskan (Sweden), A-League (Australia), Primera A (Columbia), Ekstraklasa (Poland), Serie A (Ecuador), Pro League (United Arab Emirates), Primera División (Paraguay), Premier League (Scotland), Premier Soccer League (South Africa), and Primera División (Uruguay).

Football (North American)

The North American sport of football is a much different game technically than soccer (known as football in the rest of the world). There are two versions of the game played in North America. American football is played in the professional league known as the National Football League (NFL), while Canadian football (some differences in rules, number of players, size of field, and other elements) is played in the Canadian Football League (CFL). The NFL, according to most published reports, has the highest average club values of any league in the world, with the average club valued in excess of US $1 billion. Although there are clubs in other sports (e.g., Manchester United, Real Madrid, New York Yankees, and Los Angeles Lakers) that are worth more than most NFL clubs, it is the high average value across all clubs (due largely to a strong revenue sharing structure) that distinguishes the NFL from other professional leagues. Notably, both the NFL and the CFL have made unsuccessful attempts to globalize their leagues, both NFL Europe and the CFL expansion into the United States having failed.

Lacrosse

Conceived by the Aboriginal peoples of North American many centuries ago, lacrosse has developed into a sport with a following in North American and a professional element in the continent as well. There are two versions of the game—box lacrosse and indoor lacrosse—that are similar technically but are played in different environments. Professionally, the National Lacrosse League (NLL) uses a franchise model, where clubs play in arenas in the United States and Canada. Headquartered in New York and founded in 1986, the NLL is the most prominent lacrosse league with indoor arena attendance numbers that are approximately 50% of those of the NHL and the NBA The NLL has 9 clubs that play 20 games in the regular season and average nearly 10,000 spectators per game (Kojima, 2014). In 2014, the players' average salary in the NLL was $19,672 per year. Major Series Lacrosse (MSL) and the Canadian Lacrosse League (CLL) play in Canada, where the sport is Canada's national summer sport. Major League Lacrosse (MLL) is an outdoor (box) league.

Rugby

Rugby is a major global game, but its reach (the number of countries that play) is less than football/soccer and basketball. The Rugby World Cup (played quadrennially) is one of the world's major megasporting-events and its cultural importance is high in about a dozen countries of the world. There are a number of high-caliber professional leagues around the world, in which the athletes are well compensated and games are televised. The National Rugby League (NRL) in Australia and New Zealand, and the Super League (England and France) are the largest and draw the best players from around the world. The RaboDirect Pro12 league has clubs in Italy, Scotland, Ireland, and Wales. Other professional/minor leagues play in the United States (USA Rugby League), Russia (Professional Rugby League), Spain (Super Ibérica de Rugby), and Canada (Canada Rugby League). Rugby's presence globally is expected to increase when the *Rugby 7s* version of the sport (i.e., played with only 7 players per side, as opposed to the traditional 15) debuts at the 2016 Olympic Games in Rio de Janeiro. Rugby 7s is expected to draw increased attention to the increased pace and action compared to the traditional game with 15 players per side.

In Australia, the sport of Australian Rules Football is "somewhat" like rugby and the elite professional league—the Australian Football League (AFL)—is one of the most popular in Australia, with an average league attendance of 32,566 spectators per game. The AFL is structured much like some of the North American professional leagues with a salary cap, highly paid players, and a playoff format. Its Grand Final is a major event in Australia each year. The AFL has expanded in recent years and now comprises 18 clubs, all based in Australia, although talk of a possible AFL club in New Zealand is common.

© Carmeta | Dreamstime.com—Handball Player Photo

Handball

Very popular in Europe, the sport of handball has a number of professional leagues around the world and is played at the Olympic Games. These leagues include the Danish Handball League (Denmark), the German Bundesliga, Liga ASOBAL (Spain), and Iran (Iranian Handball Super League). The European Handball Federation (EHF) Champions League is the top team handball club competition in Europe, with clubs from the top European nations. A total of 148 matches were played by 24 clubs in the 2011–2012 EHF Champions League, attracting more than 700,000 spectators in the arenas across Europe and more than 300 million TV viewers. The tournament culminates with the best teams playing in the Final 4 tournament, which draws approximately 20,000 spectators per game. Since 2010, VELUX Group became the title sponsor for the league (http://www.velux.com/velux_group/sponsorships/ehfchampionsleague).

Volleyball

Volleyball is a sport that is contested indoors by two teams of six players each and outdoors on the beach by teams of two persons each. Both the male and female games are popular, similar to tennis or golf from a gender perspective. Volleyball has strong followings in pockets around the world and is a popular sport on the Olympic program. Global in its scope, the Association of Volleyball Professionals (AVP) is the league for beach volleyball globally with events held all over the world. Professional leagues for the indoor game operate around the world for both men and women. Examples include the Chinese Volleyball League, which has both women's and men's leagues, the Iranian Volleyball Super League (men only), the Japan Volleyball League (men and women), the Dominican Republic Volleyball League (men and women), the Korean V-League (men and women), the Pro A men's league in France, Brazil's Superliga Brasileira de Voleibol (men and women), and the Plus Liga /Plus Liga Kobiet leagues for men and women in Poland.

Water Polo

The sport of water polo, although an Olympic sport, has only a small global professional presence. England (British Water Polo League) and Australia (Australian National Water Polo League) are home to the only professional leagues.

PROFESSIONAL INDIVIDUAL SPORT LEAGUES/ASSOCIATIONS

Individual sport leagues include professional sports leagues where a single athlete participates on behalf of him/herself versus one or more competitors. The individual sport leagues are presented here in this section. The term *league* is used in a broad sense here to represent a series of events under the same banner. They are presented in alphabetical order.

Automobile Sports

Automobile racing, or motorsports, has a major role in global sport. In motorsports, there are a variety of leagues for different types of vehicles, tracks, and technical requirements. These leagues range from the high-profile global Formula One (open wheel racing) to the US-only National Hot Rod Association. In North America, IndyCar (open wheel) and NASCAR (closed wheel) are the high-profile leagues, both with very high-profile lead events (Indianapolis 500 for IndyCar and the Daytona 500 for NASCAR). The Indianapolis 500 Indy Car race is the best-attended sporting event in the USA, yearly attracting more than 300,000 spectators (Busbee, 2014); however, NASCAR is the most prominent car-racing circuit with more than US $3.1 billion in revenue.

The most famous NASCAR race, the Daytona 500, draws more than 250,000 spectators while the average NASCAR attendance is nearly 100,000 spectators per race (Statistic Brain, 2014). NASCAR has nearly 75 million fans. NASCAR fans are known to be loyal, with 66% of fans willing to pay more to buy a sponsor's product. It is estimated that 36% of fans could name every sponsor of the top 30 ranked teams. There are the Le Mans Series (American, European, and Asian), arena racing (Arena Racing USA), touring car (Britain, German), stock cars (Brazil, United States), motorcycles (e.g., AMA Superbike Championship) and many others.

Boxing

One of the world's oldest (and most controversial) sports, boxing is characterized by high-profile stars, pay-per-view revenue, and influential promoters. The promoters, who could be considered to be leagues, include well-known sport organizations such as

Top Rank Boxing, Golden Boy Promotions, Don King Promotions, and DiBella Entertainment. Top boxers can earn very large salaries. In fact, it is reported that eight boxers have earned more than US $25 million for just one fight. Oscar de la Hoya, also known as "The Golden Boy," earned US $53 million for his fight against Floyd Mayweather Jr. in 2007 through a guaranteed prize purse plus a percentage of pay-per-view revenues. The fight was the highest rated and highest revenue generating per-per-view fight of all time. Oscar de lay Hoya is currently the highest earning boxer of all-time, with earnings of an estimated US $696 million (The Richest, 2014).

Golf

Golf is a global game that is played at a high level in many countries around the world. Like rugby, golf will join the Olympic program in 2016. The international professional organization of the game of golf is by tours, where players play a series of events throughout the year, often in many countries of the world. There are tours for male players, female players, and senior (age 50+) players. For men's golf, there are many tours for professional players, with the PGA (Professional Golfers Association) Tour being the pinnacle, followed by the European Tour, the Japan Golf Tour, and the Asia Tour. In addition, there are a number of minor tours or development tours around the world. At the female professional level, the Ladies Professional Golfers Association (LPGA) tour is the pinnacle of the women's game, followed by the Ladies European Tour, the LPGA of Japan Tour, and the LPGA of Korea Tour, amongst others. A May 2013 article in *Forbes* reported that the PGA Tour, a not-for-profit organization, has revenues of around US $2 billion annually, with events that have prize purses in the US $5 million to US $10 million range, and top athletes (e.g., Rory McIlroy, Phil Mickelson) who command endorsement deals well into eight figures.

© Ukrphoto | Dreamstime.com—Match In Mixed Martial Arts Photo

Mixed Martial Arts

Mixed Martial Arts (MMA), a newer combat sport, is structured much like boxing, but participants can draw from many of the martial arts during the one-on-one competition inside an octagon shaped ring. It is characterized by pay-per-view, star athletes, and high-powered promoters. The Ultimate Fighting Championship (UFC) is the premier league, although there are many smaller ones around the world. As of 2014, UFC is arguably the dominant combat sport organization in the world. Numerous reports have it valued at US $2 billion (up from original purchase price of US $2 million in 2001), much of which is driven by its high pay-per-view (PPV) television presence (average PPV event draws 3 million subscribers), with an estimated following of more than 100 million around the world and a series of blue-chip sponsors including Nike, Coca-Cola, Samsung, Everlast, YouTube, and Microsoft. Globally, the UFC has a very international following led by Brazil, the US, China, Canada, and Africa. Top fighters reportedly make close to US $1 million annually.

Tennis

A global game, tennis is arguably the most gender balanced of all professional sports. Indeed, at the major events, men and women both participate and the sport's high-profile stars are from both genders. According to *Forbes* (2014), there are five males and five females in the top 10 highest-paid tennis players in the world. Roger Federer earned the most money with a total of US $54.3 million in earnings (US $9.3 million on-court and US $45 million offcourt). His sponsors include a list of blue-chip companies such as Credit Suisse, Gillette, Mercedes-Benz, Nike, and Rolex. Maria Sharapova was reported as the world's highest earning female tennis player and third highest tennis player behind Federer and Rafael Nadal (US $32.4 million). She earned US $5.1 million on court and US $22 million off court. Her eight-year deal with Nike reportedly will bring US $70 million in revenue.

GLOBAL SPORTING EVENTS

Another major component of the global sportscape, international sporting events showcase teams and athletes from all over the world to a global audience. These events are often powered by funding sources that are also global in nature (e.g., sponsorship, media rights, merchandising). As noted, the Olympic Games, the FIFA World Cup, the IAAF World Athletics Championships, and the Rugby World Cup are all examples of the *mega* versions of these. Other prominent global examples include the Champions League tournament for the winners of European premier football league, and major horseracing events like the Royal Ascot (US $8 million in prize money for a five-day race in England), as well as the Dubai World Cup Night and Breeders Cup (each with more than US $20 million in prize money for a series of races). The tennis and golf grand slam

© Adeliepenguin | Dreamstime.com—America's Cup World Series, San Diego Photo

events (e.g., The Masters, Wimbledon) and unique one-off events, e.g., the Stanford 20/20 for Twenty (US $20 million prize purse) cricket match between England and the West Indies where each player gets a US $1 million payout for winning. Finally, the America's Cup sailing event, which attracts major sponsorship investment and large, global audiences, is a mega-event in a sport that otherwise does not receive much mainstream global attention.

Outside of the *mega* versions, there are thousands of sporting events every year that are global in one respect or another. These include events for non-Olympic sports. The primary examples here are The World Games, held first in 1981, a growing multisport event for non-Olympic sports (e.g., duathlon) and the X Games, both the summer and the winter versions. There are also global multisport events that are based on the occupation of the participants, such as Universiade (university students), Military World Games, and the World Police and Fire Games, or on some other national origin/characteristics, such as the Commonwealth Games (for the Commonwealth group of nations), the Francophone Games (for nations committed to the speaking of French), the World Masters Games (for mature athletes), the Pan Arab Games (for Arabic-speaking nations), and the Maccabiah Games (for Jewish athletes). Global multisport events are also held based on political/historical allegiance (e.g., Games of the Small States in Europe (for the small European countries), Island Games (for small island nations), and geography (e.g., All-Africa Games, Afro-Asian Games, Pan American Games, Central American and Caribbean Games, Asian Games, European Youth Olympic Festival, Mediterranean Games, Arctic Winter Games, and the Indian Ocean Island Games).

SPORTS ON THE RISE

Globally, new sports are also emerging in various international markets, depending on the availability of equipment, geographic location, inherent cultural interests and attractiveness for media/youth markets. Examples include windsurfing, skateboarding, and slope skiing (skiing in terrain parks with twin-tipped skis). Windsurfing, a non-Olympic sport invented in the USA in the 1960s, combines a surfboard, a mast, and a sail, while an individual, or sailor, is attached to the equipment via a harness line around the waist. Despite the modest exposure of the sport worldwide, windsurfing is growing, with major events in freestyle and racing, including the Professional Windsurfing Association's (PWA) World Tour (Professional Windsurfers Association, 2013), a tour—or league—of professional athletes (both men and women).

Many of the sports that are on the rise in popularity, have almost nonexistent barriers to participation in the sport in terms of sex, age, and body type (McLeary, 2007), providing for an increased opportunity for international growth and possible future inclusion on the Olympic program. As any one of these sports continues to grow in both participatory and financial capacities, it will attract increasing exposure. This is evident in the sport of skateboarding, which is growing quickly, especially in the USA, due to its attractive, rebellious subculture and attractive youth demographic (Nichols, 2011). Athlete line-ups indicate that skateboarding is popular from Brazil to Australia (ESPN, 2013).

Technological advances in sports media enable creation of platforms from which these sports can grow in a mainstream market. This is of particular importance to more established sports, which seek to attract younger followers and the sports media. In turn, the sports media seek ways to attract the attention of younger audiences in order to keep and grow ratings and revenues.

CHAPTER SUMMARY

This chapter acts as a brief, high-level encyclopedia of global sport organizations, federations, leagues, and events. Its aim is to show how fast the growth of the worldwide sport industry has been and how that growth continues. Downstream, each of these global organizations adopts policies, organizes events, and undertakes activities to help guide national, state/provincial, and regional sport systems. These sport systems connect with fans, participants, sport organizations, and media partners, all of which provide opportunities for marketers.

Chapter Activity: Pick 5!

Complete the following:
1. Pick five sports that you know nothing about, but that have worldwide footprints, list them and assess their global reach/presence.
2. Pick five sports that would make for great TV and identify the particular contributing features to great TV.
3. Identify five sports with the greatest worldwide participation and conclude why this is so.
4. Pick five sports you wish you played. Why?
5. Ask a classmate or friend to do the same exercise. Did you have some sports in common? Where did you disagree? And why?

Chapter Questions

1. Contrast the global structure of professional sport (Chapter 5) with that of the Olympic/government sport system (Chapter 4). List at least five core differences.
2. What differentiates global sport marketing from sport marketing?
3. Identify three important marketing concepts and how they apply to sport.
4. Choose two sports and prepare a "one-pager" for the President of that organizations' NSO regarding the marketing potential.
5. What are the greatest marketing risks for organizations? How would you mitigate against such risks?
6. What are the greatest marketing opportunities for emerging sports?

6

Leadership and the Olympic Games

I f, as they say, all things start at the top, it is more than interesting to note that Barack Obama, elected as the 44th President of the United States, is a frequent recreational basketball player, and a man who subsequently selected his first Cabinet of government officials in 2009 where it seemed almost every member had, at one time, played basketball professionally or at an American university in the highly competitive National Collegiate Athletic Association (NCAA).

President Obama's Secretary of Education, Arne Duncan, played at Harvard University and then professionally in Australia. His former Attorney General, Eric Holder, played one year at Columbia University while National Security Adviser, retired general James Jones, played at Georgetown University. The President's Ambassador to the United Nations, Susan Rice, played for Oxford University in England during her time

PRESIDENT BARACK OBAMA'S CABINET

FRONT ROW (L-R):Retired Gen. Eric K. Shinseki (Veterans Affairs),Rep. Hilda Solis (Labor),Arne Duncan (Education), Robert Gates (Defense),President Barack Obama,Hillary Clinton(State), Retired Marine Gen. James Jones (National Security Adviser),Timothy Geithner (Treasury), Steven Chu (Energy)

BACK ROW (L-R):Former Gov. Tom Vilsack, D-Iowa, Agriculture, Former Sen. Tom Daschle (Health & Human Services) Rep. Ray LaHood (Transportation),Eric Holder (Justice),Sen. Ken Salazar (Interior),Gov. Janet Napolitano (Homeland Security) Shaun Donovan (Housing & Urban Development)

as a Rhodes Scholar. Even the President's brother-in-law, Craig Robinson, a two-time all-Ivy League (a conference of elite academic schools in the eastern United States) Player of the Year at Princeton University and the man who checked out the future president for his sister by staging a pick-up basketball game, is connected to the sport. Robinson was most recently the head basketball coach at Oregon State University. (Harnden, 2008)

Noting the prominence of basketball in his life, President Obama often joked during his first term that he believed he had appointed the "best basketball-playing Cabinet in American history" and did so because he believed "a team of rivals" would deliver what the American people needed most as they faced the worst economic conditions their country had seen in 75 years.

Many insiders believe President Obama's love of basketball, a sport he played in high school, is one of his greatest enjoyments. So much so, that on Election Day in November 2008, Obama and 40 of his political associates played a series of round-robin games while Americans went to the polls. He would play basketball again during the tense 2012 election as he sought (and won) a second term as US president.

The love of sport by political leaders extends far beyond President Obama and the United States.

Long time Australian Prime Minister, John Howard, was revered for his support of all Australian sports and stood as the primary patron for soccer and basketball while fully supporting the Australian Football League (AFL), rugby union, rugby league, and cricket. Howard was famous during his time in office (1996–2007) for fast-paced morning walks (usually with a very small security detail) in and around the Sydney

US PRESIDENTS WHO PLAYED OR PARTICIPATED IN SPORTS BEFORE OR DURING THEIR PRESIDENCY

George Washington—played *rounders* (early version of baseball) with his troops at Valley Forge and played quoits (similar to horseshoes) while serving as America's first president

Abraham Lincoln—played horseshoes

William Howard Taft—threw out the first pitch in 1910 at Washington Senators baseball game and thus started the hallowed American tradition involving US presidents

Grover Cleveland—fished

Theodore Roosevelt—boxed

Dwight Eisenhower—played football at the U.S. Military Academy (West Point) and golfed frequently while president

John Kennedy—sailed (and was famous for playing touch football with his brothers)

Richard Nixon—bowled and ordered a bowling alley installed in the White House in 1970

Gerald Ford—played football at the University of Michigan and was team MVP in 1935

Ronald Reagan—played football, ran track, and swam for Eureka (Illinois) College from 1929–1932

George H. W. Bush—captain of his Yale baseball team in 1948 and played in the first two College World Series

Bill Clinton—golfed and jogged while president; frequently golfed with Australian professional Greg Norman

George W. Bush—played on the Yale First XV rugby union team in 1968 and later became a part-owner of the Texas Rangers (MLB) baseball team

Barack Obama—played basketball in high school and installed a basketball court at the White House to facilitate recreational basketball (Winkler, 2008)

Harbor Bridge and rarely missed a big sporting competition when Australia was playing long-standing rivals like New Zealand, England, or India.

In Canada, the current Prime Minister Stephen Harper (2006–current) is an openly devoted hockey fan and often seen in attendance at key games

(pictured right is Prime Minister Harper attending the Rogers Cup). In 2013, while in office, Prime Minister Harper published a book on professional hockey titled *A Great Game: The Forgotten Leafs and the Rise of Professional Hockey* (Harper, 2014). Notably, while his government has pushed for smaller government and reduced spending over his tenure, investment in sport has continued to rise. Former Prime Minister Jean Chretien (1993– 2003) was an enthusiastic golfer, who was famous for having meetings with then US President Bill Clinton over a round of golf.

In other countries such as Spain, where members of the royal family have been Olympians and whose Prime Minister, Jose Luisputin Rodriquez Zapatero, plays basketball, and Russia, where former Russian President Vladimir Putin is a black belt in karate and an avid sambo and judo participant, it is obvious sport can be critically important to a nation's self-image, global aspirations, its political system, and economic welfare. On occasion, investment decisions by governments suggests that sport can and will make a difference for a nation in this regard. This was certainly the case for Russia following the Sochi 2014 Winter Games where unconfirmed reports suggest Russian organizers spent more than US $50 billion to build the new infrastructure needed by Russia to develop its winter sports and used to stage the Games. By spending this amount, Sochi's Games became—by most accounts—the most expensive Olympics ever, far surpassing the estimated $42 billion allocated by China in hosting the 2008 Beijing Summer Olympics. [It is important recognize that the decisions to invest in a Games beyond the necessary

facilities and infrastructure improvements is at the discretion of the host committee and government(s). Thus, the reported US $60 billion is not the cost to host the Winter Games but was the price tag for the way that Russia and Sochi chose to undertake the hosting, which included virtually 'creating' a new tourist resort city as one of their key priorities. The Olympic Movement has no role in

judging the appropriateness of national infrastructure priorities (Burton & O'Reilly, 2014b; Lettner & Burton, 2014).]

Interestingly, while much of that US $50 billion for the 2014 Games came from Russian Federation governmental coffers, a significant amount (reportedly in excess of US $1.2 billion) came from Russian-based sponsors such as Aeroflot, Bosco, Rostelecom, MegaFon, Rosneft, and Sberbank of Russia. Sponsorship of Sochi 2014 set a Winter Games revenue record and even surpassed the amount raised by London 2012, a larger scale Summer Games.

LEADERSHIP APPLICATIONS IN INTERNATIONAL SPORT: POLITICAL AND CORPORATE

There is no other way to view these political realities and sponsorship investments than to acknowledge that sport is a critical part of today's world. This is especially evident in the highest-profile worlds of the Summer and Winter Olympics. But how should students of sport marketing place this in the proper context? What can they learn? What does it mean?

Admittedly, for a sports fan, attending a sport (or even enjoying a particular sport and following it on television or the internet) is quite common and is a behavior that applies to a large proportion of the world's more than 7 billion habitants. But imagine doing this as the president or prime minister of a country. It can send a powerful message to almost every citizen that sport is part of that country's official agenda. In cases where governments fund sport and Olympic teams (which is the case for all but a few of the more than 200 nations who participate in the Games), this leadership interest may affect funding and allocation of government resources towards (or away from) sport or sport-related initiatives such as physical activity, health, and youth.

Just such an outcome was evident in 2008 when more than 80 global heads of state attended the opening ceremonies of the Beijing 2008 Summer Olympic Games, thereby demonstrating to their own citizens official support for the Olympics and how sport was the vehicle that brought them all together.

But incorporating the values of sport into a business plan or corporate culture of a sponsor is much different from symbolically telling a country's citizens that sport is good. And using sport strategically, particularly with expensive sponsorships, is different from just liking sport. It is about marketing, about reaching particular targets with specific messages. It is about brand. It is about value propositions. It is about return on investment (ROI).

Beijing 2008 is a good example of this difference. In China, which won the right to host the 2008 Olympics in 2001, the leaders of the Chinese government wanted very much to use the Olympics to showcase their country (think of it as a global *coming-out party*) and to boost their economic development in construction and retail businesses (linking to global sponsors) by staging the largest Olympics ever. So money was no object (unconfirmed reports were that there was no limit to the budget) and by some estimates, the Chinese government spent more than US $42 billion building stadiums and other elements of Beijing's Olympic operational infrastructure. This level of expenditure

had been unprecedented until the Sochi Games in 2014.

It is also likely China's leaders saw the Olympics as a positive investment for every Chinese citizen and projected what the Olympics would be worth, not just from 2001 (when China won the right to host the Games) to 2008 (when the Olympics were held), but far into the future. China's government officials undoubtedly wanted the Olympics to give their country 100 years of economic and cultural value, but also to send an internal message (to its people) of an ascendant China, one that was going global.

From a leadership theory standpoint, this is not surprising. And, from a historical standpoint, it was effective.

On the private sector side, corporate leaders often see sport as an easy vehicle to drive their organization's core philosophy both internally and externally. In fact, many CEOs believe the use of sport, in the form of sponsorship, advertising, or even in common everyday language, most easily informs their department heads or division managers and ultimately increases the firm's true capacity. The reason is simple: CEOs want to win. And the competitive component of sport ensures that alignment with sport means all parties can connect quickly with the goal of winning.

LEADERSHIP AND WINNING

The desire (or urge) to win is imperative in today's highly competitive marketplace and finding common themes or familiar language to inspire employees is needed more than ever. Some CEOs establish their operating style as soon as they start, expressing their management values in executive staff meetings or at company-wide gatherings.

Just a few years ago, in 2007, one of this book's authors had the chance to attend a Coca-Cola Board of Directors dinner. It was a private affair in Atlanta and hosted by Neville Isdell, the chairman of Coca-Cola and incoming president and CEO, Muhtar Kent, as well as Coca-Cola board member Peter Ueberroth, former president of the LAOOC (Organizing Committee of the Los Angeles Olympic Games), former Commissioner of Major League Baseball and then Chair of the Board of Directors of the U.S. Olympic Committee (2004–2008).

Following the dinner, a senior executive from China was asked to detail for the Board all that Coca-Cola would do in China during the run-up to the Beijing Olympics. The report was comprehensive, featuring numerous strategic and tactical advertisements and promotions that would solidify the company's standing in the world's largest country. It was a thorough presentation of business plans designed to help Coca-Cola win the beverage battle in China during 2008 and the years to follow.

When the presentation was finished, Kent complimented the presentation and noted that Coca-Cola has always believed in the value of the Olympics and would remain a sponsor of the Olympic Games for as long as he was in charge. The Olympics, he commented, were "ingrained in Coke's DNA."

Not surprisingly, Coca-Cola. have been associated with the Olympics since 1928 and is already signed on with the IOC through 2020. That suggests Olympic sponsorship, or alignment with the Olympic Games, is important to Coca-Cola and is fully understood by its leadership and many of its employees. These employees know the Olympics are integral to their collective success. A review of Coke's portfolio of sponsored properties, which includes the FIFA World Cup, a stable of athletes, NASCAR, and many others, illustrates its corporate attachment to sport.

It is undeniable that Coca-Cola's various brands of soda, juices, isotonic beverages, and water are, at some level, simply refreshing beverages. Coca Cola's bottlers combine water with different ingredients and the

COCA-COLA'S MUHTAR KENT ON THE IMPORTANCE OF SPORT TO COKE

Coca-Cola has a very special and vested interest in ensuring that the noble ideals and values of Olympism live on and grow. We have been associated with the Olympic Movement since the 1928 Amsterdam Olympic Games—longer than any corporate sponsor. During the last 81 years, we have worked hand in hand with the Olympic family to reach new audiences, support athletes, promote the ideals of global peace and friendship, and provide economic support to the communities served through the Olympic Movement. At the same time, our coveted Olympic partnership has provided us with a powerful and complementary platform to advance our mission to refresh the world through our 500-plus beverage brands . . . to inspire moments of optimism and happiness . . . and to create value and make a difference. The strength of our Olympic partnership is directly related to the relationships we have cultivated over the years with the International Olympic Committee (IOC) and with all the stakeholders touched by the Games. (Kent, 2009)

final products themselves have nothing to do with sport. However, they are portfolio segments that must be marketed. Coca-Cola's soda is Coke or Diet Coke or Coca-Cola Zero. Water is Dasani. Their energy drink is Powerade. So, when Coca-Cola and its brands are combined with sponsorships of the Olympics, World Cup, UFC, high school and college football, rugby and hundreds of other sport events, with resulting impacts on consumer choices, it comes as no surprise to learn that sport matters greatly to Coca-Cola as an organization. In some ways, sport can be as important to Coca-Cola bottlers as the water and syrup (Arshad, 2014).

SPORT AND *SMALLER* CORPORATE LEADERS

But, what if you are the CEO of a smaller company that doesn't have Coca-Cola's resources and can't afford to sponsor numerous (or any) sport properties or events? What if you only operate in 6 countries of the world and not 200? Can sport still serve your organization's strategic needs? Should sport, let alone Olympic sponsorship, be part of your consideration set?

For starters, each company or organization is different. Further, the best CEOs understand that aligned values with partners and customers are better than incongruent messages and unclear brands for growing market share, stock price, and earnings. In this regard, many leaders see sport as providing a logic or language by which they can best communicate to stakeholders (internal and external) what they want their organization to achieve. In the best cases, it starts with the founder, chairman, or CEO who projects or enacts the competitive (and proven) values they have seen in sport. By doing so, they advance effectiveness holistically across the breadth of the firm and to their suppliers, partners, and customers.

Smaller partners can learn from very large global organizations who were once much smaller. Phil Knight, the founder and current chairman of Nike, believed that his upstart company of the 1960s should be filled with former athletes designing products for active athletes. His theory was simple: real athletes would know what real competitors (and those who hoped to become serious athletes) would want and need. From the very beginning, Knight brought an athlete's energy and competitive nature to his initial hires and the corporate culture he established. Not surprisingly, that competitive orientation led to monumental advertising campaigns with phrases like *Just Do It* or *Bo Knows* and endorsement relationships with American athletes like Bo Jackson, Michael Jordan, Lebron James, and Tiger Woods. But Nike also has significant endorsement deals with international athletes in tennis (Rafael Nadal, Roger Federer, Li Na, and Maria Sharapova), soccer (Cristiano Ronaldo), and golf (Rory McIlroy) (Arshad, 2014).

In his well-documented leadership role, Knight knew early on how athletes ticked because he had competed in track at the University of Oregon for famed coaching taskmaster Bill Bowerman. And while Knight was not a star runner (he was considered more of a squad man), Knight stood as one of Bowerman's "Men of Oregon" due to his quick ability to grasp key concepts like competitive response and unfailing loyalty and commitment to the team. Thus, and not surprisingly, when Knight formulated his idea to build a better running shoe and sell it to the world's best runners, he went back to Bowerman and asked him to be a partner. One of their first employees, Geoff Hollister, was another Oregon runner who had run for Bowerman.

The Bowerman mantra was simple: "Work hard. Train hard. Hone your competitive response. Be a good squad man. Don't let your teammates down." To this day, it does not matter what sport an individual may prefer, if that person is going to work at Nike, he or she must bring a Bowerman-style passion that will ultimately benefit the company (Strasser & Becklund, 1991). Nike's world headquarters in Beaverton, Oregon, features acres of playing fields and miles of running trails for their employees to use every day of the year. The courts, fields, and tracks are rarely empty.

In new employee orientation, it is explained why Nike's office buildings are named after athletic greats and why athletic busts of past Nike endorsers and museum-like displays of athletic memorabilia sit in or alongside every building. Performance excellence is revered and expected. And by having excellence visible all the time, in the form of athletic achievements, employees can easily grasp what is remembered and what is rewarded. Today, Nike is the 24th most valuable brand in the world in all categories (Arshad, 2014).

SPORT, LEADERSHIP AND PASSION

Passion, of course, can be confused with talent, and that is possibly why sport is so efficient at helping identify winners and losers. Athletes must perform and it is on the scoreboard or box score that their natural talent, ongoing commitment, and acceptance of coaching are revealed for all to see. The same is true for a leader of any organization, where leadership must not be confused with passion. Although passion can drive effort, motivate, and inspire, it also can distract, render one inefficient, and cloud rational decision-making. For example, one needs only to look at ownership decisions in professional sport regarding investments in player salaries, where elite businessmen and women often have made irrational financial decisions.

At the fan level, fans are passionate, but are not held responsible for winning. In fact, fans, even those who once played the sport, are not involved in the playing arena and, thus, have chosen to be fans as a result of some other set of factors, such as enjoyment, civic loyalty, interest, or social/networking reasons. Fans may cheer and be avid supporters who believe they are personally part of the team, even though they cannot physically contribute to the team or an individual player's actual performance. In the corporate environment, that type of avid alignment can be harnessed when employees think that they are personally part of their company team. A good leader seeks employees who want to be part of the team and its success. Or, as Green Bay Packers (NFL) football coach Vince Lombardi was reported to have famously said in an interview in 1962, "Winning isn't everything but wanting to win is." He also said, "If you're not fired with enthusiasm, you'll be fired with enthusiasm."

When employees know what the score is (and this involves a later discussion of open communication to all team members), they can better understand the benefits in winning. This can mean job security, promotions, increases in pay, more comfortable morale, better employee benefits, and less job-related stress. Human resources professionals have shown the value of these various benefits over and over, sector by sector.

So do not think for a moment that employees do not care about winning or, for that matter, sports. A variety of research studies conducted over many years show that about three-quarters of Americans have engaged in sport—participation, spectating, reading, streaming, or watching—in the past year. Given the huge recent increases in the use of personal digital communications devices, such as cell phones, laptops, and iPods, it is possible that number is now closer to 80% and is likely to continue to grow as access to sport becomes easier and easier and more diverse.

We know, as Don Tapscott notes in his book, *Grown Up Digital* (2009), that a generation has grown up "bathed in bits." Its members have ingested Facebook, Twitter, MySpace, Wii, Guitar Hero, and Xbox. They are digitally fast, getting faster every day, and are just as competitive in their interests as were previous generations.

We also know sport is everywhere and not just in the workplace. It permeates life in many aspects around the globe. Whether you are Australian,

Chinese, Canadian, Korean, Kenyan, Russian, Polish, or Brazilian, sport has a role in society and when your country's team plays in a major sport (for your country), you are likely interested. If they experience success, everyone (or almost everyone) gets engaged. Almost everyone likes being identified with a winner. Social psychologists have long called this phenomenon "Basking in Reflected Glory" (Cialdini et al., 1976). It always feels good to be associated with a winner and perhaps no country serves as a better yardstick than Australia, a country that by population standards (approximately 20 million residents) is a small country. Notably, Nike's Knight once reortedly joked that if Nike was a country, it would have to be Australia because the love of sport is so ingrained into almost every Aussie citizen. So it is that the Melbourne Cup horse race at Flemington in Victoria is referred to as "The Race that Stops a Nation" and most companies either stage Melbourne Cup parties or give their employees the day off. But, before giving Australia the title of greatest sporting nation, one must consider that almost every country has its own event or game that *stops a nation*, whether it is the FIFA World Cup final in Brazil, the Super Bowl in the United States, the men's Olympic gold medal ice hockey game in Canada (nearly two-thirds of the population tuned in in 2010), or the IPL final in India.

THE RIGHT PEOPLE IN THE RIGHT PLACES

Embracing sport does not require a sponsorship, but it does require understanding the values that sport represents and the values of stakeholders, employees, retailers, and consumers that an organization is trying to reach, motivate, encourage, and satisfy. Each stakeholder wants to be associated with growth and sustainability. It is the values in sport, however, that may prove beneficial in putting together the best team. That is what matters. Each employee should be seen as playing a role for the team to which he or she is assigned. In many companies, that concept is sadly overlooked.

One area in which any organization can employ sport is in human resources (HR), where the task of employee screening and selection is known to be critical to a firm's future performance. This is an internal area that interacts with every division of a company, but is often overlooked when marketing, sales, or public relations make decisions that face out toward partners, customers, or clients. From a leadership perspective, HR is an area that CEOs must influence, because reduced resources due to layoffs or reduced hiring rates are common in many organizations today. This means that selecting the right hire, someone who will fit immediately, is more important than ever. It is not unlike picking from players on a playground before a game starts. To complicate matters, today's young professionals, including those in the sport industry, are much more selective in their job choices and less loyal to an organization that does not treat them well. Leaders beware: treat your talent with high attention or they will soon be working for your competitors.

Interestingly enough, most recreational basketball players believe an intelligent man or woman can tell everything needed to know about a teammate (read: potential new hire) simply from playing a pick-up game. The same analogy holds for any sport any of the authors have ever played! These transferable work values from the recreation basketball example can include concepts such as the following:

1. Is an unknown person a team player?
2. Do they pass the ball or puck to others or tend to just take shots?
3. Do they make the other athletes around them better?
4. Can they be counted on when the game or meet is close?
5. Do they encourage their teammates or denigrate them when a shot is missed or a three-meter dive is blown?
6. Are they humble in victory or desire another chance in defeat?
7. Do they call fouls or make excuses every time and believe the other team is cheating?
8. Do they cheat when they think no one is looking or, even, cheat when they know everyone is looking?

This is not to say that every potential employee should be asked to play a sport or engage in pick-up basketball to get a job. But, many executives believe that only by playing golf with key employees or noon ball on a local court can they determine leadership potential or organizational fit. The same can be said for a morning jog, an after-work game of squash, or a doubles game of tennis with the boss and her husband.

On the down side, this desire to use sport or incorporate sport into a company's operational ritual can easily morph into exclusionary actions and some employees are likely to feel intimidated if the boss's reliance on sport, or the CFO's sport of choice happens to be a sport where an employee is not particularly talented or interested. Excellence in sport participation does not necessarily make someone the best employee to hire or promote.

That said, however, in a free enterprise system, competition is a fact of life and for employees to appreciate that and to be willing to compete, both personally and as a member of a team, will almost certainly prove to improve the team effort.

Where organizations embrace a concept of greater good—of winning—sport provides a wide range of metaphors, clichés, and truisms that have stood the test of time. David Falk, Michael Jordan's agent during his playing days, embraced this concept in his 2010 book, *The Bald Truth*, when he used sports phrases uttered every day by business leaders around the world: "See the whole court" or "Don't just see what is happening; anticipate what will happen" (Falk, 2010). A similar phrase from the father of professional ice hockey great, Wayne Gretzky: "don't skate to where the puck is, but to where it is going," further supports this ideal.

© Wickedgood | Dreamstime.com—Wayne Gretzky Edmonton Oilers Photo

So whether your favorite sport is one of the long-standing Olympic sports such as athletics or swimming, or one of the new Olympic sports, rugby sevens or golf, or a non-Olympic sport like cricket or duathlon, this book should provide something for an upcoming staff meeting or your next entrepreneurial effort. Take it from another US president, Theodore "Teddy" Roosevelt, who wrote in 1899:

> "FAR BETTER IT IS TO DARE MIGHTY THINGS, TO WIN GLORIOUS TRIUMPHS, EVEN THOUGH CHECKERED BY FAILURE, THAN TO TAKE RANK WITH THOSE POOR SPIRITS WHO NEITHER ENJOY MUCH NOR SUFFER MUCH, BECAUSE THEY LIVE IN THE GRAY TWILIGHT THAT KNOWS NOT VICTORY NOR DEFEAT."

Or as Roosevelt reportedly later said in a speech at the Sorbonne in Paris on April 23, 1910:

> "IT IS NOT THE CRITIC WHO COUNTS: NOT THE MAN WHO POINTS OUT HOW THE STRONG MAN STUMBLES OR WHERE THE DOER OF DEEDS COULD HAVE DONE BETTER. THE CREDIT BELONGS TO THE MAN WHO IS ACTUALLY IN THE ARENA, WHOSE FACE IS MARRED BY DUST AND SWEAT AND BLOOD, WHO STRIVES VALIANTLY, WHO ERRS AND COMES UP SHORT AGAIN AND AGAIN, BECAUSE THERE IS

NO EFFORT WITHOUT ERROR OR SHORTCOMING, BUT WHO KNOWS THE GREAT ENTHUSIASMS, THE GREAT DEVOTIONS, WHO SPENDS HIMSELF FOR A WORTHY CAUSE; WHO, AT THE BEST, KNOWS, IN THE END, THE TRIUMPH OF HIGH ACHIEVEMENT, AND WHO, AT THE WORST, IF HE FAILS, AT LEAST HE FAILS WHILE DARING GREATLY, SO THAT HIS PLACE SHALL NEVER BE WITH THOSE COLD AND TIMID SOULS WHO KNEW NEITHER VICTORY NOR DEFEAT."

CHAPTER EXERCISE: *So, You Have the Keys to IOC HQ!*

Imagine, if you can, that you are the new president of the IOC. Yes, you have been elected leader of—arguably—the most important sport organization in the world. It is a big job with big responsibility. Massive pressure. Complex politics. Unrelenting media coverage.

Now, to give you context, let's go back in time to February 2014. Let's assume you are the IOC president. Your name is Thomas Bach and you have just taken the reins at a relatively good time for the IOC. The corruption problems around the 2002 Games have largely been addressed, the World Anti-Doping Agency (WADA), an IOC creation, is fighting doping in sport with some success, and the financial situation for the organization has never been better.

Unfortunately, you have stepped into your CEO's role just months before the Sochi 2014 Winter Olympic Games are set to begin. Controversy is in the air. Immediately, you can see that your predecessor, the Belgian Jacques Rogge, had just finished what many viewed to be a successful tenure as president. He had also presided over awarding these 2014 Winter Olympics to a country (Russia) that brought with it some risk. This risk has been magnified by two major issues that the country is dealing with just as the Games are about to begin (Burton & O'Reilly, 2014b).

The first is that the 2014 Olympics are slated to take place in a country that has been threatened by rebels who are vowing to use terrorism to disrupt the Games. Threats have been issued and they are real. The Russian president has vowed to prevent any acts of violence and has established what the media is calling "Rings of Steel" around the city of Sochi. Other countries, including the United States, have partnered with Russia on security. Certainly, security and terrorism have threatened every Olympic Games in recent memory, with instances such as the deaths of Israeli athletes and team officials at the 1972 Munich Games still in people's minds.

The second issue deals with a Russian law that has been understood to mean it is illegal to distribute gay propaganda literature in Russia, but particularly in Sochi during the Winter Olympics. The law discriminates against homosexuality. This has caused a worldwide furor as attention builds leading up to the Games and the issue (the existing law) has become a lightning rod for activists who believe Russia's human rights record is unacceptable. Russia has refused to amend the law leading up to the Sochi 2014 Games and many athletes from around the world are threatening to use the Games as a podium to voice their displeasure with Russia's laws and treatment of gay individuals. This issue has the capacity to turn the Sochi Olympics into one of the most politicized sporting events ever held.

As the new president, you have been briefed on these issues and are now getting ready to give your inaugural remarks at the Opening Ceremonies on the 7th of February 2014. This is a delicate balance for you. What leadership message do you want to tell the world about the International Olympic Committee (IOC) and its many sport federations? How do you respect the view that the Games should not be political but also embrace their role for positive change? What do you want the National Olympic Committees (like the U.S. Olympic Committee, the Canadian Olympic Committee, or the Australian Olympic Committee) from more than 200 countries to hear? How do you earn their trust and support as your stewardship of the IOC begins? What are your first steps?

And, remember, billions of fans worldwide will be watching you and the media will analyze every verbal nuance in every language spoken on the globe. To enhance your written answer, we welcome your review of President Bach's actual remarks and the response of many journalists by way of an internet search.

Chapter Exercise Questions:

1. In reviewing Bach's speech on February 7th, 2014 (please find via an internet search), how do you rate it? What was good? What was not so good? What was he trying to achieve?

2. If you were him, what would you have done differently and why?

3. Go online and do a search about Thomas Bach, the IOC President since 2013. What are the key elements of his background that suit him for this role? Are there any particular experiences that may have added to his background? Here are a few sources to help:

   http://www.washingtontimes.com/topics/thomas-bach/

   http://www.dosb.de/fileadmin/Bilder_allgemein/Praesidium/lebenslauf_bach_thomas_englisch.pdf

   http://www.sports-reference.com/olympics/athletes/ba/thomas-bach-1.html

4. In his first year on the job, Bach was faced with additional challenges—including the controversial multibillion dollar investment in hosting the 2014 Games and the subsequent fallout where 5 bid cities for future Games have pulled out. How would you advise him to deal with this issue?

Case Study 6.1

Why Vancouver Should Host the Olympic Games
By: Richard W. Pound

Case Context

In order to illustrate the functioning of the global sport system and its interrelated nature with governments, citizens, and sport organizations, we are sharing this case study of a situation that faced Vancouver prior to the 2010 Games when the city voted on whether or not it wanted to host the Games.

2010 is approaching, Vancouver has been awarded the Games, but the city's citizens need to agree (via plebiscite vote) if they want to go ahead with the Games or not, given the risk and expected costs of the Games. An op-ed piece written by one of the authors of this book—Richard Pound—for a major Vancouver newspaper follows here.

There are many reasons why Vancouver should hope that, this July, the International Olympic Committee (IOC) selects it as the host city, together with Whistler, for the 2010 Olympic Winter Games.

As a former Olympic athlete (a product of the superb Ocean Falls swimming program!), past president of the Canadian Olympic Committee and a member of the IOC, it may not be surprising that I support the Vancouver effort. Nor is this the first time that I have supported bids from Vancouver, but this is by far the best we have ever managed.

Nothing in the world can compare with the Olympic Games and the host cities of the Games share a wonderful history that stretches back three thousand years. The finest athletes in the world will gather, in an unprecedented climate of peace and goodwill, to compete with each other and to demonstrate their awesome feats of athletic excellence, while we watch history being made and heroes emerging before our very eyes. Our own athletes will have better than ever chances to succeed, as a result of more focused efforts to assist them with their training and the opportunity to compete before home crowds, instead of being Road Warriors in foreign lands. There is nothing to compare, as well, with the magic that takes over an Olympic city. Those who have experienced the Games never forget the occasion. If I were King for a Day, I would undertake to host the Games for those reasons alone.

But there are those who believe that hosting the Games will place a financial burden on the host city. They are reluctant to support any such initiative. "The Games will cost too much," they say. "They are too expensive." It becomes a mantra, an endless chant that defies any effort to break through the noise to expose facts and not illusion and myth. Sadly, some elements in Vancouver have fallen under this thrall. They produce heat, but shed no light. This issue is a mere paper tiger. It needs to be "de-mythified."

A large portion of my Olympic responsibilities over the past quarter-century have centered on the financial aspects of the Games and the Olympic Movement generally. There are, if one insists on looking solely at the crass financial reasons for hosting the Olympics, several *billion* reasons why a city should aspire to host the Games. Well over one billion of these reasons are the non-tax base revenues that will be generated from television rights, sponsorships, licensing, and ticket sales. In the case of Winter Games, these revenues alone should more than cover the operations of the Games.

I live in Montreal, but have never, and will never, forget my formative years in British Columbia. Montreal has long been criticized for its so-called Olympic "deficit." This, too, is a myth. Montreal's principal mistake was not to separate its infrastructure investment budget from the Olympic operational budget. Everything was lumped together, with the

(Continued on next page)

Case Study 6.1 *(continued)*

result that the media, for reasons of their own, decided to portray the investments in a Metro system, highway upgrades, construction of facilities that would benefit several generations of Montrealers, and other investments as "costs" of a sixteen-day event. This was arrant nonsense that even a first-year bookkeeping student would recognize as such. Citizens of Vancouver should not let themselves be conned by similar demagoguery. Montreal made an operating profit from the Games that exceeded by far, on a per capita basis, the much-vaunted profit of Los Angeles in 1984.

Quite apart from all that, the economic model of the Olympics has changed enormously—the television rights fees for the 1972 Winter Olympics in Sapporo were $8.5 million; in Torino in 2006, they will exceed $810 million. In 1976, the worldwide rights for the Montreal Games were $35 million; in Atlanta, only twenty years later, they were $935 million, and in Beijing, in 2008, they will be more than $1.5 billion. And as an American once said to me, "we're talkin' dead Presidents, here, son, not your piss-ass Northern peso." If your city cannot make a profit from hosting the Games these days, then you just aren't doing it right. Vancouver can do it right.

As to the other billions of reasons, hosting the Games can provide access to funding programs from all levels of government that might not otherwise be available, for infrastructure improvements in and around the host city. In some cases, these infrastructure improvements, even though they are needed, might not happen for decades without the Olympic focus. The fact that the Games start on a specific date means that comprehensive, time-sensitive, planning can take place, with none of the usual dithering and uncertainties that so often surround any significant community project. This infrastructure will exist for many years after the two-week period of the Games, as a living legacy of the Games. Just look at what the Games did for Calgary in 1988. Properly viewed, the infrastructure improvements are investments; they are not "costs"

of the Games. Over and above the pure investment, the multiplier effect of the Olympic-related activity is ploughed back into the community, producing many times the actual investment costs in economic impact.

The Vancouver team that is working on your behalf has given much thought to the economic aspects. Their financial forecasts have been judged as reasonable and conservative by their consultants and by your own Auditor General. They deserve your confidence.

As for Vancouver itself, one of the key objectives is to attract people who are decision-makers, who will decide where businesses are to be located or expanded, where conventions and meetings will be held, where vacations and tourism will be directed. The natural assets of British Columbia are among the most spectacular in the world. But, for maximum exploitation of these extraordinary resources, people have to see them for themselves. Civic and Chamber of Commerce brochures and web sites are all very well, but they cannot compare with the visceral effect of first-hand experience, or with the immensely powerful impact of concentrated worldwide television coverage of the world's leading sports event. The Olympic sponsors and broadcasters are the most influential, not only in our country, but in the world at large. When they come to the Games in Vancouver and Whistler, they will leave thinking not just about two weeks of great Games; they will think about Vancouver and British Columbia as a desirable place to do business in the future.

One of my other Olympic responsibilities is to chair the IOC Commission that is charged with studying the organization of the Games, to find ways to reduce the Olympic-related investment and operational costs to the minimum required to stage the Games. Many of our conclusions, which will be presented to the same IOC Session that will decide on the location of the 2010 Games in July, can provide valuable guidance to the Vancouver Organizing Committee, if Vancouver is successful. They will include guides on construction, design of Olympic

(Continued on next page)

Case Study 6.1 *(continued)*

facilities, comprehensive environmental planning from the outset of the project, reduction of accreditations and services to a reasonable level and many other features that have gradually risen to levels that are not necessary. There is another myth that the IOC demands grandiose plans and facilities. This is not true. Many host cities have gone far beyond what is necessary for the Games, and we want to discourage any excesses. We do not want Olympic White Elephants. If you do not need it and do not want it for the future, use temporary facilities. At the same time, think of the legacy that can be left for the future. Look at Calgary as an example of a fabulous legacy, in the city, at the University of Calgary and in the surrounding areas.

If you live in Vancouver, if you love your city, if you are thinking about the future, if you are thinking about those who will follow you, if you want your city to win a place on the world stage and to become part of history, then get out and vote in favor of hosting the Games on February 22nd. Better still, bring a friend with you. Or two. Or three.

Seize this opportunity and "go for it" with all of the energy and enthusiasm that has been the hallmark of this great country. The chances, when the stars and the planets are lined up in our favor—and they are— come around only once in a while. Don't be left behind to watch Olympic television coming from Austria or Korea in 2010. You'll regret it for the rest of your lives.

Case Questions

1. The editorial written by Richard Pound is clearly in favor of Vancouver hosting the Games.
   - First, take the side of proponent for hosting the Games, how would you use the editorial in your communications to convince Vancouverites to vote "Yes"?
   - Now, take the side of someone working for an organization who does not want the Games, how would you respond to the editorial?
2. Throughout his editorial, Pound mentions a number of organizations, some global and some national, who can influence the success of an Olympic Games. Name each one, describe their role, and outline how they can have a positive impact on the success of the Games?
3. An important accounting point is made in the editorial about attributing major capital investments (i.e., roads, airports, etc.) to the hosting of a 16-day event. What is your view on this? From a marketing perspective, how can sport marketing overcome the established beliefs that cities (like Montreal) have lost billions hosting the Games when, in fact, if you remove the capital infrastructure investments, the Games were profitable?
4. Research the Games since 2010 and report on whether or not they had plebiscites and what the key issues were in those votes.

7

Managing National Olympic Committees[1]

T he international sport landscape, as described, is operated by thousands of organizations that work directly in sport and thousands of others who work through sport, as sponsors, suppliers, or associates. Marketing, sponsorship, and the law are the daily realities for these organizations and their management. However, when taking a global perspective, the roles and importance of these organizations differ on many levels. Certain organizations have more influence on international marketing and legal aspects than do others. Much of this influence lies with the National Olympic Committees (NOCs), international sports federations (IFs), and members of the IOC who represent the Olympic Movement in their own jurisdiction. As of December 2014, there are 204 NOCs recognized by the IOC. NOCs can play very important roles in sport in their own country and represent their country on the global stage. They name Olympic teams, partner with IFs on global event hosting, work with governments on policy, fund athletes, support coaching development and sport science, and protect the Olympic marks in their home country. This chapter, therefore, is devoted to NOCs.

The management of NOCs is often believed to center almost completely around the health, well-being, and Games-based performance of that country's athletes. In many ways, that synthesis is true. But the actions that take place away from the Games, the behind-the-scenes efforts of hundreds (if not thousands) are significant and this chapter discusses the enormous preparation, discipline, and commitment that come into play for any organization as complex as an NOC and particularly for an NOC that may coordinate in excess of 45 National Sport Organizations (NSOs), also known as National Governing Bodies (NGBs). An important point here is that the Olympic Charter stipulates that voting control of the NOC must rest with the NSOs. These NSOs are the specific sport arms of the IFs within the Olympic movement at the national (or country) level (e.g., British Triathlon Association), and without them, most NOCs could not exist, or at least they would be much less effective.

The reader should know that organizational leadership is a critical part of the Olympics and it requires a comprehensive sense of every possible outcome and the constant responsibility to manage every challenge that an athlete or NSO might face. These challenges can range from deciding to bid to host an Olympic Games to dealing with an athlete unable to attend a sponsor event due to a family conflict. Regardless of the challenge faced, effective leadership is required. And, at the NOC level, leadership is ultimately about committing to a proactive orientation, decisiveness, and measured responses that lead to elite performances, when the entire world is watching, and effective decisions in the best interests of the NOC, when no one is watching.

Rick Burton, one of the authors of this book, learned about the commitment first hand during his tenure as chief marketing officer of the U.S. Olympic Committee. Burton held this position during the 2008 Beijing Summer Olympic Games. Those Games were forever time-stamped, not only for the heroic performances the world witnessed that August, but also for the very cleverly aligned starting time of the Opening Ceremonies, which took place on August 8, 2008 at 8:08 p.m. Written another way, these were the Olympic Games that started on 8/8/08 at 8:08. For the host country China, the number eight (8) is a very favor-

© Catthesun | Dreamstime.com—The EOC 40th General Assembly Photo (Yes, listed on site same as above)

able number and Chinese athletes certainly excelled on their home grounds by winning the most gold medals (51) and 100 medals in total. The Chinese were also magnificent hosts for this massive competition and their slogan reflected this in the words selected for Beijing 2008's motto: "One World, One Dream."

The United States (winning 110 medals) also performed well at the 2008 Games, highlighted by swimmer Michael Phelps who won an unprecedented *eight* gold medals at China's stunning Water Cube (otherwise known as the Beijing National Aquatics Center). In fact, the United States' medal haul was, at the time of this publication, the highest total ever for a fully contested Games (i.e., there were no countries boycotting the Olympics). But, as any NOC administrator will tell you, the marketing side of NOC operations has a very limited direct role in athlete performance. In the case of an NOC chief marketing officer, the role in the run-up to the Games is typically to work with the NOC's sponsors (e.g., AT&T, Budweiser, Kleenex, and others for the USOC) as well as the IOC's TOP sponsors that are based in the NOC's country (e.g., brands like Coca-Cola, Visa, McDonald's, Johnson & Johnson, and General Electric). An NOC chief marketing officer (particularly one located in a large market, like the US) is also typically involved in meeting with potential future Olympic TOP sponsors like Proctor & Gamble and Dow, which might be investigating the worldwide value of the Olympic movement.

Know this: the use of the word *worldwide* is not a cliché.

Estimates for the Beijing Games suggested that more than 4 billion people around the globe saw or read about the events that featured 204 countries (or jurisdictions), 10,942 athletes, 302 events, 28 sports, and 43 world records. Eighty-six nations actually won medals (some like Afghanistan and Sudan for the first time ever) and 54 different countries won at least one gold medal (a then Olympic record). The Beijing Games also attracted visits from more than 80 heads of state including presidents, kings, queens, and prime ministers.

The Olympic Games and Paralympic Games are important and are watched closely. But an NOC marketer is watched by many groups who gauge the organizational efforts of the NOC, including the NOC's Board of Directors. As Burton would say about the 2008 Games: "all around us swirled the intense focus of large national and international entities." Specifically, at the time, the US media were lauding the athletes and scrutinizing the USOC in general. The US-based NSOs wanted more funds from the USOC to help develop their athletes and the appeal of their sports. The NSOs wanted the USOC to promote their respective agendas. The IOC wanted all of the NOCs to have their operational houses in order. The sponsors wanted their brands to grow because of their association with the Olympics and wanted the USOC and IOC to aggressively prevent other competitive brands from ambushing their investments. The national broadcast network (NBC in the United States) wanted all the USOC and IOC sponsors to buy large blocks of advertising on their telecasts and to ultimately fill up all the available advertising slots. Last, but not least, America's Olympians, selected during a grueling process of Olympic Trials, wanted as little disruption of their heightened training regimens as possible.

On the other hand, these athletes also knew and understood that sponsors wanted endorsers, network broadcasters wanted feature stories, the print media wanted interviews, and the White House might ultimately call, because the US President George W. Bush wanted to host a send-off party in Washington, DC.

Said another way, the emails were pinging away, the phones were ringing and executive meetings were scheduled from early morning until late at night.

So how does a sport marketer need to view the role of an NOC (or a National Paralympic Committee)? If the role is no more than to develop medal winners and inspire future athletes, then an understanding of the many connected elements that must be in place for the full development of national Olympic and Paralympic teams is required.

To that end, for purposes of the material that follows, these elements include—regardless of country, NSO size or budget—the following 14 activities:

1. Development of Athletes—including the training and selection of elite coaches, the development of athlete training schedules and the organization of pre-Olympic Games competitions.
2. Dedicated Training Facilities—where athletes can be gathered and work for blocks of time with a minimum of distraction or interruption in a centralized, fully-supported environment with coaching, sport science, and technical infrastructure.
3. Athlete Services—including nutrition, medical services, injury prevention, and injury recovery. Access to medical expertise, supplies, and equipment to support these services is a key element of these services.
4. Operational Areas—including coordinating services such as athlete security, athlete/team transportation, and outcome-focused technology.
5. Communications—a vast set of activities to ensure the proper and accurate transfer of information with all key NOC stakeholders, including athletes, coaches, NOC administrators, NSOs, government officials, media, sponsors, donors, and other supporters.
6. Government Relations (with ministers of sport or governmental-funding arms) and political affairs (which may include lobbyists or agents enhancing or protecting governmental support or investment for the national team).
7. Executive Relations—including management of an NSO's executive board, senior advisors and/or NSO CEOs/executive directors.
8. Marketing (including sponsorship sales and servicing)—broadcasting, licensing, social network management, merchandising, hospitality, public relations (PR), and special events. This activity will often also coordinate services provided to sponsors or the NOC by advertising agencies, sports marketing agencies, PR agencies, event ticketing firms, and hospitality coordinators.
9. Legal—including athlete dispute resolution, formal contracts, real estate acquisition, and property management. The NOC typically will engage counsel or have a lawyer on its board or executive board to help in these activities.
10. Financial—including all NOC budgetary management and NGB accounting.
11. Fundraising—covering any incremental revenue sought from nongovernment agencies, nonbroadcasting partners, or nonsponsorship sources. This could involve such initiatives as donation programs, event hosting, charity tournaments, and other fundraising programs.
12. International Relations—including interaction with the IOC, IFs, and any groups associated with bidding to host the Olympics, the Youth Olympic Games, world championships, or international meetings related to the Olympic movement, such as SportAccord.
13. Human Resources—including the recruiting, hiring, motivating, training, development, and firing of employees and volunteers associated with the NOC.

14. Educational Services (which may include providing materials to educate key constituents, plus current or future athletes) and employment services (which may be used to help athletes during their training or after their Olympic careers have been completed)—an important aspect, particularly in developing countries, of the NOC role here is focused on Olympic education and working with schools to promote the values of the Olympic Movement.

The 14 working areas listed above are typically familiar to the management of larger NSOs such as the British Olympic Association, the USOC, the COC, or the Australian Olympic Committee. However, given the diversity amongst NOCs, the management of an NOC necessarily varies by country and with the historical importance associated with athlete performance during Summer and/or Winter Games. Some countries with large populations such as the USA, China, Russia, Japan, England, Canada, Germany, France, and Brazil have consistently sought to earn as many medals as possible. Other countries (with much smaller populations than those shown above) such as Australia, New Zealand, Norway, Sweden, Finland, Hungary, Austria, Switzerland, and the Czech Republic have often chosen to focus on or target specific sports. Nonetheless, they have still enjoyed great medal-based success despite far smaller populations to draw upon. In many of these countries, Olympic accomplishment appears to hold great value for that country's population (via the concept of national psyche) and for its government.

In other countries (both large and small), Olympic medal success has often been difficult to achieve. This may stem from a government not viewing sporting success as materially valuable or because it has been traditionally difficult to train elite athletes to compete at the global level. A strong example of this might be the country of India, which, while a dominant power in global cricket and home to more than a billion people, has rarely enjoyed any individual success inside the Olympic world. Interestingly, both international and domestic observers have suggested that given its population, India should be able to compete and capture medals at the Games. But there is a long-standing belief that India's NOC has not been able to harness and master the many facets of global sport governance for sports other than cricket and field hockey. In fact, since India first competed in the 1900 Summer Olympics in Paris, only one Indian individual athlete (Abhinav Bindra won the 10m air rifle gold in shooting in 2008) has ever won a gold medal (as of August 2014).

By exception, some athletes attend the Olympic Games as independent Olympic athletes when their home countries do not or cannot support an official Olympic team. For example, at London 2012, marathon runner Guor Marial entered as an independent when his country, the newly recognized South Sudan, was still not organized in its first year of nationhood to create an NOC. By rule, without having an NOC recognized by the IOC, countries cannot officially send competitors. During the difficulties experienced in the former country of Yugoslavia in 1992, the IOC allowed athletes from certain of the republics to compete as individual athletes during the Barcelona Games. In some developing countries, the national priorities, such as infrastructure and

© Steven Crum | Dreamstime.com—Lead Marathon Group Photo

ensuring the availability of food, shelter, and education, may be such that they simply cannot afford to devote scarce resources to an activity such as organized sport.

The difficulty inherent in the challenge of winning medals should not be underestimated. From the NOC perspective, it can be extremely costly to train an elite athlete. This cost must either be borne by individual families that can afford to provide access to training and sporting competition, by sponsors who support high-profile athletes, or by countries that have developed athlete-identification systems that spot young talent and steer those competitors into state-run systems. There are many examples of athletes who had strong family support, but examples of sponsor and NOC/government support are less common, although they do exist. In the case of sponsor support, typically it is directed at athletes who have already "made it," such as snowboard legend Shaun White, whose sponsors, first Red Bull and then GoPro, famously built him a secret half-pipe training facility leading up to the 2010 Vancouver Games. At the NOC/government level, Canada's Own the Podium (see Chapter 4) program achieved considerable medal success via government and NOC funding to support cutting-edge sport science and training support for athletes. Such combinations of support have, in part, contributed to Canada's Olympic success improving significantly from the 1970s and 1980s to today. Other examples (described in more detail in earlier chapters) include the efforts of the Australian government (Australian Institute for Sport) and the British government (UK Sport) and the resulting increases in their Olympic success.

In rare cases, support and assistance from family, corporate sponsors, IOC solidarity, NOCs, and government are not the only ways that athletes reach the Olympic Games (e.g., an inner-city boxer who sees fighting as a "way out," or a long-distance runner raised in high-altitude settings where it is common to run long distances to reach schools or medical facilities). However, the fact remains that athletic equipment, facility access, qualified coaching, sport science support, and entry into larger-scale competitions (i.e., state/provincial or regional championships) is essential, as well as costly. In many cases, access to these resources may exceed the capacities of athletes, families, and sport federations, particularly in sports where equipment, facilities, and coaching are more costly (e.g., equestrian, yachting, alpine skiing, triathlon, rowing, and track cycling) as opposed to sports such as athletics, boxing, and soccer where barriers to participate are lower.

To fill these resource gaps is a role that many NOCs seek to achieve. Often, an NOC will work with other partners to develop programs to identify athletes with elite potential and then work to place these candidates in subsidized training programs that can improve individual performances, but also weed out candidates who may not be able to compete at higher (or the highest) levels. This kind of institutional support is usually costly since

© Nayaav | Dreamstime.com—Olympic Village In Sochi Photo

the athlete must be fed, housed, transported, trained, and ultimately inspired. However, although costly, this approach is known to be effective and can be observed in a number of settings, including government-run national sport centers, collegiate sport (e.g., scholarships to NCAA Division I schools in the United States), and private programs (e.g., private sport schools for youth in England).

For NOCs like the USOC (headquartered in Colorado Springs, Colorado, USA), the acquisition of funds to underwrite these athletes is an ongoing process. And because the USOC does not receive direct funding from the US government (unlike most other NOCs), the USOC must develop revenue streams from sources such as broadcast rights, sponsorship, merchandising, fundraising, and in-kind gifts. These funds, once procured, are then distributed to either all of the USOC's NSOs, or to the USOC's three main training facilities in Colorado Springs, Lake Placid (New York), and Chula Vista (California). The USOC also enjoys (and invests in) relationships with 16 other elite training sites in cities including Milwaukee, Wisconsin; Birmingham, Alabama; Oklahoma City, Oklahoma; Carson, California; and Marquette, Michigan. The COC, with offices in Toronto, Ontario and Montreal, Quebec, follows a similar model and invests its resources through NSOs to athletes, via the Own the Podium high-performance support program or through its network of National Training Centers located across the country.

At each training center supported by the USOC and the COC, but generally for any NOC supported center anywhere around the globe, year-round staffing is required since the Olympic Games are staged every two years (alternating between the Winter and Summer Games). Further, since the difference between winning a medal and failing to place on the podium can be measured in the smallest increments (i.e., hundredths of seconds, one kilogram, one centimeter), athletes are traditionally involved with intense training for years before an actual Olympiad takes place. This means the NOC is typically active 365 days a year to facilitate the performances of current and

potential future national team members, and that NOC administrators must be pre-pared to work as hard as the athletes to maintain and/or improve the funding, training facilities, coaching, and comprehensive services.

From a marketing perspective, the efforts to support high-performance sport devel-opment take on numerous applications. Sponsors of an NOC are frequently looking for ways to connect with an NOC's top athletes, particularly during non-Olympic win-dows, when their investment is not as visible as during qualifying periods and the Olympics themselves. Food and beverage sponsors like Coca-Cola, McDonald's, Kel-logg's, Chobani, and Smuckers want their products or brands in front of the athletes in the training center cafeterias while technology or telecommunications sponsors such as AT&T, Bell, or Adecco want athletes using their products during their nonpractice time. Athletic equipment providers or performance-based companies (think 24 Hour Fitness, Nike, Under Armour, Oakley, Roots) want to know that athletes are being exposed to their latest products, technology, services or developments.

Additionally, NOC marketers need to build and leverage a dynamic website, launch creative social media programs, develop attractive advertising and promotional materials for use in mainstream media, maintain a team store for visitors to a training center, and be constantly on the lookout for new sponsors that might wish to draw upon the posi-tive image transfer that can come from associating with world champions. This imagery, that of a competitive individual or team committing both physically and socially for the right to represent their country, is powerful and many Olympic sponsors adopt this im-agery in activating their sponsorship. Three Olympic sponsors in particular (Coca-Cola, McDonald's, and Visa) have been sponsors of the Olympic movement for decades and have traditionally made it clear that the Olympics are a central platform or initiative of that brand's consumer communications in hundreds of countries around the world. Other brands, such as General Electric, are sometimes less visible via mainstream media, but have leveraged the business-to-business benefits of Olympic sponsorship worldwide.

CHAPTER SUMMARY

The leadership and management of an NOC strenuous and require a nearly super-human level of support for highly dedicated and talented athletes in a fiercely (and in-creasingly) competitive arena. It is not enough to say that an NOC simply helps athletes train or provides them with tuition vouchers post career. That would fail to acknowledge that NOCs stand as institutions that help inspire future generations of athletes, who bring sponsors into play (who build on the positive images of the world's best athletes), who communicate the greatest attributes of champions, and who make it possible for the world to see itself through the lens of peaceful competition and goodwill for others. Further, NOCs have the responsibility to steward the IOC brand and brand messages (peace, harmony, etc.) in their own jurisdiction, a responsibility that requires careful marketing, smart decisions, and risk management.

That may sound like a cliché, but the Olympic movement is unique among all sports (and properties) and it requires a significant team of professional administrators and agents to help place the right athletes on (or in) the right courts, tracks, pools, ice rinks, streets, fields, or mountains of the world. The Games may take place every two years, but the training is daily, the timing is tricky, and the list of international competitors who are also seeking medals is growing longer and longer. In such an environment, the management of an NOC is about supporting holistically the health, well-being, and Games-based performance of that NOC's athletes. Leadership, here, requires a comprehensive sense of every possible outcome and the ability (and responsibility) to manage every challenge, including the ability to respond quickly and effectively to field-of-play decisions. Thus, NSO leadership, as described, thus, is ultimately about proactivity, decisiveness, and measured responses.

Case Study 7.1

An NOC and a Tourist Incident

NOCs play very important roles as operators of their Olympic Team and trustees of the Olympic brand in their home country. In any Olympic Games, all but one of the NOCs is visiting another country. They invest thousands (and often millions) of dollars or euros preparing for the team operations, high-performance support, family and friends of athletes programs, and more for their teams as the Games approach. For example, the Canadian Olympic Committee has an expert team that works on operations, athlete preparation, performance tracking, and family/friends hospitality whose work starts more than two years before any Games. They make multiple advance trips to obtain suitable accommodation, supplies, training facilities, and other necessities, all designed to ensure that the athletes' experiences will enable them to maximize performance, and work to provide the right messaging back home pre-, during, and post-Games.

The USOC is one of the most prominent NOC's in the world for several reasons. First, and perhaps most importantly, the television rights fees coming from the United States are, by far, the largest in the world, thus providing the USOC with an added importance within Olympic circles, as well as added pressure for US athletes to perform well at the Games. Second, the United States has, since their inception, been consistently one of the top performing countries at the Summer and Winter Games. Finally, the United States is the world's largest economy and home to the head offices of a number of TOP sponsors, including Coca-Cola (Atlanta), McDonald's (Chicago), and Visa (San Francisco).

As in almost every country, many Americans pay close attention to the Olympic Games in and around their two-week schedule of events. Pre-Games, this attention often includes a focus on security issues, cultural differences, and preparedness of the

(Continued on next page)

Case Study 7.1 *(continued)*

host country. As noted, the 2008 Summer Olympic Games in Beijing China were one of the most impressive Games ever held. Within the excitement and grandeur of the 2008 Games, an incident occurred just days before the 2008 Summer Olympic Games began. The incident took place in Beijing, China's largest city and—as noted—the host of the Games, where an American tourist visiting China, who was also a close relative of a top US team coach, was killed during a sightseeing trip to a local Chinese temple. The USOC was informed of the incident immediately. The news rocked the US Olympic Team because many of the athletes, support team, fans, and friends had come to Beijing at a time when the United States' global popularity had been shaken by the Iraq War and the interna-

tional policies of the president at the time (George W. Bush). Indeed, given this context, some relations were strained and worldwide perceptions were often negative. The same could be said for the Chinese, whose human rights policies were an issue with much of the world, and had been under the global media's microscope leading up to the 2008 Games. Now, an American citizen was dead and there was a multitude of ramifications at many levels.

Put yourself in the shoes of the CEO, COO, or CMO of the USOC. In the aftermath of the tourist's death, you are faced with intense media responsibility, concern for all coach and athlete safety, concern for the potential performance of your athletes, and with fear amongst all Americans (family, friends, spectators and tourists) in Beijing.

Case Questions

1. What do you think is the role of a non-host NOC on the ground during an Olympic Games? How about before the Games officially start?

2. Review the USOC's structure and mandate via internet research and suggest who would be responsible to deal with the media, to communicate to athletes, tourists, families, and friends during the Olympic Games.

3. In your opinion, do you think the USOC should have expected that American tourists might be targeted in a country like China? If so, what would be the responsibilities of the USOC relative to nonteam members? Do you believe a policy should be instituted for future Games?

4. Were all American athletes, coaches, and staff safe, or could this matter escalate into a situation like the horrific Israeli hostage situation of the 1972 Munich Games when 11 Israeli athletes and team officials were killed by terrorists during the Games?

5. What measures might the USOC have taken to accommodate the US coach and his grief-stricken family?

6. How should the USOC help, if at all, with the return of the deceased to American soil and the well-being of the coach just days before his team's first event?

7. What messages must the USOC share with the world's media as it attempts to properly address this matter but also not intimidate or distract its athletes who must still compete. Who should give this message?

8. Finally (although there were many other issues to consider), what message should the USOC send to the IOC, to the Beijing Organizing Committee (BOCOG), to the Chinese government, and to the US government? Is this matter an outlier or does this matter require the holistic management by every C-level employee of the USOC (Chairman, CEO, COO, chief of performance, chief marketing officer, chief communications officer, etc.)?

9. Review online what the USOC did in 2008 and offer your view on if they responded appropriately and suggest if there is anything that they could have—or should have—done differently?

KEY CHAPTER TAKEAWAYS

1. A National Olympic Committee (NOC) is responsible for the Olympic movement in its country and, in turn, must deal with that country's perception of its athletes and response to their actual performances at the Olympics. For that reason, NOC employees must understand their role in supporting a larger vision that showcases how the Olympics can benefit entire nationalities.

2. While the number of medals won at an Olympic Games may give the media an ability to *keep score*, an NOC must always remain cognizant of how the Olympic movement is portrayed by the media, sponsors, and governmental agencies responsible for sport or health and education. Not winning medals (or winning the most) does not tell the whole story.

3. Securing and helping sponsors leverage the assets of an NOC, NGB, or elite athlete is a critical requirement for an NOC because the consumer-facing optic created by sponsors traditionally endorses the very best attributes of international sport. Said another way, when major sponsors *activate* their investment in the Olympics by creating Olympic-related advertising or by placing Olympic imagery on their product packaging, sports fans and non-sports fans alike are shown the high-profile value of Olympic sport inside their local community.

4. For any athlete to win an Olympic medal requires a super-human commitment to athletic excellence. To beat every athlete in the world at a particular event (or to win silver or bronze) requires an efficient infrastructure that enables the athlete focus on training and performance, free of distractions. For large countries competing in many sports, this efficiency is like multidimensional chess. For some countries, even bringing a single athlete to the medal stand is a herculean achievement that still requires enormous physical and financial resources.

8

International Sport and the Law

In the absence of common language or culture, people from around the world have the ability to communicate through sport by following a universal set of rules. Each sport has its own set of rules that is determined and administered by its IF and NSOs. If the established rules are not followed, then what is being played is not an official version of that sport. The importance of law is similar to the importance of having rules to a game. If there are no rules, the game no longer has meaning.

> The rules define the essential elements of sport: the objective of the sport or game, measurement of performance, scoring, duration of contests, the field of play, the equipment used, non-permitted actions or tactics, and any applicable gender, weight or age classification. In short, the rules constitute a code governing all aspects of a particular sport. (Pound, 2008)

When writing a chapter on the topic of international law and sport, the first event that came to mind was the Olympic Games (which may not come as a surprise, given the overall focus of this work). The Summer and Winter Olympics constitute the broadest expression of international competition for countries to demonstrate (among other things), which may have the best programs and athletes across the various sporting disciplines. The Olympics have also showcased the development of a sense of civic and/or national pride from participating countries, not only from a sport perspective, where entire countries get behind their athletes and their quest for gold, but also from a legal perspective. They have been used as a platform to promote or protest certain laws and basic human rights conducive to fairness, equality, discrimination (and non-discrimination), and various political interests. The 2014 Winter Olympic Games in Sochi, Russia, is the most recent example. The focus in this chapter is to examine international law and judicial bodies within the context of sport, focusing on the 2014 Olympic Games as a case study.

WHAT IS THE ROLE OF LAW IN SPORT?

Before delving into international sport and its legal implications, it is worth commenting on the extent and frequency of litigation in sports. Although there is no public ledger or record of all the related events in all sport organizations, the authors' collective experiences in a variety of roles in sport (i.e., IOC, IFs, WADA, NOCs, NFs, athletes, coaching) includes regular contributions from the expertise of lawyers, either external to the organization or via a board member who possessed legal expertise. This is likely similar to the experiences of others in sport. But why does sport end up in the courtroom (or at least in the presence of lawyers) so often? And, how big are these cases?

To answer these questions, one only needs to consider recent high-profile examples, such as the decade-long doping/anti-doping Lance Armstrong saga in which millions of dollars, thousands of hours, and dozens of cases characterize a behavior that, in addition to the ruination of Armstrong's personal credibility, has also severely damaged the reputation of the sport of cycling.

A quick scan through television and newspapers can provide a good sense of the importance of law in sport. The international digital publication, *LawInSport*, provides insights and analysis of hot topics related to legal issues of contracts, competition, corruption, doping, intellectual property, regulations, and more across the entire world of sport. *LawInSport*'s homepage illustrates the enormous presence of law in sport at the national, international, and professional level, with articles, among others, related to ambush marketing at the 2014 FIFA World Cup, corruption leading to the award of the 2022 FIFA World Cup to Qatar, recent decisions of the Court of Arbitration for Sport (CAS) Ad Hoc Division around the 2014 Sochi Olympic Winter Games, litigation by National Football League (NFL) players over painkiller usage or concussions, and sport sanctions in the Russian Kontinental Hockey League (KHL) (LawInSport, 2014). Law and sport are intricately intertwined, with an important impact in the global sport world.

WHAT IS LAW?

In basic form, laws are rules adopted by an organization or institution having the juris-dictional capacity to do so that members of a particular community are expected to know, understand, and follow. Failing to do so may result in a variety of sanctions. As stated briefly above, the laws of a country govern in much the same manner as do rules for sport. An interesting component of law is that it is constantly evolving to reflect the changing values of a community. One of the leading Canadian cases, *Edwards v. Canada (Attorney General)*[1], also known as the "Persons Case," describes the ever adap-tive nature of the law as "a living tree" because it "accommodates [and] addresses the re-alities of modern life." Laws are created to benefit and protect the people the lawmak-ers seek to govern. Sometimes, however, legal issues can arise because of the way a particular law is written (ambiguity), interpreted (lack of uniformity), or applied (arbi-trarily and without due process). In these cases, the issue is often brought to a court and is heard in front of an impartial judge who examines the issue from a neutral perspec-tive to determine the matter or to find a solution. The legal process is important be-cause it allows laws to have a flexible quality. International federations (IFs), described in detail in previous chapters, operate with laws/rules and processes involving internal dispute resolution bodies.

In the global political and legal context, only countries are considered to be sover-eign, which means they have the full authority to govern themselves (but not other countries) as they may see fit. On the other hand, while there are laws that only purport to govern a particular community, there are also laws that apply to all countries. These laws are called international laws. Some examples are the *Universal Declaration of Hu-man Rights* and the *UNESCO International Convention against Doping in Sport*. Repre-sentatives of various countries meet together to draft and adopt these laws, which are then incorporated within the domestic law of each country. There are also specialized courts that deal with issues relating to many of these international laws.

Sport has domestic governing bodies, as well as international governing bodies, be-cause it needs the capacity to deal with sport-related issues at a variety of levels. *Sports law* is a modern term used to describe legal issues that emerge in relation to sport. There is often confusion around this term because it is thought to be a distinct area of law. However, in reality, sports law is, conceptually, no different than any other area of law. Lawyers who have sports clients will often be required to advise on contract law, tort law, criminal law, intellectual property, labor law, and legal ethics. Sport courts are also relatively similar to regular courts. The decision-makers are trained for the operation of a sport court and are familiar with international law and the context of sports-related disputes.

The laws of a particular country are important for the functioning of any organiza-tion in that country. The governance, or the overall operation of an organization, is a huge task; it requires the assembly of committees, cooperation of people, and the proper application of laws at different levels in order to operate effectively. Having a lawyer on your team—either via board membership or under contract—who is familiar with inter-

national law and sport law is never a bad idea. The most successful marketers and managers in business are those who have such a strong knowledge of laws that they are able to achieve their organizational objectives while operating within the terms of the law.

INTERNATIONAL LEGAL STRUCTURE OF THE OLYMPIC MOVEMENT

The Olympic Charter

International law and sport in the context of the Olympics cannot be discussed without mentioning the *Olympic Charter* (Charter). The first version of what is now the Charter was drafted in 1908 and since then, there have been many amendments adopted by the IOC. The Charter is "constitutional" in nature because it is the supreme law that governs the Olympic Movement (IOC, 2013a). Functionally, it has become the international Olympic law, in the sense that participation in the Olympic Movement is conditional upon acknowledging that the Charter governs such participation.

The Charter's first chapter defines the Olympic Movement and the symbols that go along with it, such as the flag, torch, anthem, and rings. Previous chapters in this book have described the functions of the major players within the Olympic Movement: the IOC, IFs, and NOCs, as well as outlining the major components of celebrating, organizing, and participating in the Olympic Games and discussing the protocols for disciplinary procedures and dispute resolution.

Important International Players

There are a number of key "players" that each have separate functions but that together, make up an essential team that is responsible for the governance of the Olympic Movement. These key players are described briefly in the section that follows here.

International Olympic Committee (IOC)

As supreme authority for the Olympic Movement, the IOC recognizes the national and host committees and promotes the values of the Olympic Movement (Official Website, 2013a). Note: in their capacity as IOC members, the members do not represent the interests of the countries from which they come, but, instead, are considered to be representatives of the IOC in those countries. It is a significant difference from the normal situation in international organizations, in which membership is derived on the basis of representing the members' countries.

International Federations (IFs)

Oversee the governance of a particular sport at the international level. The IFs also control the technical operation of their sports at the Olympics (Official Website 2013b).

National Olympic Committees (NOCs)

Control player development, in most cases through their member national federations, within their own country, choose (within certain limitations imposed by the IOC and IFs) which athletes will represent the national delegation at the Olympics, and are responsible to the IOC for choosing a city from their countries to compete for the right to host an edition of the Games.

Organizing Committees of the Olympic Games (OCOGs)

Responsible for organizing a particular Olympic Games. At the time of publication, two OCOGs are in the full swing—Rio de Janeiro, Brazil (2016 Olympic Games) and PyeongChang, South Korea (2018 Olympic Winter Games). The OCOG for the 2020 Olympic Games to be held in Tokyo, Japan is in the early stages of preparation. The rights and obligations of these players are set forth in the Charter, to which they are obliged to comply as a condition of participation in the Olympic Movement and Olympic Games.

Case Study 8.1

Illustration of the Court for Arbitration in Sport:
David, Goliath and how an Athlete can "Slingshot" into
Success at an Olympic Selection/Eligibility Dispute.

Selecting certain athletes and not selecting others for Olympic teams can easily become hotly contested issues, especially as eligibility deadlines approach. Such disputes inevitably pit the affected athletes, particularly those not selected, against their respective national federations. The consequence is that they no longer enjoy the support of the body that has the power to determine their admission to compete on the largest international stage. Herein lies the proverbial battle between David and Goliath.

This case study considers a recent decision made by the Court of Arbitration for Sport (CAS), *ad hoc* Division, during the Sochi Olympic Games. It may provide guidance to help athletes have the best chance for success in challenging selection/eligibility decisions. In general, selection decisions rendered by the *ad hoc* Division in Sochi demonstrated the difficulties for athletes in succeeding with their applications. Applications will only be successful if the CAS is convinced that the national federation (and, occasionally, an international federation) clearly breached the selection/eligibility rules.

Note: The CAS is a specialized arbitral body that facilitates the dispute-resolution

(Continued next page)

Case Study 8.1 *(continued)*

process for sport-related matters, and, in the *ad hoc* Division, with the help of on-call pro-bono lawyers, especially for the benefit of athletes. The CAS *ad hoc* Division decides upon matters beginning ten days before the Olympics Games, continuing until the end of the Games. Selection, eligibility, and challenges to certain decisions made during the competitions are three common types of disputes.

Daniela Bauer v. Austrian Olympic Committee (AOC) and Austrian Ski Federation (ASF) No. CAS OG 14/01

Daniela Bauer is an Austrian halfpipe freestyle skier. Prior to the Sochi Olympic Games in January 2014, she received an email from the high performance program administrator in the Austrian Ski Federation. This email informed her that she would participate in the Games if Austria received a "quota place" for the halfpipe freestyle skiing discipline. She was sent a travel schedule and a pre-Olympic training schedule. In the end, the ASF decided against awarding a quota place to a female halfpipe freestyle skier.

The ASF did not recommend Ms. Bauer because a younger athlete demonstrated greater potential to perform (Court of Arbitration, 2014b), and her performance and results were not sufficient for her to compete for Austria in her discipline (Court of Arbitration, 2014b).

She challenged this dispute on the basis that the ASF's actions gave her a legitimate expectation she would be selected for the Sochi Olympics (Court of Arbitration, 2014b), and its actions were unreasonable and unfair (Court of Arbitration, 2014b).

Ms. Bauer applied to the *ad hoc* Division for an order that she be admitted to the Austrian halfpipe team participating in the Sochi Olympic Games.

The Panel dismissed the application for the following reasons:

- The Olympic Charter states that a National Olympic Committee may only

© Andrew Burton

select athletes who have been recommended by a national federation. It would be a breach of the Charter for the AOC to select Ms. Bauer without approval of the ASF.

- The ASF does not have to select all athletes who meet the minimum qualification criteria of the International Ski Federation.
- The ASF has wide discretion to recommend athletes, despite having rules that set out qualification criteria. This is not unreasonable or unfair.
- The ASF was entitled not to recommend Ms. Bauer based on an assessment of her performance and likelihood of success at the Sochi Olympic Games (Court of Arbitration, 2014b).

CAS did not award Ms. Bauer a place on the Austrian ski team for the Sochi Olympics.

(Continued next page)

Case Study 8.1 *(continued)*

What Do Athletes Need to Know?

1. Be informed of all rules governing you as an athlete.

   Athletes are required to follow sporting rules at domestic, national, and international levels in order to compete in the Olympics. Sometimes these rules may overlap. Other times, they may conflict with each other. Every athlete has the right to a fair arbitration before the CAS in order to iron out these conflicts in law, usually only after exhausting all internal processes and appeals. Understanding how the rules work and being aware of how national federations interpret these rules are key elements of success.

2. The personal is political—The selection process can be a game just as much as the sport is.

   There is no set procedure for interpreting rules. Despite the presence of selection/eligibility rules as seen in *Bauer*, the national federation has discretion, if properly exercised (i.e., without bias, arbitrariness, consideration of irrelevant factors, or procedural unfairness) to make recommendations for athletes based on outside reasons. Much may depend on the specific terms of any se-

   lection policy and procedure. Speak to other athletes within your national federation to hear about their experiences and those of others. It is also important to have a good relationship with your national federation, in the event that a selection/eligibility dispute does arise.

3. Knowledge is power . . . and so is reliable evidence.

   Prior to submitting an application to the CAS to challenge a decision, look at previous cases that have dealt with similar situations. Find out how some athletes succeeded, and why others failed. Make the arguments that align your case with those who have succeeded, and distinguish your case from those that have failed. The way to prove this is by presenting reliable evidence in favor of your position. Show the panel through letters/emails, witnesses, statements, media announcements, and other records that the national federation breached its own rules, and that such breach was drastically unfair and abusive to the athlete and his/her career. The right piece of evidence can be the bull's-eye for a David vs. Goliath success story.

Case Questions

1. The article portrays Ms. Bauer as David and the national federation as Goliath. Do you agree?

2. What do you think about rules being discretionary? Is it effective for making decisions and handling disputes? Why?

3. Pretend you are the CAS Panel in *Bauer*. Would you have come to the same decision? Explain why or why not.

4. Why do you think it is important for each Olympic Games to have a CAS *ad hoc* Division available to hear urgent disputes?

5. What other recommendations would you suggest to athletes in order to bolster their chances of success before the CAS?

6. Was there evidence that Ms. Bauer might have brought to bolster her case, but failed to do so?

7. The CAS Panel said it would be a breach of the Olympic Charter for the NOC to have named Ms. Bauer to the team without the approval of the ASF. To which provision of the Olympic Charter did it refer?

8. Although this information is now shared in the case, how do you think the CAS dealt with the legitimate expectation issue on the assumption that ASF received a quota position and chose not to accept it, or gave it to someone else?

COURT OF ARBITRATION FOR SPORT

With the success from the Olympic Movement during the 1980s, the international community saw an increase in the number of sports-related disputes as a result of the emerging number of IFs and the ever-growing intensity of competitions. In 1981, Juan Antonio Samaranch, the IOC President at the time, saw the need to produce binding decisions for disputing parties and decided to create a "sports-specific jurisdiction" (Court of Arbitration, 2014g). With the help of Judge Kéba Mbaye, an IOC member in Senegal, who sat on the International Court of Justice in The Hague, a working group prepared the preliminary documents to create the "Court of Arbitration for Sport" (Court of Arbitration, 2014g).

The Court of Arbitration for Sport (CAS) is an efficient and cost-effective alternative to trials within the system of state courts for "athletes, clubs, sports federations, and organizers of sports events, sponsors or television companies" (Court of Arbitration, 2014a). Specifically, "any disputes directly or indirectly linked to sports" may be submitted to the CAS (Court of Arbitration, 2014a), thereby avoiding trial before state courts. Conveniently, in disciplinary matters, the services of the CAS are freely offered to athletes and federations. Up until 1994, the IOC was responsible for all of the operating costs of the court (Court of Arbitration, 2014e). However, with the formation of the International Council of Arbitration for Sport (ICAS), CAS now operates with an independent status, supervised by ICAS, and funding is derived from all of the user groups (Georgetown Law 2014).

The purpose of the CAS is to facilitate a sports-related dispute resolution process and provide a fair decision to all sport stakeholders. To maintain efficiency in the context of many legal actions and to hear urgent cases, the CAS has two *ad-hoc* arbitration centers in Sydney, Australia, and New York, United States, in addition to the main center located in Lausanne, Switzerland (Court of Arbitration, 2014h). Regional hearing centers have also been established in Shanghai and Kuwait City. These arrangements make the CAS more accessible to athletes and international organizations in all parts of the world. Disputes heard by the CAS are settled through the most common methods of alternative dispute resolution: mediation and/or arbitration.

Mediation is a nonbinding process where parties come together in an effort to settle disputes informally. They present their interests to each other and discuss ways that the issue can be solved cooperatively, with the help of an appointed mediator. Mediators are neutral parties who have no direct influence on the outcome of the mediation. They are called upon to identify issues, help find common ground between parties, and keep the negotiation process moving in a positive direction—towards resolution. One advantage of the mediation route is that it is a confidential process, where whatever is discussed in the room will stay in the room. Thus, mediation is often a popular choice for parties who want to keep their legal disputes out of the public eye. Another benefit of choosing mediation is that the decision-making power lies completely with the parties themselves. Mediators are not like judges, and do not make judgments. The CAS Mediation Rules are published on the CAS website. It is advisable to review the rules before participating in a CAS mediation to ensure that you and your clients are able (and willing) to comply with the rules. For example, certain matters, such as doping, matchfixing, and corruption, are excluded from the CAS mediation process (see Article 1—CAS mediation)[2].

Arbitration, on the other hand, is more similar in nature to a confrontational court process. The CAS Arbitration Rules are also available on the CAS website. Arbitration decisions are made by a single arbitrator in the first instance, and by a panel of three arbitrators in subsequent appeals. CAS decisions are binding, and CAS decisions are recognized as enforceable decisions of an arbitral court in approximately 140 countries, in accordance with the New York Convention on the Recognition and Enforcement of Foreign Arbitral Awards (Court of Arbitration, 2014b). While arbitration may seem less preferable than mediation, it may be the only option if attempts at mediation fail. An important advantage of the arbitration process is that the resulting decisions are helpful for lawmakers, lawyers, and the legal community. These decisions create useful precedents for sport-related dispute, which become references or guides that can be considered in the future if a similar situation arises.

There are two divisions of the CAS that deal with arbitration: the Ordinary Arbitration Division and the Appeals Arbitration Division. The appeal procedure is reserved for disputes that have resulted from previous internal decisions made by sport organizations such as IFs and NOCs. In these cases, parties can file an appeal, arguing that there is sufficient evidence to suggest that the arbitrator made a mistake interpreting the law or considering certain facts. Until recently, the CAS could be called upon to provide an

Case Study 8.2

International Sport Law in Action: CAS[3] Decisions in Sochi 2014

The *ad hoc* division of the CAS received an urgent appeal from the Canadian Olympic Committee (COC) and the Slovenian Olympic Committee (SOC) contesting a decision made by the Competition Jury of the International Ski Federation. During the Men's Ski Cross competition on February 20, 2014, the French team allegedly altered their uniforms to become more aerodynamic (Court of Arbitration, 2014f). This alteration is contrary to the International Freestyle Skiing Competition Rules (Court of Arbitra-tion, 2014f). However, the CAS Panel rejected the appeal because it was filed six hours late. The competition ended at 3:00pm. The SOC and COC submitted their applications at 9:47pm and 10:33pm, respectively (Court of Arbitration, 2014f). The rules are that the application must have been made within 15 minutes after the end of competition (Court of Arbitration, 2014f). The disciplinary process before the CAS does not prevent athletes from concurrently being charged under civil or criminal proceedings.

Case Questions

1. Do you think the CAS Ad Hoc Panel's decision was fair?
2. Is the timeline under the ICR appropriate?
3. Why do you think 15 minutes was the chosen timeline for making an appeal?
4. If you were part of the Canadian or Slovenian Olympic Committee, what would be your next step?

advisory opinion on a legal issue, such as when legal clarification was required, without having to bring a full case to the CAS. These advisory opinions were not binding, but could help the sport community clarify confusing areas of international sports law and policy. Because the opinions were normally given with no counter argument, they had limited value and CAS has ceased giving them.

The CAS will accept for arbitration any sports-related disputes, so long as the parties agree in writing. This can also be accomplished by including an arbitration provision in the contract or by putting the provision into a regulation or statute of a sports federation, or by having a separate agreement to arbitrate, even if the contract or regulation contained no arbitration clause. To register an application with the CAS, court fees for submitting a dispute amount to 1000 Swiss francs, approximately equivalent to US $1,150.

CAS ARBITRATION PROCESS

The applicant (a party who brings an issue to the attention of the CAS to seek a remedy) will begin the process by filing an arbitration request or a statement of appeal to the CAS. A copy of the *ad hoc*

Case Study 8.3

The XXII Olympic Games in Sochi, Russia

High-profile Olympic events attract television viewers from far and wide—billions of them. For instance, when looking back at the telecasts of the semifinal and gold medal men's hockey games during the 2014 Winter Olympic Games, one particular memory that many global television viewers have is watching their local Olympic broadcaster telecasts in locations around the country where people were able to gather and watch these high-interest games. For example, in Canada, the Canadian Broadcasting Corporation (CBC) showed camera shots of large groups of Canadians gathering in typical locations, such as pubs and bars, across the country. In addition, however, less expected locations—such as a mosque—were also featured as a prime spot for viewing hockey competitions. This is convincing evidence of the sense of unity and pride that the Olympic spirit can bring to countries all around the world as they cheer on their athletes. This large-scale attention is unique to the Games and a few other global mega events. Thus, with such attention possible, the Games can also be used as platforms to advance personal/political agendas.

Division Application Form for the Sochi Olympics is located at the end of this chapter. Upon receiving a notice of arbitration or appeal request, the respondent (a party who responds/opposes the applicant's application) will submit a "reply" to the CAS. A reply is a document that outlines the respondent's version of events in response to the initial application. If the dispute is accepted by the CAS, the parties are notified of the hearing date. At the hearing, the parties are permitted to argue their case and present relevant evidence. The arbitration decision is communicated to the parties, normally within a few weeks of the hearing. In the case of an appeals procedure to the *ad hoc* Division, because of the urgency of final decisions during the Games, the decision is rendered on the same day.

CAS case law and recent decisions may be accessed at the Court of Arbitration for Sport website at http://www.tas-cas.org/.

ATHLETE DISCRIMINATION AND SEXUAL ORIENTATION

In June 2013, Russia's Upper House of Parliament under Russian President, Vladimir Putin, enacted a statute that banned "propaganda of nontraditional sexual relations" to minors (CBCNews, 2013). Those who did so, contrary to the legislation would be subject to fines and potentially stronger sanctions. This law adversely affected the lesbian, gay, bisexual, and transgender (LGBT) community in Russia, because they are, they argue, prevented from acknowledging their sexual orientation in public. The intent of the law was to strengthen traditional Russian values over western liberalism. Signed just over six months from the start of the 2014 Sochi Winter Games, this law received considerable attention and backlash from the international community.

One of the reasons for this enhanced attention was related to the issue that, during the 2014 Games, foreigners who would enter Russia would be bound by this law for the duration of their stay. In other words, all athletes and visitors who enter the host country for the Olympics are expected to comply with the laws of the host country. LGBT athletes who qualified to compete in Sochi were worried that they might be subject to harsh treatment for their sexual orientation, including arrests, fines, and possible depor-

© Paulmckinnon | Dreamstime.com—Canadian Olympians At Gay Pride In Ottawa Photo

tation. As a result, some of the athletes who identified as LGBT considered boycotting the Games prior to their trip to Sochi. Soon after the announcement of the new legislation and the widespread global response, the IOC issued a statement from Russian President Putin assuring all concerned that the new "legislation would not affect those taking part in the Games" (CNN, 2014). This anti-LGBT law conflicted with the Olympic Charter. Fundamental Principle 6 states that "any form of discrimination with regard to a country or a person on grounds of race, religion, politics, gender, or otherwise is incompatible with belonging to the Olympic Movement" (IOC, 2014b). The new Russian law ran contrary to the fundamental principles governing the Olympics. The Charter is in place to govern against discrimination of any kind, including sexual orientation and other human rights violations during the Games period. As per the "contract" between the IOC and the host country, Russia was expected to adhere to the Charter in its entirety as a condition to the IOC's acceptance of its bid for the Olympic Games.

As noted, laws must be constantly revised in order to accommodate a changing landscape for new legal issues. Russia's anti-LGBT law is a good example. In December 2014 the IOC amended Principle 6 of the Charter to include discrimination on the grounds of "sexual orientation" and "sexual identity" (Deseret News, 2014). The IOC will also evaluate its current contract with respective host countries and include clauses that prevent/sanction them from introducing laws or polices that would violate human rights for any aspect of celebrating the Olympic Games. This change would ensure that the fundamental values of the Olympic Games are upheld.

From a marketing perspective, the Canadian Institute of Diversity and Inclusion's ad titled "The Games have always been a little gay" and related Facebook campaign to "Keep the Games Gay," along with Norwegian sports apparel retailer, XXL All Sports United, who used Sochi's anti-LGBT controversy in their "Airport Love" marketing ad, drew significant media and social media attention, and garnered praise for their witty response of the anti-LGBT sentiments around Sochi.

AMBUSH MARKETING:
THE BEST DEFENSE IS A GREAT OFFENSE

Ambush marketing will be explained in close detail in multiple chapters later in the book, however it is introduced briefly here given its importance from a legal perspective.

> THE IOC AND ITS PARTNERS IN THE OLYMPIC MOVEMENT TAKE THE THREAT OF AMBUSH MARKETING VERY SERIOUSLY. WE WANT TO PROTECT THE INTEGRITY OF THE OLYMPIC RINGS, THE OLYMPIC VALUES AND THE FUTURE VIABILITY OF THE OLYMPIC GAMES. CORPORATE SPONSORSHIP PROVIDES ESSENTIAL SUPPORT FOR COMPETING ATHLETES AND CONTRIBUTES TO THE OVERALL SUCCESS OF THE GAMES. PUT SIMPLY, WITHOUT THE SUPPORT OF OUR OFFICIAL COMMERCIAL PARTNERS, THE GAMES WOULD NOT BE ABLE TO HAPPEN (IOC, 2012).
> —*Gerhard Heiberg, IOC Marketing Commission Chairman*

It goes without saying that the IOC is extremely protective of the Olympic brand, and for good reason. The development of commercialization transformed the IOC from an organization operating on a "shoe-string budget" to one that generates billions of dollars in revenue through the "sale of television broadcast rights, sponsorships, licensing, ticket sales, coins and philatelic programmes" (Martyn, 1996). Indeed, the Olympic Games have proven to be a profitable endeavor, and companies find it attractive to use the Olympic symbols in conjunction with their marketing efforts. Notably, sponsors make large investments in exchange for the ability to align their products with the Olympic brand. Since the IOC depends on sponsorship for event sustainability, it understands the value of including legal protection of the Olympic brand in the Charter.

Ambush marketing is marketing without official sponsor status, in which a marketer will associate its brand with the Olympics without paying a sponsorship fee. Ambush marketing can be "legal," unless certain intellectual property laws are broken. There are various laws in place to prevent ambush marketing of the Olympic brand both at the domestic and international levels. Ambush marketing rules are identified by the IOC, which are then enacted into law by various host countries. See, for example, the laws regarding ambush marketing adopted for the 2014 (Russia), 2012 (England), and 2010 (Canada) Games for an idea of what these different legislative provisions intended to prevent. The "Olympic Law" passed in Russia protects against ambush marketing by banning unofficial marketing within 1km from the stadiums, and allows local authorities to have jurisdiction investigating misleading sponsorship (Feldman, 2014). The principal legal work for Russian lawyers during pre-Olympic preparations was drafting this legislation.

The NOCs of nonhost countries are also expected to respond to ambush marketing in their own countries, regardless of whether they are hosting the Games. In the case of Sochi 2014, Budweiser extended its Red Light Campaign to Olympic hockey games in Canada. The campaign was normally most prevalent during professional (i.e., National Hockey League) ice hockey games where the Red Lights are connected to an app that flashes and makes noise when a goal is scored for your selected team (Andrews, 2014). For the 2014 Games, a giant Red Light was designed to fly over Canada during the Sochi Olympics and light up when Team Canada scored a goal (Andrews, 2014). However, the maker of Budweiser, Anheuser-Busch, is not a Canadian Olympic Committee (COC) sponsor. Another beer brand, Molson Canadian, is. Bill Cooper, now the chief operating partner of the TwentyTen Group, led the anti-ambush campaign for the 2010 Vancouver Olympics OGOC. He provided the following response to Budweiser's ambush marketing tactic:

> It is brilliant, but it's not great for those who actually invested in the Canadian Olympic Team. So you invite people over for a potluck and your guests bring carefully prepared dishes and present a nice bottle of something as they enter. Then one guest walks in with a bag of chips and proceeds to eat everyone else's food and drink their wine and beer. You know immediately what kind of guest is on your hands. Well, somebody just brought a bag of chips to the Olympic party and is planning to hang out and soak up consumer love on the sponsors' dime. Classy. I wonder how the chips will taste if the tables get turned during that FIFA World Cup thing they sponsor. (Andrews, 2014)

Clearly, ambush marketing creates a significant legal issue because there are special rights given to official sponsors to use the Olympic brand. Today's technologically savvy consumers render marketing campaigns easily accessible across the world. With ambush marketing, brand protection laws and regulations in place at the domestic and international levels, the IOC has recognized the importance of having a united front, involving itself, the NOCs, and OCOGs. Thus, the IOC amended the Charter to include brand protection bylaws.

NO DOPES AT THE OLYMPICS

Doping in sport is another serious legal issue faced by the international community. Athletes train their entire lives to compete in major international events, including the Olympic Games. There is an obligation on the part of the IOC, NOCs, IFs, trainers, coaches, and the athletes themselves to be aware of the substances ingested in their bodies. Antidoping regulations are designed to preserve the integrity of sport and protect those who compete "clean;" the honest way. Promoting a level playing field in and out of competition is the core of any antidoping philosophy (WADA, 2014c).

In any well-administered doping control protocol, the doping control sample collections are strict, and there are severe penalties and sanctions associated with breaching these requirements. The threat of suspension from the athlete's sport has become a common penalty in cases of clear breach of an athlete's responsibility to become available and to submit to doping tests. A full discussion on doping tests would be a separate book in and of itself; however as an example of legislation in sport it is ideal here. A perfect balance between upholding an athlete's rights and obligations with respect to doping tests has proven to be a difficult, but not an impossible task. Antidoping legislation has been amended to place greater emphasis on the interests of protecting clean athletes.

THE WORLD ANTI-DOPING AGENCY (WADA)

WADA IS COMMITTED TO PROTECTING THE RIGHTS OF CLEAN ATHLETES, WHERE HARD WORK AND TALENT ARE JUSTLY RECOGNIZED AND DOPING CHEATS ARE EXPOSED FOR WHAT THEY ARE. CLEAN SPORT IS FUNDAMENTAL TO A HEALTHY SOCIETY AND SETS THE BEST EXAMPLE FOR FUTURE GENERATIONS OF ATHLETES. (WADA, 2014C)

—*John Fahey AC, WADA President*

WADA was established in 1999 as an independent agency with a mission to lead a worldwide campaign for doping-free sport (WADA, 2014a). The Agency operates on a public-private model, in which 50% of its funding comes from the Olympic Movement and the other 50% comes from various countries and their governments. WADA pursues a number of activities, such as "research, education, development of antidoping capacities, and monitoring of the World Anti-Doping Code (Code)" (WADA, 2014a).

From a legal perspective, WADA developed protocols for collecting and preserving evidence, assisting governments in creating anti-doping laws, and updating the Code to comply with new changes in sport. The "drafting, accepting and implementing" of the Code is a significant accomplishment (WADA, 2014b). The Code contemplates five international standards, including testing, laboratories, therapeutic use exceptions (TUEs), the list of prohibited substances and methods, and the protection and privacy of personal information. WADA believes that these international standards promote a joint and concerted effort to tackle doping. WADA has a system of governance in place. The Foundation Board is the supreme decision-making body and the executive board is WADA's policy-making body (WADA, 2014a). These boards are comprised of equal members from the Olympic Movement and governments (WADA, 2014a). The IOC complies with the Code and holds the ultimate authority on doping cases that are in connection with the Olympic Games, subject to any appeals that may be directed to the CAS. As the Code is put into practice, revisions are needed to ensure that sport remains clean and free of doping, but also to suit the changing conditions of the global sport community. The whole purpose of the Code is to ensure that athletes internationally are held to the same standards and afforded the same protections as they engage in any sport (WADA, 2014a).

The Code has become a successful document in sport as it harmonizes antidoping policies in all sports in all countries by setting out universal rules (WADA, 2014a). The purpose of the WADA is to "promote and coordinate at the international level the fight against doping in sport in all its forms including through in- and out-of-competition" (WADA, 2009). The agency carries out its legal objectives by working with intergovernmental organizations, governments, athletes, and other public and private bodies, such as the IOC, IFs, and NOCs, to prevent the illegal behavior of doping in sport (WADA, 2009). As of 2010, the Code had been adopted by 630 sport organizations and national antidoping agencies (Georgetown Law, 2014). The main ongoing adaptation of the Code is to update the prohibited list of substances banned by athletes in all sporting events. Athletes who are in breach of the antidoping rules are subject to sanctions in accordance with Articles 10–12 of the Code. The most recent version of the Code came into effect January 1, 2015.

In Sochi, six positive doping tests were recorded at the 2014 Olympic Games. One of the most prominent cases was that of Nicklas Backstrom, a Swedish hockey player. He tested positive for a substance found in allergy mediation—pseudoephedrine—and was prohibited from playing in the gold medal game against Canada (Boston Globe, 2014). Even unintentional ingestion of drugs on the prohibited list is subject to disciplinary procedure. The IOC carried out more than 2,630 drug tests at the 2014 Olympic Games in Sochi (Sydney Herald, 2014).

CHAPTER SUMMARY

International laws in sport are designed to establish standard rules to be followed by every athlete. Sport disregards nationality, ethnicity, religion, and culture. It is a gathering of people who come together for a common purpose, to put aside differences and compete—equitably, honorably, and fairly—to see who is the best at the game or event. The Olympics are progressive in this way because they seek to achieve what individual countries are unable to do on their own. Sport will always have those who seek to operate outside of the law. The Sochi Olympics case study demonstrates this through the presented examples of human rights violations, ambush marketing, and doping.

The purpose of these international laws is to deter those who act outside of the law by confronting them with sanctions, penalties, and other disciplinary measures. The Games teach the world much about culture, education, perseverance, determination, accomplishment, teamwork, and pride. For 17 days every two years, people around the world forget about their political alliances and support their own athletes, their own teams, and their own country. Citizens celebrate under their nation's flag, and many feel a powerful emotional response when they hear their country's national anthem played. Olympic championship is the ultimate sign of sport greatness, motivated—in part—by those athletes who achieve a gold medal and are admired by their fellow countrymen and women. International law seeks to protect this and the integrity of the Olympic Movement

Key Chapter Questions

1. Why are rules important in sport?
2. What is international law?
3. Pretend you have a client who has a legal issue that must be brought to the CAS. How would you describe the CAS procedure to them?
4. Do you think it is important to have a court that hears only sports-related disputes? Please explain why or why not.
5. Why is antidoping important for international sport?
6. What are two suggestions that you would recommend to WADA for improving the regulated use of prohibited substances in sport?
7. Using the Sochi 2014 Olympic Games case study, do you think laws should be amended to reflect changes in society?

Key Chapter Takeaways

1. Law in sport is similar to having rules to a game; if there are no rules, the game no longer has meaning.
2. The International Olympic Committee exercises the supreme authority within the Olympic Movement, recognizes the national committees, selects the host cities, and promotes the values of the Olympic Movement.
3. The Court of Arbitration for Sport provides a sports-related dispute resolution forum and process and provides fair and independent decisions to all sport stakeholders.
4. Global sport marketing must consider the law entrenched in global sport, as evidenced in recent legal actions around ambush marketing.

CASE ILLUSTRATION:
DOPING IN SPORT[4]

This chapter presented content related to international sport and the law. The following illustration concerns doping in sport and the role of the law from a global perspective. The topic of doping in sport is very important for sport because the worldwide situation of doping is a major concern. This case illustration tells the story of how this situation came to be.

Picture an international system of sport, sport itself being an activity governed by rules agreed to by the participants. The rules relate to matters of the field of play, the equipment used, the allowable techniques, protection against injuries, age, gender, and weight classifications in certain sports, penalties for breaches of the rules (such as penalty shots, removal for specified periods, penalty laps, even disqualification), and all of the other aspects of the particular sport. The rules apply to each sport, no matter where it may be played throughout the world. Add to all this, a rule that prohibits the use of certain performance-enhancing drugs and methods.

Now, compare this idealized concept to the reality that many athletes, despite specific rules prohibiting the use of drugs and methods, regularly and deliberately engage in doping. They are often assisted by coaches, trainers, medical and scientific personnel, their entourages and, sometimes, even the public authorities in their countries. Doping, no matter what may be alleged by someone caught doping, is very seldom accidental. It is done to gain a competitive advantage over athletes who play in accordance with the agreed-upon rules. It is cheating and, often, dangerous cheating.

Athletes who do not cheat need to be protected against those who do cheat. This requires an approach designed to ensure that the same rules apply to all athletes in all sports and in all countries and a system of sanctions to be applied in a consistent and even-handed manner. It requires testing and the application of scientifically reliable tests, as well as any other form of reliable evidence as to doping. It requires a system that will provide any person accused of doping with a fair opportunity to defend him- or herself, and an independent arbiter who will determine whether a case of doping has been made on the basis of the available evidence. And it requires a commitment on the part of everyone connected with sport to insist that the rules will be applied—to everyone.

That is the situation in 2015, at the time of the publication of this book. And the thesis of this case illustration is that a parallel universe—different from the usual legal and social order in each country—has been created around the issue of doping in sport.

But, how did that happen? An adaptation of a speech by Richard Pound, book author, provides an applied story that illustrates the marriage of international sport and the law.

(Continued on next page)

DOPING IN SPORT (Continued)

The Beginning

For me, it began in Rome in 1960. I was a swimmer and, so far as any of the swimmers we knew were concerned, there was no doping whatsoever in swimming. We did know that weightlifters were using steroids and that this had spread to track and field, especially in the throwing events. There was nothing *illegal* involved (however unhealthy it might have been), since there were no sport rules that prohibited the use of steroids, or anything else. There was some diffuse anxiety expressed by the odd international federation, such as the IAAF, and by the IOC, but this was more at the level of a concern, and had not grown to adoption of any enforceable rule.

The 1960 Olympic Games, Doping, and International Law

It was during the Games in Rome [where Pound competed as a swimmer], however, that the change began. A Danish cyclist died during the road race, at least partially as the result of using a performance-enhancing drug. This event spurred the IOC into action. It established a Medical Commission, as well as a subcommission on doping and biochemistry. It recruited leading scientists to the subcommittee and set about attempting to determine what drugs were being used and established a list of those drugs, declaring them to be prohibited. It is fair to say that while this was a beginning, it had very little impact. The IOC has only one event—the Olympic Games—that occurs only once each four years for Winter and Summer Games (i.e., taking place every two years). It has no authority to test athletes between Games; the IFs and NOCs are very jealous of their respective autonomies. In-competition testing is less likely to be effective than no-notice, out-of-competition testing. The latter did not exist.

National laws did not prohibit the use of many of the substances used for sports doping. Even controlled substances could be obtained by physicians willing to administer or prescribe them for nontherapeutic use. Life went on, as before, except that no one talked about doping, now that it was prohibited, and most sport organizations consistently denied that the practices existed in their sports. The one-universe world was almost completely ineffective. Clean athletes were constantly cheated out of the success they deserved by athletes who doped.

The Parallel Universe

The parallel universe that exists alongside the sport cheaters is that administered by the World Anti-Doping Agency (WADA), which was established in 1999. WADA has a unique hybrid governance structure, in which 50% of its members are governments and 50% are drawn from the sports movement. It has a unique revenue structure—also 50-50. WADA has drafted and adopted the World Anti-Doping Code ("Code"), which, in turn, has been incorporated into the rules of the IOC, every Olympic IF, and every NOC. It has worked with governments to put in place the International Convention Against Doping in Sport, which has now been ratified by

(Continued on next page)

DOPING IN SPORT (Continued)

about 180 countries, in which governments agree, among other things, that the Code will be the basis for their actions against doping in sport. WADA also ensures that the final arbiter in matters of doping is the Court of Arbitration for Sport (CAS) and not the state courts in each country. This has a number of advantages: CAS arbitrators are expert as well as independent, the process is faster and cheaper than in state courts, and CAS awards can be applied in some 140 jurisdictions, pursuant to the New York Convention, whereas state court awards can only apply within the territory of the state in which they are issued.

The sporting world has recognized the dangers inherent in doping, both to the health of athletes and to the integrity of sport competitions. The essence of sport is the uncertainty of outcome based on athletes or teams competing by a certain set of rules. This uncertainty is compromised if those rules are not observed.

The recent example of Lance Armstrong in cycling is a perfect example. What should be seen as sport becomes, at best, mere entertainment, without meaning. When cheating is rampant, people will stop watching or participating in what amounts to a fraud against the spectating public and the 'clean' athletes involved. Sport has, therefore, an inherent interest in preventing and eradicating doping. The mechanisms now exist to cause that to happen. The available science is reliable and robust. What is lacking, despite considerable lip-service about the need for action, is a genuine desire, at the level of athletes, team officials, sport organizations, and governments to be aggressive in the fight against doping in sport.

The 1998 Tour de France

During the 1998 Tour de France cycling race, the Festina team was discovered by the French police to be in possession of industrial quantities of doping substances and equipment. It was a huge scandal. There was almost universal recognition that cycling was unwilling or unable to control doping in its own sport and that this was likely true in other sports. The same was true regarding countries being willing to administer stringent control over their own athletes. The IOC was seen as too weak to control the Olympic Movement. It was against that background that the idea of an independent international antidoping agency was born. Specifically, the idea was to ensure that all stakeholders necessary to achieve effective anti-doping measures were involved and that no stakeholder could be in a position to control the agency. These principles led to the creation of WADA in November 1999.

A Uniform Set of Rules

Early in the 21st century, WADA undertook the most ambitious project ever attempted in the fight against doping in sport. That was the development of a single set of rules, applicable to all sports, all countries, and all athletes. This is the Code. It took two years of constant work and unparalleled consultations, but WADA suc-

(Continued on next page)

DOPING IN SPORT (Continued)

ceeded in March 2003 following a World Conference on Doping in Sport, held in Copenhagen. The Code came into force on January 1, 2004, and it was agreed that all Olympic parties would incorporate the Code into their internal rules prior to the Athens Games.

A further challenge was to ensure that governments made the Code the basis of their portion of the fight against doping in sport. This took the form of an International Convention Against Doping in Sport, under the aegis of UNESCO, which was adopted by the Conference of Parties in November 2005 and which came into force once 30 countries had ratified it. Today, some 175 countries have ratified the Convention. There is a system of accredited laboratories, international standards, a regular review of the List of Prohibited Substances and Methods, peer-reviewed research funding and educational programs now in place. There is CAS that provides quick, expert, impartial and generally inexpensive recourse in the event of appeals.

Current Status: The Parallel Universe

Today, all of the necessary structural elements are in place to mount an effective fight against doping. So, why is it that there are so few positive cases, when we know that doping is widespread? In fact, most of the major breakthroughs in doping have not been as a result of analytical positive tests, but investigations by the public authori-

ties. How is it possible, for example, that Lance Armstrong was able, for a period of almost 10 years, during which he acknowledges that he doped, under the eyes of the most expert officials in the sport of cycling, to avoid testing positive? How can that be explained? It was not as if he was never suspected of doping. Any winner of the Tour de France, let alone a multiple winner, is (or was) suspected of doping. The question simply will not go away—how was this possible?

In short, there is little or no incentive to catch cheaters, no appetite for Code compliance, no desire to expand anti-doping measures, no willingness to impose appropriate penalties, and no commitment to investing sufficient resources to create an outcome of doping-free sport. The cheating continues. It puts the health of athletes at risk. It certainly

© Alek0505 | Dreamstime.com—Cyclist Lance Armstrong Photo

(Continued on next page)

DOPING IN SPORT (Continued)

forces many of them to have to lie about their conduct. It penalizes all athletes who play by the agreed-upon rules. It defrauds the spectating public, just as any other form of corruption does. It puts the integrity of sport at risk. If the public loses confidence in sport, it will stop watching and supporting sport. This has happened before and can happen again. There are no sports and no countries without risk—including mine and yours. The substances and methods may vary from sport to sport and the degree of doping may vary from country to country. But to deny the possibility that doping occurs requires willful blindness.

Yes, this is a parallel universe:

1. We have our own laws (rules).
2. We have our specialized science.
3. We have our own governance.
4. We have our own penalties and sanctions.
5. We have our own court system.

The CAS is a showcase of this parallel universe. One of the most recurrent expressions of concern surrounds the so-called protection of athletes—although much of this is often focused on protection of the guilty, as opposed to protection of those who are being cheated. You can be certain that no one in the antidoping field wants an innocent athlete to be sanctioned. Cases are only brought where there is a genuine belief that doping has occurred. Let us look, therefore, at the protections available to anyone charged with an antidoping rule violation.

- The right to have a B sample analyzed, which, if it does not confirm the analysis of the A sample, completely exonerates the athlete
- The right to know all of the details of the laboratory process
- The right to have had a continuous chain of custody of any sample
- The right to access to any internal appeal process within an IF or NOC
- The ultimate right to appeal to CAS, in which any panel must find, to its "reasonable satisfaction," that the antidoping rule violation has been established (the burden on the part of the athlete is the lesser burden of a "balance of probabilities")

Alternative dispute resolution (ADR) has become an increasing part of a worldwide system for the resolution of disputes. Most lawyers will be aware of such processes and there are many such systems available, especially in matters of commercial law. Examples are the American Arbitration Association (AAA) and the International Chamber of Commerce (ICC). There are several advantages to such a process. They include speed, confidentiality, expertise, and the ability to have some input into the selection of the arbitrators who will decide the matter. Until 1984, there was no comparable ADR system for international sport. Some countries had domestic procedures that lent themselves to sport matters, but these were few and not sophisti-

(Continued on next page)

DOPING IN SPORT (Continued)

cated. One of the outcomes of the Olympic Congress in Baden-Baden in 1981, and the arrival of a new IOC president, was the desire to have an ADR mechanism for sport. This led to the creation of the CAS by the IOC. Its initial purpose was to provide a service for the resolution of sport-related disputes, entirely funded by the IOC. Modest offices were provided for purposes of administering CAS and a list of arbitrators was prepared.

Sport, like almost any other segment of society, is somewhat change-averse and it took some time for sports organizations to develop familiarity with CAS and to have confidence in the quality of the arbitral awards, but this has grown over the years, and many such organizations now include provisions in their rules and even in their contracts to the effect that disputes will be brought to CAS for decision. Even the IOC, a notoriously conservative organization, now agrees that disputes involving the decisions of the IOC (formerly not subject to any appeal—as the supreme authority of the Olympic Movement) can be heard before CAS.

Once the IOC agreed to allow such disputes to come before CAS, the structure of CAS had to be somewhat modified, since CAS had to be independent from the IOC in order to be recognized as an independent arbitral body. This led to the establishment of the International Council of Arbitration for Sport (ICAS), which consists of 20 members, all with legal backgrounds. Four members are appointed by each of the IOC, IFs, and NOCs. Four additional members are then appointed, with attention paid to the need to have members familiar with the concerns of athletes involved in many disputes, and an additional four members are selected from the international arbitration field, to be sure that CAS is well guided in the best practices of arbitration.

CAS has its official "seat" in Lausanne and, as such, is subject to the supervision of the Swiss Federal Tribunal. This tribunal, the highest court in Switzerland, has recognized CAS as an independent arbitral body, the decisions of which are entitled to deference on the part of state courts. It will generally only interfere in circumstances in which there have been errors as to the jurisdiction of CAS or where the rules of natural justice or due process have not been followed, including the full right to be heard. A particular advantage (for an international sport system) of an arbitral body is that its decisions can be enforced in countries other than Switzerland. The New York Convention applies to the decisions of CAS, which can be enforced in approximately 140 countries. This is quite different from decisions of state courts. For example, the Jamaican courts have complete competence to decide on any matters brought before them—but, only in Jamaica. Their decisions have no effect anywhere other than in Jamaica. If you wanted to enforce a judgment of a Jamaican court in Canada, you would have to convince a Canadian court to issue its own judgment to the same effect, which basically amounts to re-trying the case.

In the case of CAS, its awards will be enforceable in any country that is a party to the New York Convention. This removes a great deal of uncertainty in sport. Imagine

(Continued on next page)

DOPING IN SPORT (Continued)

the case where an athlete is declared ineligible to compete in a certain sport. The athlete may appeal to the courts in his or her country and the courts may disagree with the international decision and decide that the athlete is eligible. That judgment only applies in that particular country, so you would have the anomalous result of the athlete being allowed to compete in his or her country, but nowhere else in the world.

As it relates to doping, pursuant to the Code, CAS has the exclusive jurisdiction as the final court on such matters. Impressions are that state courts are quite happy with such an outcome. First, it relieves the pressures on crowded court schedules and, second, the state courts recognize that they do not have the expertise required for such matters. Doping appeals can be highly technical, where challenges regarding the science are involved, where the laboratory procedures followed are examined, and where expert evidence evaluations are required.

State courts will always remain, for their citizens, the court of last resort. But, those courts will require that the same citizens first exhaust their recourses in accordance with the applicable rules. If, as in the case of international sport and doping, those rules require that appeals be arbitrated before CAS, the state courts will say that such process must be followed. If, at the end of that process, there is a claim that natural justice has not been followed, they may then step in, but they will not, in the absence of such a failure, purport to substitute their opinion for that of the arbitral court.

Back to the Lance Armstrong saga—you may recall that Armstrong tried to have his case brought before the US courts, rather than arbitrate, as required under the Code. The court refused and said he must follow the sport rules. Armstrong did not wish to arbitrate and his results were annulled and he was declared ineligible for life. Ultimately, he confessed that he had doped all along.

CAS has taken steps to ensure that it keeps up with technological advances, so that, for example, users can file their documents electronically from anywhere in the world. Hearings can also be held anywhere in the world, at the convenience of the parties. CAS even has a fund designated to provide some financial support for athletes who cannot afford to pay for legal assistance. One might conclude that CAS serves the needs of the stakeholders in international sport quite well.

9

Sport Marketing and the Law

Depending on their backgrounds, readers of this portion of the book might be relieved to know that it is not intended to be a legal text, but merely a brief summary of how marketing attracted the attention of lawmakers, and how these interests are addressed and protected by law. In particular, the focus of the chapter is on the protection of economic and property interests. Some of these issues can be considered classic, and others were invented for the purposes of protecting newer forms of property resulting from the evolution of more sophisticated means of doing business. Protection of consumers took much longer to develop than protection of property and producers of goods and services. Indeed, it is only in the past few decades that governments created watchdog organizations to make sure that consumers are not taken advantage of by unfair marketing efforts. For example, an organization cannot have "sales" that last forever or work with a competitor to fix prices that are to the detriment of the consumer. These government watchdogs will make sure this does not happen and will institute legal or regulatory proceedings if such conduct is discovered.

From the perspective of 21st century society, it would not be unfair to suggest that few areas of human activity have attracted as much legal attention as marketing, especially when it attempts to influence human behavior. "Behavior" in these circumstances is the influencing of decisions relating to the acquisition of goods and services, rather than, say, political behavior in the larger sense. This commercial focus requires an understanding of some historical background, especially in England, where the foundations of the Anglo-American law originated and from which some of the earliest legal principles were evolved.

MARKS ON GOODS

The marking (not marketing) of goods has been a factor for almost as long as trade has existed. Originally, this was not so much for the purpose of generating goodwill (although that did develop as a consequence), but rather for the assumption of responsibility with respect to inferior products. Marks include guild marks, proprietary marks (to establish ownership and a right to recovery), clothiers' seals (usually to indicate the origin of goods), printers' and publishers' marks, cutlers' marks, patents, and trademarks.

The early (circa late 1800s and early 1900s) significance of trademarks was, therefore, not as an asset of an individual owner related to the goodwill of the business, but rather as a liability, in the nature of a compulsory disclosure of the source of the wares, which disclosure enabled guild authorities to regulate trade, impose and enforce standards of quality and workmanship, and suppress competition among guild members. During this time, royal authorities used marks to organize domestic and international trade, and to repress commercial fraud. The protection and enforcement of marks was in the public interest. As time went on, the concept of a private interest slowly took hold, aided by the concept of property in proprietary marks, particularly cutlers' marks in London. The secondary message of marks, as a guarantee of quality, was also now important.

Because the consequences of infringement were penal in nature and were intended to protect the public from deception, two basic principles distinguished early marks from modern trademarks. First, the defendant trader must have put the wares on the market knowingly. Second, the wares must have been of an inferior quality. When combined, these two principles were felt to protect the interests of the public.

REGULATION OF MARKETING

As is often said, big reward comes with big risk. Marketing is the product of a form of economic competition in which success in the marketplace is rewarded—often handsomely—and failure is often costly, if not fatal. The unfortunate reality in marketing is that success is never permanent, although failure certainly can be. For example, a massive success with the launch of a new product could be followed by years of product failures leading to the eventual failing of the business. However, a start-up that never encounters success will disappear very quickly.

This reality is reflected in the laws of supply and demand, which have their own special calculus. They may be elastic or inelastic. From the supply side, monopoly is an ideal state, permitting the supplier to engage in uncontrolled fixing or manipulation of prices. This has never been popular from the perspective of those on the demand side, who require or purchase a product or service. In a monopoly circumstance, there is no incentive for the supplier to improve quality or lower prices. Most argue that these situations are not good for the consumer.

Each generation has a tendency to believe that its own problems or challenges are new and unique, but control of markets has been a feature of the human condition since before recorded history. Farmers, granary owners, shippers, and monarchs have profited at the expense of consumers in every era of human existence, ever since society moved away from a pure hunter-killer model to a market-driven model where people exchange resources of one form for resources of another.

Today, in a mercantile society, the forces of competition have accelerated beyond anything imaginable 200 years ago. At that time, the Industrial Revolution increased the production of consumer goods at a rate exceeding the wildest dreams of producer and consumer alike. Society was just slow to respond. The legal institutions necessary to regulate trade did not exist. The early 19th century society did not have a pressing desire for such regulation. The reason for this was that, at the time of the Industrial Revolution, it was property (i.e., land ownership) that led to political power, not people. The idea of universal suffrage was then completely unthinkable, and considered akin to revolution and anarchy. It took almost a century of political developments to wrest away control from the landed gentry. First, it evolved into the hands of the industrial elite, and only much later was it available to the working classes. It was not until that shift of power began to occur that society was able to begin to address the important matters of education, public health, and protection from the deplorable conditions under which a great percentage of the population lived.

As a result of these shifts, three principal lines of legal thinking emerged. Bear in mind, however, the very limited social and legal apparatus that then existed.

THREE LINES OF THINKING IN THE EMERGENCE OF MARKETING REGULATION

1. Protection of the State and Its Revenue

    The first line was protection of the state and its revenue. Some of these included the Navigation Acts and the Corn Laws, and others used customs and trade barriers as incentives to protect the local markets and manage preferred access to colonial markets. The colonial connections were valued, but ignored in the course of domestic politics.

2. Protection of Commerce

    The second line was protection of commerce towards ensuring that businesses could survive and meet consumer needs. As the volume of goods available for sale increased, certainty of the contractual rules applicable to the sale of goods had to be ensured, the use of negotiable instruments for payment or for credit needed to be developed, financial institutions needed to be created, currency regulated, and commercial practices generally standardized.

3. Protection of Property

The third line of thinking was the protection of property. This was in addition to the traditional notions of property, such as real estate, transmission on death, mortgages, boundaries, and the like. Gradual recognition was afforded to what modern lawyers know as intellectual property. At this point, there were no concepts of trademarks, trade names, copyright, or patents.

PROTECTION OF INTELLECTUAL PROPERTY

Four general means by which the law protects the products of human intellect:[1]

Absolute monopoly: the right of the owner of the intellectual property to prevent all other persons from using that property (e.g., patents);

Qualified monopoly: the right of the creator of intellectual property to prevent others from copying or otherwise exploiting the work actually produced by him (e.g., copyright);

Compulsory license: the right to use intellectual property by all who wish to do so, provided they pay a certain license fee to the creator (e.g., compulsory license schemes in patent and copyright statutes); and

Unfair competition: a fragmented collection of creators' rights built around the principle that the creator has the right to prevent others from using his property in an unfair manner (e.g., passing-off or breach of confidence).

UNFAIR MARKETING PRACTICES (Passing Off)

As time passed, as markets developed, and as competition increased, the law had to catch up with commercial developments in the marketplace. Legal recognition was given to the concept of goodwill—an intangible aspect of a business that did not appear among the recorded assets and liabilities of the business. Nevertheless, goodwill was an important aspect of the business, representing the likelihood that a satisfied customer would return to that business for goods or services in the future. Goodwill had value, often in significant amounts.

DEFINITIONS OF "GOODWILL"

There have been many efforts to describe or define goodwill, two of which are included here. The first is an early judicial pronouncement by Lord Macnaghten in 1901:

What is goodwill? It is a thing very easy to describe, very difficult to define. It is the benefit and advantage of the good name, reputation and connection of the business. It is the attractive force which brings in custom. It is the one thing which distinguishes an old established business from a new business at its first start. Goodwill is composed as a variety of elements. It differs in its composition in different trades and in different businesses in the same trade. One element pay preponderate here, and other there.[2]

The second is somewhat more modern:

> The advantages of a trademark may include consumer satisfaction with the product identified by the trademark, the impression created by advertising, favourable reports from consumers' groups and regulatory bodies, and the visual and verbal attributes of the trademark. These advantages share a common propensity to increase the sales of the product bearing the trademark. The monetary value of the goodwill of the trademark is thus the additional profit made by the owner of the trademark over the profits which would have been made without the trademark. (Cairns, 1988)

The actions of other traders can have an impact on the goodwill of the business. It is considered to be a normal business risk that another trader might have a superior product or service and that customers who might otherwise have returned to the original business would, instead, patronize the other. It was different, however, if another trader were to attempt to pass off his own goods as those of the original business. The first reported case of passing-off was *Perry v. Truefitt*[3] in which the court stated, "A man is not to sell his own goods under the pretense that they are the goods of another man."[4] The legal and economic concern was that the goodwill of the business which was affected by the passing-off would thereby be diminished. Passing-off became the first strictly economic tort at common law, not far off from the tort of deceit.

FIVE CONDITIONS TO A PASSING-OFF ACTION

Over the next century and a half, the concept of passing-off was refined as more complex trade actions tested its limits without, however, disturbing the original conceptual basis for the tort. By 1980, five conditions had been identified as essential to a passing-off action:

(1) misrepresentation;
(2) by a trader in the course of trade;
(3) to prospective customers of his or ultimate consumers of goods or services supplied by him;
(4) which is calculated to injure the business or goodwill of another trader, and
(5) which causes actual damage to the business or goodwill of the trader bringing the action.[5]

In the interim, there has been considerable statutory evolution, particularly through the adoption of specialized statutes that introduced specific legislative schemes to provide protection from improper actions by others, which might adversely affect businesses having certain types of intellectual property. These include statutes dealing with trademarks, trade names, industrial designs, copyright, and patents. In general, there is a system of registration, which provides public notice of the intellectual property of the registrant, and a process by which infringements of the registered rights can be prosecuted. These systems tend to be cumbersome and fairly rigid, but reasonably successful in achieving their objectives. There can be crossover between the statutory systems and the original tort of passing-off, which may lead to a choice between remedies sought and the particular forum in which the action will be pursued, but passing-off is most often invoked where the intellectual property sought to be enforced is not in the form of a registered right.

CANADIAN TRADE-MARKS ACT (1985)

Globally, most developed countries started protecting trademarks more closely, especially in the late 1900s. While every country has its own manner of drafting legislation, the Canadian Trade-marks Act[6] provides a good example of a statutory scheme designed to codify (and somewhat expand) the concept of passing-off.

7. No person shall
   (a) make a false or misleading statement tending to discredit the business, wares or services of a competitor;
   (b) direct public attention to his wares, services or business in such a way as to cause or be likely to cause confusion in Canada, at the time he commenced so to direct attention to them, between his wares, services or business and the wares, services or business of another;
   (c) pass off other wares or services [as/for] those ordered or requested;
   (d) make use, in association with wares or services, of any description that is false in a material respect and likely to mislead the public as to
      (i) the character, quality or composition;
      (ii) the geographical origin, or
      (iii) the mode of the manufacture, production or performance of such wares or services: or
   (e) do any other act or adopt any other business practice contrary to honest industrial or commercial usage in Canada.[7]

The nature of the right of the owner of a trademark is proprietary and it appears easier to characterize that right as one of property in the trademark itself than in the goodwill of the business.

Part of the evolution of the law has been a shift away from the traditional view of trademarks as attaching to the particular traders or merchants toward a broader public interest. This shift has occurred in other developed countries as well. The Supreme Court of Canada has expressed this idea in the following terms:

The role played by the tort of passing-off in the common law has undoubtedly expanded to take into account the changing commercial realities in the present day community. The simple wrong of selling one's goods deceitfully as those of another is not now the core of the action. It is the protection of the community from the consequential damages of unfair competition or unfair trading.[8]

INCREASING REGULATION OF COMMERCIAL PRACTICES

As trade and consumption became more ubiquitous, they also became more sophisticated and competition in the marketplace became more intense. The opportunities (and the temptation) to increase trade by any means, whether misleading or not, multiplied. Purchase on credit became a way of life and has produced more than its share of economic crises. The cost of credit to consumers became especially difficult to determine as recourse by sellers in respect of sales on credit and installment became increasingly draconian. It is beyond the scope of this work to identify and canvass each element of troubling market behavior and the particular response by each jurisdiction over time. However, it is important to note generally that the outcome of the efforts to protect consumers has produced a set of bewildering statutory and regulatory frameworks that is all but impenetrable, especially to the consumers it is designed to protect.

STATUTORY AND REGULATORY FRAMEWORK

In continuing to use Canada as an example, a wave of federal statutes to regulate commercial practices emerged in the 1980s and continued into the 2000s. Some of these include the Food and Drugs Act (1985)[9], the Fruit, Vegetable and Honey Act[10], the Canadian Agricultural Products Standards Act (1985)[11], the Canada Grain Act (1985)[12], the Feeds Act (1985)[13], the Fertilizers Act (1985)[14], the Fish Inspection Act (1985)[15], the Livestock and Livestock Products Act (1990)[16], the Seeds Act (1985)[17], the Boards of Trade Act (1985)[18], the Canada Shipping Act (2001)[19], the Railway Safety Act (1985) (formerly named the Canadian National Railways Act)[20], the Excise Act (1985)[21], and the Royal Canadian Mounted Police Act (1985)[22]. In addition to these, statutes dealing with such matters as consumer protection, product liability, safety, and many other areas, at both federal (Canada) and provincial levels, saturated an already-complicated environment. The breadth of these statutes gives some idea of the many areas in which marketing has or may have an impact on the public interest.

To focus, however, on some of the principal regulatory aspects in a commercial system which bears on marketing, it suffices to identify the major statutory schemes. While there are variations from jurisdiction to jurisdiction, they are relatively minor. As trade becomes increasingly global, and consumer rights must be protected more than ever, they must be consistently exercised in all applicable jurisdictions in order to withstand any potential conflicts.

INTELLECTUAL PROPERTY AND MARKETING TRADEMARKS

A trademark is defined in section 2 of the Canadian Trade-marks Act:

a. a mark that is used by a person for the purpose of distinguishing or so as to distinguish wares or services manufactured, sold, leased, hired or performed by him from those manufactured, sold, leased, hired or performed by others,

b. a certification mark,

c. a distinguishing guise or

d. proposed trademark.

There can easily be some overlap, depending on the circumstances and the artistic or literary character, between a trademark and copyright. Unlike copyright, however, a trademark may be extended indefinitely and does not expire 70 years after the death of the author.

A certification mark is a concept created by the statute, one that did not exist in the common law. Some such marks have appeared in the context of sports clothing and equipment (e.g., Nike swoosh, Adidas three-stripes). The definition:

> a mark that is used for the purpose of distinguishing or so as to distinguish
wares or services that are of a defined standard with respect to:

> the character or quality of the wares or services,

> the working conditions under which the wares have been produced or the services performed,

> the class of persons by whom the wares have been produced or the services performed, or

> the area within which the wares have been produced or the services performed, from wares or services that are not of that defined standard. (CIPO, 2014b)

A distinguishing guise is defined as

> a shaping of wares or their containers, or a mode of wrapping or packaging wares the appearance of which is used by a person for the purpose of distinguishing or so as to distinguish wares or services manufactured, sold, leased, hired or performed by him from those manufactured, sold, leased, hired or performed by others. (CIPO, 2014b)

An obvious example of a distinguishing guise is the shape of the classic Coke bottle, the Heinz ketchup bottle, or a Tropicana orange juice container.

PATENTS

Patents are defined similarly in developed countries throughout the world, but again the Canadian example is used to explain the concept. A patent provides the owner with an absolute monopoly for the exploitation of the subject-matter of the patent for a limited time. Patents are issued in respect of "inventions," which are defined as "any new and useful art, process, machine, manufacture or composition of matter, or a new and useful improvement in any art, process, machine, manufacture or composition of matter."[23] The keys to the issuance of a patent are novelty and usefulness.

The owner of the patent has the exclusive right of making, constructing, using, and selling the invention to others for the full term of the patent. When the patent expires, others are free to manufacture and sell the subject-matter of the patent. Efforts are sometimes made to try to obtain practical extensions of such period by registering the name of the subject matter as a trademark. This may or may not be successful, but if it is, the inventor gains a market advantage from continuing to manufacture or sell goods with a recognition value due to the monopoly enjoyed during the validity of the patent.[24]

A vast majority of sports equipment has been patented. Modern issues regarding the ability to patent computer software, medical treatments, genes, business methods, biological sequences, living matter, and others remain unsettled to some degree. Compulsory licensing applies to such inventions as patented medicines. Infringement of patents by violating the terms of the patent (think knock-offs) exposes the infringer to damages sustained by the patent holder as a result of the infringement.

TRADE NAMES

A trade name is defined as the name under which any business is carried on whether or not it is the name of a corporation, a partnership, or an individual. "Shell" is a trade name used by the Royal Dutch Petroleum organization, and is closely connected with its trademark. Both words (e.g., trade names and products) and phrases (e.g., slogans or company catch phrases) can be trademarked, with trademarking preference for words and phrases that are unique. Images can also be trademarked and for some companies, like Coca-Cola, their trade name also appears in their trademark image.

INTELLECTUAL PROPERTY STATUTES COPYRIGHT

Copyright legislation provides that copyright subsists in every original literary, dramatic, musical, or artistic work. It arises automatically with the creation of the particular work and there is no requirement that the author must first register it. Copyright is a creature of statute, as the Supreme Court of Canada has noted:

> copyright law is neither tort law nor property law in classification, but is statutory law. It neither cuts across existing rights in property or conduct nor falls between rights and obligations heretofore existing in the common law. Copyright legislation simply creates rights and obligations upon the terms and in the circumstances set out in the statute.[25]

For the purposes of this legislation, copyright carries with it the sole right to produce or reproduce the work or any substantial part thereof in any material form whatever, to perform the work or any substantial part thereof in public or, if the work is unpublished, to publish the work or any substantial part thereof, and to authorize such acts.

INDUSTRIAL DESIGNS

The protection granted in respect of industrial designs is essentially a variation of general copyright law, but one of the differences is that it requires registration. The statutory description of "design" or "industrial design" means features of shape, configuration, pattern, or ornament and any combination of those features that, in a finished article, appeal to, and are judged solely by, the eye (CIPO, 2014a). Ideas or concepts are not registrable and designs must be rendered in a concrete and visible form before any registration is possible. There are also rules regarding originality as a prerequisite for registration. Protection is granted for a period of ten years from registration (CIPO, 2014a).

COMPETITION STATUTES

Competition Acts prohibit, among many forms of commercial behavior, the use of trademarks for the purpose of unduly restricting competition and misleading advertising.

CRIMINAL LAW

The provisions of the Criminal Code prohibit forgery, falsification, defacing, and removal of trademarks, as well as misleading advertising.

CONSUMER PROTECTION

Statutes generally require the provision of adequate information to enable consumers to make informed decisions regarding purchases. Particularly, information is needed that pertains to how much interest they are paying in respect of credit or installment purchases, precisely what it is that they acquire, what recourses they may have against vendors, what liability exists in respect of defective goods, and how recourses can be exercised.

PRODUCT LIABILITY

There is an implied warranty that goods are suitable for their purpose. Statutes have been adopted to codify those principles and to provide particular recourses.

SPECIALIZED NATIONAL STATUTES—SPORTS MARKETING

© Olgavolodina | Dreamstime.com—Sporting goods with symbolic Olympic Games in Sochi 2014

As sport developed on both domestic (most countries of the developed world) and international fronts, it attracted commercial interests seeking to capitalize on its growing popularity with consumers. Support was both financial and promotional in nature. Companies sponsored teams and athletes, as well as events. In some cases, the contribution was in the form of products or services for athletes, events, coaches, or associations. The sponsoring corporations used the names and logos of teams and their players. Standard means of protecting the applicable intellectual property were available.

With the rapidly expanding importance of the Olympic Games in the late 1900s and early 2000s, there was an equal growth of commercial interest in the Games and the opportunities of sponsors and licensors to become associated with the event. As stated elsewhere, marketing is an empirical exercise of trial and error, in which more is often learned from failure than from success. Dealings on the part of Olympic organizers with corporations were often conducted on the basis of far less business experience on the Olympic side of a transaction than was possessed by the corporations. Generally, Olympic organizers were doing things for the first time, in contrast to traders who spent their lives promoting their goods and maximizing their profits. Consequently, Olympic organizers often came out on the short end of business-related transactions. In particular, the definition of rights granted was often much looser than it ought to have been, the permissible statements of connection with the event not sufficiently limited, and even the duration of the rights granted was not specific. Then too, the Olympic organizers faded from sight (and even existence) following the Games, since their only responsibility was to organize the event, leaving only the NOC of the host country in place thereafter, usually as a party that had not granted the marketing rights in respect of the Games.

HELMS BAKERY V. UNITED STATES OLYMPIC COMMITTEE

One notorious example occurred in the United States, arising out of the 1932 Olympic Games in Los Angeles.[26] Helms Bakery had a licensing arrangement with the organizing committee to supply Helms Olympic Bread to the Olympic village. The owner of the bakery, Paul Helms, saw this as an opportunity to gain additional advantage by claiming a greater association with the Games. He took out a full-page advertisement in the *Los Angeles Sunday Times*, claiming that the bakery was the official supplier of "Olympic bread."[27] A long saga occurred when the bakery refused to withdraw its advertising and use of the Olympic rings following the Games and Helms went so far as to seek registration of the IOC and United States Olympic Association (USOA, the precursor to today's USOC) marks, including the Olympic rings, the word "Olympic," and the Olympic motto.[28] Inexplicably, the Los Angeles organizing committee, although notified of the registrations, did not object to the registrations. In the end, once the IOC and USOA woke up to the fact that there was a gap in US law that allowed such actions to occur, they were forced to reach an agreement with Helms that would allow the USOA to register its own emblems and other Olympic marks.

The eventual solution was that in 1950, the United States Olympic Association became federally chartered by an Act of Congress[29] and, in addition to having general responsibility for Olympic matters, was given the exclusive power to consent to commercial use of the USOA shield, the IOC's five-ring symbol, the Olympic motto, and the words "Olympic" and "Olympiad" in the United States and its territories.[30]

Following a review of the often conflicting jurisdiction of the National Collegiate Athletic Association and the Amateur Athletic Union, the USOC was effectively rechartered by Congress in 1978 through the Amateur Sports Act and its right to consent to the use of the five-ring symbol and other Olympic designations was continued.[31] This legislation is one of the most comprehensive in the world regarding jurisdiction of an NOC, particularly as it relates to the economic aspects of the use of Olympic-related materials.

Because there is a concentration of commercial interest in the Olympic Games, normally in the months preceding the celebration of the Games, OCOGs often seek special legislation to assist in the protection of rights they grant to sponsors and licensees. Such legislation normally identifies the marks adopted by the organizing committee and may provide for expedited recourses in the event of violations. Protection may extend to permission to seize any unauthorized goods or counterfeit items. Most special legislation of this nature will have a "sunset" clause, bringing the protection to an end at a certain date.

Using the Canadian Olympic experience again as an example, special federal legislation was adopted to protect the 1976 Montreal Organizing Committee logos and other Olympic usages. Calgary did not request any legislation in relation to the 1988 Olympic Winter Games and simply relied on the normal legal protections and enforcement mechanisms. Vancouver sought and obtained enactment of a federal statute to protect its marks for the 2010 Olympic Winter Games. Globally, Sydney, Australia, had earlier benefitted from special legislation for the 2000 Olympic Games and London, England, did the same in 2012.

If it is legally possible and politically feasible, the better course for organizing committees is to obtain such legislative protection, as it will serve as effective judicial notice that the marks are protected. It will also eliminate any possible gaps in the normal legal mechanisms that could be exploited by others who might wish to assert a connection with the Games.

NOTABLE AMBUSH MARKETING/SPONSORSHIP LEGISLATION

For reference, here is a list of the legislation from various large event host countries that will be helpful to those who are practicing in the area of ambush marketing and sponsorship:

1. In Canada, the *Olympic and Paralympic Marks Act 2007* protects Olympic and Paralympic related marks, and restricts businesses from using misleading associations with these marks. See more at
    http://www.parl.gc.ca/HousePublications/Publication.aspx?Docid=3297628&file=4
2. In Australia, the *Sydney 2000 Games (Indicia and Images) Protection Act 1996* provides regulation for using images associated with the Sydney2000 Games. See more at
    http://www.comlaw.gov.au/Details/C2004A05042
    http://www.comlaw.gov.au/Details/C2012C00403

3. In South Africa, the *Merchandise Marks Act, 1941*, was amended for hosting the FIFA World Cup and Cricket World Cup to protect both words and emblems and prohibit false descriptions and misrepresentations of goods being sold and made in South Africa.

   http://www.info.gov.za/view/DownloadFileAction?id=68152
   http://www.info.gov.za/view/DownloadFileAction?id=68099

4. In the People's Republic of China, the *Regulations on the Protection of Olympic Symbols Relations 2002*, protects Olympic names, emblems and symbols, such as the five rings, mascot, anthem, Olympic-related terminology and abbreviations of the Chinese Olympic Committee and the Beijing 2008 Olympic Games Big Committee. See more at

   http://en.beijing2008.cn/bocog/ipr/n214071828.shtml

5. In Brazil, *The Olympic Act* protects distinct Olympic symbols of the Rio2016 Games and RIO2016 Paralympic Games and restricts any use of the symbols by nondesignated groups or individuals (even if not for commercial use). See more at

   http://www.inta.org/INTABulletin/Pages/BRAZILCongressAdoptsLegislationto
   CurbAmbushMarketingDuring2016SummerOlympics.aspx

Case Study 9.1

Protecting Your Marks

Case Study Context

In an effort to outline the close ties between the law and sport marketing, this short case is included to illustrate the importance for a sport organization to use the legal tools provided in an effective manner to maximize the marketing value/benefit of their property. Similar to the case following Chapter 4, this case study is set in the years leading up to the 2010 Vancouver Olympic Games, when the issue of protecting the Olympic, Para-lympic, Vancouver and Whistler (joint host city) marks was dominating the local media and political discussions. The decision was getting attention from politicians, citizens, marketers, corporate Canada, and the sport community. Another editorial written by one of the authors of the book—Richard W. Pound—for a major Vancouver newspaper follows here.

PROTECTING YOUR MARKS
By: Richard W. Pound

I have been following with interest the media coverage relating to the Vancouver National Olympic Committee's (VANOC) efforts to prevent the use of Olympic marks and Olympic designations, including suggestions that VANOC is acting unreasonably when it seeks to prevent such usage.

From 1968 until 1982, I was secretary, then president, of the Canadian Olympic Committee (COC) and from 1983 until 2001, responsible for the marketing and television activities of the International Olympic Committee (IOC), during which time Canada hosted two Olympic Games: Montreal in 1976 and Calgary in 1988.

In both positions, one of the principal lessons I learned was the need to protect the trademarks of each organization. VANOC now faces the same challenge.

To raise the funds necessary to stage the

(Continued on next page)

Case Study 9.1 *(continued)*

2010 Olympic Winter Games, VANOC will rely on funds from the public authorities, in the form of grants or services from the three levels of government, municipal, provincial, and federal. These public funds are directed to specific purposes, such as construction, security, and infrastructure. They have no commercial connotations. But government contributions fall well short of what is required to host the Games. All parties, especially governments, are anxious—and properly so—to ensure that no burden of any funding shortfall falls on taxpayers.

The other source of revenues is the private sector, which will support the Games with sponsorships (broadcast and other) and similar commercial relationships, as well as ticket sales. To avoid any financial shortfall, it is essential that VANOC's ability to generate revenues not be compromised. Companies and broadcasters will only invest shareholder resources if they are able to obtain a commercial return on their investment in Vancouver's Games. These are not charitable donations, but calculated commercial and marketing decisions. Return on the investment comes from association of their brands with the imagery and symbols of VANOC and the Olympic Games.

This association takes the form of making the Olympic marks created by VANOC and those already in existence from the COC and IOC available for use by sponsors (Bell Canada, for example, whose commitment to the Games has been exemplary). The five Olympic rings are the most widely recognized symbol in the world today. VANOC must be in a position to guarantee to its broadcasters and sponsors, as well as to manufacturers of licensed merchandise, that they will be the only entities permitted to use the Olympic marks. The value of Olympic partners' association is derived from the exclusivity that can be granted by VANOC. If this usage is not exclusive, and VANOC cannot assure its Olympic partners that others, including their competitors (who pay nothing toward the Games) will not be able to use Olympic marks, the value of the rights that VANOC can grant will be drastically reduced and its revenues will be greatly diminished. Why would anyone pay for rights to use the marks if anyone can use them for free?

There is a spill-over impact on ticket sales as well, as we saw from the recent Athens Olympics. There was uncertainty as to whether the Greeks could complete all the work necessary to stage the Games, because of construction delays and funding shortfalls. People who might otherwise have attended were unwilling to risk paying for tickets to an event that might not happen. If people become concerned that VANOC cannot meet its financial obligations (and governments have made it clear that their contributions are capped), the uncertainty will cause potential ticket buyers to make other choices and the downward spiral will become even worse.

VANOC needs a policy that is clear and unequivocal: any unauthorized use of the Olympic marks, whether deliberate or inadvertent, is prohibited. Any unauthorized commercial or organizational suggestion of some connection with the Games (such as "Vancouver 2010," "Whistler 2010," the "Vancouver-Whistler Games," "Team 2010," etc.) must be prevented and it must vigorously enforce its rights, with legal action, if necessary.

Failure to implement such a policy puts the Games in jeopardy. This is no joke. There are a lot of parasite marketers and ambush marketers out there, waiting like vultures to seize any opportunity to exploit weakness in enforcement of the Olympic marks, or even to attack their validity. The stakes for everyone connected with the Games are too great to permit exceptions.

CHAPTER SUMMARY

This chapter has outlined that sport marketing is profoundly impacted by laws that aim to protect economic and property interests and the interests of consumers. Clearly, sport and its major properties—such as the Olympic Games—are contexts in which infringements are possible and sometimes intended, thereby requiring additional legal considerations. This chapter helps round out the core foundations of global sport marketing and is applicable to the chapters on sport sponsorship and tactical ambush marketing in the chapters that follow.

Key Chapter Questions: *Case Discussion*

1. What is your view on legislation and sponsorship?
2. Research two topics: (i) what the resulting legislation was around the Vancouver Games and (ii) how successful VANOC was at generating sponsorship. Based on this research, answer the following questions:
   a. In your view, how important was it to protect VANOC's marks?
   b. Do you think the resulting legislation impacted the sponsorship sales results?
   c. Was the resulting legislation fair to (i) sponsors, (ii) nonsponsors who are competitors to official sponsors, and (iii) to VANOC?
   d. Would you recommend that other sporting events pursue similar legislation?

Key Chapter Takeaways

1. Marks on goods are a key component of protecting intellectual property.
2. Marketing regulation can provide protection of state commerce and revenue to support the survival of business to meet consumer needs and provide the protection of property.
3. Protection of intellectual property protects the products of human intellect.

Part II

Sponsorship

10

Sponsorship as an Element of Marketing Strategy

With the ability for great impact from the local community to a global level, sport sponsorships are now an integral element of many marketing strategies. Relationships between sponsors and their sponsees are ever-growing, with very large commitments of financial and in-kind resources invested in exchange for access to audiences, community support, association to a cause, and positive images. When combined with the ever-increasing costs of sport participation and sport spectatorship, sporting events, teams, and athletes are looking more and more to sponsors to help defer costs and mobilize their plans into action.

In a formalized sponsorship relationship, there are several elements of sponsorship agreements (contracts) that have a bearing on its success. These elements include the level of association between the sponsee and sponsor, the means by which the sponsorship will be activated, the level of exclusivity that the sponsors can be guaranteed in relation to the competition, as well as details on evaluation plans and servicing aspects. Sponsorships are sometimes measured in terms of the amount of media attention they attract, or by the way they encourage audiences to link some of the sponsee values to the sponsor. For most sponsoring organizations, however, determination of the real value of sponsorships is by measuring positive impact on the financial bottom line.

AN INTRODUCTION TO SPONSORSHIP

For the ten worldwide Olympic sponsors (the "TOP sponsors") of the 2014 Sochi Olympic Games, sponsorship—given their multi-million dollar investments—is obviously important to their businesses. This can be attributed to the Olympic Games' ability to draw massive levels of local, national, and worldwide attention, offering an almost unparalleled opportunity for companies to showcase their brands. Even 3,000 years ago, in the times of the ancient Olympic Games, athletes benefitted from the contributions of chariots, horses, and equipment from wealthy members of Greek society, in exchange for special seats, heightened social status, and other privileges (Mullin, Hardy, & Sutton, 2000). In modern times, in the six years leading up to the 2010 Winter Olympics in Vancouver, US $756 million was raised through sponsorship at the national level, not including international sponsorship revenues from the TOP sponsors or investments made directly through national sport organizations (e.g., Hockey Canada) or indirectly via professional sport leagues (e.g., National Hockey League).

In the 1970s, sport sponsorship was typically a philanthropic endeavor, as companies sponsored events, teams, and athletes without much attention to what was gained in return other than public goodwill (Sleight, 1989) or the interests of senior management. In the 1980s, the use of sponsorship started to shift and, increasingly, financial and other resources were devoted to sponsorship, along with a greater awareness of the potential impacts of sponsorship, and especially, as Otker (1988) and Meenaghan (1991) suggested, a way for companies to break through the clutter of other advertisers that were jamming radio and television stations at the time. This began a trend in sponsorship away from its philanthropic roots towards becoming a legitimate member of the marketing mix (Séguin & O'Reilly, 2007).

Today, sponsorship is big business, with the total global investment in rights fees estimated to be over US $53 billion and nearing US $20 billion in North America alone (IEG, 2014). Over and above this would be additional billions of dollars invested in activating these rights. If corporate contributions to philanthropy are also considered (i.e., donations and giving, as opposed to sponsorship), which was estimated to be about US $11 billion (Giving USA Foundation, 2013), total North American spending (sponsorship plus corporate donations, but not including activation) is approximately US $30 billion annually.

Alongside advertising, sales promotions, and other promotional tactics, sponsorship is now a standard part of an organization's marketing and public relations plan, to help generate a greater awareness of its goods or services, support a positive corporate image, increase sales, or gain exclusive rights that provide an advantage over its competition (Cornwell, Roy, & Steinard, 2001). Sponsorship, according to Mullin, Hardy, and Sutton (2000), can be an important strategy in helping companies reach specific target markets by associating their brands with audiences' leisure and lifestyle activities. Importantly, sponsorship differs from the other tactics in the promotional mix of organizations. For example, sponsorship differs from advertising, due to the type of relationship between a sponsor and sponsee, and the ability to reach a wider or more targeted audience. A sponsorship aims, according to Meenaghan (2001), to connect with audience emotions related to a sponsored event, team, or athlete allowing them to reach their target audience more indirectly than through direct advertisement (Crimmins & Horn, 1996).

In a typical sport sponsorship, the sponsor hopes to be seen as part of the event or program and that, through that association, audiences will equate (or transfer) the sponsee's positive images to the sponsor and help it develop a deeper bond with consumers (Kover, 2001; Gwinner, 1997). Thus, sponsors can be rewarded, as audiences may believe that supporting the sponsor (by purchasing the sponsor's product) will in some way help support the sponsee. For example, it is known that some proportion of the population of developed countries will support sponsors who support their national teams at Olympic Games (Séguin, Lyberger, O'Reilly & McCarthy, 2005). Practically speaking, when a sponsor is viewed to be part of an event or program, particularly in today's reality of the wide adoption of personal video recording

and online video streaming, it allows for clear demonstration of their association with the event, teams, or athletes when television/streaming audiences can easily fast-forward commercials or limit their viewing to sport highlights.

SPORT SPONSORSHIP 101

As a growing and effective marketing strategy, sport sponsorship is an essential part of the promotional mix of organizations. Through effective activation, sponsorship of a sport property can generate a sense of awareness about the sponsor to the target audience, and can generate the consumers' positive feelings about the sponsor brand and image (O'Reilly & Lafrance Horning, 2013). Sport sponsorship can help promote a corporate brand and image, support marketing objectives through increases in sales, and be part of a formal media strategy to reach target markets (Sandler & Shani, 1993). By being more aware of the brand, consumers may also pay more attention to supporting advertisements about the brand, have better brand recall, or feel an emotional link to the sponsor (Meenaghan, 2013).

The opportunities for sponsorship through sport are considerable. Indeed, attractive sport event platforms, such as the Olympic Games, FIFA World Cup or professional sports leagues like the NFL, EPL, AFL or NHL offer businesses significant prospects for showcasing their goods and services to build their images and brands with specific (and sometimes multiple) target audiences. This chapter explores the role of sponsorship in an integrated marketing plan by examining the definitions of sponsorship and related terms, the way sponsors partner with sport organizations and use tools used to activate and evaluate the objectives of a sponsorship.

DEFINING SPONSORSHIP

By definition, a sponsorship refers to an organization (the sponsor) providing financial contributions (or products or services) to another organization (the sponsee) in exchange for the ability to promote its brands to its target group(s). Fahy, Farrelly, and Quester (2004) noted that sponsorship is a strategic activity that allows businesses to develop sustainable advantages over their competition, and Rifon, Choi, Trimble, and Li (2004) added that sponsorship is a way to link with external issues as a way to influence audiences. Despite the stagnation of marketing budgets since the global financial crisis of 2007–2008, sponsorship has continued to grow (IEG, 2014; CSLS, 2013), revealing that many businesses see sponsorship as an efficient and cost-effective tactic to reach their target audience(s).

THE SPONSORSHIP RELATIONSHIP

The relationship between sponsee and sponsor is not always direct. Intermediary agents can represent clients (e.g., athletes or teams) who are seeking sponsorships, or represent the interests of businesses (i.e., sponsors) or organizations (e.g., marketing agencies or market research firms) who view sponsorship as a valuable part of their marketing strategy. The sponsorship can also benefit from the recruitment of a "champion," on both the sponsee and sponsor side, to act as an internal and external leader to communicate and draw support for the goals of the sponsorship. For example, in the case of a corporate sponsor, the champion could be a senior executive who drives activity related to a given sponsor.

An effective sponsorship relationship can help organizations on several fronts. Through sponsorship, businesses can demonstrate their community support, increase public awareness, build their public image, improve relationships with corporate partners, motivate employees, differentiate from the competition, reach target markets, and, ultimately, increase sales (Irwin & Sutton, 1994). Sport sponsorship agreements, according to Séguin and O'Reilly (2007), allow organizations to exchange resources for promotional exposure at events, through sport teams, and through sponsorship of individual athletes.

Being a sponsee seeking sponsorship is difficult as there are more demands for sponsors than there are available resources for sponsorship. In fact, for most sponsees, achieving sponsorship revenue is very challenging. Unless the sponsee has the opportunity for vast reach or specialized target marketing opportunities, such as the Olympic Games, Super Bowl, FIFA World Cup, or the Stanley Cup NHL playoffs, sponsees typically find themselves facing significant competition in find-

© Zhukovsky | Dreamstime.com—Pepsi Official Soft Drink Of Super Bowl XLVIII Billboard On Broadway During Super Bowl XLVIII Week In Manhattan Photo

ing, securing and retaining sponsors. Indeed, it is strongly recommended that sponsorship-seeking sponsees need to think of sponsorships as two-directional and offer benefits to the sponsor and commit to building strong relationships by delivering on the commitments made to the sponsors (Séguin & O'Reilly, 2007).

Through sponsorship, sponsors provide financial resources or goods and/or services to the sponsee. Normally, however, the sponsor does not have input in establishing the goals and objectives of the sponsee. For example, a national sport organization will not typically engage its beverage sponsor in deciding how it sets its annual strategy and allocates its high-performance resources. However, since sport sponsorship can provide a financial contribution to sport organizations, athletes, teams, or events, the sponsor is certainly supporting the efforts of the sport property to achieve its goals. Sponsors are from all types of industries and typically seek a variety of their own objectives (O'Reilly & Madill, 2008) with the sponsorships in which they do engage. In some cases, corporations adopt sponsorship as a way to balance social responsibility with corporate success, such as sponsoring a property that is a charity or a not-for-profit, or that has a charitable component.

THE ROLE OF SPONSORSHIP IN THE MARKETING MIX

As noted, sport sponsorship is a communications tool that many organizations are embracing to reach current and potential target markets. Although it enables specificity in terms of messaging to particular market segments, sport sponsorship does not replace traditional marketing or promotions. Today, it is part of an organization's broader marketing mix, alongside any established marketing tactic (e.g., advertising, public relations, event hospitality, and social media). Akin to any tactical element of the marketing mix, sport sponsorship, as a marketing strategy, implies that the organization is identifying the needs and wants of its target consumers, trying to find the best way to

© Trueffelpix | Dreamstime.com—Marketing Mix, Product Place Promotion Price Photo

meet these needs and wants relative to the goals of the organization. The *best way* is normally accomplished by considering the marketing mix of tools available under the 4Ps of the marketing mix of product, price, promotion, and place. Many scholars view sport sponsorship, and its ability to reach consumers in a satisfying way (McCarville & Copeland, 1994), to fit within the promotions *P*.

Through the inclusion of sport sponsorship in their marketing mix, organizations can communicate their functions, services, objectives, and values (Barrett, 1993), in hopes of persuading potential consumers and influencing their decisions for future purchases. In an integrated marketing approach, according to Tripodi (2001), organizations may look for additional ways to support a unified message and build synergy between the brand and the sponsee. For example, integration in the marketing mix may include the organization being linked to individual athletes, sales promotions, media advertising, and corporate hospitality, all within the same sport event or series.

Contra or in-kind sponsorship is an additional strategic consideration for an organization, which may include in-kind donations through the provision of free or reduced-cost products and/or services. A contra/in-kind investment can be done in combination with a cash sponsorship or in an exclusively product/service contribution. Examples include the support of sport sponsees through the provision of clothing, sport gear, event equipment, supplies, training, support staff, marketing expertise, communications channels, and media.

A strategic element of a sponsorship for a corporation may include employee volunteering, which can enhance the sponsorship partnership and image. This occurs when the sponsor allows its staff to participate in the sponsorship and enjoy the events, the experience, and the sports with which it is associated. This can lead to internal marketing (i.e., targeted to employees) benefits, such as employee motivation and decreased turnover of staff. For example, a multinational technology company, Intel, promotes employee volunteering through its Encore Fellowship Program, and provides funding to match time devoted by employees to community nonprofit organizations (Intel, 2014), and 65% of Microsoft's employees contribute to community volunteering with more than a billion dollars donated through the company's corporate matching program (Microsoft, 2014). Similarly, telecommunications firm Bell Canada, sponsors its own employee volunteering by providing $500 to local organizations when their employees volunteer 50 or more hours to the organization (estimated to be a total contribution of more than US $600,000 per year) (Bell, 2013).

TACTICAL ELEMENTS OF GLOBAL SPORT SPONSORSHIP

An analysis of dozens of sponsorships (Institute of Sport Marketing, 2005) determined that there are four key steps in creating and maintaining successful sponsorships.

1. Each of the sponsee and the sponsor much clearly define priorities, objectives, and primary target markets, which requires an understanding of the behaviors, interests, and motivations of the sponsor's (potential) consumers.

2. Both the sponsor and the sponsee should leverage the power of volunteers through formal training to help drive the sponsorship's return on investment (ROI).

3. Both parties need to ensure a coordinated and consistent brand message to be able to influence consumer impressions.

4. A sponsorship needs to be measured. Detailing what success means to both the sponsee and sponsor helps create formal plans to measure the benefits and ROI.

Additional aspects of the sponsorship that are important to its success include the strength of the association between the sponsee and the sponsor, the activation of the sponsorship by both parties, the use of social media in sponsorship activation, and the exclusivity that the sponsee offers to the sponsor.

SECURING A SPONSOR

It is important, tactically, to emphasize that the task of finding sponsors is not easy for the majority of sponsees, as the number of sponsees seeking sponsorships is disproportionate to the number of available sponsorships (Hoek & Gendall, 2002b). For example, in 2012, the multinational bank, the Royal Bank of Canada (RBC), based in Canada, had more than 30,000 requests for corporate donations or sponsorship, according to Melanson (2011), and could only support 4,000 of those initiatives with total investments of approximately CDN $120 million to charitable causes and sponsorship agreements.

Sponsorship is a regular part of business operations for most large companies, with names such as Adobe, Emirates Airlines, Nintendo, among thousands more, dedicating web space to information about requesting and securing sponsorship. However, as noted, acquiring substantial sponsorship is a difficult feat for all but the most attractive properties. Prior to searching for a sponsor, a sponsee must be clear about its own objectives, in order to identify potential sponsors where mutual interests may intersect. The sponsee should complete thorough market research to create profiles of potential sponsors that may highlight areas of mutual interest and possible mutual gain. Defining mutual gains is a step that cannot be overlooked; far too often sponsees approach sponsorship by telling a prospective sponsor what they need, rather than placing emphasis on what they can offer (e.g., reaching target audiences; benefits to stakeholders) and

what resources can be shared (e.g., expertise, resources, and assets). The sponsee must, therefore, clearly communicate its goals and objectives in a way that is accurate, concise, and distinct, in order to help distinguish itself from other competing potential sponsees (i.e., why we would be a better bet for sponsorship by an identified company than some other organization seeking to compete with us for its sponsorship).

An important note is that mutual interests and mutual benefits do not imply that the sponsee and sponsor need to have the same interests or seek the same benefits. On the contrary, as O'Reilly and Brunette (2013) pointed out, a disconnect in values is sometimes what sponsors "are willing to pay a premium for" (p. 177). Sometimes the value in the sponsorship lies in association with something that is normally disconnected; for example "Hershey's Track and Field Games," which is a 35-year partnership between chocolate manufacturer, the Hershey Company, and the National Recreation and Park Association, USA Track and Field, and Athletics Canada, seems disconnected if the goal of Hershey's is to sell chocolate, while its partners value health and physical fitness initiatives for kids (see O'Reilly & Brunette, 2013). The sponsorship concludes with an opportunity for "qualifying" children to attend the national games, with a free trip to Hershey, Pennsylvania, along with a visit to Chocolate World park and the Hershey's chocolate factory (Hershey, 2014). When a candy chain sponsors a healthy kids initiative, both may gain, even though the sponsor and sponsee interests and benefits are very distinct. In fact, sponsors must also be aware that some audiences may find their sponsorship offensive if a party deems that a soft drink, cheeseburger, sugared cereal, or chocolate bar is not "healthy" and therefore should not be associated with children.

If both partners agree to a sponsorship, an agreement needs to be drafted and signed by both. A draft of any sponsorship agreement should include the term of the partnership, the logistics of the shared resources, policy related to any disconnect if relevant, and accountability. Importantly, both organizations need to be certain that they can devote the required time, resources, and energy to the sponsorship, and have a clear understanding of how that time, resources, and energy will be sourced. An assessment of risks to both the sponsee and the sponsor should also be made, considering how the sponsorship can affect the brands of each positively and negatively, and by thinking through best and worst case scenarios.

THE SPONSOR-SPONSEE ASSOCIATION

A sponsorship is like a dance, with each partner adding an important element to the overall product. Both the sponsee and the sponsor have important roles and each one's efforts impact the image of the other. This dance is described as the *association* between the sponsee and sponsor, and it is a crucial element in any sponsorship agreement. Sponsees, through their hosted events, teams, or participation in events (e.g., sponsorship of an individual athlete), can provide the platform for a sponsor to associate its brand with an image or value that can benefit the sponsor. These benefits are enhanced when the sponsee and sponsor share interests, objectives, and values, and—as noted earlier in this chapter—even when a disconnect exists in the sponsor's interests.

On the sponsee side of the association, the sport property benefits by receiving financial and/or in-kind product/service contributions from sponsors wanting to associate with them, by providing a platform for higher sponsor visibility and its images for association. In the case of a disconnect, however, these associations may be controversial if the media and public question the ethical implications of the sponsorship. For example, Olympic athletes at the 2014 Sochi Olympic Games including Canadian figure skater Patrick Chan and ice hockey player Drew Doughty received criticism from children's health and rights advocates who admonished the athletes' sponsorship agreements with McDonald's feeling that the messages were misleading audiences and contributing to the obesity epidemic (Weeks, 2014). Restaurant chain Hooters, known for its "tacky" look and scantily clad servers, was also criticized for its sponsorship of a NCAA Division I Men and Women's golf tournament, as critics debated whether support from a corporation with values that conflicted with intercollegiate athletics was appropriate (Athletic Management, 2004).

Similar concerns about disconnected associations exist when sponsors who sell unhealthy products sponsor sport events to target youth markets with accompanying associations to gambling, alcohol, and obesity-related food and drinks (Maher, Wilson, Signal, & Thomson, 2006; Boone, 2004; Butterworth, 2011; Freedhoff & Hebert, 2011). The disconnect is something that sponsors are often willing to pay for, even amidst public criticism due to the benefits it can provide for the sponsor's brand and sales, as well as the fact that it is normally the sponsee who received the negative media backlash that may result (O'Reilly & Brunette, 2013).

ACTIVATION

To promote the sponsorship and the association between the sponsee and sponsor, each partner may implement *activation* strategies to reach the target market(s) and support the transfer of images between the brands. Activation is critical in implementing a successful sponsorship. Without activation strategies, other marketing approaches would be more profitable than sponsorships. Activation tools are diverse and, although normally supported by the sponsor, can be funded by either the sponsor or sponsee to make the sponsorship most effective. For example, Nicholls, Roslow, and Dublish (1999) noted that activation included creating and funding television commercials with cobranding leading up to a sponsored event. Other activation strategies include using a sponsor's brand name in an event, league, or team name (e.g., Scotiabank Ottawa Marathon and Barclays Premier League Football); brand

© Mingchai | Dreamstime.com—Barclays Asia Trophy

names on athlete uniforms and gear; cobranded displays at point of purchase that target consumers in a certain location; signage at events and sport venues (e.g., advertisements on the boards or ice of ice hockey championship games); related publications such as newsletters, blogs, and fan packs; on-site product samples; and using sponsee logos on sponsor product packaging. Modern activation strategies include cobranded social media campaigns and contests.

SOCIAL MEDIA

Like any communication or marketing tactic of today, social media is increasingly important. This is no different in sponsorship, where studies have shown an increase in the proportion of sponsorship activation investment in social media from about 3% in

2009 to more than 15% in 2013 (CSLS, 2013). As new technology continues to emerge and as new users adopt existing and more sophisticated platforms, the ability for sponsors to reach target audiences improves. Mangold and Faulds (2009) report that social media takes the control of marketing messages out of the hands of marketers, and puts it in the hand of participants and audiences.

The importance of developing and articulating a social media strategy around the sponsorship, in particular sponsorship activation, cannot be underestimated. Consider, as Meenaghan (2013) did, one major sponsor, Nike, which invested US $771 million to create a social media presence (including direct marketing, paid internet search results, and more) with results that are difficult to measure. If sponsorship has the ability to generate public goodwill and promote a corporate image, then companies like Nike, and many others, must harness the tools of social media (e.g., Twitter and Facebook, plus their inevitable successors) to convey the message about their sponsorship activities. As O'Reilly, Gibbs, and Brunette (2014) explained, the use of social media to "break news, share pictures, provide followers with advance access, and share live updates during games or events" creates platforms with enormous public reach, including Twitter with more than 500 million active users and over 3 million integrated websites. Through social media, the transfer of sponsorship images can be global and in real time, creating a win-win situation for the sponsor and sponsee who both can reach each other's social media followers in showcasing their sponsorship and related events to the world.

EXCLUSIVITY

In today's cluttered marketplace, perhaps no part of an integrated marketing strategy is as important as a brand's ability to stand out above the crowd. *Exclusivity* in a sponsorship agreement refers to the right of the sponsor to be the only sponsor in its category (i.e., no competitor will be present) of the particular sport sponsee/property (termed *category exclusivity*). This means that no other similar organizations can be associated with the sponsored event, team, or athlete. In return for the financial or in-kind contributions of the sponsor, the sponsee allows the sponsor brand to be associated with theirs, exclusively, without competing for attention with other comparable brands. Exclusivity blocks the competition from using the event, athletes, logos, taglines, products, and activities in their own marketing messages.

Exclusivity in the sponsorship agreement can legally regulate and reduce the influence of direct and indirect ambush marketing by other nonsponsee brands who try to associate with an event, especially a large scale event, to reap marketing benefits without the financial commitment to the sponsee. In ambush marketing, as will be explored further in Part III of this book, the ambushing company tries to utilize the public attention around an event for its own marketing interests and, in turn, divert the attention away from other sponsors (Meenaghan, 1996). However, consumers can find ambush marketing confusing, and potentially offensive, which can hurt the relationship between the sponsee and sponsor since the sponsor may lose brand and sales benefits due to the confusion and the sponsee will risk being able to renew the sponsorship.

The exclusion of the competition can mean big business for the exclusive sponsors who gain clean access to a particular target market and the resulting opportunities for direct sales, increased traffic, and emotional connections. Pound (1996) noted that since the 1980s, exclusivity in Olympic sponsorship has created high-level demand, since exclusivity in sponsorship brings on strong competition from sponsors and, along with it, high price tags. The exclusive Olympic sponsors, named The Olympic Program (TOP), invest, on average, more than US $100 million per quadrennium for their exclusive sponsorship rights. Since consumers do value brand-sponsee associations, that exclusivity can have a positive influence on consumer purchasing decisions.

WHAT MAKES A GOOD SPONSORSHIP?

There are both tangible and intangible methods of evaluating a sponsorship, which typically include a mix of sponsorship-associated sales, media coverage, image transfer, and on-site hospitality elements.

Tracking Sales

Arguably the single most important question about a sponsorship is, did it generate ROI or increase sales? Within an integrated marketing plan, sponsorship should be able to influence consumers in their decision to purchase, increasing sales (Mullins, Hardy, & Sutton, 2000). Often, the benefits of sponsorship can be assessed through tracking sales via the measurement of the capacity of the sponsorship to increase sales, product distribution, leads, retail traffic, and return customers, as measured through sales in a short-term (e.g., 2–3 month) period surrounding the sponsorship compared to previous years, sales in the region of the sponsored event compared to national averages, and/or sales directly at events (IEG Sponsorship Report, 2011).

ROI can be part of determining the positive outcomes of a sponsorship. Wilkinson

(1993) noted that four measurements can contribute to the sponsorship ROI including i) the level of sponsorship activation (or activities) such as promotions on site, sold merchandise, sold events, and samples distributed; ii) the change in consumer attitudes and level of sponsee-sponsor image transfer; iii) comparing to other internal or external sponsorships to determine sponsorship benchmarks in relationship to rights fees, communication process, support, and integration of the marketing plan; and finally, iv) an evaluation of the efficiency and cost of the sponsorship in achieving a certain ROI and specific sales objective relative to other marketing strategies. Just like for-profit sport properties, not-for-profit and charitable sport organizations engage in activities that will increase sponsorship to support their future work, bring in new contributors, and build strong relationships with current contributors. Sponsorship may not be the most direct route for sales, but in the end organizations use it as a marketing strategy to ultimately, and hopefully positively, impact their bottom line.

An important point that emerges when taking an ROI/sales perspective to sponsorship is that the status of the property as for-profit or not-for-profit becomes largely irrelevant from the perspective of the sponsor. In particular, the sponsor is interested in the attractiveness of the property and not whether it is not-for-profit or not. Some of the biggest and most important sponsorships are derived from not-for-profit organizations (e.g., the Olympic Games, FIFA World Cup). The challenge, therefore, is not the status of the sponsee, but the values of its property and its ability to communicate the values.

Media Coverage

Well-constructed sponsorship agreements (or aspects of larger sponsorship arrangements) often include strategies to attract substantial media coverage for the sponsor (Howard & Crompton, 1995). Monitoring this media coverage is part of understanding the success of the sponsorship. Since sport events, teams, and athletes can garner considerable media attention, sponsorship can provide cost-effective media spotlights for the sponsor. Some sponsors (or their agencies) look to professional media or marketing research firms to implement formal monitoring systems and to help guide press conferences or media releases. Especially important is a good social media strategy and monitoring system.

Strategies to monitor media coverage can include a count of the amount of television/screen time that the sponsor received via the sponsee event, or the number of times that the sponsor brand appeared visibly on screen images or in still photos distributed through social media. Central to the valuation of media coverage is how much media attention a sponsee can make possible to the sponsor (Crowley, 1991), as well as the power of the media coverage (i.e., a brand mention during a national TV broadcast in primetime is more valuable than a mention on a low traffic web blog). Unfortunately, noting that the sponsor must activate effectively to take advantage of the offering, the media coverage promised (or expected) as part of the sponsorship agreement is not always fulfilled. It must, nevertheless, be evaluated accordingly, whether the outcome of the evaluation is positive or negative.

Image Transfer

As noted, an important aspect of sponsorship is its ability to create a lasting corporate image that supports corporate objectives for a sponsor. The images (or perceptions) that consumers have about a brand are the general feelings, ideas, impressions about an organization or its services or products (Kotley & Andreasen, 1995). The image is part of the brand's reputation, and the sponsorship can use a sport sponsorship to try to capitalize on the sponsee's positive image and emotional connection with its audience via a transfer of these images to the sponsor's brand.

Sponsorship can also help separate the sponsor's brand image from that of its competitors. The image transfer can be influenced by the type of event being sponsored, along with its history, the characteristics, venue and size of the event, and individual factors (Gwinner, 1997). The leveraging of image transfer between a sponsee and sponsor, if positive, can be beneficial to both partners (Gwinner, 1997). For example, the sponsorship between car manufacturer Subaru and World Endurance Canada to create the Subaru Triathlon Series and sponsored Ironman events link the Subaru brand with images of fitness, strength, sport, and endurance. Subaru also offers participants incentives for future car purchases, with a distinct (yet subtle) message: *If you are a triathlete or an ironman, you will drive our cars.*

Hospitality

Increasingly, major sponsorship agreements include significant hospitality and entertainment packages within the sponsorship. Notably, hospitality can be a part of relationship marketing in sponsorship, as Berrett and Slack (1999) described, as it can help sponsors attract, retain, and grow relationships with target consumers, as they reinforce the image and experience associated with their product and/or services. Offering hospitality to support the sponsorship can create a space for informal networking and reinforcement of the brand. Hospitality agreements expose the sponsor and its consumers to unique access that may be unavailable to other consumers (e.g., an exclusive sponsor can run contests to win trips to sporting events that it sponsors or a sponsor of a high-profile event can offer tickets to key customers and/or potential customers).

In small sponsorships, hospitality is also a key component as it can provide important internal marketing objectives. For example, individual runners can sponsor charitable organizations to obtain an entry into a sold-out, or qualifying-restricted, marathon event. This includes charity programs related to the Ironman Foundation that provide guaranteed entry to Ironman triathlon events in exchange for this *sponsorship*.

Overall, sponsors may also be attracted to sponsorships if the sponsee can provide exclusive tickets or accommodations, backstage access, luxury boxes, and/or other exclusive benefits that they can share with prospective consumers, or use to reward loyal customers or employees. An important point is that, from a corporate governance perspective, there are risks inherent in hospitality where use of funds to 'wine and dine' VIP guests could be construed as a misuse of funds. Similarly, from an operational perspective, there are security risks when VIP guests are invited to an event. This was observed at the 2014 Olympic Games in Sochi when a number of VIP politicians and sponsors decided not to attend over security concerns.

EVALUATING SPONSORSHIP SUCCESS

Determining the success of a sponsorship agreement is only possible with an appropriate method of evaluating that sponsorship. For the sponsor, in particular, formal evaluation of a sponsorship allows for the determination of whether or not the sponsorship provided a good ROI, sales or otherwise (depending on the sponsor's objectives). ROI is normally quantified in financial terms, but can also be measured using other generated business benefits that are not easy to quantify through specific attribution to the sponsorship, such as an increase or decrease in the number of customers (see Becker-Olsen, 1998).

Sponsorship evaluation can yield quantifiable (tangible) results that are based on a variety of metrics, including formal documents such as presence on websites, posters, and product labels, or communication strategies such as public announcements and broadcasts. Less quantifiable or attributable to the sponsorship are the benefits derived from the sponsee lending its image and audience loyalty to the sponsor. However, both tangible and intangible benefits can deliver advantages that contribute to generating brand awareness, changing consumer attitudes, increasing sales, and generating media coverage (IEG, 1995). Whether tangible or intangible, the evaluation of sponsorship benefits is a critical feature of a sponsorship agreement, yet quality evaluation strategies that have pre-sponsorship benchmarks, the appropriate metrics, and clear outcomes are rarely part of sponsorship agreements.

In an effort to provide a better method to evaluate sponsorships, O'Reilly and Madill (2012) suggest a seven-step process, summarized here.

1. The first step is to "set the stage" by completing a pre-assessment of the objectives of the sponsorship and building relationships before deciding to go forward (or not) with the sponsorship. Part of the pre-assessment provides a lead-up to what type of data will be analyzed in later stages of the sponsorship. This includes defining sponsee and sponsor objectives, internal and external organizations involved with the sponsorship, spectator demographic, audience ratings and engagement (e.g., active Twitter followers), media coverage, competition, restrictions (e.g., no alcohol sponsors), and prospective conflicts or biases.

2. The second step in the sponsorship evaluation process includes interviewing the key personnel on the sponsorship (both sponsor and sponsee) and a formal sponsorship contract review. The purpose of this step is to ascertain what the sought objectives for each party in the sponsorship are.

3. Step three involves clearly defining the objectives to be measured in the evaluation that result from the data collection/contract review in the second step. This includes summarizing both the formal (i.e., written in the contract or other strategy document) and informal (i.e., provided in an interview) objectives that each party is seeking.

4. Step four outlines—based on the review in the second step—the target market(s) that the sponsorship is seeking to reach.

5. Step five provides the data collection plan (methods and metrics) to assess the achievement of all the outlined objectives (step three) for each of the target markets (step four), and includes the resources and implementation of that data collection.

6. Step six is the analysis of the data collected in step five.

7. Step seven is to summarize the analysis to determine the outcomes and impacts of the sponsorship. It allows for a summary evaluation of the sponsorship.

The seven steps can help organizations in determining whether to consider renewing the sponsorship agreement or not.

SPONSORSHIP TERMINATION

Sponsorship agreements should include mutually agreed start and end dates (e.g., the sponsorship may start before the sponsee event and end at the conclusion of the event activities). The specific process to terminate a sponsorship, for any involved party, should be explicitly included in the agreement or contract, whether the sponsorship is successful or not.

Positive sponsorship experiences can lead to a legacy of mutual trust and support that should allow for ongoing renewals and perhaps very long partnership (e.g., the Olympic Games and Coca-Cola). Of course, not every sponsorship agreement can end well and sponsorships are normally terminated for two reasons: the contract ends and is not renewed due to issues such as dissatisfied partners, change in strategies, key contacts leaving, better offers or poor results; or the contract is terminated due to unsatisfied contracts, lack of activation, or other conflict. Some will not meet the goals and objectives of one or both partners, and will be learning experiences for future scholarships. Thus, the sponsorship agreement should include formal exit strategies for both parties, who need to both think through worst case scenarios, and the potential impact on brand image and legacy, as they evaluate prospective sponsorship agreements.

CHAPTER SUMMARY

A strong relationship between a sponsor and a sponsee is crucial to building any successful sponsorship. This relationship will often extend to include third parties (often agencies) who represent the sponsor or the sponsee on some element (e.g., media agency, agency-of-record, digital agency, etc.). The sponsorship relationship can have lasting impacts on future associations with sponsees/sponsors, and impact future sales, media coverage, consumer images of the organizations and events. Well-established plans at the onset of the sponsorship with a mutual understanding of each partners' goals, objectives, and values, along with continued contact through the life of the sponsorship is a key lesson for future sponsees and sponsors. Having a key contact on both of the sponsor and sponsee sides can be valuable in the communication process, and help ensure professionalism throughout the life of the sponsorship. As described, the value of hospitality for sponsors at events should not be discounted, and is a growing standard practice in the sponsee-sponsor relationship. In the end, sponsees should aim to deliver more than what is expected. Too often, sponsees see sponsors as a source of money but forget to highlight (and deliver) what they can provide in return.

Sponsorships have much value and appeal in an integrated marketing plan. The ability to connect with an audience through target approaches or offer mass appeal is a coveted piece of the sponsorship world. The Toyota TOP sponsorship is a great example of a sponsor seeking to leverage a global sport property. Nevertheless, the sponsee-sponsor relationship is delicate and needs to include much thought regarding the mutual gains and possible pains. Sponsorships offer a cost-effective and exclusive way for business to gain positive attention and meet financial goals.

Key Chapter Questions

1. What makes a good sponsorship? Please provide an example of a good sponsorship.
2. Find an example of a sponsorship being showcased through social media. What has the public reception been on Twitter? On Facebook?
3. Describe an example of a desired image transfer between a sponsor and a sponsee. Was the image transfer effective? Why or why not?
4. What is the appeal of sponsorship exclusivity on the side of the sponsee?
5. Find an example of a sponsorship termination with negative impact on the sponsor and sponsee. Could this negative termination have been avoided?

Key Chapter Takeaways

1. Sponsorship is a regular part of doing business, yet the demands for sponsorship far outweigh the available sponsor resources.
2. Typical sport sponsorship allows sponsors to become an integrated part of the event or program.
3. Sponsors and sponsees do have to share values; nevertheless, the disconnect between values is sometimes something for which sponsors are willing to pay a premium.
4. Sponsorships are effective if they increase the sponsor's sales, achieve good media coverage, and tightly link sponsor-sponsee images.

11

Olympic Sport Sponsorship Sales: An NOC Perspective

"AS THE OLYMPIC MARKETING PROGRAMMES CONTINUE TO GROW AND DEVELOP, THEY ENSURE THE FUTURE VIABILITY OF THE GAMES AND PROVIDE ESSENTIAL SUPPORT NOT ONLY FOR THE OLYMPIC GAMES, BUT ALSO FOR THE OLYMPIC MOVEMENT AND THE OLYMPIC ATHLETES."

—*Gerhard Heiberg, IOC Marketing Commission Chairman*

National Olympic Committees (NOCs) have the principal responsibility on a quadrennial basis to qualify athletes in their respective sports and send a team to represent their jurisdiction at the Olympic Games (Chappelet, 2008). According to the Olympic Charter, the NOCs' mission is to "develop, promote and protect the Olympic Movement in their respective countries" with the recommendation

© Ukrphoto | Dreamstime.com—Olympic Superstore in Sochi

that each NOC seeks "sources of financing in a manner compatible with the fundamental principles of Olympism," (IOC, 2013). The Olympic Games and national pride provide the basic fuel for the establishment and the ongoing development of NOCs, yet financially, they rely on the basic business formula of revenue less expense equals income. A more apt view, as not-for-profit organizations, may be that NOCs focus on revenue that, in turn, determines their budgets/expenses. The revenue generated is what sustains the ongoing operations of the NOC and any growth initiatives it may seek.

Although the IOC and NOCs are not-for-profit organizations, without a reasonable surplus of funds to provide the ability to promote training, transport, organize, and manage their Olympic organization, most would be unable to exist. Each NOC has, by its own organizational constitution, a nationalistic set of responsibilities that are traced back to the Olympic Charter. Many are funded fully by national governments and work closely with the NSOs in their community. Many others have a hybrid public-private business model and a few, such as the United States Olympic Committee (USOC), have a model totally based on its ability to generate its own revenue streams. Although profit may not be the overall objective of these organizations, without revenue streams that equal or exceed expenses, most NOCs would find it impossible to function. An important element of these revenue streams is the establishment of relationships with commercial entities to provide financial support.

RELEVANT MARKETING CONCEPTS

Marketing consists of the development and implementation of programs designed for the purpose of generating revenue for the particular organization. Contextual models of the field include discussion of the marketing mix, which is synonymous with such marketing elements as product, price, place, promotion, consumer, cost, communication, convenience, commodity, and channel or distribution, all of which have found their way into the language of basic marketing concepts. To generate revenue, marketing starts and ends with the consumer, without whom there would be no financial capacity to organize global Olympic competitions.

Athletic competition in and of itself was a noble pursuit, recognized as such by the ancient Greeks as an event worthy of attending, but in today's sport entertainment marketplace, consumer involvement with sport has evolved to a complex relationship driven by a variety of factors (see O'Reilly, Nadeau & Kaplan, 2011). In turn, the sales of sponsorship—which is based on providing a platform for engagement with people as previous chapters have outlined—is even more complex (and challenging). Just compare for a second the ancient stadium in Olympia with uncomfortable seats and no technology to capture an event for any other kind of consumption, versus today's world in which more than four billion people can watch the opening ceremonies of the Olympic Games, and all of those people plus many of the three billion who did not watch can view the event at a later date in a variety of different formats.

Promotion, as one of the four elements of a typical marketing strategy (the 4 Ps), in the NOC context, is a matter of communication with its customers and partners, using the elements of the promotional mix such as advertising, personal selling, sales incentives, and public relations. However, it is easy for an NOC to fall into the trap of expecting sponsors to seek them out for the development of a partnership that would enhance the sponsors' market visibility and therefore allow them to promote their products. Without a significant investment in an outbound marketing (promotional) strategy to develop national long-term sponsorship relationships, an NOC puts itself at risk if it needs sponsorship revenues for its success.

An important—yet underresearched—area of sponsorship is sponsorship sales, or the process of selling sponsorship of a sport organization (athlete, event, association, team, etc.) to a corporate partner. This role—in the case of an NOC, the development of national and mutually beneficial long-term sponsorships—is often a result of a personal selling effort building on the previous marketing efforts of the NOC. In this context, personal selling is defined as a business-to-business (B2B) and person-to-person activity that uncovers and satisfies the needs of the sponsorship partner to the mutual long-term benefit of both parties. This chapter seeks to provide the background and tools needed to understand sponsorship sales, with particular emphasis on sponsorship sales at the NOC level.

© Denyskuvaiev | Dreamstime.com—Denys Yurchenko
On The Samsung Pole Vault Stars Photo

THE SPONSORSHIP SALES ECOSYSTEM

In general terms, an ecosystem is an ecological community linked together with its environment that functions as a unit. In a business context, the system is all about the interactions between the community of organizations in a particular area and their environments. Specific to the sponsorship sales situation, a *sales ecosystem* can be viewed as a complex set of relationships and interactions of individuals and organizations who have an interest in (e.g., a fan), can impact (e.g., member of an NOC Board of Directors), or are impacted by (e.g., the NOC's high-performance director) the potential sponsorship. At the core of the NOC sponsorship sales ecosystem are the sponsor(s) and the NOC. Since sponsors of NOCs typically have many alternatives for their marketing dollars, the skills and knowledge for developing long-term partnerships fall on the shoulders of the NOCs marketing department, often led by the CMO, a vice-president or director of marketing.

For an NOC marketing department, or any unit tasked with sponsorship sales, there are four key elements at the core of the organization's promotion foundation, each of which directly impacts the organization's ability to represent itself successfully in the sales process and to maximize its ability to create sponsorship partnerships. The four elements are (i) knowledge of a potential partner's industry, (ii) understanding the potential partner's customer's product(s) and/or service(s), (iii) knowledge of the potential partner's customer base, and (iv) possessing the ability and assets to provide value to the potential partner. The intersections of these knowledge base components along with a personal selling approach/skill set are what comprise the foundations of a successful sponsorship selling campaign. Of course, if the organization or its property has no marketing value, sponsorship sales are impossible, but assuming that sport properties have some level of attractiveness to corporations, this should not be an issue. The sales professional responsible for developing this relationship must maintain the highest level of professionalism, knowledge, and skill when developing long-term sponsorship relationships.

When selling national sponsors at the NOC level, it is important to remember that, typically, the primary objective of sponsorship for the potential sponsor is ROI, often in the form of increased sales and resulting revenues. Sponsors want the property to help them sell their product(s) and/or service(s). They want to use the property's equity and reach the property's membership or spectators in a way that allows them to navigate existing market clutter (Séguin & O'Reilly, 2008). Therefore, it is important not only to understand the target potential sponsors' business(es) and product(s) but also to understand who are the customer(s) of the potential sponsor (and the competitors in their category). Understanding what makes a customer buy from the sponsor will be one of the ultimate goals of understanding the sales ecosystem. Most sponsorship sales professionals consider this a vital step before even considering connecting with a potential sponsor.

The sponsorship sales ecosystem, however, goes far beyond understanding the potential sponsors' customers and those of the competition, but also considers the people who are not currently purchasing from prospective sponsors. If market research can identify a group of future potential clients for the potential sponsor, this may become the new business segment that the potential sponsor would like to develop and that can be emphasized in the sales process. Clearly, any potential sponsor's new customer base must be articulated with respect to its competition. Knowing with whom the sponsor competes and how it will approach the market in a competitive manner is an important aspect of the sponsorship sales ecosystem. It is not "all about the money" but understanding that the primary source of interest for potential sponsors begins with the customers (or potential customers) and developing a relationship.

WORKING WITHIN THE OLYMPIC CHARTER

In sponsorship sales for any NOC or Olympic-related organization, one must not forget about the uniqueness of the Olympic business model, which includes the requirement to maintain consistency with the fundamental principles of the Olympic Charter. Here, a sponsorship sales professional must have a clear understanding of these guidelines and the responsibilities that the NOC has within the Olympic system, contracts, treaties, and other governance realities. This understanding of the system is the guide that the NOC (and the sponsorship sales team/person) must adopt. An important point is that existing sponsors and suppliers of the IOC, OCOGs and NOCs play a major role in identifying and developing new sponsorship business. TOP sponsors may seek national-level activation (and have sponsorship rights that the NOC must respect, even if they choose not to activate them) while other NOC sponsors may be interested in co-sponsorships or joint activations. It is vitally important to remember that the business environments of each country (and each NOC) differ, and may differ considerably, as explored in Part 1 of this textbook.

NATIONAL OLYMPIC COMMITTEE ASSETS

In any sponsorship sales situation, the organization that is seeking sponsors must initially review its *inventory* (i.e., what it has available to sell). In the case of an NOC, these are described as the NOC assets, which are anything tangible or intangible that is capable of being owned or controlled to produce value for a sponsor and, therefore, is considered to have positive economic value. This process involves asking and responding to/researching a number of questions.

- What are the things of value that the NOC owns?
- Does it have any intangible value in terms of reputation, image, and brand?
- What specific products and services does the NOC have to offer?
- What does it have that would allow a sponsor to reach its stakeholders, or better reach its own customers, or expand its base?
- Would association with its marks (e.g., NOC logo with the five rings) attract the interest of any consumer groups?

Typically, the assets of an NOC fall into two general categories that align with the two main thrusts of marketing: business-to-business (B2B) and business-to-consumer (B2C). First, B2C assets are what the NOC is offering to the general public, and—second—the NOCs B2B offering is what assets it has to offer to business entities that could, in turn, reach the B2C assets through a potential sponsorship/partnership relationship. The primary focus of this chapter is B2B and sponsorship assets.

© Ukrphoto | Dreamstime.com—Samsung Pavilion In The Olympic Park During Winter Olympics Photo

Examples of NOC assets that may provide sponsorship sales opportunities include those that are facility-based (e.g., parking, facility tours, renting out meeting rooms, assigning pouring rights to a beverage organization, etc.), image-based (e.g., logo, title sponsorship, associations), event-based (i.e., ability to put in place joint/group ticket sales, special events, in-game promotions, public address announcements, scoreboard and advertising ribbon boards, etc.) and platform-based (i.e., the sponsor uses the NOC's assets (e.g., athletes, brand name, Olympic trials, etc.) around which to activate.

NOC ASSETS AND THE TOP PROGRAM

The TOP Program is a highly effective global sponsorship model, with a limited number of categories/sponsors, a program that provides these sponsors with category exclusivity across the Olympic family, including NOCs. During an Olympic Games, these TOP sponsors can reach billions of people (estimates for London 2012 exceed 3.5 billion total viewers) (IOC, 2013) with clear Olympic associations and activations. However, for an NOC, the TOP Program provides both opportunities and challenges for sponsorship sales. The same issues impact OCOGs, IFs, and NSOs/NGBs but at a considerably lower degree of magnitude.

From the sponsor (or potential sponsor) perspective, an NOC has many high-quality assets, which certain sponsors may be interested in engaging with for their own purposes of achieving marketing, promotion, and relationship building objectives. Some of these NOC assets include but are not limited to naming rights, the use of the NOC's database, the use of the NOC marks (e.g., images, athletes images, logo), access to on-site facilities (e.g., hospitality tents, rink boards, activations), broadcasting rights, exterior signage, and advertising. This list of marketing concepts is limited only by the creativity of both the NOC's and a potential sponsor's marketing departments. Realistically, for sponsorship sales, it is often the responsibility of the NOC to identify the marketing assets and accompanying creative activations that will be most beneficial to helping the potential sponsor promote its offerings, grow its business, build its brand, retain its employees, or achieve its key objectives.

SALES TACTICS

Once the assets have been identified, the sponsorship sales process accelerates. For the purposes of outlining the steps, consider the example of an NOC with a group of potential products to offer a sponsor. Assume that the NOC is in a strong market with a basket of high-value Olympic assets to offer sponsors. An important decision is whether to group together an integrated package of naming rights, digital signage, and hospitality suites along with printed program inserts and the use of the image and logo of the NOC, or to offer a basket or list of options to a potential sponsor so the sponsor can evaluate and choose those which are most appropriate to its needs. An advantage of presenting a group of assets together is that it may encourage the participation of a sponsor's marketing department to evaluate and determine how best to use the relationship on all its levels, thereby, at least in theory, increasing the sponsor's activation of the property.

When the NOC presents its basket of high-value assets, it is not unusual for a conversation to result in which the potential sponsor asks for extensive details, historical information, and colorful descriptions of the proposed offering. It is important for the sponsorship sales team to remember that initial interaction with potential sponsors should not be all about the NOC, the Olympics, or the athletes' needs, but about the needs of the sponsor and the objectives of the sponsor's marketing department. The process of selling is not a matter of telling stories; it is one of asking questions and uncovering what the potential sponsor wants and needs. The quality of a question asked in determining the true needs of the potential sponsor may be more beneficial to the NOC than a list of the Olympic medals won by its athletes. The focus should be on providing a "value proposition" (i.e., why a sponsor should engage in a sponsorship relationship with the property and how that relationship will add more value or better solves a problem than alternative options available). Thus, the primary focus for the sponsorship sales team is to demonstrate the value to the potential sponsor. Some examples of the types of questions to ask are listed below here.

1. How should the sponsorship be evaluated? From the perspective of the sponsor? From the view of the property? What about through a sports marketing or research agency?
2. What steps does the potential sponsor typically take in reviewing and deciding on a sponsorship proposal?
3. How does the potential sponsor typically establish a sponsorship partnership?
4. What is motivating the potential sponsor to engage in a sponsorship relationship? If it is an upcoming Olympic Games (or other major event), dig deeper to seek a longer-term reason.
5. What is the potential sponsor's pain (e.g., has a compelling event happened recently?)? And how can our property help with it?
6. Get a copy of the potential sponsor's fiscal calendar of marketing activities.

The sponsorship sales team needs to realize that a potential sponsor who is considering engaging in a sponsorship with the NOC will be evaluating that property within the framework of its existing marketing strategy and versus alternative promotional/marketing options available to it at similar cost/effort. Often, a potential sponsor will have numerous marketing goals within a comprehensive marketing plan, and a sponsorship

opportunity will be considered only if it falls within that. A corporate sponsor will likely only make a major sponsorship decision (such as an NOC sponsorship) after undertaking extensive market research and ensuring that the sponsorship fits in its mix of marketing elements directed at achieving its objectives. Ideally, therefore, the NOC sponsorship sales team should try to obtain a copy of the potential sponsor's marketing strategy, so that it is thoroughly understood prior to starting the sales process.

In many developed countries of the world, including North America, Europe, Australia, and Asia, corporations

are often publicly owned, where its securities such as stock or bonds are offered for sale to the general public, typically through some form of stock exchange. As part of this process, these organizations are required to provide reliable information about their business to the investing public. This can be a very important source of information for the sponsorship sales team, along with the corporate's website, industry reports, and assessments of their previous sponsorship activity. Additional sources of information can be found via government publications (e.g., census data, industry reports, industry classification systems, etc.).

Another important tactic for the sponsorship sales team of an NOC (or other Olympic organization) is to consider the long-term value of the potential sponsorship relationship. This could be classified as a *relationship marketing* approach, where the offering to the potential sponsor emphasizes customer retention and satisfaction for current and future customers of the potential sponsor. Our experience is that this focus (i.e., establish a long-term relationship) is much more likely to lead to a sponsorship sales success than focusing solely on the sales transaction to *sell* the sponsorship. An additional important sales consideration is that a number of potentially important smaller relationships (e.g., individual event sponsorship) may be in the best interest of both parties and may be used as a stepping stone to further more extensive partnerships where retention and satisfaction of the relationship will produce long-term benefits to both parties.

INTEREST IN OR IMPACT ON A SPONSORSHIP SALE

A sponsorship sales professional always considers all of the potential influences on this relationship by considering range of persons, organizations, business, and other influencers that may have a significant impact on the outcome of the sponsorship are important even though they may not be under the direct control of the NOC. Decision influence may come from within or from outside of a prospect organization (potential sponsor).

Within the organization, the first constituents to be considered are the internal decision-makers, who represent the most important component of the decision-making process. Often these internal decision-makers rely on the opinions of organizational influencers prior to making a decision. These influencers are other persons in the potential sponsor's organization who are connected to the prospect's organization and have the power to influence and persuade the ultimate decision-making group. The role and power of influencers in any organization largely depend on the culture and politics of that organization. Thus, it is important to direct sales resources towards the important influencers, particularly those involved in the marketing function. Usually more than one person will influence executive decisions in an organization.

In the B2B sponsorship sales decision, external influences outside the sponsor and the property may include a much larger set of constituents, such as event consumers, legal consultants, industry experts, competitors, and sport fans. These groups can have a major impact on the success of a sponsorship relationship and, as such, influence the sale process and may have an impact on the success of the sponsorship sales team's efforts. In order to enable the sponsorship sales person to better understand and prepare for these groups of influences, a framework that groups them into five categories is presented below.

1. Customer/Consumers: ticketholders, the local public, the general public, media outlets, other sponsors, and broadcast rights holders.
2. Input Organizations: suppliers, regulatory authorities, government, and sport leagues.
3. Intermediaries: merchants, brokers, facilitators, marketing firms, management firms, sports agents, and advertising agencies.
4. Competitors: any competitor or substitute to the potential sponsor.
5. Internal NOC stakeholders: management, staff, board members, venue management, volunteers, and current/former athletes.

Each of these constituents can influence the sponsorship sale in a positive and/or negative way, where any influencer has the ability to impact the process from *closing the deal* to *derail a sponsorship campaign*.

PERSONAL SELLING COMPETENCIES

The sponsorship sales team's background and skills play an important role in the sponsorship sales process. In fact, unless this group or individual or external agency or combination of these groups have the network, the skills, and the background to build a relationship and convince a potential partner of the value of the property, a sale will not occur, or at least not one that is fair for the NOC.

© Evgenyi44 | Dreamstime.com—Banknotes issued 100 Russian rubles for the Olympics in Sochi Photo

It is essential to ensure that the sponsorship sales team has the requisite skills and abilities. The NOC must ask itself what are the key competencies in the selling process necessary to produce long-term, strategic, sponsorship relationships? What specific experiences and skills must the sales team possess? If there are any abilities that it does not possess in-house, must it hire or engage an agency? Depending on the size and scope of the sport property (NOC), these needs will vary. For example, the sales needs of the United States Olympic Committee (USOC) versus those of the Ivory Coast (Comité National Olympique de Côte d'Ivoire) differ considerably due to the size, media, and development of their respective national markets. To simplify the competencies required for sales, they are organized into five major categories:

1. **Network/Pipeline:** Does the sponsorship sales team have the ability to access and build relationships with potential sponsors through personal contacts, pipeline building (e.g., fostering early or new relationships), and cold-calling (e.g., creating relationships where none exist)?

2. **Presentation Skills:** Does the team have the ability to do both informal (e.g., lunch meeting) and formal (e.g., official pitch to a potential corporate partner) presentations of the highest quality, both in terms of oral delivery and presentation materials?

3. **Research:** Does the team have the research ability to find data and analyze it for effective understanding of a potential partner's value proposition, its market, and the property's sponsorship value? This will include benchmarking analyses to come up with pricing, case studies to determine potential activations, and secondary research to determine international comparable properties, as well as to understand the potential sponsor's marketing strategy and promotional goals. Prior to approaching any potential prospect it is important to establish a baseline of knowledge prior to each and every interaction. This baseline should include key components of the prospect's current business situation and identification of their marketing objectives that can normally be sourced by a web search. This, in turn, will call for clearly established objectives around the goals of the proposed sponsorship.

4. **Negotiation:** If a potential sponsor expresses sincere interest and a possible partnership develops, it will eventually reach the negotiation stage on price and deliverables. Often a corporate sponsor will engage an agency to negotiate on its behalf, thus the property's sales team needs to be experienced and informed for a negotiation to ensure a fair deal that provides value to both parties.

5. **Sealing the Deal:** As a potential sale works through the process, the sales team needs 'closers' or those who have expertise in finalizing the deal and getting both parties to say yes to an agreement.

KEY ELEMENTS OF A SPONSORSHIP SALES APPROACH

This section identifies a series of important considerations that may help the sponsorship sales process, depending on the context and the situation.

1. **Corporate Social Responsibility (CSR):** Today, many corporations are seeking to give back to society and seek sponsorship partners who will help them to do this. *Sustainability* and *legacy* are similar terms to describe CSR in the sports world. As such, potential sponsors may assess a sponsorship proposal and evaluate its ability to allow the corporate to support a positive social outcome such as the environment or childhood obesity. CSR is also a value creator, as it has the potential to have marketing impact for both the sponsor and the property. This type of benefit can be observed in many TOP sponsors who activate around their support of Olympic athletes and their ability to lend operational impact to the Games' events, such as computing, timing, food and beverage, and management support.

In considering a potential partner, a corporation will look at the property's ability to allow them to do this (and to tell their costumers and potential customers about it). Essentially, they will ask if the sponsorship opportunity provides the ability to align with their CSR strategy. Also referred to as *corporate citizenship*, CSR can involve incurring short-term costs that do not provide an immediate financial benefit to the company, but that, instead, promote positive social and environmental change. Thus, for sponsorship sales, the potential sponsor's past interests in CSR,

© Nasir1164 | Dreamstime.com—Corporate Social Responsibility Photo

what the specific topics of interest are/could be (e.g., environment, sustainability, water, health, community legacy, etc.), need to be researched and built into both sales conversations and proposals so that the potential partner can see how it will be able to better promote itself in a positive social context. This is a critical consideration when establishing sponsorship opportunities.

2. **Source of Budget:** Many corporations today have budgets that *could* go to sponsorship organized under separate marketing and philanthropic units. Sometimes, there may be additional budget *units* specific to corporate donations and/or public private partnerships (O'Reilly & Brunette, 2013). Although many properties are not normally aware of or that concerned about which of their partner's budgets the resources come from, this is a major flaw in many sales efforts, as the source will often be tied to the objectives that the potential sponsor may be seeking. For instance, if the budget is coming from a philanthropic, cause-related marketing, or donations source, although ROI may be relevant, the impact on the cause and the resulting association to the CSR brand will likely be the key driver. Conversely, if the source is a marketing or sponsorship budget, ROI will be the key approach. For a public-private partnership, a mix of ROI and CSR is normally suggested, however in cases where marketing budgets are considerably higher than philanthropic budgets, the better the business case, the greater the

possible sponsorship. For philanthropic budgets, there is always a risk of falling into the wrong pool and having to compete with hospitals, cancer, mental illness, relief of poverty, and other impactful causes, where sport is more likely to come out on the short end. For example, as described in the Chapter 3 case study, the Canadian Paralympic Committee has a mixed-value proposition of high-performance sport (linked to ROI) and disabled athletes with tremendous stories of overcoming adversity (linked to CSR).

3. **Risk:** The sponsorship sales team must consider if any risks (and, if so, the level of risk) that the potential partner could face via the sponsorship. This may or may not be related to CSR. It may be about potential brand risks if an athlete misbehaves or a poor result/tragedy occurs. In response, the discussions and proposals need to address/mitigate any potential risks and include language on what happens should a nontrivial risk with the sponsorship be identified. An additional recommendation to NOCs is that an internal evaluation (i.e., for the NOC's own consideration) should be undertaken to assess the potential of risk to its own brand and thereby avoid entering into partnerships with the *wrong* sponsors. As former star baseball player for the New York Yankees Yogi Berra famously advised, "Don't make the wrong mistakes".

4. **Organization Analysis:** As noted, research into the potential partner is a key component of sales process/success in sponsorship. It has been said that companies do not sell to companies, but rather that people sell to people. It is critical, therefore, to understand the who's who of your potential sponsor's organization. An organizational analysis is a tool by which to achieve this, since it provides the sponsorship sales team with a clear understanding of the organization. Although the format can vary, it should—at a minimum—include (i) a review of the company's directory to identify the key contacts (e.g., CMO, VP Sponsorship, sponsorship/marketing staff) and their backgrounds, (ii) an understanding of the firm's organizational chart over time to identify the priorities, changes, and identify key staff members who are rising in the organization (and who should become targets for relationship building), (iii) an analysis of strategic plans, corporate websites, and annual reports to determine strategic focus of the potential partner and possible fits for sponsorship.

5. **Targeted Relationship Building:** With an organizational analysis in place and the targets identified, the sales team can seek to build relationships with the decision makers at the potential sponsor. This process views relationships on a continuum from *adversarial* (i.e., negative) to *trusted advisor* (i.e., positive), with requisite plans to minimize the influence of nonsupporters and engage the support and coaching of supporters. Establishing these individuals' buying influence and the roles they play will further help establish the key players in an organization. Primary candidates are the financial decision makers ("those who hold the purse strings"), sponsorship decision makers, technical influencers (e.g., information), end-users (e.g., sponsor employees who will work on it, customers, and consumers), and third-party opinion generators and influencers (e.g., consultants,

legal representatives, industry experts). It is important to understand that each group is looking for "What's in it for me?," so discussion and proposals should include both features and benefits focusing on the "What's in it" for the individual as well as for the organization.

6. A recommendation to properties and/or agencies in building relationships with sponsorship-related objectives is to focus on building the relationship with *the key marketing executives*, as they are the ideal persons to champion the potential partnership and if they can be convinced that there will be ROI for the sponsor, there will be, in theory at least, a significant amount of money they could pry loose (which is not the same situation in a CSR or corporate donation situation).

7. **Features and Benefits:** In sales of sponsorship, the features—or benefits or details—of the deal are vitally important to its success. These details allow the potential sponsor to determine if the proposed opportunity will enable them to achieve what they need to achieve—a price-point within their budget. From the NOC or property perspective, articulation of the specific benefits/features is a key element of discussion, proposals, and negotiations in the sponsorship sales process. It is in the NOC's (or the property's) best interests to draw a connection between the features and benefits of the sponsorship and the specific benefit to the individual and organization providing the sponsorship resources in monetary or product/services. Notably, it should not be forgotten that a deep understanding of a sponsorship features/benefits package is in the eye of the beholder, so the sponsorship sales team needs to clearly outline/describe the related details (e.g., licensing, hospitality, etc.), incentives, and specific actions. As previously noted, the sponsorship sales team must focus not on the benefits for its organization (the NOC) but on what the benefits are for the potential sponsor. For example, if the potential sponsor is interested in market exposure, the features of the proposal would include specific deliverables that would outline how the sponsorship will help the potential sponsor achieve exposure and to what extent.

TARGETING POTENTIAL SPONSORS

Although many NOCs (and sport properties in general) have a very challenging task to sell sponsorship, there are those (e.g., British Olympic Association, USOC, COC), that have high sponsorship value and that can be more selective in approaching sponsors. In these cases, attractive potential partners can be those that have geographic, strategic, and personal relationship fits. Does the potential sponsor share markets with fans/participants? Do the available images and offerings match with the sponsor's objective(s)? Is there a relationship in place with someone at the sponsor to connect with or get a meeting? If positive answers to all three of these questions are not there, then it is likely futile to proceed with a sales effort until such a time as all three answers are positive. If the answers are appropriate, then a consideration of the interest in/need for sponsorship by the prospect and its ability to afford the revenue sought should be undertaken. Simply put, does the sponsor need what the property offers and can they pay sufficiently for it? A *no* answer to either will present difficulty, if not impossibility, in furthering the relationship.

CHAPTER EXERCISE: SPONSORSHIP SALES

Sport organizations with more diversified revenue bases are more likely to enjoy stable financial conditions. However, many not-for-profit organizations rely on only a few revenue sources for the majority of their budgets. Given the uncertain and varied environments of internal, public, and private funding for not-for-profit sport organizations, this puts the financial sustainability of the sport organization at risk if one of those sources is negatively impacted. Thus, it has been a normal occurrence in recent years for these organizations to pursue sponsorship to diversify their revenue sources. This often results in the identification of sponsorship, or expanded sponsorship, as a priority.

Assume you are the sponsorship manager for a sport organization and have been assigned the task of increasing sponsorships. As you embark on this effort, four considerations should govern your approach.

- First, you need to conduct an environmental survey of your current sponsorship partners. Do you have any? If so, who? What categories? What categories are empty that might be interested in your sports property? Who does your organization have that is at current risk of nonrenewal?
- Second, step back from your day-to-day view of your organization and consider what the customer (sport fan) considers to be your organizational profile, image, and reputation. Then think about what potential categories and sponsors could match that profile. Do your participants, members, or other stakeholders match the customers of those categories/sponsors? For example, a polo or tennis club event may align with high-end fashionable products, and skateboarding with the energy drink market.
- Third, do some research to better understand your market. You can never have too much data on a potential sponsor prospect or its category. Talk to people close to your prospect, chat with an industry expert, run a focus group of your membership, research your prospect online, find a sample of consumers of a potential prospect and ask them why they purchase that product. The opportunities for collection of data are vast and possession of such data will allow for a strong level of understanding of a prospect's customer base.
- Fourth, plan your approach. Build the relationship. Set a meeting. Figure out who should be there. Articulate how a partnership will benefit both organizations. Be creative. Look for opportunities to develop the relationship over time. Sometimes it takes a small start with a long-term plan to develop a major relationship.

Exercise Questions

1. Select a sport organization you will represent and go through the four steps of the approach using online and publicly available resources. If you work for (or have worked for) a sport organization, use that organization.
2. Identify 20 components of your property's inventory that may be of interest to a sponsor. Distill that list down to your top 3 and select the best features of your property.

3. Match each of those features of your property to a benefit that you will be able to provide a prospect. How will each feature of your property be able to provide the sponsor with a cost-effective marketing solution?
4. Identify your prospect's needs. What are the business challenges currently facing your prospect, and how will your partnership help to address those needs?
5. Clearly state what your organization hopes to gain from this relationship.

Key Chapter Questions

1. Should every sport property pursue sponsorship? Should every NOC?
2. What are the key steps in the sponsorship sales process?
3. Why (and how) should the sponsorship sales process differ for a high-value NOC versus one with limited marketing presence?
4. How important are the Olympic rings/marks to NOC sponsorship sales?

Key Chapter Takeaways

1. Sponsorship sales is very difficult and requires a sponsorship sales team with specific competencies.
2. Selling a sponsorship is a process that involves prospecting, researching, targeting, negotiating, and servicing.
3. If you want to get value, you must be able to give value.

Case Study 11.1

Executive Perspective

Tyler Mazereeuw, Senior Director, Business Development,
Canadian Football League Chair, Sponsorship Marketing Council of Canada

Topic: Sponsorship Sales

Last time I checked, there wasn't a manual for selling sponsorship, and how could there be when every sponsorship by its very nature is fundamentally different. Based on my experience, the best sponsorship development executives use a balance of creativity combined with the persistence, patience, and relationship building skills that you would find in a traditional sales person. Most of these executives would also consider themselves marketers first and fans second; they craft compelling stories that resonate with brands and win with consumers. If you're too busy focusing on why you love the sport and who your favorite team was growing up, you could lose sight of what's important to the potential sponsor

and client sitting across the table from you, who may or may not be a fan. Objectivity is critical. If you can separate your own personal interests and focus on what's important to your prospect, you'll fast-track the sales process and enhance your probability of closing the deal.

It's paramount that you become an expert in sponsorship before you start to think about which property you're selling. Would you feel comfortable if your doctor wasn't an expert in the medical field? Whether it's the Olympics or a local festival, if you can't articulate why sponsorship works, how can you possibly convince a brand to invest in a sponsorship? If you want to sell sponsorship, understand the mechanics that drive

(Continued on next page)

Case Study 11.1 *(continued)*

it. Ask yourself, Why should I buy sponsorship over a more traditional advertising vehicle such as television, print, or radio? One way to position sponsorship is to help articulate why it's different or how it could be used to amplify other marketing tactics. Advertising shows your customer who you are, but sponsorship demonstrates what you have in common with them. This shared-interest and common ground provides the foundation to create a meaningful dialogue, which ultimately builds a relationship and trust. This leads to an emotional connection that is unmatched by other marketing options. If you can't get them past first base (why sponsorship works) you'll never get them to home plate (closing the sponsorship deal).

Relationships and big ideas make the sale. Marketers like shiny new toys and sponsorships are a perfect match since they come equipped with an unlimited supply of new concepts, relevant promotions, and other compelling stories to share. These in turn create a unique point of differentiation—a hallmark of sponsorship. Everyone wants the next "Kraft Hockeyville" or the new version of what P&G has created with its Olympic-inspired "Mom" platform. Helping your prospect understand why there's a fit and how it can impact their business is critical, but in order to take it to the next level, identify how this sponsorship can be activated across multiple stakeholders and business units.

It's important to help the prospect understand how to activate the sponsorship. Create the concepts and ideas that demonstrate how the sponsorship will come to life. How they can engage different business units (e.g., with a bank, think about retail banking, credit card, wealth management, and insurance) and how different stakeholders will benefit. The more business units and stakeholders who can benefit from the sponsorship, the higher the probability that

you can access more budgets and close the deal. More importantly this creates sustainable value that keeps the sponsor engaged and invested in the long-term. It's one thing to capture a sponsor, but it's another to keep them. In sponsorship, what happens after the deal is signed is equally if not more important in retaining them.

Although sponsorship isn't your typical sales job, it's still selling, and a strategic numbers game. Eighty percent of your opportunity is going to come from the top twenty percent of your prospects. Basic understanding of the sales process should be mastered in order to maximize your time and overall effectiveness. Prospect, present to the prospect, and follow-up as they say. How you determine who to call, when to call and how much time to spend with each prospect, combined with the time and creativity you invest during the sales process, is the art behind the sale. Creating an ideal customer map that helps you understand what your ideal sponsor would look like will help streamline the process and allow you to focus on the high-probability partners, and more importantly, the ones who will stay. Spend some time understanding what the ideal sponsor looks like. Do they have the wherewithal to buy, but more importantly, do they have money left to activate the partnership? Do they understand the value of sponsorship? Are their customers your fans? These are just some of the guideposts you can use when prospecting.

Preparation is the true mark of a pro. What happens when a quarterback doesn't prepare, or a coach doesn't watch the game tape of their next opponent? You work in sports; you should know that the greatest champions invest everything on and off the field of play. It should be no different in sports business. Whether it's a presentation, cold call, or other form of communication, prepare yourself for success and plan (don't "hope") to win.

12

Olympic Sponsorship: 1896 to 1984

Despite the magic of the Olympic Games, there is nothing magic about the basic marketing principles that apply. Nor is there any major difference between sports marketing (a mere subset of marketing) and the Olympic version. Olympic marketing is so remarkable because of its ability to draw worldwide interest, the consistency of the messages, the extraordinary outcome of concerted efforts, and the dramatic increase in the value of the Olympic brand. The multidecade sponsorship partnerships of some TOP sponsors are testament to this.

UNCERTAIN AND LOCAL BEGINNINGS

Modern Olympic sponsorship has evolved in directions and to an extent unimaginable at the time the Greeks struggled desperately, in the period leading up to 1896, to assemble the funds necessary to organize the first Games of the modern era in Athens. It was a close-run effort, saved in large measure by the intervention of leading local businessmen, the Greek Royal family and a few businesses. As an example, Kodak was a modest supporter of those Games, evidently aware of both the photographic potential of sports events and its own role as an international corporation that could potentially benefit from additional recognition in the Greek market.

Sponsorship of sports events, teams, and clubs was not new, even in the 19th century. At the time, sponsorship was, however, essentially a local phenomenon. This was not altogether surprising, since sport at that time was itself essentially local. Apart from a very few cross-border matches and a few intercity matches, until the means of mass transportation made the movement of large numbers of people simple and fast, sport audiences were generally small and stayed close to home. The harnessing of steam proved to be the essential impetus to greater and greater popularity of sport, bringing with it an increased interest on the part of the business community. Growth of the railways met the needs of players and spectators alike and the replacement of sailing ships by steam-powered vessels made even the prospect of intercontinental sport seem closer at hand.

The revival of the Olympic Games can now be seen as the first significant effort to provide an international platform for competitive sport. The idea for such a platform was an audacious concept, driven by a young French educator, Pierre de Coubertin, well ahead of its contemporary time, and extended well beyond the classic limitation of the ancient Games as a festival restricted to Greeks who could reach Olympia. This notwithstanding, from a marketing perspective, the modern Games remained essentially local in nature as an event worthy of commercial support: They were important to the host community, but were of marginal interest to the business communities in countries from which visiting athletes came to compete. If those countries had any interest in the Olympic Games, it was only because athletes from their countries were going abroad to participate. Sponsors at home might have been willing to provide modest support for their athletes, in return for limited public recognition of such a gesture, but not for the event itself.

MARKETING AND THE INTERNATIONAL OLYMPIC COMMITTEE

The concept of marketing—in any sophisticated form—came relatively recently to the International Olympic Committee (IOC). Part of the reason for this was its general and philosophical distaste for any activity that smacked of commercialism, part was that the characteristics and power of the Olympic brand had not been identified, and part arose from the peculiar organization of the Olympic Movement on the basis of national participation. The IOC has always held itself out as the supreme authority of the Olympic

Movement and the arbiter of all matters relating to the Olympic Games, including ownership of all rights in and to the Games, appropriate use of the term *Olympic* and use of the five interlocking rings, described by it as the Olympic Symbol. Its position in that regard has never been seriously challenged and the IOC has managed to occupy the self-declared role at the head of the Olympic Movement since its inception in 1894.[1] This authority has included adopting and amending the Olympic Charter, designating the host cities for the various editions of the Games, determining the sports, disciplines, and events comprising the program of the Games, establishing the rules for participation in the Games, and managing all ceremonial aspects of the Games.[2]

THE STRUCTURE OF INTERNATIONAL SPORT

The IOC has adopted a form of quasidiplomatic recognition as its means of validating participation in the Olympic Movement. Thus, it recognizes various international federations (IFs) as organizations that have demonstrated their ability to organize and control a particular sport on an international basis.[3] It also recognizes National Olympic Committees (NOCs) in countries and territories, in accordance with a set of criteria determined by the IOC.[4] The NOCs are accorded the responsibility of choosing the delegations from their territories that will represent the NOC at the Olympic Games.[5] They are also given an exclusive right, within their territories, to the use of Olympic designations, including the incorporation of the word "Olympic" into their name, and are given the right to create one or more Olympic "emblems," which involve a combination of the Olympic rings and a distinctive national identification.[6] IFs have no similar Olympic-related rights and their members, the National Sport Organizations (NSOs), recognized as such by the IFs, have a similar lack of access to Olympic identification in their countries or territories. The NSOs are, however, pursuant to the Olympic Charter, included in their NOC and have, in fact, IOC-mandated voting control of the NOC.[7] This is a policy decision by the IOC, intended to ensure that control of the NOC is exercised by persons knowledgeable in matters of sport. The NOCs are directed by the Olympic Charter to obtain legal protection of the word "Olympic" and the five ring symbol within their territories.[8] It has not always been possible to accomplish this objective and the IOC does not apply sanctions against those that have been unable to obtain such protection.

ORGANIZATIONAL CONTROL OF GAMES

When awarding the Olympic Games to a host city, in recent years, the IOC has developed and imposed increasingly complex requirements of an organizational nature. During the early history of the modern Olympic Movement, the IOC tended to content itself with designating the host city and then leaving all responsibility for the organization of the Games to the local authorities. This resulted in several early editions of the Games that were poorly, if not chaotically, organized, to the point that continued existence of the Games was in serious doubt. It was not until 1912 that the Games were well-enough organized to be considered a fixture on the international sport scene, only then to have the next edition in 1916 be canceled due to World War I.

The essential laissez-faire attitude of the IOC continued for many years thereafter. To some degree, this was understandable, since the IOC was a small, impecunious, organization of volunteers, with almost no full-time staff. The IOC had no revenue-generating programs of its own. Its members were assessed annual membership fees to cover the costs of a miniscule secretariat and they paid, personally, all their travel and accommodation expenses when attending IOC Sessions and the Olympic Games. The host cities were essentially left to their own devices to arrange for the financing of the Olympic Games, including any required infrastructure. As late as 1974, the *contract* between the IOC and the Moscow authorities in relation to the 1980 Games was only two double-spaced pages.

PUBLIC-SECTOR FUNDING

Government funding of Olympic Games costs did not involve the usual market-driven commercial elements, although some promotional recognition of contributions was a normal byproduct of public sector activities. It became increasingly typical, however, for government contributions to fall short of defraying the full costs of organizing the Games and local organizers sought assistance from the private sector for such purposes. Competitive sporting events had enjoyed private sector support well before the revival of the Olympic Games, although not on an international basis in competitions of the nature of the Olympic Games. There were well-developed, commercially supported, professional sports circuits, in a number of sports, dating back to the middle of the 19th century. Indeed, a general concern about the abuses that developed from such professionalism provided an important part of the momentum leading to the revival of the Olympic Games and the obsession of the early leaders of the Olympic Movement with amateurism as the antidote to those abuses.

Beginning with Athens in 1896, private funding of the Olympic Games proved crucial to their celebration. No doubt part of the reason for this was the uniqueness of the concept of international Games at that time, as well as no history of government support of athletic competitions. Part was undoubtedly the refusal to contemplate, as a matter of Greek national pride in its emerging statehood, the possibility that a revival of the ancient Greek Games could be allowed to fail. In the event, significant individual donations were made and the first Olympic commercial sponsors appeared for the Athens Games.

ATTRACTING PRIVATE SECTOR SUPPORT

As the Olympic Games grew increasingly important on a world scale, the ability to attract commercial support for them also increased. The IOC allowed the organizers of the Games to create their own emblems, consisting, as in the case of the NOCs, of the five rings with a distinctive element identifying the particular Games.

Sponsors of the Games were allowed to identify themselves or their goods and services by use of the emblem (often with descriptive language identifying the sponsorship) and licensees were permitted to manufacture and sell goods and souvenirs identified

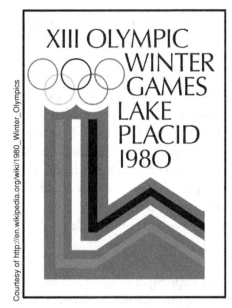

Courtesy of http://en.wikipedia.org/wiki/1980_Winter_Olympics

with the Games. In time, this would become a significant factor in the generation of revenues necessary to defray the organizational costs of the Games.

This development contained, however, the seeds of some difficult commercial problems, which became increasingly apparent as time went on. One problem related to the IOC itself. In a system based on geography, it had no territory over which it had jurisdiction. It was in the anomalous position of controlling the Olympic Movement and the use of the five rings, but had no place in which it could, on its own accord, use those rings for its own commercial purposes.[9] Another related to the NOC of the host country, which had its own emblem and which could continue to use that emblem, even when its country was the host country of the Olympic Games and there was an organizing committee, with its own emblem, commercially active in the same market.

The potential for confusion in the marketplace, whether innocent or deliberate, was obvious, and the value of any rights granted by either the organizing committee or the host NOC would be diminished as a result of the confusion, unless a sponsor had the right to use both emblems. In 1968, while not an official sponsor, McDonald's flew in hamburgers to Grenoble, France, generating good press for supporting and feeding athletes, yet without sponsorship rights. Obtaining both sets of rights entailed making an arrangement with both the organizing committee and the NOC. The main event was the Games, of course, and the short-to-medium term value of a Games sponsorship was much greater than one with the NOC. Where the real collision occurred was when a sponsor became a sponsor of the organizing committee and one of its competitors became a sponsor of the NOC. While the nature and extent of rights that could be granted were quite different, the confusion between which company was a sponsor of the Games (and what that meant) and which was a sponsor of, say, the national team in the same Games (and what that meant) had the effect of diluting the sponsorship value of each. These proved to be some of the original examples of ambush marketing. A well-cited example is from the 1984 Olympic

GAMES OF THE XXIVTH OLYMPIAD SEOUL 1988

Courtesy of http://en.wikipedia.org/wiki/1988_Summer_Olympics

Games in Los Angeles, where Kodak sponsored the US track and field team and purchased broadcast time advertising spots to undermine the official Games sponsorship of Fujifilm, a major competitor that had successfully outbid the long-time film sponsor.

A further difficulty arose from the national and territorial organization of the Olympic Movement. An NOC had the right to use its emblem in its own country. If it wanted to use it in another country, it required the permission of the NOC in that other country. The same was true of the Olympic organizing committees. They had the right to use their emblems in the countries where the Games were being organized, but nowhere else, unless they got permission from the NOCs of those countries in which they might want to use the emblem. Naturally, any such permission came with a cost, as well as with the complications and expense of negotiating the separate agreements with each NOC.

At the beginning of the modern era, the limitation of resources and the limited confidence that the Olympic Games would continue to increase in importance were reinforced by less than impressive organization of the 1900 and 1904 Games, the bail-out by Rome from its 1908 commitment, with London stepping in to take its place, and World War I and the Depression in the early 1930s. The successes of Stockholm (1912), Paris (1924), and Berlin (1936) were not perceived as any long-term guarantee that the Games were viable, especially with World War II about to provide a further 12-year gap in their celebration. All in all, it was not a reassuring commercial proposition. Notwithstanding the many setbacks, however, glimpses of the potential role of the Games as a unique platform in world sport could be seen, and sports authorities persisted in their quest of that potential.

The post-World War II world was as complex as the post-World War I period, although, counterintuitively, somewhat more stable, because of the promise of mutual assured destruction, a dynamic of the stocks of nuclear weapons in the hands of the major powers. The rise of the Soviet Union as a world power required considerable political adaptation by other countries, but its self-imposed isolation (at least in sport) began to diminish once it decided that it wanted to become part of the Olympic Movement. The subtext of Olympic competition as a continuation of a Cold War, combined with the increasing phenomenon of television, with its ubiquitous reach, its immediacy, and galloping technological advances, became increasingly interesting to the commercial world.[11] The vast audiences, the *good guy–bad guy* positioning, and the media-based *scoring* and medal counts made the Olympics larger than life. Business was much more enthusiastic about involvement with the Olympics, even though the commercial focus remained essentially domestic, rather than international.

This state of affairs continued for many years. The Games were regarded as the responsibility of the host country or city, both financially and organizationally. The IOC had nominal control, but no money. International federations provided sport expertise, but no funding. The NOCs were responsible for the expenses of their teams in relation to the Games. In both organizing the Games and getting athletes to the Games, private sector support was essentially local: Businesses and individuals in the host country might be prevailed upon to assist the organizers to discharge their duties of staging the

Games, while private sector support of the visiting Olympic teams was generally provided by nationals of each country.

TRENDING TOWARD INTERNATIONAL INVOLVEMENT

On the other hand, there was an international creep that could soon be discerned, largely through the ubiquity of television, but also, to some degree, as a result of increasing international expansion of businesses. Companies were carrying on business around the world, led in large measure from the United States, although it was not alone, and other countries also had international businesses, or were at least contemplating the advantages of scale that could flow from operating on an international basis. Japan launched itself, from its position as host of the Olympic Games in Tokyo in 1964, as a country that could now be perceived as highly organized and highly competent. Gone was the pre-war and post-war image of a country struggling to produce even second-class goods.[12] Mexico attempted the same in 1968, with less commercial success, but did manage to demonstrate that, architecturally and culturally, it ranked in the top echelons of the world. The new Germany showed itself in 1972, Canada organized excellent Games in 1976, despite a seriously flawed financial plan to support the new infrastructure. By 1974, following a failed attempt to win the 1976 Games, the Soviet Union bid for the 1980 Games with enough self-confidence to invite the world for a glimpse behind the Iron Curtain. Los Angeles would finally get its chance to host a second Games in 1984 (having tried unsuccessfully to win 1976 and 1980) and set the stage for genuine international commercial sponsorship.

OLYMPIC MOVEMENT RESPONSE
TO MARKETING CONSIDERATIONS

As this was occurring, commercial interest in the Olympic Games was increasing, and the amounts of money available were beginning to become more and more significant. Television rights, especially for 1984 and beyond, escalated dramatically, as did domestic sponsorships of the Games themselves. The growing commercial interest in the Games was driven by increasingly sophisticated television broadcasts, particularly in jurisdictions where commercial advertising was allowed. Broadcast sponsors used language such as "the Olympic Games are brought to you by . . ." to create vicarious *ownership* of the Games in the broadcast territory. The massive fascination of the viewing public with the Olympics made investment in such broadcast sponsorships extremely worthwhile. Such positioning, in the United States, would eventually lead to growing tension between the USOC and the IOC, based on the assertion by the USOC that such broadcast statements were diminishing its ability to attract sponsors for the US team, especially when coupled with a demand for a share of the US television rights to compensate for its alleged losses of potential team sponsors.[13]

In the midst of this was the IOC, still a small organization with no experience in either television or marketing. It also retained the mental set, derived from an elderly male membership wedded to the concept of amateurism that the earning of money

from sport, no matter how, was essentially distasteful. Despite this, the IOC was nevertheless fully aware that the NOCs had to be able to raise funds to ensure that they could participate in the Games. It had therefore allowed each NOC to have an Olympic *emblem* that could include the Olympic five-ring symbol, which the NOC could then use to raise funds. The IOC did what it could to obtain legal protection for the Olympic Symbol and the five rings, and even encouraged a largely unsuccessful effort to obtain protection under an international convention known as the Nairobi Treaty. Virtually every important country declined to participate.

ORGANIZING THE HOST COUNTRIES

Additional difficulties soon developed in host countries, where the local organizing committees (known as Organizing Committees for the Olympic Games, or OCOGs) had the marketing rights regarding the Games and were permitted to have their own Olympic emblems, but where the NOCs also maintained their rights to use to use their approved emblems in relation to the national Olympic team and other activities of a fundraising nature. This proved to be a minor problem for the 1976 Games in Montreal, when the NOC competed for sponsorships with the OCOG. The potential confusion between the different roles and responsibilities was less than it would otherwise have been, due to the enormous market clutter created by the OCOG, which had literally hundreds of different sponsors, so many and so small that their contributions were closer to donations than genuine platforms for marketing programs. The result was marketing cacophony, from which the sponsors derived little, if any, commercial benefit. The activities of the NOC, selling team sponsorships were more of an irritant than serious competition. But there was a clear warning of potential trouble in the offing.

The situation was much more severe in Los Angeles, eight years later. The 1980 Moscow Games had not been a practical problem, given the Soviet government's tight central control of both the OCOG and the NOC, a negligible domestic market, and limited commercial interest in much of the developed world in anything having to do with the Soviet Union. This was exacerbated once the movement began to boycott the Games as a result of the 1979 Soviet intervention in Afghanistan. The particular 1984 situation is described elsewhere, but the Los Angeles Games eventually led to a number of important changes in matters relating to Olympic marketing.[14] The first was that by the time the 1992 Games were awarded in 1986, the NOC of any host country was required to have to have a single joint marketing agreement with the OCOG, to prevent destructive competition between two Olympic-related organizations in the same country in relation to the same Games.

INTERNATIONAL SPONSORSHIPS ARE BORN

The second major change was the realization that the IOC needed to give serious attention to the manner in which Olympic marketing rights could be obtained by sponsors on an international basis, an issue that had never been addressed from a conceptual perspective. International corporations would assure the IOC that they *loved* the Olympics, but that it was too difficult and too expensive to deal with the Olympic Movement. This arose from the territorial manner in which the Olympic Movement was organized. Each country or territory had an NOC, which had exclusive rights to the use of Olympic emblems in that country or territory.

As an example, The Coca-Cola Company was an international company with great interest in and a long history of continuous support of the Games, dating back to 1928. If, however, it wanted to develop a worldwide campaign for its product category in relation to both Games in the course of an Olympiad, it would have to do all of the following:

- Obtain the sponsorship rights from the OCOG of the Olympic Winter Games
- Obtain the sponsorship rights from the OCOG of the Summer Games
- Obtain the sponsorship rights from the NOC of the Winter host country
- Obtain the sponsorship rights from the NOC of the Summer host country
- Obtain, one by one, the sponsorship rights from the NOC of each country in which it proposed to activate its campaign (at the time, there were some 160 NOCs—as of August 2014, there are 206)

In the process of accomplishing the latter, Coca-Cola would be dealing with countries having greatly differing commercial sophistication, often exaggerated expectations of what the marketing rights might be worth, and the high likelihood that many NOCs would be bargaining against Coca-Cola with its competitors. Many of the markets would be too small to justify spending the time, money and effort to arrive at an agreement. Arrangements of this nature were also fraught with the competitive dangers in markets like the European Community, with its principle of free movement of goods. This meant that, if its competitor(s) could obtain rights even in the smallest, least important member state, any such competitor could flood the European market with Olympic-related packaging and other publicity bearing those marks, in order to try to blunt the Olympic advantage of Coca-Cola.

© Alaksandr Stzhalkouski | Dreamstime.com— Coca-Cola can with Sochi 2014 symbolic photo

While it was good news for the IOC and NOCs to hear that sponsors loved their Olympic involvement, it was bad news to learn that the Olympic Movement was too expensive to deal with. Having established a Commission for New Sources of Financing (which later became the Marketing Commission), and having come to the conclusion that the Olympic Movement was too dependent on a single revenue source (television) and that it needed to diversify its revenues, the observations by the potential marketing partners were particularly troubling.

CHAPTER SUMMARY

In the field of global sport marketing, the Olympic Games offer the opportunity to reach the world; opening sponsors to new markets or reaffirming old markets. Yet, despite the growth and sophistication of the Olympic brand, there are still huge challenges which face both organizers, as they try to control the messages around the brand, and sponsors as they try to navigate the levels of control on the brand. As the expenses of hosting Games grow to ever more Olympic proportions, attracting massive private funding is imperative. The high costs of sponsorship, even combined with the major legal issues, as explored in Chapters 8 and 9, that surround (and protect) the Games, is nevertheless worth the high rewards that can be achieved through the Olympic sponsorship. Unfortunately, the official Olympic sponsors may not be the only ones that reap the rewards; the ambush marketers are constantly looking for ways to get into the *ring*. On to the next section: ambush marketing.

Key Chapter Questions

1. What characterizes Olympic sponsors in the period of 1896 to 1984? Could you break down this 88-year period by different *eras*?
2. Describe in detail how the 1984 Olympic Games *changed* Olympic sponsorship forever?
3. Typically, how does private sector support differ from public sector support for an Olympic Games?
4. In your opinion, why did it take so long for international sponsorships to become part of the Olympics?
5. Research other global mega-sporting-events online (FIFA World Cup, Rugby World Cup, IAAF World Championships, etc.). How do their timelines compare to those of Olympic sponsorship? Did these events adopt similar approaches as the IOC?
6. Review the bid process for a city seeking to host the Olympic Games. How is it different today, from a sponsorship perspective, than it was in 1960?

Key Chapter Takeaways

1. Sponsorship of sport is not new. It has been around for centuries but has expanded dramatically in the past two or three decades.
2. The growth of Olympic sponsorship relied on changing market dynamics, technological change, IOC strategy, and increased financial requirements that could not all be defrayed by governments.
3. Sponsorship was slow to be adopted by the IOC due, in part, to an organizational philosophy (pre-1984) that commercialism and television should not be part of the Games.
4. International sport—IOC and IFs—has become increasingly influential in recent years. It relies on both public and private sector funding and support in most countries of the world (with the US as a notable exception).

13

Olympic Sponsorship:
1984 to 2015

As the Lake Placid and Moscow Olympic Games of 1980 came to a close, the IOC recognized the need to expand its revenue base to multiple sources beyond television. It is considered smart business sense to not be single-sourced in terms of revenue. This led to the idea of marketing, about which the IOC knew very little. With the 1984 Games hosted in Los Angeles, it was operating in the most sophisticated market in the world. The US television rights had reached the dizzying amount of US $225 million, but marketing revenues, although greater than in Moscow and Montreal, still lagged far behind those from television.

As mentioned in the previous chapter, in discussions with many of the major sponsors, the IOC had learned that those sponsors thought the Olympic "property" was

superb, but that it was just too difficult to deal with the Olympic Movement (i.e., all organizations and individuals involved in sport related to the Olympic Games). The result was that they only activated their

sponsorship rights in a few countries, since it was too time-consuming, complicated, and expensive to chase around getting agreements with most of the NOCs.

Activating the sponsorships in only a few countries meant that their competitors could blunt the impact of their sponsorships by signing up NOCs in neighboring countries. Given the structure in place and the conscious decision of Games sponsors not to activate in certain countries, it was possible for competitors of Games sponsors to be opportunistic and strategic in their own choices for sponsorship. For example, for the Los Angeles 1984 Games, Nike outfitted the USA men's basketball team as a result of its USOC sponsorship agreement, which provided visibility through the Games, yet made no financial commitment to the organizing committee. It would be inaccurate and unfair to describe this conduct as pure ambush marketing, since the markets available to them were unoccupied by the Games sponsors as a result of the latters' own choices, but it certainly provided opportunities to gain a significant Olympic profile at a much lower cost than becoming a Games sponsor. The designations used could, in addition, give the broadest possible impressions.

THE 1980s PARADIGM SHIFT

The promotional and revenue gaps around the Games were all too obvious. The question facing the IOC was how to solve the problem. It required some thinking *outside the box*. IOC leaders asked whether it might be possible to turn the territorial marketing conundrum into an advantage. It was this thinking that led to the creation of the TOP Program (acronym for The Olympic Program), which would become a best practice of global sponsorship (see Table 13.1 below for a history of the program).

The process began in exploratory discussions with a Swiss-based company, International Sports and Leisure (ISL), owned by the Dassler family which, at the time, controlled Adidas. ISL had developed a business model with respect to the FIFA World Cup, the quadrennial world championship of football, organized by FIFA, the IF for the sport of association football/soccer. The model involved an agreement negotiated between FIFA and ISL, whereby ISL would purchase all of the television and marketing rights to the World Cup from FIFA for an agreed price and ISL would, in turn, on-sell such rights to sponsors and broadcasters. The idea was based on the fact that if the price was right, FIFA would be happy, and so would ISL, which took all of the related financial and reputational risks.

The IOC, however, was not willing to sell all Olympic marketing rights to ISL. Indeed, many of the rights were not the IOC's to sell, such as those of the OCOGs and

Table 13.1. TOP Sponsorship Program History			
TOP Edition	**Participating NOCs**	**Sponsors**	**Revenues**
TOP I			
1985–1988 (Calgary, Seoul)	159	Coca-Cola Brother Federal Express Kodak Matsushita Philips Time Visa 3M	$96 million
TOP II			
1989–1992 (Albertville, Barcelona)	169	Coca-Cola Bausch & Lomb Brother Kodak Mars Matsushita Philips Ricoh Time UPS Visa 3M	$172 million
TOP III			
1993–1996 (Lillehammer, Atlanta)	197	Coca-Cola Bausch & Lomb IBM (Atlanta only) John Hancock Kodak Matsushita (Panasonic) *Sports Illustrated/Time* Visa Xerox (Atlanta) UPS	$279 million

(Continued on next two pages)

Table 13.1. TOP Sponsorship Program History *(Continued)*

TOP Edition	Participating NOCs	Sponsors	Revenues
TOP IV			
1997–2000	199	Coca-Cola	$579 million
		IBM	
		John Hancock	
		Kodak	
		McDonald's	
		Panasonic	
		Samsung	
		Sports Illustrated/Time	
		UPS	
		Visa	
		Xerox	
TOP V			
2001–2004	202	Coca-Cola	$663 million
		John Hancock	
		Kodak	
		McDonald's	
		Panasonic	
		Samsung	
		SchlumbergerSema/Atos	
		Sports Illustrated/Time	
		Swatch (Athens)	
		Visa	
		Xerox	
TOP VI			
2005–2008	205	Coca-Cola	$866 million
		Atos Origin	
		General Electric	
		Johnson & Johnson	
		Kodak	
		Lenovo	
		Manulife	
		McDonald's	
		Omega	
		Panasonic	
		Samsung	
		Visa	

(Continued on next page)

TOP Edition	Participating NOCs	Sponsors	Revenues
Table 13.1. TOP Sponsorship Program History *(Continued)*			
TOP VII			
2009–2012	205	Coca-Cola	$957 million
		Acer	
		Atos Origin	
		Dow Chemical	
		General Electric	
		McDonald's	
		Omega	
		Panasonic	
		Procter & Gamble	
		Samsung	
		Visa	
TOP VIII			
2013–2016	205	Coca-Cola	1,000 million[1]
		Atos Origin	
		Dow Chemical	
		General Electric	
		McDonald's	
		Omega	
		Panasonic	
		Procter & Gamble	
		Samsung	
		Visa	

the NOCs. Over the course of several months, however, the broad lines of a possible marketing program were developed, which borrowed some of the features of the FIFA World Cup model. Sponsorship categories having a worldwide potential were identified and matched against what might be expected from a worldwide sponsorship. The OCOGs from both the Winter and Summer Games would contribute their marketing rights (for a negotiated price), the IOC would contribute the five-ring Olympic Symbol for the purposes of permitting more generic and less country-specific emblems (for a negotiated percentage), and the NOCs would contribute their marketing rights in specified categories in exchange for negotiated amounts per category. The result would be that sponsors would have, in effect, a one-stop sponsorship shop that would eliminate the need to proceed to the extensive party-by-party negotiations.

The IOC then went to the sponsors and said, what if it could put together such a one-stop shopping package, which, for each Olympiad, would include the marketing rights to the Winter and Summer Games and all of the NOCs and, in addition, the

IOC itself, with the right to use the five rings? The reception to this suggestion from potential sponsors was overwhelmingly enthusiastic. The IOC then said, what if, in addition to a worldwide package of marketing rights, it could guarantee exclusivity within the particular product or service category, so that during the full four-year period of the Olympiad, none of the sponsor's competitors would be allowed to have any Olympic association whatsoever? One would have thought they had died and gone to heaven. In such an eventuality, the Olympic rights, which would now be worldwide, would have a huge value. The whole would be much greater than the sum of the parts.

It was relatively simple to come up with the idea and quite another to get from where the Olympic Movement was then positioned into the mode that would enable the TOP Program to become reality. It was reminiscent of the quotation attributed again to Yogi Berra, who said, "In theory there is no difference between theory and practice; in practice there is." Starting with the organizing committees, the IOC was faced with certain sponsorship arrangements already in place for the 1988 Games in Calgary and Seoul

and would have to make transitional adjustments in respect of certain of the categories.

Next were the NOCs. Of the approximately 160 NOCs that existed at the time, perhaps thirty of them had a meaningful marketing program; the others had occasional *ad hoc* sponsors or nothing whatsoever. For the latter, anything that might come from an international marketing program would be manna from heaven, incremental income, and (the program being denominated in US dollars) provide them with much-needed hard currency. Among those NOCs with their own marketing programs, there was some suspicion, since they had comfortable sources and sums of marketing revenues, and they were not certain what impact an international program might have on these revenues. The US, in particular, was dubious, since its market was well developed and there was a tradition in the US of private sector support of the Olympics and no government funding whatsoever.[2] Further, within the IOC membership, there was deep suspicion about anything smacking of marketing and a reluctance to take the lead in an unfamiliar venture. Within the program itself, it was recognized that not all marketing categories lent themselves to worldwide sponsorship. The IOC needed to define product or service categories that were essentially the same throughout the world and that were marketed by companies with a worldwide reach.

The attractiveness of the program to the OCOGs was that their sponsorships would now be worth much more than previously, when sponsors faced the incremental costs and aggravation of obtaining territorial rights.[3] In addition, the levels of the TOP sponsorships were bell-weather indicators and had the effect of driving increases in the levels of domestic sponsorships. The NOCs, provided that they did not lose existing revenues, had opportunities to grow their sponsorship base and develop new revenues. They, too, benefitted from the bell-weather effect of the TOP sponsorships. And the IOC had a new opportunity to become directly involved in marketing as part of the broadening of its own revenue base, something denied to it until that point as a result of not having its own territory. Having the IOC involved and having access to the five rings alone, instead of merely NOC and OCOG emblems, was important to sponsors, which provided additional leverage to the IOC in the discussions and in the eventual management of the program. A single worldwide logo with the combination of the sponsor logo and the five rings was much more powerful than several different logos for Winter and Summer Games and local NOC campaigns.

ISL had been engaged in efforts to design and implement the program from its inception, but until early 1985, had been unable to reach an agreement on the program operational elements and functioning within the IOC Secretariat, which had insisted on complete control and approval of every aspect, from categories to negotiations to contract approvals. This would have made it impossible for ISL to have meaningful negotiations with a potential sponsor, since ISL would have to disclose that whatever was negotiated would then have to be approved by the IOC administration, which had not participated in the negotiations. This arrangement was (not without some internal difficulties) altered so that ISL could hold itself out as the authorized agent of the Olympic parties, which removed this challenge entirely. The IOC was really not giving up something of importance by ceding that authority, since it was clear that potential worldwide sponsors would not agree to arrangements on that scale without some face-to-face contact and assurances from the principal, namely the IOC itself.

SHOW ME THE MONEY

Leaving aside the extraordinary benefits to the Olympic Movement of the publicity generated by the worldwide marketing program, the essence of the TOP Program as a marketing program meant that the question of money could not be ignored. Assuming the program was to be implemented and could thus produce revenues from worldwide sponsors, how were these revenues to be shared? These were very difficult discussions and there were many occasions on which it seemed like no consensus could be reached. The eventual outcome has been preserved to date (see Table 13.2).

Allocating half the total revenues to the OCOGs (roughly two-thirds of that percentage to the Summer Games and one-third to the Winter Games) was not particularly contentious. The Games provide the focal point for the sponsors' marketing efforts and without some obvious connection with the Games, sponsors would have had considerably less (if any) interest. The two-to-one ratio reflected the relative size and expenses of the Summer and Winter Games, with some minor flexibility where the market sizes in the host countries justified changes from the general principle. The importance of the

Table 13.2. Distribution of Revenue	
OCOGs (Summer & Winter)	50%
IOC	10%
USOC	20%
All other NOCs	20%

IOC and its five-ring symbol accounted for the size of its share and a 40% total for the NOCs (which had no direct connection with the Games) was not unreasonable. Far more difficult was achieving agreement among the NOCs on the allocation to the USOC of a share that equaled the rest of the NOCs combined.

The brutal fact, however, was that TOP was a marketing program and that the value of each territory was a reflection of the interest of the sponsors in that marketing territory. This had nothing to do with the "Olympic" importance of a country and the performance of its athletes on the field of play, or of its size and population. It took months of negotiations to achieve that understanding—that even though the Soviet Union (as it was known at that time) and Hungary produced disproportionate shares of Olympic medals, or that China was the largest populated country in the world, their commercial markets (also at that time) were of relatively limited interest to worldwide sponsors. This point is very important to emphasize to those working in sport, as it illustrates that these decisions are business based and not sport based.

Another hard fact was that, without access to the US market, sponsors had almost no interest in a worldwide marketing program. So, without the participation of the USOC, the program would have been stillborn. All of this reality notwithstanding, there remains enormous resentment regarding this element of revenue distribution and there have been concerted efforts to revisit it, especially with the recent extraordinary developments in markets such as the BRIC countries (Brazil, Russia, India, and China) and others, all stoutly resisted by the USOC, until a new agreement was reached with the IOC in 2013.[4]

TOP SPONSORSHIP PROGRAM OPERATIONS AND CHALLENGES

Once the overall revenue percentages were fixed, the key to contractual delivery of the TOP Program was determining the categories of sponsorship, making sure that the NOCs were committed for the identified categories, and negotiating the price of the sponsorships with the sponsors. The direction of the program rested with a Marketing Coordination Meeting (MCM), a committee composed of representatives of the IOC, NOCs, OCOGs, sponsors and the program administrator, ISL.

The MCM was funded from within the program to cover the costs of administering it. Its role was overall management, including decisions on categories to be offered, likely sponsor candidates, pricing levels per category, presentation strategies, managing sponsor expectations, sponsor support, hospitality initiatives, ticketing policies, sponsor servicing, ambush and parasite marketing responses, marketing research and communications messaging, such as designations to be granted and permitted advertising statements. Its management goal was to do whatever was possible to add value to the sponsorships.

It required time and a good deal of work to cause the Olympic parties to understand that they were receiving marketing funds, not charitable donations. It was a significant step forward to move from being considered as a charity, competing with many other socially desirable causes, such as cancer research or hospitals, for a portion of a necessarily limited corporate budget, to dealing with the marketing executives of those same companies. Their budgets, unlike the charitable giving activities, depended on the value of the program to the profit-making objectives of the business. If value could be demonstrated, there was essentially no limit to the available funding where return on investment was the governing principle. So, to get value, the IOC had to be certain that it delivered value, which became the focus of its efforts with the marketing partners.

The initial choice of sponsors and sponsorship categories was based on identifying companies with a global reach and product or service categories that were more or less the same in all markets. Nor was there a great deal of nuance in the early choice of categories. Initial categories were very limited, such as film, credit cards, soft drinks, optical, audiovisual, fast food, computers, and wireless communication. Over the years, there has been considerable *category creep* and increasing overlap, particularly with the significant development of digital and computer technologies, necessitating careful designation of the real *core* element of the sponsorship. Otherwise, for example, the computer category would soon have been practically all-consuming. In the meantime, the soft drinks category morphed into non-alcoholic beverages and credit cards into payment systems. None of the original categories has remained the same.

NOC negotiations were essentially internal and conducted one by one, without disclosing the amount paid to another NOC in discussions with any NOC. Reductions in the category-wide prices of sponsorship were negotiated in the event that one or more NOCs elected not to participate in the program, based mainly on the perceived market value of the *missing* territories. As noted earlier, the *Olympic* importance (e.g., the number of athletes participating or medals won) of a missing territory was essentially irrelevant. What mattered was the marketing attractiveness of the market. Thus, when the program first began, it would have been far more serious had Korea not participated than had China not participated. In recent years, that dynamic has changed drastically as the Chinese market has expanded beyond any expectations at the time, as have those of several other important countries.

One of ISL's essential roles was to conduct the one-on-one negotiations with the NOCs, to agree on the categories they would release to the program and, in effect, to *buy* those categories from the NOCs, thus providing the NOCs (other than the USOC, which had its percentage share of the overall program) with a guarantee of the revenues they would receive. These guarantees were provided by ISL itself, not the IOC or the TOP Program, so ISL assumed considerable financial risk. While it did not matter too much to ISL if the eventual TOP agreement in a particular category did not produce enough to meet the total payments agreed per category, it nevertheless had to be sure that the aggregate program revenues offset the guarantees it provided. The program managers developed a system of reserves to help mitigate the risks. ISL itself was paid by way of commission on the program revenues.

Many of the TOP sponsors, such as Coca-Cola, Kodak, and Visa, were acknowledged as global businesses, which had been what was intended. In addition, however, others in the early days were hoping to become global and wanted to be included in a worldwide marketing program to establish their global activity, or at least their global potential. Examples of these were Brother Industries, Ricoh, and later, John Hancock. Some of the sponsors adapted to changing conditions and technologies, whereas others did not. When the TOP Program first began, for example, the Eastman Kodak Company, by far the dominant company in the field of photographic images, was, essentially, a chemical company, making the key ingredient in the photographic business, namely film. It did not seem to appreciate the advancing technological tsunami—digitization—that would completely change photography and cameras, until it was too late to recover. Now Kodak is little more than a case study of a failed market analysis, or perhaps a failure to perform an effective market analysis. Xerox had to reinvent itself, when the mere copying of documents proved to be an inadequate business model.

The computer category was a demonstration of a fundamental misunderstanding on the IOC's part (as well as on the part of IBM, the computer sponsor) regarding the ever-increasing pace of development in computing technology. The IOC had what proved to be a rather naïve idea that, once Games software had been developed, it could "unplug" that system from the Games, once they were completed, put it in a virtual suitcase, and plug it in at the site of the next Games. No one, apparently including IBM, had conceived of a pace of technological development that would make systems obsolete almost by the time they were installed, and certainly within a maximum of 18 months. In addition to that collective misjudgment, the IOC had also failed to anticipate that IBM would insist on an *IBM* solution for every IT requirement, even when the IBM solution was not as good as someone else's solution, or was much more expensive. The escalating IT costs soon began to amount to more than a third of total Games costs, which was unsupportable and caused the IOC not to renew the sponsorship. This led to a search for a systems integrator sponsor, which could become, in effect, a general contractor for IT solutions, choosing the best and least expensive, and then ensuring that the various systems could *talk* to each other.

MS-DOS version 1.25
Copyright 1981,82 Computer, Inc.

Command v. 1.1
Current date is Tue 1-01-1980
Enter new date:
Current time is 1:01:56.20
Enter new time:

A:

© Fabriciorauen | Dreamstime.com—IBM PC Operating System Photo

KEY MARKETING LEARNING

Technology and competition will always change faster than you think.

Another interesting miscalculation, both on the part of the TOP Program and on the part of the potential sponsor, occurred in the credit card category. Within the TOP Program, it had been assumed that this new idea for worldwide Olympic marketing would have been a natural fit with American Express and therefore made that company its first call (after Coca-Cola, which had been "in" from the start). The presentation touched on all the buttons that should have excited a potential sponsor: youth, universality, credit card use, sport, promotion, aspiration, achievement, indeed just about everything . . . however, to everyone's profound shock, it was summarily rejected—American Express said it was not interested.

The American Express rejection was particularly unsettling, not only because the IOC and ISL instincts had proven to have been so wrong, but also because if it became known that such a market leader had turned down the TOP Program, this would likely have a severe dampening impact on other companies and other categories. So, a quick response was required. Visa was the next most obvious choice, but it was a far more complex organization than American Express, since it consisted of thousands of different banks. Fortunately, its management, led by Visa US, liked the program and liked the idea of category leadership that association with the Olympics would bring, quickly steered the idea though the internal continental and regional organizations and the IOC was able, in a remarkably short time following the American Express rejection, to announce that Visa was the TOP sponsor in the credit card category.

Interestingly, American Express was enraged at this outcome. The Olympic parties were never certain whether its strategy had been to refuse a sponsorship, rather than to make a counteroffer, intending to negotiate a lower price, and thus force the Olympic parties to come crawling back to American Express from a position of weakness, since in its corporate view, there was no viable alternative, or whether it simply realized, once a major competitor took it up, that it had made a colossal misjudgment. The outcomes were interesting: Visa has enjoyed an extremely successful sponsorship, while no one in the American Express organization who played any part in the Olympic sponsorship refusal was still employed by the organization three years later. As if to confirm its error, American Express embarked on regular ambush programs, described in detail in upcoming chapters in this book.

The revolution in wireless communications has had a major impact on Olympic sponsorship, beginning from the early days of the TOP Program, when mobile phones were primitive and cumbersome, to the immensely sophisticated handheld devices provided by the current TOP sponsor incumbent, Samsung. These devices are not merely powerful phones, but complex platforms for communications of every type, including reception of the television signals of the Games, allowing their users to experience the Games in real time, with full audio visual applications and integrated informational backup. There can be little doubt that wireless communication will have significant ongoing impact on the way the Games are brought to Olympic audiences and this in turn will undoubtedly affect the way the Games are marketed and, perhaps, financed.

Relations with the TOP sponsors were generally quite satisfactory. Everyone was excited about the new marketing initiatives that were developing. From the TOP program administrative perspective, the main challenge was to ensure that sufficiently senior sponsor representatives attended the MCM, bringing a higher level of appreciation for international marketing strategies. It was important to prevent the MCM from getting bogged down in the minutia of delivering the program at the operational level by sponsor personnel concerned only at that level. The only low point in the sponsor relationships arose from the Salt Lake City bidding scandal in late 1998 and the first half of 1999. There was justifiable concern on the part of some sponsors that the value of their investment could be adversely affected by the fallout from the scandal and the IOC representatives were very much on the defensive for several months. They had to assure all of the sponsors (as well as broadcasters) that they would deal with the problems arising from the scandal. The data that they collected in the meantime showed, however, that public support for the Games and the Olympic athletes remained as strong as ever, despite the disapproval of the conduct of a few of the IOC members, so the marketing crisis passed, even though the IOC had important residual effects from a governance perspective. Comprehensive reforms were put in place by the end of 1999, with the result that the IOC now implements international best practices in its self-governance.

OPERATIONAL CHANGES

As with any marketing program, it is essential to maintain a high degree of enthusiasm, energy, focus, and excitement. Following the death of Horst Dassler in 1987, the focus and enthusiasm of ISL gradually began to diminish, and many of its key staff either left ISL or were reassigned. This led to an agreement to part ways with ISL in 1995. While this happened and may sound simple, the IOC learned that it is not always easy to extract a large organization like the IOC from a long-term relationship, especially one that involves existing contracts relating to events that will occur several years in the future. The program then engaged a new team of young marketing professionals in Meridian Management, a company that was largely funded by the IOC, but in which the major economic benefits accrued to the professional shareholders.

This change gave the program a new lease on life and during the first years of Meridian's stewardship, the IOC undertook its first-ever brand audit of the Olympic brand. Although it thought then that it understood what the Olympic brand was, it had never conducted an independent study to see whether the consuming public shared a similar assessment of the Olympic values. The results were very reassuring, both as to the core values of the brand and as to the willingness of consumers to accept linking those values with commercial sponsors, provided that the sponsors made it clear that they were helping to stage the Games or helping athletes train for and get to the Games.

In more recent years, the IOC has decided to take the entire TOP Program in-house and to eliminate any buffer, such as an outside agency, even one as close to the IOC as Meridian Management had been, between it and its sponsors. There are pros and cons implicit in such a decision, the former being that the IOC may save money and does not have filtered communication with its sponsors, and the latter that the aggravation of dealing with the details of the program and the often contentious negotiations with the NOCs on revenue shares can no longer be consigned to the agency.

HELP YOUR PARTNERS TO BE SUCCESSFUL

One of the main keys to the success of Olympic marketing has been the recognition by the IOC that it must assist sponsors in their activation of the marketing rights that they acquire through the sponsorship. When the TOP Program first became a reality, sponsors seemed to know, intuitively, that they had acquired valuable rights. What they did not know, however, was how to activate those rights in a manner that produced the marketing outcomes for which they had hoped. In large measure, this was because they did not know or did not understand exactly what it was that they had bought and how to use whatever it was that they had bought. (Cynics say that a sponsorship is a relationship that involves paying a fee for the right to spend even more money.)

The IOC's role, once it recognized the problem, was to help demonstrate not only what the sponsors had acquired, but also how to use it to their benefit. It worked with them to identify the values important to their businesses and then to relate them to the Olympic values.

Bringing that combination to life was the challenge, but once the sponsors understood the combination of values, it was far easier to translate the concepts into their own integrated marketing communications. Some of the Olympic-related copy, television commercials, and photographic materials produced in support of Olympic sponsorships have been quite remarkable and

> **KEY MARKETING LEARNING**
>
> A marketing property needs to fully support and facilitate the activation efforts of its sponsor(s).

immensely creative. The better the activation, the better the marketing outcomes, and the better the marketing outcomes, the more valuable the rights become. It is a great example of why an organization that seeks sponsorships should become deeply involved in making certain that its customers are successful. It creates the proverbial win-win scenario. The IOC also made certain that it did not try to squeeze the last drop of financial blood from any sponsor. It was far better for the IOC to have sponsors realize what a fine bargain they had negotiated, since it made them more likely to renew for subsequent iterations of the TOP Program. The success of their sponsorships also made it more likely that they would renew. Success is a reinforcing phenomenon. Finally, the *in terrorem* scenario was that if they did not renew, there was a risk that a competitor might step into their place and reap the same marketing rewards.

SPONSORSHIP EVALUATION

Another matter that required careful attention was the measurement of results. The IOC had achieved one objective, namely that Olympic support was no longer merely part of a limited charitable donation or corporate social responsibility portfolio. Marketing, on the other hand, was virtually limitless, provided an acceptable return on investment could be demonstrated. Results matter—feeling good about a relationship does not demonstrate anything; empirical support is needed, particularly when the investments are of the magnitude of the TOP sponsorship program.

Thus, measuring the impact of the sponsorships became particularly important and the IOC became a genuine partner with its sponsors, to ensure that it shared all infor-

mation of this nature. There was nothing to
be gained from inaccurate data and it made
certain that data regarding outcomes,
whether better or worse than hoped, were
made available to sponsors. All that said,

KEY MARKETING LEARNING
A relationship based on common objectives, trust, and confidence in each other is vital to a successful partnership.

however, what really makes a sponsorship *work* is the relationship of trust and confidence that is built through the sharing of common objectives. The IOC wanted the relationship to be successful, which could only happen if it did everything possible to make the sponsor successful.

THE CATS (IFs) WHO REFUSED TO MARCH

As part of attempting to make the TOP Program as universal as possible within the Olympic family, the IOC tried, without success, to attract the IFs to become part of the TOP Program, especially when they launched general complaints about how the NOCs were being "preferred." The fundamental weakness of their complaint was that the IFs were unwilling to provide any marketing rights to the program, whereas the NOCs, the IOC, and the OCOGs did. No one was willing to subsidize the IFs, who not only did not contribute, but also, in several sports, actively attempted to ambush TOP and other sponsors at the time of the Games. It was a somewhat backhanded way of demonstrating the marketing power of the Olympics, since the IF sponsors wanted the Olympic association (without paying for it) as much as their regular association with the IFs. As a result, the IOC has taken steps to amend the Olympic Charter to prevent nonsponsor identification during the Games, particularly on the field of play.

Looked at in retrospect, it would have been extremely difficult to deliver on any sponsorship commitments on behalf of the IFs, since they operate for three years and eleven months out of every four years solely concerned with their own programming, the overwhelming majority of which is not related to the Olympic Games. In retrospect, the failure to have reached an agreement with them may well have been a blessing in disguise.

SOME PROBLEMS ARISING FROM SPONSORSHIP SUCCESS

One of the noncommercial outcomes of the enormous success of the Olympic Games is that people and organizations often attempt to hijack the Games to advance their own agendas. Governments have done so in the past through boycotts targeted at host or participating countries and, from the other perspective, as in the case of the Berlin Games in 1936, to promote the Nazi regime and its programs. Self-promotion is a matter of degree, since every host country wants to be perceived in the best possible light, but there can be no doubt that Berlin exceeded even a chauvinistic limit. Boycotts (or the threat of boycotts) became a tool of choice for a number of years, including Tokyo in 1964 (threat), Mexico in 1968 (threat), Munich in 1972 (threat), Montreal in 1976 (actual), Moscow in 1980 (actual), Los Angeles in 1984 (actual), and Seoul in 1988 (actual, but relatively minor). After that, governments seemed to realize that boycotts

were not only unsuccessful political actions, but also that they harmed their own citizens more than the target country.

Other organizations also try to use the Games to further their own interests. Greenpeace has not hesitated to attack the Olympics, as have activists in many other fields. Coca-Cola and McDonald's have been attacked in the context of their Olympic sponsorship positions, and the IOC has been included in the attacks, principally by those concerned with sedentary lifestyles and bad eating habits. Dow Chemical was attacked in respect of an accident involving one of its current subsidiaries Union Carbide, long before its acquisition by Dow Chemical, that had caused deaths and environmental damage. Supporters of Tibet attacked runners in the 2008 Olympic Torch Relay prior to the Beijing Games. A full list of such examples would be too long to include in a work of this nature. The marketing point to be drawn from such actions, however, is that there is always an element of risk to be assessed when choosing both sponsors and host countries.

CHAPTER SUMMARY

The TOP Program is currently in its seventh iteration and many of the arrangements for subsequent editions of the program are already in place, up to, including, and beyond the 2020 Games (awarded to Tokyo in September 2013). The concept and design of the program are still sound, although the IOC undertakes a regular assessment of possible alternative programs, in order to test the relative values of the TOP Program in comparison with other formats. Some of the early sponsors have dropped out, as market conditions and their own businesses have changed. Others have changed their marketing focus from sport and the Olympics, but new sponsors have been found to replace them.

The preference within the program was always to maintain as many of the core sponsors as possible and to get the commitment to Olympic sponsorship absorbed into their corporate DNA, rather than to have sponsors with a short-term strategic involvement arising from, for example, the location of a specific Olympic Games. Maintaining excitement is always crucial, both within the Olympic Movement and the sponsor group. It is essential to avoid situations in which sponsors are not involved as a result of their positive commitment to the Olympics, but simply to occupy the sponsor position in order to prevent their competitors from gaining a foothold. Whenever that occurs, the activation and energy levels are correspondingly lower and the Olympic Movement loses the additional "lift" that comes from energetic sponsor promotion. In any program of this nature, the rights-granting parties need to be particularly aware of category creep, in which the categories of TOP sponsors become too broad and have a limiting impact on the ability to raise sponsorship revenues from other categories, now swallowed up in the TOP category, but never used by the TOP sponsors. And, finally, there has been a tendency to drift away from the view that worldwide exclusivity in a category is a huge aspect of value, commanding a premium, into a sponsor attitude that, instead, this feature should entitle them to some sort of volume discount.

As the 1980s drove the IOC to become directly involved in marketing to increase its revenue, sponsors recognized the value of having access to the five rings, rather than being limited to the NOC and OCOG emblems. The creation of a single worldwide logo used in combination with sponsor logo and the five rings proved to be a powerful draw. As with any marketing program, it is essential to maintain a high degree of enthusiasm, energy, focus, and excitement. For marketers, the appeal of the Olympics is still great, yet demands creating and maintaining enthusiasm leading up to the Games and beyond.

Key Chapter Questions

1. You are the marketing manager of a high-tech interactive company. Your president has asked you to prepare a two-page memorandum on how an Olympic sponsorship might be beneficial to the company. Draft your reply.
2. The Board of Directors of your company has decided that it will become an Olympic sponsor. You have been requested to design the marketing program. What are the elements that you should identify and how would you deal with them?
3. The President of the IOC calls you to say that he needs an independent assessment of the Olympic brand. Prepare the four-page market analysis you would send him.
4. Find five particularly effective Olympic commercial messages (print, audio, or video) used by TOP sponsors and describe why they are effective.
5. If you were the IOC Brand Manager, what recommendations would you make to maintain and strengthen the Olympic brand?

Key Chapter Takeaways

1. The better the activation, the better the marketing outcomes, and the better the marketing outcomes, the more valuable the rights become.
2. A sponsored organization/property needs to fully support and allow the activation efforts of its sponsor(s).
3. The creation of the single logo for both Winter and Summer Games was an important part of the IOC's movement toward direct involvement in marketing initiatives.

Part III

Ambush Marketing

14

Introducing
Ambush Marketing

As introduced in the chapters of Part II, the success of the TOP program and the value it provides to its sponsors led those sponsors' competitors to explore ways to mitigate the benefits derived from the program by the TOP sponsors.

SUCCESS HAS ITS COSTS

Despite the many challenges of inventing and implementing a new marketing concept, the IOC's TOP Sponsorship Program has been extremely successful and the value of the Olympic brand has increased to a huge degree. As mentioned in the previous chapter, the TOP program is now in its seventh iteration, in essentially the same format as originally presented. This success has, however, not gone unnoticed, especially by the competitors of TOP sponsors, who can see the impact of the Olympic sponsorships.

Faced with the evident success enjoyed by their competitors activating their official Olympic sponsorships, there are several courses of conduct available to non-Olympic sponsors in these circumstances. The nonsponsor can pursue its own marketing strategy, independent of what the Olympic sponsor has chosen to do with its Olympic involvement and trust that its own strategy will be more effective than the Olympic-related strategy of its competitor. Or, it can recognize that the Olympic sponsor has gained a competitive advantage that increases awareness and market share that its own strategy may not neutralize and attempt, instead, to reduce the level of that advantage. Action in that regard can take many forms. Opinion will likely be divided as to the ethical aspects (and also the legality) of certain actions.

AMBUSH MARKETING

The classic ambush marketing program is designed to be sprung on one's competitor very close to the officially sponsored event and at a time when promotion of the relationship will be at its highest. As the term suggests, the ambush strategy is kept secret until it is launched, with the objective of attempting to create as much of a link (or association) as possible with the event being sponsored, so that the consuming public

will be misled, or at least confused, as to the identity of the real sponsor, thereby reducing the sponsorship's effectiveness.

If the ambush is timed properly, the targeted official sponsor may not have enough time to adjust its own promotions to identify the ambush and to clarify its own position as the official sponsor in the minds of the consuming public. Depending upon the sophistication of the ambush program, key visual and word elements are typically used, such as photos of athletes, competitions, stadia, place names, and so forth, all designed to suggest or imply a connection between the ambusher and its products or services and the sponsored event. Nike Football's June 2014 "The Last Game" commercial was a mash up of football and cartoon characters that was viewed almost 55 million times in the first 10 days of its launch. The themes, feel, and timing of the ad were obviously tied to the 2014 World Cup, yet, as Nike was not an official sponsor, it made no specific World Cup references: is this ambush excellence? Ambushers generally try to avoid clearly false statements (such as a claim that they are, in fact, sponsors), but play in the grey and ambiguous areas of both language and illustration. By doing so, the ambusher hopes to diminish the known "lift" that its competitor, as official sponsor, may have achieved in the past or is expected to gain in its current campaign and, in the process, possibly to generate some Olympic lift of its own. The primary objective of an ambush tends, however, to be negative, in the sense that it is a direct attack against the particular competitor, rather than a positive promotion of the ambusher itself.

PARASITE OLYMPIC MARKETING

Parasite Olympic marketing, a derivative of ambush marketing, is designed to feed off the goodwill of the Olympics without contributing in any way to their promotion or the costs of staging them. This form of marketing is not necessarily directed at a competitor or an Olympic sponsor, despite being an effort to feed off the Olympic platform. It may occur even in categories that are not the subject of official Olympic sponsorships. Typical of such programs are non-Olympic sponsor companies that choose to support an individual Olympic athlete or perhaps a national team, especially (although not necessarily) in the host country, which costs far less than becoming a sponsor of an OCOG, but provides opportunities to advertise their association with and support of the athlete and/or team. The closer the connection made with the athlete's Olympic performance or the team's Olympic aspirations, the greater the opportunity for the company to draw from the goodwill accruing to those seen to be supporting the Games and the OCOG. There are many examples of this form of marketing activity, including the personal sponsorship of Roger Federer by Rolex. This was never a sponsorship directed primarily at Swiss Timing's Omega Olympic sponsorship, but when the promotions are run during an Olympic period, if Federer is participating in the Games, confusion as to Rolex's Olympic role can be created. Other examples include the clothing sponsors of certain athletes, who purport to require the athlete to wear the sponsored clothing at all times, even including the Olympic Games, as opposed to the athletes wearing the official team uniforms. The Canadian ice hockey federation has attempted to impose its logo on the competitive uniform of the Canadian Olympic team, followed by refusal to permit the use of photographs taken even during the Olympic Games without its permission and, of course, the payment of fees for such use.

Further examples might include statements such as "XYZ Company supports the dreams of Joe Smith for success in Rio de Janeiro in 2016" or "To win in Sochi in 2014 requires dedication, teamwork, and split-second timing. We at XYZ Company are proud to support Canada's bobsled team." The word "Olympic" is carefully not used, but any reasonably well-informed consumer will know exactly what event is contemplated. The Disney organization, which was definitely not an Olympic sponsor, had a program during the 1988 Olympic Games in Seoul, in which it had brief sound bites from Olympians, who would dutifully say, when asked what they were going to do now that they had won gold at the Games, that they were going to Disneyland or Disney World.

RESPONDING TO AMBUSH
AND PARASITE MARKETING EFFORTS

In many respects, the activities described validate the success of the Olympic marketing program, since, if that program were not successful, no one would bother to ambush it or try to suck value from it. The challenge thus created, however, is that the IOC must protect the rights it has granted to its own and, by extension, OCOG and NOC sponsors, which have paid significant amounts to obtain Olympic-related rights on the basis, generally, that they are exclusive. The sponsors, quite naturally, expect that the grantor of the rights (i.e., the IOC) will stand behind and protect the rights that have been granted.

Extreme cases are normally easy to detect and to resolve. Indeed, the unauthorized use of the five-ring symbol and use of the word *Olympic* along with outright false claims can usually be identified and stopped quite easily. Most OCOGs can make arrangements for expedited court hearings, if necessary, and most developed countries have mechanisms to bring obvious cases before the courts, when required. Even the threat of legal proceedings, as a matter of last resort, will normally attract serious attention from the party that might be implicated, especially if it is clear that such proceedings will, in fact, be resorted to and diligently pursued. The vast majority of infringement cases tend to be genuine mistakes, arising from a lack of understanding of the legal protections surrounding the Olympic marks and designations. Faced with confrontation, those involved will normally cease the conduct giving rise to it.

Other ambush or parasite efforts, however, especially deliberate programs, may be subtler and requests to the unauthorized users to stop the activity may not be effective. This requires development of an escalating series of responses, plus the all-important exercise of good judgment. Because the circumstances of each case may vary, the following is a nonexhaustive list of possible responses:

- Cease-and-desist letter from the granting organization, explaining that the action contravenes copyright or trademarks
- Follow-up personal contact with the infringer
- Cease-and-desist letter from legal counsel: Following the rejection by American Express of TOP sponsorship opportunity, American Express embarked on a series of ambush activities. It did not respond to a cease-and-desist letter and its management was unrepentant regarding any such programs. Legal action was successfully taken by the 1992 Albertville organizing committee, assisted by the IOC.
- Contact with legal counsel representing the infringer to try to settle the matter
- Press conference outlining the infringement and efforts to resolve the dispute and clarification that the infringer is not a sponsor and is not helping to organize the Games: In the context of the 1996 Games in Atlanta, the IOC advised American Express that, at the first sign of any ambush of the Olympic sponsor (Visa) by it, the IOC would call a press conference, in Atlanta, would have the US women's gymnastics team on hand to lament the fact that American Express was not helping the Games or them, and, as a finale, the Chairman of the IOC Marketing

Commission would take an (expired) American Express card from his wallet, state that he was no longer willing to do business with a company that acted in such a manner, and cut the card in half. American Express was advised that the media would be briefed in advance and that the photo that would go around the world would be the cutting of

© Flynt | Dreamstime.com—Cutting A Credit Card Photo

the card. American Express eventually acknowledged that it had, indeed, been given the first opportunity to be a TOP sponsor and that it had rejected that opportunity. It agreed that it would stop the ambush program. To give credit where credit is due, it did exactly what it promised and the ambushes stopped.

INSTITUTION OF EXPEDITED LEGAL PROCEEDINGS

Where infringements take the form of the visual presentation of material, such as posters or advertisements appearing in locations controlled by the IOC or an OCOG, the offending materials can simply be removed and, if necessary, the persons involved may be escorted from the premises. Removal of offending materials has been a common occurrence at Olympic Games and there is a regular sweeping of Olympic venues by the IOC and the OCOGs to ensure that such material is confiscated.

Responses to these infringements may include examination of the clothing and uniforms of athletes to be certain that there is no nonconforming use of commercial or national messages. There were several cases of

© fstockfoto | Dreamstime.com—2008 Olympic Soccer Tournament Photo

this nature in Beijing in 2008, especially by football teams from Argentina and Brazil, which insisted on using their national federation uniforms instead of the Olympic uniforms. One of the cases was resolved in favor of the IOC position only after the intervention of the president of the country. Careful definition of those venues under the control, for example, of OCOGs can go a long way to reducing the opportunities for ambush or parasite activities. The IOC has attempted to reduce some of the predictable problems of this nature by amending the Olympic Charter to require the use of NOC-approved clothing and equipment, to prohibit the use of any "messaging" other than manufacturers' trademarks (including strict limitation of the size of even the manufacturers' marks), and to provide general directions and authority to NOCs regarding team uniforms.[1]

On the other hand, the IOC is careful not to allow its marketing programs to be seen to interfere with equipment or competition clothing that might have an impact on the sport performance of Olympic athletes. If an athlete has always used, for example, Adidas spikes in athletics and the IOC (or organizing committee) sponsor happens to be Nike, neither would force the athlete to wear Nike spikes during the Olympic Games. Other aspects of competitive equipment and clothing may fall within the rules of international federations, as technical or safety considerations that apply to all competitors. But performance is not affected by the parade or podium clothing of a national team sponsor, whether or not a different sponsor happens to have clothing agreements with individual athletes or teams. The IOC protects the NOC in such circumstances. It is unlikely (but not impossible) that any athlete sponsor would attempt to prevent an athlete from competing in the Olympic Games on such grounds.

Prohibited commercial material within Olympic venues extends not just to ambushers, but also even to the official sponsors, since it has been a fundamental position of the IOC that Olympic venues should be *clean*—free from all such commercial materials. The IOC has also adopted the policy that Olympic-based advertising by its sponsors should not be "comparative" advertising, which, in essence, attacks or denigrates competitors of the sponsor. The IOC supports the products or services of its sponsors, but does not want to be seen as associated with or supportive of attacks against other companies or their products or services. An example of such advertising might be: "When you come to the Olympics, be sure to bring your Visa card, because the Olympics don't take American Express." This was, initially, a difficult concept for sponsors to accept, since all other sports events in which they acted as sponsors allowed such identification. In time, however, they understood that one of the special and differentiating features of the Olympic Games was that they were not occasions for attacking their competitors, merely that they were for promoting their own goods and services in the unique ambiance of the Games.

HOW MUCH IS TOO MUCH?

Marketing is an empirical exercise. There are certain common disciplines that apply to any marketing initiative, without which success is unlikely. Marketing is also highly competitive: The objective is to influence choice in the marketplace, which ultimately involves convincing consumers to choose one product or service (the marketer's) from among many other possibilities (those of its competitors). Left to their own devices, most marketers would be quite content to have their competitors disappear from the face of the earth, on their own account or with the help of successful efforts by the marketers. There are, however, legal and other restrictions regarding anticompetitive activities and a general philosophy in most countries with developed markets that healthy competition leads to better goods and services and lower prices for consumers. In fact, this is accepted economic theory that competition is good for an economy and a society. This view, of course, does not, however, diminish the desire for greater market share and profits, so competition remains fierce.

Within the Olympic field, sponsors often purport to take the extreme view that no competitor in their particular sponsorship category should be entitled to have any sports-related (as opposed to Olympic) marketing program that might compete with their own. Such demands made on the IOC and OCOGs may be quite unreasonable and require careful management by Olympic parties. Both sponsors and OCOGs need to develop an understanding of exactly what rights have been granted, what constitutes infringement of those rights, what the limits of reasonable free speech are, and what the appropriate remedies are—or, perhaps more accurately, what solutions can be envisaged—in particular circumstances. These, too, are empirical judgments for which no formulaic cookie-cutter answers can be provided.

Case Study 14.1

The Vancouver Winter Olympics in 2010

Recent Olympic experience with sponsorship and ambush marketing can be found in relation to the 2010 Olympic Winter Games in Vancouver.[2] The OCOG for these Games was generally known by its acronym, VANOC. Public sector funding sources for VANOC included the governments of Canada, British Columbia, Vancouver, and Whistler.[3] Funding obligations and the permissible application of the public funds were defined in a formal multiparty agreement. The principal private sector funding sources included television and other broadcasting, webcasting or interactive rights, sponsorships (TOP Program and domestic), licensing arrangements, and ticket sales.

Leaving aside broadcast rights granted, which can be subject to their own forms of ambush activities, all the other revenue sources could be subjected to ambush or parasite marketing depending on the non-sponsor(s) involved. Given that the special nature of Olympic marketing combines both the event and the ability to use Olympic-related designations and marks, both are important revenue generation considerations. For example, the 2010 Vancouver Games had both community and commercial aspects where rights were granted for commercial aspects (e.g., Rona as the official home improvement partner of VANOC)

or community purposes (e.g., Tourism Vancouver's "Keeping the Flame Alive: Experiencing the Games in Vancouver" campaign), which supplemented the general ability of the public to refer to the Games as a matter of public notoriety and fact.

From an Olympic marketing perspective, however, a key consideration is the protection of commercial rights granted by the IOC. In the case of the Vancouver 2010 Games, the IOC and VANOC both granted commercial rights to sponsors and were responsible for the management of reasonable commercial expectations by the sponsors, the Olympic parties, and the public at large. Since it is always easier to avoid a problem than to have to solve it, efforts to prevent infringements were viewed as good investments. Similarly, the expectations of sponsors can be managed:

- a careful definition of the rights granted;
- agreement in advance as to responsibilities for identifying possible infringements;
- the degree to which the rights-granting parties will themselves undertake remedial action (as opposed, for example, to merely supporting the party to which the rights were granted);
- actions that the parties may agree upon in specified circumstances;

(Continued on next page)

Case Study 14.1 *(continued)*

- financial responsibilities of each party regarding the costs of remedying infringements, or the failure to *deliver* the full package of rights granted; and
- publicizing criteria regularly for public and private sponsorship stakeholders to promote wide understanding of both commercial and community expectations.

Specific to the 2010 Vancouver Games, knowing that it would certainly be faced with possible infringements, VANOC developed a matrix that enabled it to assess the degree of concern that the conduct should trigger, namely whether it would be a matter of low concern, high concern, or borderline. The following examples are based on an article published in *Journal of Sponsorship*, November 2008 (vol. 2, no. 1) by Bill Cooper, then VANOC's Director of Commercial Rights, to whom the authors are also indebted for provision of examples and strategic considerations within VANOC.

XYZ Hotels Welcome You to Vancouver, Host City of the 2010 Winter Games. We offer hotels close to every Olympic venue. Reserve Now.

or, a sign posted on the door of ABC Pub

Come enjoy a drink while you watch the 2010 Olympic Winter Games.

The matrix developed by VANOC to assist it in determining its appropriate level of concern had six criteria including an assessment of whether the mark was factually accurate, relevant, commercially neutral, unduly prominent, used Olympic visuals, or provided unauthorized association. By using the six criteria, the level of concern over the two Cooper examples can be assessed in Table 14.1.

Table 14.1. Assessing Concern Over Use of Olympic Marks

Criteria	Descriptions	Level of concern relevant to example 1: *XYZ Hotels Welcome You to Vancouver, Host City of the 2010 Winter Games. We offer hotels close to every Olympic venue*	Level of concern relevant to example 2: *ABC Pub Sign Come enjoy a drink while you watch the 2010 Olympic Winter Games*
Factually accurate	marks must be factually and accurately used without distortion of modification	High	High
Relevant use	usage of marks must be factually relevant to a larger initiative/creative/storyline and not an overtly promotional manner to create or contribute to unauthorized association	High	Low
Commercially neutral use	marks must be used in an environment clean of third-party logos or company names	High	Low
Undue prominence	mark usage should not be unduly prominent within overall message and should be within an editorially relevant manner within a larger story	High	Medium
Use of Olympic visuals	usage of such marks is the exclusive right of Olympic rights holders, or those with noncommercial license agreements	High	High
Unauthorized association	no association created between third party and the Olympic brand	High	Medium

(Continued on next page)

Case Study 14.1 *(continued)*

Assessing the two messages sourced from Bill Cooper's article against this matrix shows clearly that the hotel advertisement creates a high degree of concern, while the pub sign is of less concern. In the hotel example, an association between the brand name and the Games is implied, while the pub is showcasing the opportunity to watch the Games. Common sense judgment must be exercised in certain cases that may well be flagrant violations of Olympic rights, but that have limited commercial downside and in which the unauthorized users are hoping to become popular martyrs, self-portrayed as the "little guys" who take on the Olympic juggernaut. Many such violators will be self-represented in court and undoubtedly attract disproportionate (adverse) media coverage that does nothing but distract the Olympic parties and add to their legal bills while offering no commercial return. Typical of such cases was an "Olympic" Pizzeria in downtown Vancouver, in clear violation of Olympic rights, but which seemed to relish the idea of the publicity that would come from a resort to legal proceedings. VANOC was careful not to fall into the trap and the matter rested where it was, with the public increasingly aware of the clumsy attempt to cash in on the cachet of the Olympic Games while contributing nothing to their success and of such mean unimportance that it was not worthy of notice. This is a practical example of the analysis inherent in the proper management of commercial rights and the balance required to separate acceptable community usage or references from those that may have commercial consequences for authorized rights holders.

Often more difficult to manage is the degree to which public authorities, having contributed to the funding of the Games, should be able to position their involvement. There can be no legitimate objection to providing appropriate recognition in respect of such contributions, which are often significant, sometimes as much as or even more than the private sector contributions, provided that such recognition does not result in market clutter, nor create misleading impressions regarding direct connection with the Games.

Contributions and the applications of funds provided by governments are normally specified in multiparty agreements and quite often are directed towards infrastructure and capital investments, as opposed to organizational expenditures pertaining to the event itself. Commercial partners will, understandably, want to position themselves as contributing to the staging of the Games and helping athletes to prepare for them. They will not want governments to take all of the promotional oxygen out of the air (since politicians, particularly hosting political leaders, will also want to communicate their support of the Games and the athletes), so organizing committees (like VANOC) must tread a fine line to accommodate the recognition of both public and commercial partners.

Ambush Beyond Sponsors?

Although the term *ambush marketing* is typically used in relation to sponsorship, there are other situations in which it can occur. OCOGs derive significant revenues from licensing agreements in which third parties are permitted to use Olympic marks and designations on products, such as clothing, equipment, and souvenirs. Licensees pay considerable amounts for the right to do so, usually a combination of a minimum guarantee against specified royalties based on actual sales. Apart from the OCOG's normal commercial management of license agreements, such as quality of the goods, accuracy of mark use, and accounting for sales, Olympic licensees need to be protected against counterfeit goods, whether produced in the host country or elsewhere. Special arrangements need to be made to be able to identify counterfeit goods and their sources, to seize such goods preemptively when they enter the host country or are found in it, and to determine how the parties will share the responsibility for acting in relation to counterfeit goods.

(Continued on next page)

Case Study 14.1 *(continued)*

In considering, again, the 2010 Olympic Games, VANOC generated many millions of dollars from the sale of admission tickets to Games events. In furthering the revenue objective and venue management during the Games, tickets had to be designed and produced for hundreds of sport sessions and hundreds of thousands of spectators, each for a specific session and with a specific location (seat or viewing area) within the Olympic venues. In addition, elaborate arrangements were made to ensure equi-table distribution of the tickets as between domestic spectators, foreign spectators, and the Olympic family. This ticketing aspect of the Games is also subject to counterfeiting. Today, modern Olympic tickets include state-of-the-art anticounterfeiting measures and devices that rival even paper currency security measures. In this regard, OCOGs tend to delay the physical production of the tickets as long as possible and refrain from disclosing the appearance of the tickets as part of their efforts to reduce the risks of counterfeit tickets appearing in the marketplace. Other types of fraud affecting Olympic tickets include credit card fraud, in which the public is invited to purchase tickets from vendors by way of credit card. In relation to the 1988 Calgary Olympic Winter Games, one fraud was exposed when the perpetrator failed to include sufficient space in the order form for the intended victims to insert all the numbers on their credit cards.

CHAPTER SUMMARY

Today's world is increasingly complex, regulated, and litigious. Few areas of law and regulation are as complex and uncertain of application as intellectual property. Modern forms of communication have revolutionized not only communication, but also the ability to (mis)appropriate intellectual property. Regulators are uncertain as to solutions to these problems and to the related enforcement of rights. Many of the applicable legal principles are derived from centuries-old modes of communication and business models that have diminishing or marginal relevance.

Notwithstanding this plethora of uncertainty, it is precisely the segment of the legal and technological spectrum in which Olympic marketing must operate. The central *assets* of the Olympic Movement are the IOC, OCOGs, NOCs, IFs, NSOs, and the intellectual property they possess—the five rings, the word *Olympic* as a qualifier of its event, and the various Olympic emblems of organizing committees (such as VANOC) and the NOCs. Protecting those rights against unauthorized use or appropriation is a full-time concern and of the utmost importance. Indeed, the failure to protect these rights may lead to their legal extinction and, most certainly, a diminution of their marketing and sponsorship value.

Faced with the uncertainty of the legal principles and recognizing that resorting to the courts for legal solutions is usually lengthy, expensive, and uncertain, litigation should remain the last resort as recourse for sport organizations and their sponsors.

Alternative solutions can be more effective and have the additional benefit of being tailored to particular circumstances. Voluntary compliance regarding Olympic rights is much preferred to forced compliance. Media can be used to identify nonauthorized use and the impacts of such use. In any mutually dependent relationship, there are elements of deterrence and leverage available. And finally, if not primarily, is the matter of education to precondition the marketplace and to identify limits of acceptable behavior.

In the end, faced with possible infringements, it will be essential to conclude whether commercial harm is being suffered or whether the conduct falls within the broader community engagement. VANOC, for example, expended considerable political and social capital in an effort to make the 2010 Winter Games "Canada's Games." This was easier said than done, especially in a country with Canada's physical and cultural configuration and the particular location of the Games in Vancouver, at the western end of the country and continent. From a community perspective, therefore, the more attention and commitment to the 2010 Games, the closer VANOC could come to realizing its objective. This meant that it had to be especially careful in its characterization of conduct engaged in for that purpose, as opposed to conduct designed to create an unauthorized commercial advantage.

It is perhaps appropriate for modern Olympic parties, including commercial partners, to reflect on the *big picture* and overall objectives when considering ambush marketing. What, exactly, are the parties trying to achieve? How can ambush marketing adversely affect these goals? How do they identify ambush marketing? How should they respond to it in order to further their legitimate commercial and societal objectives? What, indeed, are the interests to be promoted, protected, or discouraged? How can all parties work together for mutual benefit to each participating organization? In the remaining chapters of section III, answers for these questions are provided and implications for the global sport marketing world presented.

Key Chapter Questions

1. Find three definitions of ambush marketing. Which do you prefer and why?
2. Your president wants your four-page SWOT assessment as marketing director regarding how to ambush a particularly successful promotion of your biggest competitor. How would you frame your advice?
3. What improvements would you suggest to VANOC's Commercial Rights Management Mission?
4. You are the marketing director of one of Visa's major competitors. What kind of Olympic-related parasite marketing program might you design? What would be the elements of it? The tag lines you might suggest?
5. If you had the same position at Visa and expected either an ambush program or a parasite program to come from a major competitor, what steps would you take to counter both?
6. How would you, as marketing director, respond to severe media criticism of an ambush or parasite program enacted by your company?

Key Chapter Takeaways

1. Official sponsors can reap many benefits, including increased visibility and high reach, but nonofficial sponsors can pursue their own, independent, marketing strategy.
2. The choice to be a nonsponsor can be a deliberate choice.
3. The cleanest way to deal with the limitations of public sector advertising is to ensure that no commercial elements enter into noncommercial licensing agreements that specify the permitted usage of any Olympic marks, designations, and statements.
4. The vast majority of infringement on the Olympic marks is unintended, yet the most effective might be the most subtle but deliberate.

15

Ambush Marketing:
A Research Perspective

This chapter builds on the previous 14 chapters, which established Olympic sponsorship, outlined sponsorship sales, and introduced ambush marketing. This chapter adds a depth to the story by reviewing the growing body of research on ambush marketing to further inform our understanding of this particular topic within the global marketing context. The term *ambush marketing* is sometimes used interchangeably with the term *parasite marketing* as described by a former IOC marketing director "seek[ing] to leverage off the goodwill and worldwide reputation of the Olympic Movement at the expense of official sponsors" (Payne, 1998, p. 326). Specifically, this chapter focuses on sharing some of the attributes, nuances, and realities that define ambush marketing.

THE OLYMPIC BRAND

As previously established, the Olympic Games—often represented by the five interlocking rings—is a highly recognized international brand that represents a set of ideals/values (e.g., respect, excellence, friendship) that have been communicated as the core values of the modern Olympic Games since their creation in 1894. The brand is also represented by the Olympic flame, the Olympic torch relay, the Olympic motto, and other images of the Games. This brand is portrayed by various stakeholders, including TOP sponsors, OCOG sponsors, broadcasters, NOCs, OCOGs, IFs, and governments. In the case of sponsors, the strength of the brand has attracted high levels of interest, particularly at the TOP sponsor level, including the interest of non-sponsors—or ambushers.

The rich imagery linked to the Olympic brand and the compelling emotional stories of athletes cer-

© Ukrphoto | Dreamstime.com—Olympic Flame in Sochi Photo

tainly make large market connections possible, as consumers understand what the Olympics mean and find it relevant in their lives. In such an environment, sponsors are able to bond via the Olympic brand on a deep emotional level with consumers regardless of culture, language, or gender and in the 200+ jurisdictions of the IOC (Ferrand, Chappelet and Séguin, 2012).

OLYMPIC PROPERTY RIGHTS

Ambush marketing is a strategic alternative to the sponsorship of mega-events such as Olympic Games. Particularly, the notion of ownership determines which alternative is more likely. As the *owner* of the official rights to the Olympic Games, a sponsor is provided by the IOC with exclusivity for its category in terms of associating with the Olympic brand. In return for the investment the sponsor makes, the IOC undertakes efforts to protect the exclusivity of those sponsorship rights to deliver on its promise to the sponsor and ensure a positive outcome from the sponsorship to maintain its revenue base and pursue renewal. The efforts to protect exclusivity occurs around the Olympic properties: Games, Olympic symbol, flag, motto, anthem, identifications, designations, emblems, flame, and torches (Ferrand et al., 2012), all of which can be targets for ambush marketing, although the Games and the symbol (the five rings) are most likely to be ambushed.

Rule 7 of the Olympic Charter describes the IOC's position with respect to rights.

Rights over the Olympic Games and Olympic properties

1. The Olympic Games are the exclusive property of the IOC, which owns all rights and data relating thereto, in particular, and without limitation, all rights relating to their organization, exploitation, broadcasting, recording, representation, reproduction, access and dissemination in any form and by any means or mechanism whatsoever, whether now existing or developed in the future. The IOC shall determine the conditions of access to and the conditions of any use of data relating to the Olympic Games and to the competitions and sports performances of the Olympic Games.
2. The Olympic symbol, flag, motto, anthem, identifications (including but not limited to "Olympic Games" and "Games of the Olympiad"), designations, emblems, flame and torches, as defined in Rules 8–14 below, shall be collectively or individually referred to as "Olympic properties." All rights to any and all Olympic properties, as well as all rights to the use thereof, belong exclusively to the IOC, including but not limited to the use for any profit-making, commercial or advertising purposes. The IOC may license all or part of its rights on terms and conditions set forth by the IOC Executive Board.

The Charter defines an Olympic designation as "any visual or audio representation of any association, connection or other link with the Olympic Games, the Olympic Movement, or any constituent thereof" (IOC 2010, Rule 14). The inclusion of visual associations is often what characterizes the marketing efforts of nonsponsors as ambush

marketing, since a visual association with imagery is a common ambush tactic. Consequently, as seen in the previous chapter, the IOC must, on occasion, fight to protect its control over its properties.

The principles that govern the management of Olympic properties and rights are described in the Olympic Charter, and the IOC works closely with the sponsors, media partners, OCOGs, and NOCs to implement these principles (Ferrand et al, 2012). For example, for the Games, a "Host City Contract" is signed by the IOC, the host city, the host country NOC, and the OCOG once officially formed. The OCOG copyrights all the Olympic properties and these rights are transferred back to the IOC after the Games.

In order to protect the marketing value of the rights, the IOC and its official rights holders are the only authorized organizations that can use the Olympic symbol by itself with certain, strictly enforced restrictions. NOC and OCOG emblems must be distinct from other Olympic emblems and be designed in a way that clearly identifies the emblems being connected with the country of the NOC. For example, the emblem of the USOC includes the Stars and Stripes and the Olympic rings, thus clearly identifying the US flag with the Olympics. The rings are clearly separated from the other emblems (e.g. flag) or designation (e.g., United States Olympic Committee, United States Olympic Team). NOCs/OCOGs are also required to registering the mark with the proper authorities in their jurisdiction.

Great Britain and Japan are additional examples of NOCs who include country associations in their logos and team clothing.

OLYMPIC SPONSORSHIP ACTIVATION AND RIGHTS

Olympic sponsorship was described in detail in Chapters 12 and 13. From a brand perspective, TOP sponsors can link their brands to the Olympic brand and their rights include partnerships with all the recognized National Olympic Committees (NOCs) and their Olympic teams, the OCOGs and the organizers of the Youth Olympic Games (YOCOGs). TOP sponsors can connect with consumers locally by activating their sponsorships with national Olympic teams and by signing agreements with athletes and/or specific NSOs. With the revenue from TOP VIII (2013–2016) expected to generate more than US $1 billion, the success of this program is clear. As noted, sponsorship is also an important source of revenue for OCOGs and NOCs. In the case of OCOGs, domestic sponsorship support[s] the operations of the OCOG, the planning and staging of the Games, the host country NOC and the host country Olympic team. The Olympic Games domestic sponsorship programme grants marketing rights within the host country or territory only. The host country NOC and the host country Olympic team participate in the OCOG sponsorship programme because the Marketing Plan Agreement requires the OCOG and the host country NOC to centralise and co-ordinate all marketing initiatives within the host country. (IOC 2011a: 17)

Although the domestic marketing rights are restricted to the country of the OCOG, the revenues from these programs are now comparable to those derived from the TOP program. For example, the 2014 Sochi Olympic Winter Games raised US $1.3 billion in domestic sponsorship while US $957 million was generated by TOP VII (2009–2012) (IOC, 2014). OCOGs also grant the use of Olympic marks, imagery, or themes to third-party companies to create Olympic Games-related products, merchandise, and souvenirs for consumers. See example below. These licensing-agreements promote the Olympic image, the host country's culture, and are now an important source of revenues for OCOG.

NOCs often devise their own sponsorship programs in product categories that do not compete with TOP partners. Sponsors can link their brands with the NOC's brand, its activities, and its Olympic team. Some NOCs (e.g., USOC, British Olympic Association, German Olympic Sport

TM/MC
PREMIER NATIONAL PARTNER

© RBC

Confederation) have sophisticated sponsorship programs generating millions of dollars in revenue. It is important to note that sponsorship rights at all three levels do not include the rights to athletes, the IFs, and the NSOs. In other words, competitors of official sponsors can create relationships with star athletes and/or with a high-profile sport in a specific country (e.g., soccer in Brazil, baseball in Japan) and activate those in a way that indirectly creates close associations with the Olympic brand. This is arguably a weakness within the Olympic system and much effort is undertaken by the IOC along with NOCs and OCOGs to manage this issue. Thus, although the success of Olympic sponsorship can be credited in part to the IOC's efforts to manage and control its brand, a few challenges remain.

OLYMPIC BRAND—CLUTTER AND AMBUSH MARKETING

Sport events with global appeal have been successful at creating their own brands with their loyal fans and larger audiences via the media. As discussed in Chapter 14, the IOC's decision to adopt brand management principles to its business in the mid-1990s has contributed to making the Olympic brand one of the strongest of these brands. The

Olympic brand essence consists of ideals and values (e.g., excellence, friendship, community) with a highly emotional aspect that connects to these values which have been shown to be relevant to consumers worldwide (Ferrand et al, 2012).

The power of Olympic brand results from a system that has been carefully led and managed by the IOC building a system that is one that *cocreates value*—in other words, value to the Olympic brand and value for the brands of its stakeholders is being created concurrently (Ferrand et al., 2012). To illustrate this concept, consider that the TOP sponsors' associations with the Olympics are a form of brand alliance. When sponsors integrate/align their activation programs with the Olympic brand (e.g., Visa and Olympics), significant promotional value for sponsors results, including such benefits as brand recognition, access to markets worldwide, emotional extensions, and differentiation from competitors. These extensive benefits, in turn, attract the interest of nonsponsors who are competitors (or not) of official sponsors, thereby encourage ambush (or parasite) marketing.

While these brand alliances bring great value to the Olympic brand, it is paramount that a brand governance structure manages and controls the brand and its many assets. The objective here is to preserve the uniqueness of Olympic brand despite a highly cluttered marketplace, where the amount of competing communications messages trying to get the attention of fans, spectators, and potential consumers is beyond what people are able to digest (O'Reilly & Séguin, 2009). These brand alliances or partnerships (or sponsorships) can also occur at the NOC level. For example the USOC currently (as of August 2014) has 25 sponsors and 23 licensees (see http://www.team usa.org/sponsors).

OLYMPIC STAKEHOLDER—
AMBUSH MARKETING AND CLUTTER

NSOs, athletes, and other national/international events can claim (or create an impression of) ownership over specific stories and/or images that may be related, directly or indirectly, to the Olympics. For example, a large NSO, such as USA Basketball and the Football Federation of Australia, is able to own numerous stories and images that generate strong emotions within their country and their sport community. In the Canadian context, Hockey Canada is able to build associations via the public's deep roots with hockey. In turn, these images/stories provide value to the NSO brand (e.g., Hockey Canada), which can be activated by their own sponsors (e.g., Esso). The same is true of high-profile athletes (e.g., Usain Bolt and PUMA), who could launch a promotional campaign that could create associations with the Olympic brand and possibly mislead consumers to believe that an official sponsorship exists (Séguin & O'Reilly, 2009). Dr. Dre received much publicity for providing Beats by Dre headphones to certain athletes in their national colors during the London 2012 Olympic Games.

The strength of these brands and association with the Olympics are what set the stage for ambush marketing. A nonsponsor can launch a related and confusing promotion that coincides with the lead-up to or during the staging of Olympic Games (see Dr. Dre example). Consequently, confusion over who is the official sponsor may result, given the clutter and the perceived association to the Olympic brand. In such circumstances, it may be difficult for an official Olympic sponsor to stand out. In turn, this provides for an environment in which a nonsponsor could adopt ambush marketing to help navigate a cluttered marketplace by making Olympic brand associations, which could threaten and dilute the effectiveness and value for official sponsorships.

While activation programs are the best method for sponsors and nonsponsors to break through the clutter, engage consumers with their brands, enhance brand reputation, and ultimately achieve positive return on investment, they require important investments (sometimes 3–5 times more than the basic rights fees) and, typically, are more effective for sponsors. Thus, clutter and ambush marketing are highly linked and together pose a serious threat to the value of sponsorship as they could impact its marketing value of the property unless contained. It is, therefore, in the IOC's best interests to protect its brand and its sponsors.

BRAND PROTECTION

The IOC's efforts to protect its brand beyond traditional means (i.e., trademark laws, activation) have changed the way mega-events approach ambush marketing globally. These efforts are known as brand protection, which consists of protecting both the tangible (i.e., words, symbols, the Olympic motto, etc.) and intangible aspects (i.e., image, values, reputation, etc.) of the brand. The tangible aspects of the brand are protected via such tactics as trademark law. However, protecting the intangible brand characteristics is more complex, since key stakeholders (internal and external) of the Olympic brand must be mindful of their actions, which may impact the integrity and potentially the image and value of the brand (Séguin, 2013). For example, when a few IOC members were found to have accepted inappropriate benefits from the Salt Lake City bid committee, the negative worldwide media coverage that resulted was a threat to the brand and sponsors. While the IOC ultimately recovered, such actions from within the organization often have a negative impact on the brand and, by extension, sponsorship.

The same could apply to external stakeholders such as the 2014 Games host country government, Russia's, antihomosexuality legislation, where Russia did agree that there would be no discrimination during the Games, and did deliver on that promise. In this regard, the Olympic Charter (p. 11) states, "The practice of sport is a human right. Every individual must have the possibility of practicing sport, without discrimination of any kind and in the Olympic spirit, which requires mutual understanding with a spirit of friendship, solidarity and fair play."

Other threats to the Olympic brand and Olympic sponsors include doping, cheating, lack of interest of youth towards the Olympics, excessive commercialization, and ambush marketing. All are well-recognized by the IOC and managed within the organization's brand protection strategy. For example, the issue of excessive commercialization around the Games (official or not) is closely related to the issue of clutter discussed earlier. The IOC's ability to control the level of commercialization around its brand is directly tied to its commercial value for sponsors. Consequently, the requirements of the IOC on cities wishing to host the Olympic Games have increased significantly now

providing (i) that all marketing rights within a host country be under the control of OCOG (not the host NOC) and (ii) that host cities must guarantee that all outdoor, public transportation, and airport advertising space used for the Olympic Games be under the control of OCOG (IOC, 2008: 127). Tactically, these advertising spaces are then integrated into what is commonly known as the cityscape, which provides a clean (i.e., no nonsponsors) visual landscape. This is also known as the "Look of the Games" (see picture above). Further, bid cities are now required to guarantee that their country's government put in place legislation against ambush marketing of the Olympic Games and its sponsors. These demands, although significant, are now common practice for mega-events such as the FIFA World Cup, Commonwealth Games, and the World Cup of Rugby.

AMBUSH MARKETING ACTIVITIES

Ambush marketing activities are now an expected part of the commercial landscape of mega-sport events like the Olympic Games. While academic research on ambush marketing has grown rapidly over the last two decades, there remains no accepted definition of what constitutes ambush marketing. Sandler and Shani (1989) initially defined ambush marketing as "a planned effort by an organization to associate itself indirectly with an event in order to gain at least some of the recognition and benefits that are associated with being an official sponsor" (p. 11). While this definition is often cited, it really never obtained consensus amongst academic or practitioners (Crow & Hoek, 2003; McKelvey & Grady, 2008; Meenaghan, 1994). In 1998, Sandler and Shani suggested that the real problem related to ambush marketing was "the consumer's lack of knowledge and confusion about the sponsors and their contribution to the sponsored event" (p. 381). More recently, Burton (2011) defined ambush marketing as

> a form of associative marketing which is designed by an organization to capitalize on the awareness, attention, goodwill, and other benefits, generated by having an association with an event or property, without the organization having an official or direct connection to that event or property. (p. 714)

The Chadwick and Burton definition clearly emphasize the "intent" that a nonsponsor must have to undertake a true ambush. Practically, former American Express marketing executive Jerry Welsh views ambush marketing as "a marketing strategy with its programmatic outcomes, occupying the thematic space of a sponsoring competitor, and formulated to vie with that sponsoring competitor for marketing pre-eminence" (Welsh, 2002, p. 1). In these terms, those without official sponsorship rights would likely agree with such a view and believe that ambush marketing is little more than good business strategy, hence forcing sponsors to fully activate their partnerships (Séguin & Ellis, 2012). On the other hand, sponsors and property owners (e.g., IOC or FIFA) are most likely to take an opposing view. Their definitions of ambush marketing tend to be negative in tone and often question the ethics of those using such strategies.

As long as ambush marketing continues to pit ambushers against sponsors and property holders in the commercial field of play, there is likely to be little consensus on a definition. But perhaps it really does not matter, as ultimately it remains the property's responsibility to ensure that the sponsors' rights are protected. As suggested by the Brand Protection Manager for VANOC following the 2010 Games:

> I didn't have a lot of patience for the debate of what constitutes ambush as it might be defined legally, as it might be defined in marketing textbooks because those aren't really relevant. What's relevant is—is there a risk of confusing the consumer and perhaps more pertinent to the property is there a commercial risk? And if the answer to either of those two questions is yes then it doesn't really matter if [it is considered] ambush or not, you as a property owe it to your sponsor to do something about it and if the law doesn't support you to process it as a legal case that doesn't necessarily relieve you of the duty to do something about it on behalf of your sponsors. You still have to pick up the phone and call the advertiser and try and coax them into a position that's, you know, more conducive to the exclusivities you sold to your sponsor. (Bill Cooper, personal communication, June 29, 2014)

Ambush Marketing Strategic Frameworks & Tactics

Over the years, a number of researchers have described various tactics of ambush marketing (c.f. Crompton, 2004; Meenaghan, 1994, 1998) including the sponsoring of media coverage (e.g., Kodak's sponsoring ABC's broadcast of Olympic Games), advertising that corresponds with an event (e.g., purchasing billboards in host city and major inbound routes, sweepstakes, media buy), sponsoring subcategories (e.g., athletes, national teams, national sport federations), and thematic advertising and implied association.

Recently, Burton and Chadwick (2011) proposed a typology of ambush marketing with three broad classifications: direct ambushing, indirect ambushing, and incidental ambushing. The first, direct ambushing, occurs when a brand intentionally tries to make itself appear to be associated with an event for which it has no official rights and in the process directly attacks a rival who holds the official sponsorship rights. There are three types of direct ambush marketing identified by Burton and Chadwick, including *predatory* (i.e., deliberate ambushing of a market competitor to gain market share and confuse consumers), *coattail* ambush marketing (i.e., nonsponsor association with an event through a legitimate link other than becoming a sponsor), and *property infringement* (i.e., intentionally using protected intellectual property). The second classification, indirect ambush, is described to exist when an association with an event is made, but the motives are not to attack a rival's (official sponsor) plans. The five types of indirect ambush are (i) *associative ambushing* (i.e., the use of imagery or terminology to create the illusion of being an official sponsor), (ii) *distractive ambushing* (i.e., promotional presence at or near an event without infringing on the event's marks), (iii) *values ambushing* (i.e., use of event central's theme to imply association without infringing on event), (iv) *insurgent ambushing* (i.e., use of street-style guerilla promotions at or near an event), and (v) *parallel property ambushing* (i.e., the creation of an event related to the ambush target and competes for public attention). The third type of classification from Burton and Chadwick (2011), *incidental ambushing*, is when consumers associate the ambusher's brand with an event without any attempt by the ambusher to do so. Although not intentional in nature, this type of ambush marketing still contributes to cluttering the marketing environment around the event. The two types of incidental ambushing are *unintentional ambushing* (mention of a product by media leading to consumer associating the company as a sponsor) and *saturation ambushing* (i.e., increase in advertising spending around an event without suggesting association with event).

When examining the classifications above, we note that for the most part, mega-events properties such as the Olympics have been able to manage/control these ambushing tactics. For example, by ensuring that all marks, emblems, and Olympic symbols are properly registered with appropriate legal authorities (e.g., trademark laws), the IOC protects—at least in part—its assets and can legally pursue infringers and seek compensation for damages incurred. In addition, by working with its official broadcasters, the IOC is able to ensure that official sponsors get first right of refusal to purchase ad time during broadcast of Olympic Games and also dictates how the Olympic symbol can be used hence preventing *sponsorship* (and possible ambush) of the broadcast. Further, by demanding guarantees that all outdoor advertising space, advertising space on public transport, and all advertising space at airports be under the control of OCOG, the IOC prevents much of the guerrilla marketing tactics. However, the predatory, coattail, associative, and value ambushing techniques are much more difficult to control and offer nonsponsors numerous points of entry to create associations with the Olympic brand.

For example, despite Reebok being the official sponsor of the 1996 Olympic Games, a rival competitor, PUMA, ended up grabbing the headlines when defending 100m Olympic champion Linford Christie appeared at a well-covered press conference wearing contact lenses that contained Puma's logo. This photo was featured on the front page of newspapers around the world.

In addition, thematic advertising or implied associations corresponding to the event used imagery and/or wording in their advertising without including restricted trademarks, symbols, or words. This is the case of Nike's "Risk Everything" campaign around 2014 FIFA World Cup using numerous athletes as well as its "Find your Greatness" campaigns around the 2012 and 2014 Olympics. Obviously, for companies such as Nike, ambush marketing has gotten increasingly strategic and is directed at specific publics, which makes sense. View a video from this campaign at https://www.you tube.com/watch?v=Iy1rumvo9xc.

Ambushers understand the value of using intangible brand associations to link themselves to the Games while not contravening the laws protecting emblems, words, and other symbols hence making it more difficult for the authorities (in the case of legalized anti-ambush legislation), OCOGs, and the IOC to shut them down. Nike's ad campaign that appeared around the 2012 Olympics and the 2014 Olympic Winter Games tested the limits of the Olympic rules on ambush marketing. In 2012, Nike launched a global TV campaign "Find Your Greatness" featuring everyday athletes competing in places around the world named London. The campaign, launched in 25 countries, was timed to coincide with the Opening Ceremony of 2012 Games. Although there was much skepticism about the motivation of the campaign, Nike's Chief Marketing Officer, in an article published by *The Guardian* newspaper two days prior to the Olympic ceremonies, publicly stated

> The idea is to simply inspire and energize everyday athletes everywhere and to celebrate their achievements, participate and enjoy the thrill of achieving in sport at their own level (Nike's Chief Brand Officer, in Sweeny, 2012).

Nike's 2012 multimillion dollar campaign was backed with a Twitter marketing push using the hashtag #findgreatness. The campaign was supported with outdoor and print advertising as well as online film featuring London-based everyday athletes. Its minute-long ad was reloaded 36 different times onto various video sharing sites such as YouTube and Daily Motion, making it the most pirated ad campaign in August 2012. While this would not be a sought outcome for some (i.e., video uploaded and repurposed by other users) for Nike, this was a good thing (Wei, 2012).

Nike was back in the spotlight with a number of targeted marketing campaigns around the 2014 Olympic Winter Games in Sochi. Russia's specific ad campaign—aptly named "Play Russian"—portrays the harsh Russian winter and celebrates the athletes who are out moving despite the temperature in a bid to inspire movement in the streets of Moscow and around Russia, building momentum around a "Winter of Sport." Showing the world how to embrace sport and "Play Russian," local athletes take center stage in the campaign, which features an ice hockey star player as well as other well-known Olympic athletes (West, 2013). Nike adjusted its campaign for the Canadian market with an ad featuring a Team (Olympic) Canada player that attempted to fuel the Canadian pride with the message that Canadians own hockey. The ad entitled "All Ice Is Home Ice" features clever references to playing other countries, including a shot of a cheering fan with the Russian flag on his cheek (Krashinsky, 2014).

The two previously presented examples of Nike's marketing activities around the Olympics illustrate the challenges of protecting the intangible aspects of a brand. It is obvious to many in the field that ambush marketing has become a strategic alternative to sponsorship for many firms. The number of occurrences and the number of sport properties that have been subject to it has grown immensely. While its long-term effect has yet to be determined, some argue that it diminishes the value of sport properties. But as shown in the Nike's example above, managing ambush marketing has become a complex undertaking by properties. It is an essential element of an overall brand protection strategy with the ultimate goal of protecting/enhancing brand equity. This will be examined in detail in the next chapter.

CONSUMERS PERCEPTION AND RESPONSE TO AMBUSH MARKETING

A key part of debate and discussion around ambush marketing has focused on consumer perceptions and responses to the practice. Since the late 1980s, there have been numerous studies that take varying approaches to this discussion and have produced a similarly variable group of conclusions (e.g., Koenigstorfer & Groeppel-Klein, 2012; Lyberger & McCarthy, 2001; MacIntosh et al., 2012; Mazodier & Quester, 2010; Sandler & Shani 1993; Shani & Sandler 1998). One element of this discussion that many agree on is the fact that there is a general lack of awareness related both to the practice of ambush marketing (Séguin, et al., 2005) and Olympic sponsorship (see Hoek & Gendall, 2002a; Lyberger & McCarthy, 2001; Shani & Sandler, 1998).

However, there remains limited understanding about consumer confusion and how it could be influenced by ambush marketing (MacIntosh et al., 2012). On one side of the discussion, there is a trend in the literature towards research demonstrating consumer apathy and indifference towards ambush marketing (e.g., Koenigstorfer & Groeppel-Klein, 2012). In one particular study, it was noted that when looking at thematic ambush marketing tactics in particular, consumers were able to draw a line between the deceptive and the merely suggestive. They did not feel as though ambushers sought to confuse them; in fact they felt like they were just doing their job as marketers, taking part in typical business practices (Moorman & Greenwell, 2005). A study by Koenigstorfer & Groeppel-Klein (2012) further noted that although official sponsors received more long-term benefits from their partnerships than ambusher's did from their strategies, there was little negative impact on consumer's perception of an ambusher's brand and thus little reason for an ambusher to stop what they were doing.

Conversely, other studies support the potentially negative impacts of ambush marketing on consumer perception and response-based examinations of the impact of ambush marketing strategies on consumer purchase intentions and brand attitudes toward ambushers. For instance, Mazodier and Quester (2010) found that the disclosure of a brand as an ambusher resulted in three negative impacts. The first was the creation of a negative perception around the brand's integrity. This could create a feeling among consumers that the brand could not be trusted, decreasing perceived sincerity and honesty of the brand. Second, it was found that if consumers were informed an ambusher was potentially having a negative impact on the event they were ambushing it would lead to the development of a negative consumer perception of the ambusher's brand (i.e., brand affect) (Mazodier and Quester, 2010). Third, as a result of the negative brand impressions created through the above impacts, Mazodier and Quester (2010) noted that this lessened a consumer's intent to purchase the products of an ambush marketer.

Mazodier and Quester (2010) further argued that there are two modifiers to these results. First, they noted that "involvement in the event significantly increases the negative impact of disclosure on brand affect, perceived integrity and purchase intention" (p. 59). This finding is reinforced by another recent study conducted by MacIntosh et al. (2012) who found that high-interest consumers perceived ambush marketing more negatively than low-interest consumers, indicating that level of interest acts as a moderating influence of ambush evaluation on purchase intention. The second modifier discussed by Mazodier and Quester (2010) was attitude towards sponsorship, finding that while a more positive attitude towards sponsorship reinforced negative impacts of ambush tactics on both brand affect and perceived integrity, it did not negatively impact purchase intention.

CHAPTER SUMMARY

The research on ambush marketing further supports the uncertainty around ambush marketing, from both a consumer and a practitioner perspective. The modern sport marketing and sponsorship practitioner needs to be wary of these varying views in dealing with sponsors, governments, associations, and international stakeholders. For example, if you were hired by the city that the USOC selects to bid for the 2028 Olympic Games, you need to be very aware of the issues at play and the sought benefits of each stakeholder as you build out your bid from a sponsorship perspective. Clearly, the IOC wants brand protection. The sponsors want exclusivity. The NSOs and NOCs want to share. The OCOG sponsors wants profile and platform. And so on. Thus, although uncertainty remains around ambush, the practical reality is clear.

Chapter Exercise

You are a high-profile athlete in your country having won an Olympic medal and numerous World Cup and World Championships medals in the sport of speed skating. While being retired for more than 15 years, you have been an active contributor to sport as well to numerous charities within your community. A few years ago, you were invited by a few prominent community leaders to join a group interested in bringing the Olympic Games to your hometown. After a fierce *national bid competition* your city was selected by your NOC as your country's representative on the international bidding competition to host the 2018 Olympic Games. This was exciting and the prospect of hosting the Olympic Winter Games was real.

While busy volunteering for the bid committee, you also happened to be the national sport director for a major telecommunication company that had its roots in the same city. The company has also been a long-term sponsor of some of the biggest and most popular national sport organizations in the country including short-track speed skating, snowboarding, ice hockey, and alpine skiing. The agreements were in place until 2014 and negotiations for another 4-year cycle (to 2018) were well underway. It was natural for the company to become one of the biggest supporters of the bid committee by investing US $4 million as a sponsor. The company executives and its employees were proud to support the community's dream of bringing the Games home. In 2011, the dream became reality as the IOC elected your city as the host of the 2018 Olympic Winter Games.

The OCOG officially sought bids for various "domestic sponsorship" categories in the fall of 2013. After huge efforts in putting together what it considered a very strong sponsorship bid to the OCOG, the company's executives felt confident. In addition, it believed that having the better communications infrastructure in the region was giving them an advantage over its main competitor located in another region of the country. It was therefore with disbelief and immense disappointment when the OCOG announced that its fieriest competitor was selected as the best bid. Indeed, the astounding US $200 million package offered by its competitor was more than US $60 million from its offer. It was bitter disappointment especially given that the company has its roots in the host city and really wanted the sponsorship. Instead, the competitor was keen to leverage its association with the country's Olympic team competing in the 2014, 2016, 2018 and 2020 Olympic Games as well as a main sponsor for the 2018 Winter Games. Given its exclusive seven-year association with the Olympics, the company planned on increasing its market presence (especially in the region of host city) and gain market share in mobile phone and satellite TV services. The 2014 Olympic Winter Games were only five months away and plans were in place to activate its rights.

Frustrated and still bitter about losing the sponsorship rights, the Vice-President of Marketing for the company asked you to provide some advice on the next steps. She was well aware that during your university studies, you conducted extensive research on ambush marketing. Specifically, she asked you to prepare a brief on the following:

Exercise Questions

1. What are some of the key findings from research on ambush marketing? How is it relevant for the company?
2. Should the company develop an aggressive ambush marketing strategy around the 2014 Games only five months away? Why or why not? Should it also plan a long-term ambush strategy leading to the 2018 Games? Why or why not?
3. What are some alternatives to ambush marketing that could accomplish similar outcomes?

16

Responding to Ambush Marketing

C hapter 15 establishes ambush marketing as something about which the general population is uncertain, that official sponsors dub a threat, that nonsponsors consider as an alternative, and that rights holders seek to eliminate. This chapter provides direction and insight into how to respond to or react to ambush marketing or the threat of ambush marketing, something that sport marketers will inevitably face in their career, as a sponsor, a nonsponsor, a rights-holder or a participant.

YOU SENSE AN AMBUSH . . .
AND YOU HAVE SOMETHING WORTH PROTECTING

Around the turn of the present century, the IOC faced a number of important issues (e.g., bribery, cheating, doping, overcommercialization, ambush marketing) that threatened its most important asset, the Olympic brand. The decision to adopt a strategic brand management approach to its activities was perhaps not fully understood by all of its stakeholders, but was certainly a decision that aligned with the current practices in the business world of the time (Aaker, 1991; Keller, 1993). This brand orientation mind-set allowed the IOC to develop internal branding capabilities, gain a deeper understanding of its brand, and ultimately, deliver its brand in a coherent manner.

Today, the Olympic brand is arguably one of the most recognized brands in the world. It has positive brand associations (i.e., Olympic values), is perceived as a quality brand (i.e., best athletes in the world participate, blue chip companies as partners, etc.), enjoys strong and loyal support from its stakeholders (e.g., sponsors, broadcasters, fans) and has other proprietary assets (Olympic flame, torch relay, still and moving images, etc.) that contribute to its aura. With this in mind, it is safe to say that the IOC, with the support of key stakeholders, has succeeded in building a dominant brand, one with a very high level of brand equity. As such, the IOC has been able to leverage its brand and gather strong support from the private (i.e., TOP sponsors) and public (i.e., government) sectors. Clearly, it is of the utmost importance for the IOC and its partners not only to manage and control the brand but also to protect it from possible threats that could compromise its value. These threats, as outlined in the prior chapter, include ambush marketing.

While sporting issues such as doping and cheating can damage the essence of the brand, commercial issues linked to clutter and ambush marketing can be just as harmful as they take away from the uniqueness of the brand and threaten the IOC's ability to generate revenue from sponsorship (Séguin & O'Reilly, 2008). This is an important challenge for the IOC given the large sums of cash and in-kind contributions raised from sponsorship and broadcasting.

Given their size and significance, the need to protect Olympic marketing revenues has been a priority for the IOC and many of its stakeholders (i.e., OCOGs, sponsors, and governments). However, re-

> ### Inside the Dollars of London 2012 Games
>
> TOP and broadcasting contributed more than US $700 million to the London 2012 OCOG, in addition to the US $1.15 billion raised by the OCOG for its domestic sponsorship programs and the US $135 million from merchandising sales, a total of more than US $2 billion from commercial programs (IOC, 2014). With a budget of $3.5 billion, it is clear that the revenues generated from commercial programs resulting from a strong Olympic brand are significant for OCOGs otherwise, the money would likely come from the public sector (i.e., taxpayer dollars), which already makes massive investments (e.g., transport/road/sport infrastructures, security) in hosting the Games. The final cost for the London Games alone was reported at $14.6 billion or £8.921 (Gibson, 2012).

sponses to the threats resulting from ambush marketing (e.g., special legislation) must be crafted carefully given the possible (negative) impacts on other stakeholders such as athletes, NSOs, the host country, and the public (see Ellis, Scassa & Séguin, 2011).

It is clear, however, that the threat of ambush marketing has placed tremendous pressure on sport properties to develop strategies aimed at protecting their brands and their sponsors. But despite important measures taken by the IOC in recent years, non-sponsors continue to create associations with mega-event brands by navigating through the grey areas (McKelvey & Grady, 2008; Ellis et al., 2011). There are numerous established business strategies to deal with ambush marketing as presented earlier in Chapters 14 and 15. As a reminder, the main ones include the need to address clutter, develop public relations (PR) and activation programs (e.g., coordinated collaborative investment beyond the rights fees), and ensuring NOC expertise in marketing and brand management (i.e., on staff or via third parties).

The clutter that surrounds mega-events should be addressed through exclusivity. Public relations can play an important role in responding to (and preventing) ambush marketing by allowing for the opportunity for a property to educate consumers about the sponsorship as well as increasing their ability to recognize ambush marketing when they see it (Crow & Hoek, 2003; Townley et al., 1998). Public relations provides a further outlet for property rights holders to make a public example of the ambusher, in hopes of offsetting the benefits it may have received via the ambush, with bad publicity (Meenaghan, 1996). The development of strategic activation programs by sponsors is also a well-documented strategy to prevent ambush marketing through additional investment to strengthen the connection in the consumer's mind between the property and the sponsor, thus making it more difficult for ambushers to create confusion in

consumers' minds (Crow & Hoek, 2003; Meenaghan, 1996; O'Reilly & Lafrance-Horning, 2013).

The management and control of broadcast rights is yet another important aspect responding to ambush marketing (Crow & Hoek, 2003; Meenaghan, 1996). Ideally, broadcast rights would be included in the sponsorship rights package hence guaranteeing advertising spots to sponsors only and not allowing non-sponsors to purchase the spots. But such an approach could result in higher sponsorship fees and possibly lower revenue from lucrative broadcast rights for the property. Nonetheless, giving sponsors the *first right of negotiation* over advertising within the various media platforms (television, radio, internet, etc.) seems to be an acceptable compromise.

On a large scale, increasing the marketing expertise of NOCs and NSOs around the world and creating strategic sponsor recognition programs at the national level are suggested as important aspects of managing the brand, since it is essential that the Olympic brand be managed in a uniform and coherent manner around the world. A well thought-out sponsor recognition program that works in synergy with a sponsor's activation strategies may facilitate the public's ability to differentiate between sponsors and nonsponsors as well as to recognize the contribution of sponsors to the Olympic Movement (e.g., staging of Olympic Games, athletes support, etc.). In looking at each of these strategies, it is clear that stakeholders who stand to benefit the most from brand and sponsor protection can, and should, take individual and collective responsibility for ensuring said protection through sound business practices. The next section examines this further.

KEY STAKEHOLDERS: INVOLVEMENT
AND RESPONSIBILITIES IN AMBUSH RESPONSE

The stakeholders engaged in Olympic marketing are numerous and have been well articulated and described throughout the book. The IOC is at the center of this system of stakeholders and, as such, exerts great influence over them. For example, as the ultimate Olympic rights holder, the IOC allocates rights to an OCOG, which must respect the rules, such as product categories reserved for international TOP sponsors, when developing its domestic sponsorship program. In return, an OCOG can develop a national marketing program that also takes into account the wish of the host city and the local authorities, whose objective is to guarantee a sustainable legacy (Ferrand et al., 2012). But while stakeholders are interested in cocreating value with Olympic brand and benefit from such associations, they also play an active role in protecting the brand from ambush marketing. The roles and responsibilities of IOC, NOC, OCOG (including venue managers), sponsors, and governments (including custom agencies) have been described in detail throughout the book, so their roles, specific to responding to ambush marketing, are described below.

STAKEHOLDERS' ROLES AND RESPONSIBILITIES
IN RESPONDING TO AMBUSH MARKETING

IOC

The IOC is the ultimate guardian of the Olympic brand. It is responsible to establish the brand strategy and create and manage brand alliances and marketing rights with the TOP sponsors and broadcasters. In responding to ambush, the IOC has (i) made important changes to host city agreements (e.g., ensuring an OCOG/host NOC joint marketing program managed by the OCOG, taking control of outdoor advertising in

© Anka12 | Dreamstime.com—Sochi, Russia—February 7, 2014: Festivities of Maslenitsa Photo

the host city, and implementing an integrated "look of the Games" program) and (ii) encouraged legislation to protect the brand and sponsors against ambush marketing. Other IOC measures to counter ambush marketing include (i) tightened broadcast and internet monitoring, (ii) increased control of athletes' marketing rights during the Games, and (iii) dedicated resources to take ownership of official films, broadcast coverage, and still images of past Games.

An example of a specific action taken by the IOC is the creation of the Olympic Television Archive Bureau (OTAB) to manage the footage and archives that have been purchased. The IOC has also developed an extensive knowledge transfer program between OCOGs, which includes the transfer of sponsorship best practices along with key brand protection strategies from OCOG to OCOG. Moreover, the IOC engages in strategic communications/PR programs as well as the education of NOCs on marketing and brand management. Finally, the IOC has gone to great lengths to work with host NOCs/OCOGs to protect the Olympic brand, Olympic marks, and sponsors' rights though specific national legislation such as Olympic and Paralympic Marks Act (OPMA) passed in Canada in 2007 for the Vancouver 2010 Olympic Winter Games, and similar acts in both England for London 2012 and Russia or Sochi 2014.

NOCs

Each NOC is responsible for the protection of the Olympic brand within its own jurisdiction. It registers all Olympic marks and symbols with proper legal authorities, develops and implements public relations programs that adhere to those of the IOC, develops and administers educational programs for specific target markets, lobbies governments to modify or create legislation to protect the Olympic brand and control ambush marketing, works with sponsors on activation strategies, and establishes the structure of national sponsorship programs while controlling clutter.

OCOGs

OCOGs play an essential role in protecting the Olympic brand. Over its typical lifespan of seven years, an OCOG creates its own brand and marks to reflect the host country's key characteristics, values, and vision. This brand is then used to generate value through alliances with other brands within the large network of Olympic stakeholders. In recent Games, OCOG revenues from domestic sponsorship programs have exceeded the TOP program's contributions. OCOGs also develop an identity for the Games that are branded through the Look of the Games and the Olympic mascot, which is unique to each Games. The OCOG is the main watchdog against ambush marketing. It monitors and acts on all identified infringements by using legal means to protect its partners (if legislation is in place). OCOGs also work closely with law enforcement agencies to fight counterfeit merchandising and ambush marketing. Finally, OCOGs develop extensive educational programs aimed at informing stakeholders about the legislation, the need to protect its rights, what stakeholders can and cannot do in terms of associations with the brand, and possible consequences to infringements.

Venue managers

Venue managers are a subcategory of stakeholders under OCOG. They are essential in responding to and preventing ambush marketing as they monitor branding on athletes entering the field of play. Over and above this, a venue manager ensures that no ambush-based advertising signs or displays (or any other advertising, including sponsor advertising) are inside the venues, and also monitor crowd behaviors that may signal a potential ambush (e.g., blocks of fans wearing a similar shirt, banners). A well-known example (with a full case description to follow in Chapter 17) of Bavaria beer seeking to ambush Heineken's sponsorship of the 2010 FIFA World Cup illustrates the potential effectiveness of venue-based tactics.

© Sergeibach | Dreamstime.com—Shopping Photo

Sponsors

The sponsors' main responsibility is to activate their sponsorship and *claim their space*, by establishing specific objectives and working with IOC/OCOG/NOC and cosponsors to establish common communications/activation strategies and plans to prevent ambush marketing. Sponsor activations seek to create close associations with the Olympic brand and its values, include athletes in communications and messaging, and clearly communicate their role as official sponsors of the Games. Sponsors are also encouraged to purchase advertising inventories available from official Olympic broadcasters, so as to not allow their competitors an opportunity to undermine their sponsorship.

Governments

Governments, in recent years, have become quite active in protecting the Olympic brand and responding to ambush marketing. As previously noted, special legislation aimed at protecting the Olympic brand and controlling ambush marketing is now a requirement for a host country to bid. For example, in the lead-up to the 2010 Olympic Winter Games in Vancouver, the Canadian government passed the Olympic and Paralympic Marks Act (OPMA), which aimed at protecting the exclusivity of official sponsors (Ellis et al., 2011). This legislation provided, amongst other things, protection of the Olympic marks against certain misleading associations between a business and the Olympic Games (Ellis et al., 2011). The London Olympic Games and Paralympic Games Act was passed by the UK government in 2006 in preparation for the 2012 London Olympic Games. In addition to the legislation, a host city collaborates with the OCOG and other stakeholders to create viewing sites that permit the public to experience the Olympics by watching the competitions on large TV screens. Viewing sites also offer sponsors and other partners opportunities to activate and engage with fans and create a unique atmosphere around the Games.

Customs

The role of customs and border control can play an integral part in controlling counterfeit merchandises that may be entering the host country from abroad. Custom officers can seize such merchandise and make appropriate contacts with authorities.

DETERMINING WHAT MATTERS AND WHAT DOES NOT

Given the ever-growing number of areas and platforms where ambush marketing can take place, it has become more important for property owners and brand stewards to focus their anti-ambush efforts on those situations that offer the potential for real harm to the brand and avoid those where the cost to control would far exceed any potential harm. This involves looking at various ambush marketing situations and determining which of those situations really matter, and which do not, before a response is considered. This is a question of determining what matters, using the principle of commercial harm as guidance, as well as some of the conflicts of interest that have been identified as causing problems when defining significance of an ambush marketing situation.

Commercial Harm

Commercial harm is one of the key considerations in an ambush response. When an ambush marketing program has the potential to cause commercial harm, appropriate action is required. In the Olympic setting, commercial harm refers to a situation in which there is a negative consequence from an ambush marketing action that impacts on the bottom line or brand equity an Olympic stakeholder. As introduced in Chapter 15, there are three main types of commercial harm that could result from ambush marketing: (1) consumer confusion, (2) clutter, and (3) negative brand.

Consumer confusion is often cited as the main threat from ambush marketing based on the argument that organizations that participate in ambush marketing are seeking a way to cause confusion in the marketplace about who is the official sponsor of the Games. This is done in an effort to negate the benefits a sponsor will receive from its investment in the Olympics, as well as to receive the benefits of sponsorship without having to pay the price of sponsorship rights. Former IOC marketing director Michael Payne (1998) has described such an approach as "a deliberate attempt to deceive the consuming public" (p. 325). An ambush program that obviously and strategically sets out to achieve this goal represents the potential to cause commercial harm to the sponsor and the Olympic sponsorship program and, as a result, a response is necessary.

The second type of commercial harm that can result from ambush marketing is clutter. While sponsorship was originally seen to be a way to fight against clutter (Mullin, Hardy, & Sutton, 2000), the current prevalence of sponsorship messages now adds to the clutter rather than providing a unique position in the marketplace (O'Reilly & Séguin, 2011). As McDaniel and Kinney (1998) noted, this is dangerous because "awareness of official sponsorships is fleeting, especially in a highly cluttered or ambush-prone event environment" (p. 400). Specific to the Olympic Games, the perceived overcommercialization of the Games means that the marketplace may already be cluttered. Séguin and O'Reilly (2008) note that the pursuit of the highest possible price for broadcasting and sponsorship rights could come at the expense of controlling the amount of clutter and providing an opportunity for ambush marketing campaigns to add another layer to the clutter that already exists, further confusing the market and potentially weakening the associations of the official sponsors and the Olympics. With this risk in mind, ambush marketing that seeks to flood the marketplace with unclear messages and images should be considered as a potential threat and therefore approached with an appropriate balanced response.

© Priesen | Dreamstime.com—Mbango Francois Wins Gold Medal Photo

Third, the promotion of brand images and associations by an ambusher that are in contradiction to those valued by and related to the Olympic Movement could present the potential for commercial harm. Indeed, if an ambush marketing campaign presents the potential to dilute the sponsor-Olympic associations through the well-publicized promotion of contradictory images in relation to the Games, it could represent a commercially harmful situation. For instance, during the 1996 Olympic Games in Atlanta, Nike ran a well-activated ambush campaign around the Games promoting the tagline "You Don't Win Silver, You Lose Gold." This was described as being "essentially a counterculture to real sports values . . . (and) completely inappropriate at the time of the Games" (Pound, 2004, p. 162). While Nike was dissuaded from continuing to use the tagline and went on to become a future partner with the Olympics, the situation provides a good example of the perceived dangers of incongruous ambusher associations. The chance that an ambusher's brand message may influence people's perceptions of the Olympic brand in a negative context provides the potential for commercial harm and therefore an anti-ambush response is likely needed in such situations.

Conflicting Interests

When contemplating what matters and what doesn't from an ambush marketing perspective, one must consider and manage the various conflicting interests of the Olympic stakeholders. In an address to the Canadian Sponsorship Forum in March of 2010,

Bill Cooper, then the Director of Commercial Rights Management for VANOC, discussed the risks and challenges associated with trying to manage the needs and expectations of the many stakeholders who wanted access to Olympic marketing rights (Cooper, 2010). Taking a commercial rights perspective, Cooper identified six different stakeholder relationships that might cause a need to examine how to manage their conflicting interests. The outcomes of these considerations can be important for determining what matters and what does not in a given ambush marketing situation.

Three of Cooper's six stakeholder relationships offer examples of conflicting interests that are particularly interesting and need to be considered and managed going forward. The first is the conflict between sponsors and tax-based businesses. Cooper asked the question, "If your host city wants maximum engagement for the local business tax base and your sponsors and licensees want exclusivity, can the two co-exist?" (p. 6). For instance, if a local restaurant wants to engage its business in the atmosphere of the Games, OGOCs need to consider how this can be managed in a way that allows them to do so without violating the exclusivity of a TOP sponsor like McDonald's. A marketer needs to ask what types of engagement could be allowed and what types pose a real danger of commercial harm to the sponsor.

Another conflict identified by Cooper relates to the struggle between managing the conflicting interests of broadcast right holders and marketing right holders. While sponsors are offered the first right of negotiation on broadcast advertising purchases, they are not obligated to buy airtime in their product category, and perhaps after a major outlay on rights and leveraging, their budget does not permit such an all-encompassing media buy. On the other hand, official broadcast partners pay similarly significant fees for the right to be an exclusive broadcaster and their financial success depends on selling advertising airtime for a premium price. With this in mind, Cooper (2010) postulates, "If an official sponsor wants exclusivity and an official broadcaster wants to be able [sic] sell broadcast sponsorship competitively, can the two co-exist?" (p. 5). Given that sponsoring a broadcast, or thematic advertising during the official broadcast are among the most classic methods of ambush marketing (Meenaghan, 1994), this presents a dilemma when determining what matters, and what does not. Third, it is noted by Cooper that a conflict exists between media coverage and media partners. He asks, "If your communications team wants maximum coverage across all available media and your marketing budget requires you to do an official media deal, can the two exist?" (p. 5). Thus, those involved in managing commercial rights must determine the point at which media coverage becomes an unauthorized effort to associate the media company with the Olympic Games thus infringing on the rights of an official media partner.

Considering the three situations above, the suggestion can be put forth that when seeking to determine what matters and what does not, there is a need to develop strong communication channels and integrative solutions among stakeholders. The broadcast department and communications department specifically should be integrated into ambush marketing decision-making at some point in the process to help ensure the response to ambush marketing satisfies the greatest number of stakeholder needs possible.

PREVENTION: THE BEST DEFENSE IS A GOOD OFFENCE

The idea is that strong offensive action will hinder the opposition's ability to mount an opposing counterattack and is known to lead to strategic advantage. This is fitting in the context of ambush marketing as, originally, the term was used in the context of sponsorship with a military connotation to describe how a competitor or a nonsponsor would surprise the official sponsor by engaging in tactics that created confusion amongst consumers as to who is the real sponsor. In other words, ambushers successfully disrupted the exclusivity purchased by sponsors.

Although the IOC was initially reacting to ambush marketing incidents, this approach was soon identified to be too passive since it was believed that even if the IOC and/or OCOG was successful at ending an ambush after an *attack*, the damage was already done and the possible benefits associated with the sponsorship diminished. This became a serious problem for the IOC and led to the adoption of the strategic brand management approach previously described. When managing and protecting the Olympic brand became the priority, the IOC's strategy toward ambush marketing went from a defensive (passive) one to an offensive (proactive) strategy based on collaborative efforts with NOCs, OCOGs, sponsors, and governments, education, legislation, city branding/clean venue, and activation programs. These tactics are described in the sections that follow.

TACTICS TO RESPOND TO AMBUSH MARKETING

Education

Education programs targeted at specific stakeholders are a proactive strategy that is now commonly used by mega-event organizers to manage ambush marketing. For the IOC, anti-ambush marketing educational programs managed by OCOGs reflect such an approach. In fact, despite having legislation to protect its sponsors, the VANOC viewed education as the number one tool in fighting and preventing ambush marketing. The Commercial Rights Management Department (CRM) was responsible for this program and was convinced that this was to become an important legacy for sport organizations having to deal with commercial partners. Sponsors, potential ambushers, and consumers were all targeted. VANOC dedicated high-level marketing personnel to work with sponsors from the time they signed on, since they viewed it to be essential that sponsors understood exactly what rights they had purchased, how to best use those rights, the ability of VANOC to protect those rights, and the challenges to be expected in this respect.

The task of educating the various targets (consumers, potential ambushers, sport organizations, athletes, employees, volunteers, etc.) was a complex and broad undertaking. Here, VANOC created a variety of tools (e.g., brochure, PowerPoint presentations, internet site) that were communicated through direct mail, presentations at conferences (public, private, and academic), and one-on-one meetings with business/sport leaders. The goals were to outline how stakeholders could engage with the brand without infringing on the rights and what, exactly, would be considered ambush marketing in the eyes of VANOC. Stakeholders (including the general public) were also encouraged to report possible infringements by filing a form on the website or by calling a 1-800-hotline number. While education was a clear goal of this campaign, it was also the intention of VANOC to send a clear message to the business (i.e., nonsponsor) community that if ambush strategies were to be considered, it would not be tolerated.

Following the lead of VANOC, education programs targeted at national and local sport governing bodies on topics such as general marketing, brand management, ambush protection expectations, symbol registration, and protection are now becoming a common strategy in managing and responding to ambush marketing.

Legislation

Since legislation became a requirement of many mega-event bid processes, governments no longer limit their involvement to providing financial and political support. Indeed, the fierce competition between cities and/or countries seeking to host a limited number of hallmark events has made it easier for those properties to demand more from host cities and their respective governments. For example, in its candidature procedure and questionnaire for candidates interested in bidding for the Olympic Games, the IOC requires a potential host for "guarantee(s) confirming that the legislation necessary to effectively reduce and sanction ambush marketing is enacted."

For the 2010 Vancouver Games, the Canadian Government did provide such a guarantee by passing *Olympic and Paralympic Marks Act* (OPMA). The Act provided "for the protection of Olympic and Paralympic marks and protection against certain misleading business associations between a business and the Olympic Games, the Paralympic Games or certain committees associated with those Games" (Olympic and Paralympic Marks Act, 2007). OPMA was designed to add protection to permanent legislation (Trademarks Act) that already protected Olympic words, symbols such as the Olympic rings, and the words "Canadian Olympic Committee." More importantly, OPMA offered the organizing committee an increased ability to seek resolution though the law in a more timely and undemanding manner. Recently, this mode of prevention has continued to become ever more stringent. The legislation passed for the London 2012 Games, *the London Olympic and Paralympic Games Act 2006* included a "Right of Association." While this development has been criticized individually (Scassa, 2011) and as part of the placement of ambush marketing in such a rigid legal framework (Ellis et al., 2011), it arguably represents an increased opportunity to proactively attempt to protect the Games from ambush marketing. The argument is made that the creation of such strong legal measures represents an increasing deterrent for those who are considering an ambush marketing campaign (Ellis et al., 2011). It also closes loopholes that savvy and well-advised potential ambushers would have sought to exploit in other years. So while anti-ambush marketing legislation is often thought of as a reactive response, it also represents an opportunity for proactive protection by acting as an upfront, pre-Games deterrent.

City Branding/Clean Venue

The IOC now demands specific guarantees "confirming that the legislation necessary to effectively reduce and sanction ambush marketing and, during the period beginning two weeks before the Opening Ceremony to the Closing Ceremony of the Olympic Games eliminate street vending and control advertising space and air space will be passed . . ." (IOC, 2008:124).

© Faustasyan | Dreamstime.com—White Teddy Bear Symbol of Sochi Olympics in 2014

The IOC also seeks to control all outdoor advertising in the host city and those municipalities having an operational role in staging the games (e.g. venue cities, transport hub cities). Similarly, all advertising space at the airports used for the Olympic Games and in those airports having an operational role are also included (IOC, 2008). Once all outdoor and airport advertising are under the control of the OCOG, a comprehensive *Look of the Games* is rolled out throughout the city. As athletes and spectators arrived for the Sochi 2014 Olympic Games, they were greeted with signage featuring the official mascots, including the Polar Bear, right.

Outdoor billboards and other public space are used for sponsor advertising or to place a variety of signs that communicates the visual identify of the OCOG's brand.

ACTIVATION PROGRAM

As noted by Crimmins and Horn (1996), "if a brand cannot afford to spend to communicate its sponsorship, it cannot afford sponsorship at all" (p. 19). As examined in the previous chapters, the development of strategic activation programs is essential for sponsors. While this means additional investment, it ensures that sponsors are taking advantage of the numerous intangible brand associations that are linked to the Olympic Games. Effective activation also has the ability to create a connection in the consumer's mind between the Olympic Games and the sponsor thus making it more difficult for ambushers to create confusion (see Crow & Hoek, 2003; Meenaghan, 1996).

A vital tactic in combatting ambush marketing is for sponsors to ensure that they *own* the marketplace. In this context, "own" refers to being the organization that is most commonly associated with a given attribute. For example, Nike *owns* the best athletes, Visa *owns* the Olympics, Volvo *owns* safety, and Apple *owns* online music. If the corporation has done its job in making consumers aware it is the official sponsor and has fully integrated its brand with the Olympics, it does not leave much of an opportunity for a non-sponsor to launch an ambush campaign to cause confusion.

To summarize, activation should be considered as part of the cost associated with sponsorship from the beginning of the partnership and both parties should work together to ensure a leveraging program that is fully integrated into the marketing and communications program of each organization. Such a consistent and encompassing approach to building awareness for these relationships will help ensure prevention of damaging ambush programs.

REACTIVE RESPONSES TO AMBUSH MARKETING

Occasions arise when a proactive approach is not possible or plausible. Instead, to protect the brands and sponsors, three tactics may be employed including naming and shaming, legal actions, and on the ground local *brand police*.

Name and Shame

Name and shame is a well-known reactive tool used by event organizers to bring an ambusher into the spotlight. For example, in a case where strategies such as "cease and desist" letters do not have the anticipated response, the property may decide to go to the media with the intention to damage the ambusher's reputation by denouncing its perceived unethical, inappropriate, or disgraceful marketing attempts to ambush the property and steal from the event organizers. Essentially, it is a PR campaign aimed at painting the ambusher in a negative light with the hopes that they will prefer ending the ambush rather than being perceived as an untrustworthy or unethical corporation in the eyes of the consumer. Given the huge media attention around the Olympic Games, the simple threat of naming and shaming is sometimes enough to stop an ambush. This was the case famously described (see Chapter 14) by one of the authors of this book, Dick Pound, when he communicated about carrying an American Express (AMEX) credit card in his wallet and threatening to cut it in half at an IOC press conference if AMEX proceeded with its ambush campaign.

Another example is the case of Esso (Imperial Oil) prior to the 2010 Olympic Winter Games, where the name-and-shame response did end up going in front of a national audience when VANOC decided to engage an Olympic gold medalist, media partners, and government partners in condemning the promotion. Tactically, a press conference was organized at a hotel purposely chosen to be next door to Imperial Oil's headquarters. During the address to a room packed with media, VANOC's CEO John Furlong, forcefully depicted the company as using unethical/unfair means that in essence cheated the athletes. He further argued that this was done because of Esso's wish to deceive the public. The CEO was followed by the athletes' spokesperson (a high-profile Olympic gold medalist) who suggested that the company was essentially "stealing" since its actions jeopardized future funding for athletes. The CEO of VANOC was reported as saying, "How can we credibly appeal to Canadian companies to support our Games and our athletes if their competitors can accidentally or deliberately undermine those investments?" (Blaike, 2006). He continued by implying that governments (and hence, taxpayers) would be left to pay any deficit related to the Vancouver Games if sponsors became unwilling to invest. In the end, Esso dropped this specific promotion. While this was an important victory for VANOC, other such attempts were not so successful. For example, there was the case of Lululemon, a popular leisurewear company from Vancouver, who created an ambush campaign around the 2010 Games (for full details and deeper learning, a case study on the topic is included at the end of this chapter). By going to the media to name and shame Lululemon, VANOC unintentionally provided a platform for the company to talk about its support of the community and high-profile athletes and the fact that they did not intend to fool anybody.

In summary, as nonsponsors' use of ambush marketing increases in sophistication and frequency, the use of naming and shaming will likely continue to decrease as it can be leveraged by the ambusher for increased media attention. As suggested earlier, it may be that property owners are now aware that the added media attention given to ambushers may actually have the reverse effect (and a negative one for the official sponsor and the property). Thus, a name-and-shame campaign may be the objective of nonsponsor ambusher as it may provide great publicity for their campaigns, may place the official sponsor in a negative light, and could position the property as greedy and unfair to the nonsponsor. However, it is important to note that this is likely only plausible with smaller players, as major global corporations cannot generally afford the risk of a well-managed exposure à la AMEX and Esso. In the case of the Olympic brand, the ability of the nonsponsor to link to the perception of the Games being over commercialized and only about money further increases the risk associated with the name and shame technique.

As discussed, anti-ambush marketing legislation is being used as a proactive strategy to deter potential ambushers from carrying out their campaigns. However, not all ambushers are deterred and when their actions run afoul of such laws, there are legal remedies that can be applied in response. The exact legal responses available for every individual OCOG are shaped by the specifics of the law that has been created (i.e. OPMA or LOGPGA) and the constitutional and legal framework in which they are addressed (see Ellis et al., 2011). For instance, Canada's *Olympic and Paralympic Marks Act 2007* was the first to allow for an injunction to be granted against ambushers without the typical burden of proof for irreparable harm that cannot be undone through monetary compensation. The *London Olympic and Paralympic Games Act 2006*, includes such responses as a payment of damages, injunctions, the recovery of lost profits, and the delivery to the plaintiff or destruction of offending items. Some anti-ambush marketing laws go so far as to include the potential for jail time if found guilty of infringement (i.e., South Africa's *Merchandise Marks Amendment Act 61, 2002)*. While legal remedies are typically considered a last resort, they do offer a hardline (and often expensive) response to ambush marketing practices when it is needed.

Brand and Ambush Marketing Police

The main role of the brand police is to protect against the unauthorized use of marks and ambush marketing. Within Olympic venues, brand police are looking for anything that could provide advertisers with inappropriate exposure. For example, fans in the crowd are not allowed to upload clips of the day's action to YouTube or to post their pictures from inside the Olympic Village on Facebook. Brand police have the power to remove or cover manufacturers' logos that are not part of official sponsorships; examples include asking athletes to remove clothing with nonsponsor logos and taping over words, slogans, images or logos on journalists' computers, or on venue soap dispensers and toilets. They may ask ticket holders to remove some clothing if too many people are wearing similar brands that are noticeable. The mandate of the brand police also extends to counterfeit merchandise and the inappropriate use of marks. The main challenge is to find the proper balance between protecting sponsors' interests and impeaching on the public's freedom.

In such a controlled situation, there is again the danger of bringing highly commercialized issues into the public domain and, as such, linking the Olympic brand with *money* and *commercial interests* that are in opposition to the true essence of the brand. The quote below is an example of how the 2012 brand police were discussed within the UK media:

> Hundreds of uniformed Olympic officers will begin touring the country today enforcing sponsors' multimillion-pound marketing deals, in a highly organized mission that contrasts with the scramble to find enough staff to secure Olympic sites. [Y]esterday, the Culture Secretary, Jeremy Hunt, refused to rule out that even more soldiers may be called upon to help with security, but dismissed the issue as merely a "hitch." However, as well as the regular Army, the Olympic "brand army" will start its work with a vengeance today. (Hickman, 2012)

Such negative media attention must be taken into consideration and the appropriate response for these situations undertaken to ensure that the Olympic stakeholders are protecting themselves from their own potentially brand-damaging activities.

AMBUSH MARKETING EXTERNALITIES

In any ambush marketing response, three specific considerations must be taken into account. These are *time*, *proportionality*, and *public relations*. Each is described here in further detail.

Time

There is a temporary structure to the Olympic Games. Each Games is 16 days in length, each OCOG goes from foundation to termination in the space of seven years, and each bid process is about two years long. This means that there is a fixed time during which both the risks and rewards of sponsorship (and therefore ambush marketing) are at their height. The Olympic brand, while always prevalent, rises to the forefront of public consciousness in the few weeks before and after the Games are taking place, allowing for the greatest opportunity for sponsors to leverage the partnership they have built with the brand.

At the same time, this heightened interest also creates the best environment for non-sponsors to adopt ambush marketing methods (e.g., thematic advertising, subcategory sponsorship) to try and make their own association with the Games and create confusion in the market, whose effect can be heightened given that interest during this period is short and intense. Indeed, it is possible that without a quick response much confusion can be created in a very short period of time, with little time left to provide the marketplace with clarity as to who is actually the official sponsor. Thus, there is a need to ensure a rapid response to threats of Olympic ambush marketing activities, particularly during the time around the Games. The argument has been made that legislation offers one way to accomplish the goal of a fast response (Ellis, 2013). The creation of the ability for an injunction against the alleged ambusher to be granted before the standard burden of proof has been met means that ambushers can be stopped before they are able to do much *harm* and the legal details can be sorted out after the Olympic Games. While this raises many questions about the extent of the power of anti-ambush marketing legislation, it is felt to be an advantage by organizers and sponsors.

Proportionality of Response

A second consideration is the use of a response to ambush marketing that is proportional to the perceived offense. Since ambush marketing can often be difficult to define and there are plenty of grey areas involved when looking at what is or is not considered to be an ambush, caution needs to be taken and conflicts of interest considered. For instance, at what point does a small family restaurant in a host community who has put up Olympic-related signage cross the line from community and event engagement into ambush marketing?

It is argued that those stakeholders involved in Olympic marketing should recognize the need to examine each situation individually, taking the full context into consideration and then making a reasoned and informed judgment about the appropriate type and strength of response, if at all. More specifically, it is suggested that when making determinations about the appropriate ambush response one should, first and foremost, consider both the intentions of the perceived ambusher and the risks and likelihood of commercial harm potentially resulting from the ambusher's actions. A major corporate sponsor is unlikely to feel any commercial harm as a result of the actions of a small family-owned business that is merely engaging the Games with no obvious intention of taking the spotlight or market share away from the sponsor. In such an instance, if it was felt that a response was warranted that response should be proportionate to the potential for harm with perhaps a polite, explanatory phone call or a brief, polite letter outlining the issue.

During the 2010 Winter Games in Vancouver, a proportionality of response type of approach appeared to be part of VANOC's strategy. Their approach to brand protection was being "committed to enforcing [their] rights in a disciplined, sensitive, fair, and transparent manner" (VANOC, 2008, p. 10). The CRM developed and communicated a set of guidelines for various stakeholders, including the public, the local business community, and the national corporate community. These guidelines provide a two-part ambush marketing assessment process detailing the way in which a potential ambush situation would be classified as either high concern or low concern.

Despite a general move towards increased transparency, critics of this approach can argue that any determination of a proportionate response and the level of infringement assessment is still dependent on a subjective interpretation of the rules and the given situation thus there continues to be a danger of overpolicing the issue of ambush marketing.

PUBLIC RELATIONS

Discussed previously, public relations, or PR, can also be a proactive response, but it can be used as a reactive one as well. Notably, alongside any anti-ambush marketing program, there is a need to consider and manage PR concerns that might arise related to such programs since there is always a risk of creating an appearance of being a bully, especially when these actions are taken against smaller, local and/or family businesses. Indeed, in such cases, public sentiment is more likely to fall on the side of a small business than a major global corporation, even if the concerns of the official sponsor are legitimate. Clearly, any response

> **Tactical Example: The VANOC Infringement Assessment**
>
> As introduced and explained in earlier parts of the text, infringement assessments are a key component of ensuring legislation is adhered to. As a further illustration, the process used at the Vancouver 2010 Olympics is presented here.
>
> In the first part of the process, the CRM team would undertake an infringement assessment, where the guide outlined six factors: (1) factually accurate use (correct use of the brand); (2) relevant use (attached to a larger, ongoing storyline not disproportionately connected to the Games); (3) commercially neutral (does not contribute to an unauthorized business association); (4) undue prominence (brand is not given gratuitous prominence in the larger initiative); (5) use of Olympic or Paralympic visuals (using logos, historical Game imagery etc.); and (6) unauthorized association (related to timing and strategic placement of advertising in question) (VANOC, 2008). In any given case of perceived ambush, the CRM team would allot each of the above factors a rating between 1 (low) and 3 (high) to achieve a combined score on the 6 factors. A score of 8 or less was considered to be a low-risk situation that would only be lightly monitored going forward, while a score of 14 or higher was considered an infringement. A score in between 9 and 13, requires further observation and assessment (VANOC, 2008). Once the level of infringement has been assessed, the second part of the process involves a determination of the appropriate enforcement response. The measures considered in this portion of the process are less transparent than those provided for infringement assessment, just noting that such considerations will be taken.

that is perceived as disproportionate, if not properly managed from a public relations perspective, has the potential to do more damage to the Olympic (IOC) brand and sponsor's brand than the ambush marketing itself.

Furthermore, consumers do not care to see two major corporations fight their battles in public. In the end it looks good on no group, not the sponsor, not the Olympic movement, and not the ambusher for two major corporations to be trading insults in the media and attracting negative attention away from the athletes and the true values of the Games. In this case, a comprehensive public relations program is taking on the larger task of brand protection. If negative public perceptions are created by the response to ambush marketing, they could translate to negative brand associations, ultimately harming the brand value and equity of the Olympic Movement.

CHAPTER SUMMARY

This chapter outlines how to respond to ambush marketing tactically. It implies that ambush is a marketing ploy that one must respond to, however it also presents the legal responses that position ambush marketing as wrong. So, the question begs, does the de-

© Bobsphotography | Dreamstime.com—Wooden Bavaria Beer Barrels Photo

cision to use ambush marketing automatically make someone—or some organization—evil? Simply, if an organization considers ambushing a rights holder, are they practicing black magic?

Some parties—academics, politicians, and practitioners alike—have come to believe that ambushing is illegal, mean-spirited, corrupt, malicious, criminal, and an act worthy of the punishments meted out for treason or a major felony. It is positioned to be worse than forgery but not as bad as murder. So does thinking about using ambush strategies or tactics automatically make a CEO, VP, or marketing director *evil*? Can only certain business types even entertain going down this "dark hallway"? Are certain categories (such as apparel or soft drinks) allowed while others (like clothing companies) not? What about certain individuals? Is there a psychology needed to entertain the use of ambushing? And a different one to respond to it?

We know that anyone that entertains ambush is likely to be tarred with a certain stripe. Think about the Bavaria beer executive who lost his job—publicly—following his orchestrated ambush at the 2010 FIFA World Cup. Is ambush marketing a career derailment waiting to happen? And yet . . . and yet . . . ambushing tactics happen and some are brilliant and recognized publicly as brilliant. A good example is Subway's use of Olympic athletes to ambush McDonald's. What about the Pepsi Taste Test or Wendy's using real humans named Ronald McDonald or Ford running ads with people driving competitors' cars and comparing them? Are these evil or smart?

Thus, although ambushing may be evil (not to mention illegal) in certain cases, it may not be as evil as is often presented. So the smart organizations who prevent ambush (such as the IOC, OCOGs, and FIFA) are not necessarily fighting evil, they are protecting their partners' interests and, in turn, their revenue sources. Perhaps that is the best way to finish this chapter . . . intelligence, including the use of legal tactics, is the key to responding to ambush.

Key Chapter Questions

1. What are the harmful consequences of ambush marketing?
2. Who are the key stakeholders in maintaining the premium of the Olympic brand?
3. If you lead a marketing campaign, how would you advise your team to respond to an ambush?
4. From everything examined in this book to this point, and in this chapter, would you classify ambush marketing as evil?

Key Chapter Takeaways

1. The threat of ambush marketing has placed tremendous pressure on sport properties to develop strategies aimed at protecting their brands and their sponsors.
2. Given the tremendous increase in ambush marketing it is important to focus anti-ambush efforts where there is potential for real (or irreparable) brand harm and avoid responses where the cost to control would far exceed any potential harm.
3. Education and legislation can help deter ambush marketing.
4. The best defense is a good offence.

Case Study 16.1

Creative Ambushing

Vancouver Olympic Committee (VANOC)

The Vancouver Organizing Committee for the 2010 Olympic and Paralympic Winter Games (VANOC) was a not-for-profit organization responsible for planning, developing, organizing, financing, and orchestrating the 2010 Winter Olympic and Paralympics. After the 2010 Games were awarded to Vancouver, British Columbia, in 2003, VANOC was established in order to perform roles required to mandate support and promote the development of sport in Canada (VANOC, 2010).

International Olympic Committee (IOC):

Described in detail in earlier chapters in the book, the International Olympic Committee (IOC) is an international not-for-profit association based in Switzerland, which chooses the hosts and ensures the organization of the modern Olympic Games and Youth Olympic Games.

VANOC Sponsorship:

VANOC presented three tiers of national sponsorship to Canadian companies as part of the domestic sponsorship program for the 2010 Games. Tier one consisted of the airline, banking, brewery, telecommunications, and petroleum categories. Tier two represented the categories of clothing, cruise lines, hospitality, postal service and courier, computer hardware, internet, home improvement, telecom hardware (non-wireless), insurance, resources, office products, and retail companies. Tier three included the airport, catering, consulting services, consumer goods, department store, food products, freight forwarding and customs brokering, market research, lumber, hotels, health services, greeting cards, furniture, mining, network equipment, packaged goods, personal care products, rail services, heating, ventilation and air conditioning, snow-making, and grooming equipment, ticketing, temporary power, recruitment and staffing, and security equipment categories.

(Continued on next page)

Case Study 16.1 (continued)

As VANOC sponsors, companies had exclusive rights to the Olympic logo and the opportunity to develop an inclusive marketing platform around the Olympic Rings. In addition, sponsors had the advantage of market share exclusivity (in Canada), cross-selling, in-store marketing and fundraising programs, as well as benefiting from the various "halo effects" provided by the affiliation to the IOC, the Olympics, the Olympic brand, the five rings, and the Olympic core values (IOC, 2011).

In an effort to protect its sponsors, VANOC spent roughly US $40 million to buy every square inch of outdoor advertising space in Vancouver and the surrounding mainland areas, extending from billboards to transit buses during the Olympic Games. In turn, to protect the Olympic sponsors, the space purchased by VANOC was resold only to Olympic sponsors, giving them the opportunity to use prime visibility for advertising and preventing corporate rivals from ambush marketing (Bradish, 2010).

LULULEMON ATHLETICA

On Monday, December 14th 2009, Lululemon, a Vancouver-based manufacturer and retailer of technical athletic apparel for yoga, running, and exercising, launched a new line of clothing that attracted a great deal of attention. As a nonsponsor of the Vancouver Olympic Games, Lululemon launched its "Cool Sporting Event That Takes Place in British Columbia Between 2009 and 2011 Edition" at stores across Canada.

It was not long after that VANOC received word of Lululemon's creative yet audacious product line that they responded with a name-and-shame approach. Bill Cooper, director of commercial rights management for VANOC responded by stating that "we [VANOC] expected better sportsmanship from a local Canadian company than to produce a clothing line that attempts to profit from the Games but doesn't support the Games or the success of the Canadian Olympic team."

By most accounts, the marketing tactics of Lululemon would be considered to be a form of predatory ambushing, since Lululemon intentionally bombarded a competing official sponsor (Hudson's Bay Company (HBC)) with the intent of achieving market share and to confuse consumers as to whom the official sponsor was. Although, some could argue that this form of ambushing is associative (i.e., lacking any wording or images that clearly links the promotion to the 2010 Games), Lululemon's undertakings were considered by VANOC to be too dis-

tinct and calculated for their actions to be seen as anything but deliberate (Burton and Chadwick, 2010; Canada 2010, 2010).

When the Lululemon action came to light, many reviewed closely the rights that VANOC had been provided by the IOC as the host organization of the 2010 Games. Such a review showed that, when it comes to advertising during the Olympics, VANOC had exclusive Canadian marketing rights to all elements of the Olympic brand from January 1st, 2005, to December 31st, 2012. During this time, only the official (paying) sponsors were able to associate with the Olympics and use the Olympic marks. Given the amount of revenue attracted from these domestic sponsorships, OCOGs are especially protective of the Olympic brand, threatening and following through with legal action against any businesses attempting to capitalize on Games trademarks (CBC News, 2009). This was the case for Lululemon.

However, Lululemon was not the only company warned or told to stop ambush marketing. They had done their homework and were prepared. Akin to any marketer aware of the Olympic rights, they did not go as far as to use obvious trademark words such as "Olympic," "podium," or "medal" or the image or emblem of the Olympic rings. In fact, the bright and creative marketers at Lululemon were able to build awareness on the international hype surrounding the Olympics without violating the restrictions granted to VANOC by the IOC, the COC, and the anti-ambush legislation (Shaw,

(Continued on next page)

Case Study 16.1 *(continued)*

2010). So, although Lululemon's product collection and other marketing activities around this collection had caused issues and VANOC felt there was significant risk of imposing harm on the Games, VANOC did not pursue legal action against Lululemon. The reason that no legal action was pursued is that Lululemon did a very good job of researching ambush marketing legislation and strategy, and then strategizing to avoid strict consequences under the letter of the law. In spite of Lululemon's actions, VANOC tried to persuade Lululemon to change their marketing tactics while they were advertising their new clothing line.

Lululemon insisted that their clothing line was about patriotism and not ambush marketing. They noted widely that they support athletes at all levels and would continue to do so for both local and world competing athletes from across Canada.

Case Questions

1. In your opinion, is Lululemon's clothing line about patriotism or ambush marketing?
2. What can other NOCs and future host Olympic committees implement in preventative strategies to abstain creative companies like Lululemon from ambushing?
3. Was this act of ambush marketing by Lululemon avoidable from VANOC's stance? Should there have been better management with foreseeing such stunts from competing nonofficial companies?
4. What areas of educating consumers need to improve regarding the deficits linked with ambush marketing?
5. Is it possible to create a letter of law that completely blocks ambushing marketing at the Olympics?
6. What opportunities has Lululemon created for other nonofficial sponsors?

17

Ambush in Practice: A Significant Marketing Quandary for the Olympic Games

Many marketing personnel for the International Olympic Committee (IOC) and National Olympic Committees (NOCs), and executives from National Sport Organizations (NSOs), International Federations (IFs), and the TOP sponsors are often asked by researchers, students, or journalists to comment on ambush strategies and tactics. This is particularly reasonable since marketers often seem to associate the concept of *ambush marketing* with the Olympic Games (and to a lesser extent the FIFA World Cup). The reason might have something to do with some of the most memorable ambush efforts and many other attempts or defenses that are linked to specific Olympic Games. Just think about some of the classic all-time marketing rivalries, such as Visa—Master Card, Coke—Pepsi, Nike—Reebok (and recently Under Armour), Kodak—Fuji, Anheuser-Busch—MillerCoors, Molson—Labatts, and Subway—McDonald's—Wendy's.

If the reader likes all-out competition, a battle between two or more competing consumer product giants with money to spend is something fascinating to observe. It is certainly great for advertising and sports marketing agencies plus TV networks, magazine, and sports properties. Or as Steve Battista, SVP Brand Creative for Under Armour told *The Hub Magazine*, "Relentless curiosity about how to do things differently and tell our story in a better, bigger way—that's what drives innovation at Under Armour. [When we come to work] it's game on. Time to take on the big guys" (January/February 2014; p. 22).

The genesis for this feisty issue is probably drawn from the historical reality that the IOC was the first modern sport property to limit the number of categories and prioritize category exclusivity for sponsors, thus allowing them to associate with the Olympics.

This chapter builds on Chapters 14, 15, and 16 to provide a deeper and applied understanding of ambush marketing through the authors' experiences with the Olympic

Games and to frame the concept from the perspective of the ambushing party as well as the organization getting ambushed. The key objective for the reader is to grasp some of the historical origins of Olympic ambushing, some of the most noted examples, and to provide opportunity for informed discussion on whether ambush marketing is wrong, evil, or a logical counteractivity by competitive *brands* seeking to protect or gain market share.

Admittedly, there will also be some abstract concepts, such as the suggestion that a city can be ambushed by its own leaders or to suggest that some entities (e.g., the IOC, FIFA, or even a country such as Great Britain) may seek to promote government legislation to protect private sponsors and to ensure either a sense of fair play or comprehensive control. Some readers will enter into this conversation and suggest the prohibition of ambush marketing borders is a denial of free speech or dictatorial/socialistic control. The authors of this text welcome that conversation in countries where free speech is protected or provided.

A SHORT HISTORY OF OLYMPIC AMBUSHING AND SEVEN TYPES OF AMBUSH

Looking at modern brands, both Coke and Eastman Kodak have suggested that they were involved in some of the earliest Olympic Games with Kodak buying an ad in the scoring program as early as the 1896 Games in Athens and Coke providing product (1,000 cases) for the 1928 Amsterdam Games. Four years later, Omega became the official timekeeper of the 1932 Olympics in Los Angeles and started a memorable relationship with the IOC and various Olympic Games hosts since. In each of these cases and those of any current or past TOP sponsor, most argue that their

© Pindiyath100 | Dreamstime.com—Omega Clock Photo

competitors, realizing the value of an Olympic partnership, have sought to infringe— or ambush—some of this value at some point.

But what is this ambush concept? At a minimum, there are at least seven types of ambush that we have observed and some of the choices might surprise readers:

1. A Non-Games Sponsor ambushes an Official Games Sponsor before, during, or after the Olympics
2. A Non-Games Sponsor ambushes Official Games Sponsor after the Olympics conclude
3. Official Games Sponsor ambushes another Official Games Sponsor
4. Official Games Sponsor ambushes the spirit of the IOC (example to follow)

5. Official NOC Sponsor ambushes the spirit of the IOC or the NOC
6. Official IF sponsor or NSO Sponsor ambushes the NOC or IOC
7. A Non-Sponsor ambushes the OCOG

Readers should note that presenting seven types of ambush (above) might be seen by some in the sports industry as rather cavalier (or excessive), but this breadth has been created here on purpose to ensure that readers understand that ambush marketing (or coordinated ambush marketing activities) is a real and varied business concept frequently employed and often without full understanding of what is happening. It is also, in many countries, a societal concern when the right to advertise or promote a product is denied or restricted, based solely on the provision of sport sponsorship exclusivity and the intertwining of sport relying on corporate influence and a complicit government using sport to promote its own international agenda (i.e., tourism, economic stability, or political ideology).

Certainly, for our purposes, any sports organization that sells sponsorship rights or seeks to sell a concept (such as hosting the Olympic Games) that is supported by sponsorship is likely to face intentional and nonintentional matters of ambush. In a modern society, this is notable and we must therefore understand why ambushing happens. It is perhaps valuable to draw a sense of what ambushing has been from a few of the more notable ambush moments in Olympic history and to understand some historical roots.

In his 1985 book *Made in America*, Peter Ueberroth, the president of the Los Angeles OCOG (LAOOC) for the 1984 Summer Olympic Games (and later the chair of the board of the US Olympic Committee), writes about the need to privatize the hosting and presentation of the Olympics (at least in order to cost-efficiently stage them in Los Angeles where there would be no national or state public money provided to support this undertaking). In one section, Ueberroth (1985) noted,

> Everyone assumed Kodak would step forward with a big check, and the local Kodak people assured us hundreds of times that Kodak's sponsorship was a fait accompli. It [Kodak] had been a sponsor of the Games before and it had also sponsored the US team. Kodak dominated the field, and it was this strength that ruined any chance of making a deal. Kodak was smug. Kodak's lead lawyer played games with us, believing we had no other choice. He persisted in offering us only half of our $4 million floor. Kodak underestimated us. Meanwhile, Dentsu, Inc., a Japanese advertising agency, brought in Fuji Film. We asked Dentsu to put Fuji on ice. Finally, we told Kodak to fish or cut bait. Kodak missed its deadline, and we gave Fuji 72 hours to sign. Fuji came in for $7 million and agreed to process, without charge, all news photographers' film at the Games—something Kodak had never even contemplated (pp. 71–72).

In that moment, a giant of the sports sponsorship world and a long-time supporter of the Olympics were out of the Games (with numerous Kodak employees reportedly losing their jobs). But Kodak sprang back into action by becoming a sponsor of the US Track and Field team and by buying an exclusive position on ABC's television broadcast.

The net consequence?

People in Los Angeles and IOC officials would have been aware Fuji was the official sponsor of the LA Games, but fans watching at home probably saw familiar Kodak advertisements and assumed Kodak was once again the official film category sponsor.

Thirty-six years later, during the 2010 Vancouver Winter Olympics, the sandwich chain Subway, which was not an official sponsor of the IOC, VANOC, or the USOC, designed a television advertisement that showed swimmer Michael Phelps, the winner of eight gold medals during the 2008 Beijing Summer Olympics, diving off a racing platform and beginning what looked like one of his famous attempts at gold. As an unusual commercial effect, Subway showed Phelps not slowing down to make a customary flip turn at the far end of the pool but powering through the pool's wall and presumably swimming through concrete and earth. When the commercial cut to a map of the northwestern United States and southwestern Canada, a line showed Phelps burrowing through Oregon and Washington clearly headed toward British Columbia's capital of Vancouver.

For Olympic marketers, this was sacrilege. Not only was McDonald's the official restaurant sponsor of the IOC and VANOC but swimming was not even a sport of the Winter Olympics. Still, to an uninformed consumer sitting hungrily on a couch in Alberta, Texas, or Florida, the image Subway successfully created was one that violated no *rules* but clearly ambushed both the official sponsor (McDonald's) and the Winter Games.

In between these moments of 1984 and 2010, there have been numerous examples of ambush behavior that have caused varying levels of concern, outrage, and threatened lawsuits. In John Davis's 2008 book *The Olympic Games Effect: How Sports Marketing Builds Strong Brands*, Davis points out a few key examples worth sharing here:

- 1992—Barcelona: Nike sponsors news conferences with the US basketball team and when Michael Jordan [the star of the Team USA Dream Team] accepts the gold medal for basketball, [he] covers up his Reebok logo [on his medals podium track jacket]
- 1994—Lillehammer: American Express runs ads claiming "that if you are going to Norway, you'll need a passport but you won't need a Visa" [in response to Visa's legendary ad campaign that spectators going to the Olympics had better bring their Visa because it was the only credit card accepted]
- 1996—Atlanta: Nike buys out billboards around Atlanta's Olympic sites and sponsors Michael Johnson's famous golden shoes, impacting Reebok's official sponsorship
- 2000—Sydney: Qantas Airlines's slogan "Spirit of Australia" coincidentally sounds like Games slogan "Share the Spirit" to chagrin of official Sydney Olympic sponsor Ansett Air
- 2008—Beijing: Pepsi (not an authorized sponsor of the Games) changes its can color to red from blue for the Beijing Olympics ostensibly because red is an auspicious color in China [and because Coke's can has always been red]

AMBUSH MARKETING OPERATIONALIZED

Definitions of ambush marketing were presented in Chapters 13 and 14. Practically, Davis (2008) defines the concept simply as being "a practice whereby a company attempts to associate itself with a significant event, such as the Olympics, in an unauthorized and unofficial way without paying the sponsorship fees." In essence, then, an ambush is somewhat like the surprise attack that the word ambush connotes. A party that is conducting a traditional business venture is *surprised* by a hidden (or disguised) opponent that seeks something the traditionalist was not expecting. As an example, if Coca-Cola purchases exclusive partnership rights to sponsor a sports event, it should not expect to find Pepsi at the event. If they do, it means Pepsi was able to *ambush* Coke and place their product inside the boundaries of that sporting event.

What's important for readers to understand is that not all ambush activities are illegal. If Coke was sponsoring a marathon, it may want all the banners strung along the race course to reflect Coke's investment in the race. But this does not mean that Pepsi cannot (or should not) try to aggressively sell Pepsi products at every store or restaurant where they are traditionally available for sale. Coke's executives will know this in advance, however, and they would likely go to the race organizers and demand that Pepsi not be allowed to hang competitive banners saying things like "Welcome Race Fans" or "Need Refreshment from the Race? Buy Pepsi Here!" In this case, Coke executives will ask the race organizers who sold Coke an exclusive sponsorship to work diligently to ensure that Pepsi is not allowed to create the impression that they are the sponsor of the marathon.

The Pepsi vs. Coke marketing war was evident in India, Pakistan, and Sri Lanka during the 1996 Cricket World Cup, when a photo was released showing a Coke banner that stated "Coca-Cola Second Floor" with a Pepsi banner placed under it that read, "Pepsi Every Where" The photo turned out to be only an electronic generated ad, but nevertheless Pepsi's smart tagline, there is "Nothing official about it" stole some of Coke's limelight (Ad Wars, 2009). While this example is fairly illustrative of ambush marketing, readers should also consider other ambush circumstances such as the next example below.

In October 2007, less than one year from the August 8th Opening Ceremonies for the Beijing Olympics, the chief marketing officer for the USOC was confronted with a unique situation. Beer giant Anheuser-Busch (A-B), brewers of leading beers Budweiser and Bud Light had made arrangements with a number of top US female Olympic-level athletes to appear in near-naked or sexually provocative poses with giant beer bottles or parked motorcycles. These women were among the best athletes in the world and many of them were capable of winning gold medals in Beijing. This type of advertising posed numerous problems for the USOC on a variety of fronts. First, while the women had the right to sign contracts as paid endorsers for A-B and pose in any fashion they wished ("It's a free country"), conservative Americans might believe the USOC had endorsed this overtly sexual presentation and could complain the USOC was complicit in stereotyping women and helping create or allow advertising that objectified women by treating them as sex objects. Further, the "sexification" of the USOC was not an image that this conservative global sports organization wanted.

Further, if A-B were allowed to present athletes in this fashion, what might other existing or future sponsors propose for American athletes? What if a sponsor wanted to show an athlete smoking or stealing their product for comical effect? What if an athlete wanted to develop a "bad boy" or "bad girl" persona to break through the marketing clutter of *good/positive* athletes upholding Olympian values?

Second, and this was potentially more challenging, the USOC wanted to re-sign A-B as an official (and exclusive) sponsor for the next four years at an increased price. But making the decision to kill their Beijing ad campaign would cost them hundreds of thousands of dollars in economic areas ranging from endorsement fees (to the athletes) to production fees (to the photographers, graphic designers, copy writers, etc.) and in-store replacement costs. The reality was that the USOC had learned of this situation too late to stop something that was already nearing final production. This clearly put the USOC in the very delicate position of trying to tell a major sponsor that the USOC felt like A-B was ambushing the spirit of the Games as well as the USOC's athletes. The compromise? The USOC requested the St. Louis brewer air-brush more clothing back onto these female team members. As one might imagine, A-B did not like this request knowing that many of their

target male consumers did not think very much about the Olympics (and probably knew nothing of the USOC) but that they would stop in a supermarket aisle if the Budweiser point-of-purchase display material presented a pretty girl in a slinky swim suit or tank top cozying up to an ice-cold bottle of Bud. The USOC did not score many points with A-B executives during those discussions but an "air-brush" compromise was reached that allowed the USOC to believe it could defend itself against charges (if they materialized) that the organization was sexist and would do anything to accommodate a sponsor.

The USOC faced numerous other challenges and many were created by underfunded NSOs/NGBs that received part of their operating budget from the USOC but also needed to augment that income by selling sponsorships specifically for their sport. In the modern era, the pressure has mounted on NSO executives to produce more medal winners and top eight finishes at world championships, forcing them to seek out better world-class training facilities or pay larger stipends to their athletes to facilitate daily training. In short, if an athlete has to work to feed him/herself (or their family), it is not possible to train adequately. But for the NSO to generate more money, it needs to either sell more sponsorship packages or stage more events that deliver new broadcast rights revenues or generate ticket sales. For many NSOs this is not possible.

The problem in the United States has been that the USOC is held responsible for protecting the TOP sponsors, as well as USOC national sponsors like A-B, AT&T, 24 Hour Fitness, or The Home Depot. In total, the TOP and USOC sponsors probably covered the 20–25 most prominent sponsorship categories and left very few "open categories" for NSOs to consider. [*From the authors: As noted previously, the USOC is a unique NOC in that the US government does not fund athlete development or training but leaves that to the USOC and the respective NSOs. The USOC's funding, however, is protected by federal law (the Ted Stevens Act) that mandates that any use of the Olympic rings or Olympic trademarked concepts (i.e., gold, silver, and bronze) must be approved by the USOC. This explains, in part, why the USOC receives a significant payment from the IOC for a portion of the US broadcast rights and a portion of TOP sponsorship revenue. In other countries, government funding underwrites the development and training of Olympic hopefuls.*]

Invariably, the USOC's challenge is understanding that an NSO may be incentivized (or lured) to strike up relationships with a company or brand that wants the appeal of the Olympics without having to pay a major premium or serve as a global TOP partner or even as a national (USOC) partner. Further, the act of working with an NSO like track and field, swimming, gymnastics, soccer, hockey, figure skating, or skiing could give that marketer a certain Olympic grass roots appeal that allowed brand managers and advertising agency executives to project a broad appeal of endorsement by a popular sport's greatest Olympic heroes (both past and present). Such a sponsor could make it look like they were helping figure skating or gymnastics to produce future Olympians but, in doing so, they could ambush the rights that the USOC had sold to USOC exclusive sponsors.

In certain categories, this NSO sponsorship could overlap onto an existing USOC sponsorship and create a two-front war for the USOC. On one hand they would be fighting their existing sponsor (who expects exclusivity and protection) and on the other hand they would be fighting their own NSO (that desperately seeks incremental revenue to train elite athletes). Further, the potential exists that the IOC may believe that a country like the United States, Canada, Australia, or Great Britain are over-commercializing the Olympics and that appropriate government support/funding would eliminate this NSO-created activity. As always, the problem in stopping an incredibly strong NSO like USA Swimming or Hockey Canada, with a bevy of top US swimmers like Michael Phelps or Dara Torres or pro hockey players like the NHL's Sidney Crosby and Jonathan Toews, is very difficult.

One way for readers to appreciate the challenges of ambush marketing is to draw on a rather famous piece of marketing literature called "Marketing Warfare in the 1980s" by Philip Kotler and Ravi Singh Achrol that was originally published in 1981 in the *Journal of Business Strategy*. While the title of the article may make it sound dated, one of the primary tenets of Kotler and Singh's work was acknowledging that businesses consistently attack each other to claim market share, revenue, or profitability and this leads to concepts such as *frontal attack, flanking attack, encirclement attack, bypass attack* and *guerilla warfare* (which consists of making small, intermittent attacks on the different territories of the opponent, with the aim of harassing and demoralizing the opponent and eventually securing concessions).

All of these stratagems are discussed in the analogy of war and violent behavior allowing Kotler and Singh to draw analogies from military theorists like Germany's Carl von Clausewitz and Great Britain's Basil Liddell Hart. Of particular interest may be Liddell Hart's position that "the 'object' in war is a better state of peace, even if only from your own point of view" (Kotler & Singh, 1984). Adding to this, Kotler and Singh (1984) note that "such a statement seems more compatible with the business milieu, since modern competitors rarely adopt the Clausewitzian objective of 'total annihilation' of the enemy which can ultimately "run afoul of antitrust legislation." (Kotler & Singh, 1984).

It is important to note that, in certain circumstances, the idea of ambush marketing may demoralize an organization that believes it has purchased (often at a high price) exclusivity only to find itself under attack with its key customers acting confused around who the official sponsor is. Thus, ambushing, if it is not structured as a flanking maneuver, is often seen as a worthy tactical element of guerilla warfare. Imagined another way, students might recall old Western movies, as they were often shown on television in the late 1950s and early 1960s. The premise then for Hollywood was generally simplified to showing Party A (a bank or postal service) needing to drive their stagecoach through rough terrain in order to deliver a valuable commodity. Before the drivers set out on the mission, they knew there was a high likelihood that outlaws (Party B) would "ambush" them at some point along the journey.

In this way, both parties (A and B) knew what might happen next. The bank (or train) expected to be attacked and generally took appropriate precautions (cleaning guns, bringing ample ammunition, hiding support riders, or concealing a secret weapon). Meanwhile, the outlaws knew that the stage coach was coming through a specific pass at a specific time and that if they picked the right moment to attack, they could surprise the bank's agents and take their valuables. This analogy is, of course, a bit dated, but the premise that an official sponsor (Party A) is going to support an event like the Rio 2016 Olympics or the Tokyo 2020 Olympics can only result in the likelihood that a competitor (Party B) is going to know the exact route and timing of this marketing activity.

Case Study 17.1

Subway, McDonald's, and the 2010 Olympic Games

The fast sandwich chain Subway knew McDonald's would spend millions in sponsorship fees and activation efforts (TV ads, billboards, in-store promotions, etc.) throughout late 2009 in the run-up to the actual February Vancouver 2010 Olympic Games themselves. McDonald's objectives (i.e., sales growth and market share gains) and tactical actions (i.e., athlete endorsements, point- of-purchase materials visible in all franchises, on-package identification as an official sponsor) were likely to be very clear and industry media would detail much of what McDonald's was planning to do.

To combat possible market share gains that McDonald's might realize in countries like Canada and the US where these two organizations fight over share of stomach

Case Study 17.1 *(continued)*

and billions in revenues, Subway could either reduce spending knowing McDonald's would increase their efforts (and thus abdicate fighting McDonald's *frontal attack*) or Subway could attempt to bring the battle to McDonald's. By January 2010, everyone knew what Subway was going to do: they would ambush McDonald's, VANOC, and the IOC by signing Beijing 2008 swimming superstar Michael Phelps to an endorsement contract.

© Mitchellgunn | Dreamstime.com—SWM: World Aquatics Championship—Ceremony Mens 200m Butterfly Photo

As *Sport Business Journal* reporters Tripp Mickle and Terry Lefton noted in January 2011, "Subway featured Phelps in a controversial spot that ran on NBC in 2010. The spot showed Phelps swimming across land toward Vancouver 'where the action [was that] winter.' Because Phelps is a summer Olympian, Subway could use him in the ad during the Winter Games without violating IOC rules that prevent non-Olympic sponsors from developing ads that show competing Olympic athletes before or during an Olympic Games. The same would hold true with [US speed skater Apolo Anton] Ohno during the London Games."

Interestingly, Phelps photographed or filmed away from a pool might not immediately suggest *ambush* to a distracted and frequently bombarded-by-food-ads consumer. Phelps looks more like a gangly, long-armed, young adult. But Michael Phelps

in a swim suit and skin-tight racing cap suggests the power of his incredible eight gold medals from Beijing. Subway knew this and by creating an advertising plan featuring one of the greatest Olympians of all time, they purposely took actions that would either *confuse* consumers on which company was the actual restaurant sponsor of the Olympics . . . or Subway would force McDonald's to sign additional endorsers and spend more money to fight Subway's marketing plan. Since all resources are finite, this offered the potential for McDonald's to use more of their budget against Olympic initiatives and leave another area of their business vulnerable. If Subway was attentive, this shift in funding might provide a different place to attack the market leader.

As might be expected, McDonald's was not pleased with Subway's usage of Phelps and quickly contacted the USOC, the COC, and IOC to demand *protection* be given to McDonald's, the official IOC and Vancouver sponsor. In the United States, the USOC (acting on behalf of the IOC) immediately took action deploring Subway's actions, but Subway was ready for this response and responded with the following commentary:

"Subway has a successful history of partnering with elite athletes," said Subway spokesman Robert Bronfeld in a prepared statement. "Regarding our latest commercial featuring Michael Phelps, Subway does not share the USOC's perspective and the conclusions being drawn from it. Michael Phelps has been an integral part of several Subway marketing campaigns since late 2008," the company statement said. "We are proud of our work with Michael, and we look forward to working with him and other elite athletes throughout 2010 and beyond." (Associated Press, January 29, 2010)

Further, as the *New York Times'* Stuart Elliot would record, "McDonald's is upset," said Tony Pace, Subway's Chief Marketing Officer, who oversees the Subway Franchisee Advertising Trust Fund, referring to a complaint from McDonald's that Subway was

(Continued on next page)

Case Study 17.1 *(continued)*

trying to pass itself off as an official Olympic fast-food sponsor, though McDonald's had bought those rights. "My reaction to the fact McDonald's is upset? I'm lovin' it," Mr. Pace said, infamously quoting the McDonald's ad slogan.

As Subway pursued its ambush strategy, they began collectively using Olympians Phelps, gymnast Nastia Liukin and Ohno and undoubtedly aggravating various Olympic institutions that consistently point to the importance of fair play and recognition of fixed rules. In fact, by January 2012, Subway was actively using a provocative print ad in America's largest circulation national newspaper, *USA Today*, showing Phelps, Ohno, Liukin and emerging basketball superstar (and potential Team USA member) Blake Griffin with advertising copy that read, "2012 is their Year. Elite athletes are powering up for a big 2012 with temptingly tender SUBWAY Turkey Melts. Try Apolo Ohno's fresh take on turkey—double meat and boldacious banana peppers. Subway: The Official Training Restaurant of Athletes Everywhere."

What might make this advertisement interesting for readers is knowing that Subway created an official designation for which there is no authority to grant rights or challenge the appropriateness of their claim. If Subway indicates they are "the official training restaurant of athletes everywhere," there is not a sport governance organization or elite athlete body to challenge them. [*From the authors: Coincidentally, one of the book's authors, Rick Burton, was involved with a similar marketing tactic at Miller Brewing Company when the company created advertising declaring Miller Lite as the "Official Beer of Summer." Since no organization controlled licensing for the seasons of the year, it was a claim Miller could make with complete confidence no administrative body (or competitor) could challenge our claim and position.*]

Make no mistake; Subway knew exactly what it was doing. They undoubtedly understood and prepared for the likelihood they would receive negative press from trade publications or stories transmitted by national wire services like the Associated Press or Reuters. Tellingly, though, in commenting on Subway's actions, *Sports Business Journal's* Mickle and Lefton (2011) used a very revealing quote from IMG, a sports marketing agency that has long played a major role with Olympic sponsors: "While I don't support ambush marketing as a strategy, one could certainly say the Phelps campaign got people talking about Subway," said Gary Pluchino, IMG Consulting's senior vice president, Olympics. "If they decide to use Apolo the same way they used Michael Phelps, then one could assume the Phelps campaign met Subway's objectives."

AMBUSH, AMBUSH, AMBUSH—EVERYWHERE

Although the recent Subway—McDonald's example is a powerful illustration of ambush marketing, there are many other places it can be observed. For instance, a cereal brand like Wheaties, that has used athlete endorsements on its boxes since the 1930s (New York Yankee's first baseman appeared in 1934, Olympian Babe Didrikson in 1935), traditionally has waited to see which athletes will perform best at an Olympics and then, in a form of delayed ambush, place that newly minted superstar prominently on their cereal boxes.

Not surprisingly, since mothers have often played a central role in food selection for their families, US female athletes such as gymnasts Mary Lou Retton, Carly Patterson, and Nastia Liukin along with pole-vaulter Stacy Dragila, sprinter Jackie-Joyner Kersee, swimmer Brooke Bennett, diver Laura Wilkinson, downhill skier Lindsey Vonn, and figure skater Sarah Hughes have all appeared on Wheaties boxes in the United States during times when Wheaties was not an official sponsor of any Olympic organization. Why? Probably because the tactical use of an Olympian, even without official rights, has probably worked to help drive incremental sales or enhance brand imagery. The athletes mentioned above

(Continued on next page)

Case Study 17.1 (continued)

enjoyed enormous visibility secured through the reach and frequency of the Olympic Games and were only too willing to accept endorsement checks to promote a cereal brand.

The nature of Pluchino's statement above about "meeting objectives" for the Subway-Phelps case belies two powerful elements of ambush marketing that readers should consider. The first is that modern sport is very much reliant on exclusive sponsorships in order to offset the rising cost of staging major sporting events. Leagues (and the teams that comprise leagues) like the NFL, NBA, MLB, NHL, MLS, CFL, NASCAR, Indy Car, Ultimate Fighting, and others draw billions of dollars in sponsorship from various organizations seeking to associate with sports. This is not surprising and the simplest way to understand the attractive nature of sports is that most spectators enjoy themselves at a stadium (or while watching a game or race on TV) and thus the long-standing and empirically supported (see Séguin et al., 2005) belief has been that if a sponsor is considered to have supported that enjoyment, then the possibility exists that the consumer will reward the sponsor's support of the *game* with retail purchases either at the stadium/arena or in another setting.

In a study of sports fans, researchers Vassilis Dalakas and Greg Rose (2004) found this to be especially true among the die-hard fans, the ones that truly care about the team or event that is sponsored. For these fans, buying the sponsor's products is essentially a way to return the favor to the sponsor for supporting their favorite sports property. To some extent, the sense of gratitude depends on the size of the sponsored property. Fans of mega properties like the Olympics or the NFL may be less likely to see the sponsor as vital for the existence of the event, whereas it is more believable for fans of smaller local properties to buy into the idea that a sponsor *makes the event possible*.

NASCAR fans are legendary for showing reciprocity to sponsors for supporting their favorite drivers but this could backfire. Dalakas and Levin (2005) found that die-hard NASCAR fans who love the sponsors of their favorite drivers and want to buy their products, also dislike sponsors of rival drivers and are less likely to buy from them.

Second, and perhaps just as important, is that marketers now accept and recognize that ambush activities are going to take place and in some cases will be considered to have worked. This leads to a much greater demand placed on sport property organizations to protect their exclusive sponsors and to flex their considerable enforcement *muscles* when it comes to inhibiting ambush behavior and protecting official sponsors.

This is often where the figurative gloves come off.

A LEGENDARY EXAMPLE OF AMBUSH MARKETING: ATLANTA 1996

A perfect example of ambush marketing, and one that is often cited, is from the 1996 Olympic Games where Reebok and Coca-Cola were signed as official sponsors. Given that Atlanta was Coke's headquarters city, executives there were fearful that Pepsi might try any number of activities to confuse consumers or attack Coke's premier position with the Atlanta Games. To that end, Coca-Cola reportedly spent ten times the cost of their official sponsorship to ensure there was no tactical opening for Pepsi to even consider using. The general feeling among Olympic insiders was that Coke thought of everything, but paid a significant premium for that peace of mind.

Boston-based Reebok, on the other hand, was not as flush with cash and was considerably less invested in the city of Atlanta than Coke. This created an opportunity for Nike, the Oregon-based footwear giant, to come to town in a big way. Nike bought up local billboards and buildings, bought time on various TV programs and signed numerous top athletes likely to medal. They also had a tent in the hospitality area, with lots of loud music, exhibits, and activations, such as being on the receiving end of a Pete

(Continued on next page)

Case Study 17.1 *(continued)*

Sampras tennis serve. The most familiar athlete from those games was sprinter Michael Johnson and for one of his gold medal races, Nike saw to it that Johnson ran in golden shoes. For many, the most famous image of the Atlanta Games was the memory of seeing two gold shoes emblazoned with Nike-trademarked swooshes.

The net result is perhaps surprising but not unexpected. Many IOC officials were disenchanted about how commercialized Atlanta 1996 had made the Olympics. Although the sponsors were very active, it was the sprawl of tents, activations, signs, brand ambassadors, and clutter throughout the city that led to this disappointment. In some places, there wasn't an unbranded meter (or yard) of sidewalk or building. This disturbed those IOC members who appreciated (if not relished) the fact that Olympic competition was originally staged (both in 776 B.C. and 1896 Athens) in unbranded or *clean* stadiums and *clean* cities (since 1996) including busses, subways, airports, and other outdoor public spaces. Unlike FIFA's World Cup, there are no signs ringing the pitch and optimal camera-friendly locations (i.e., directly behind the goals) where sponsor logos are prominent. At the Olympics, beyond the presence of manufacturers' brands on uniforms and equipment (i.e., shoes, skis, hockey sticks, balls, timing gear), there is no in-stadium promotion.

So what of Reebok and Coke? The short answer is that most Americans came away from the 1996 Games telecast believing Nike and Coke were the major sponsors of the 1996 Games and this speaks to the power of modern sponsorship. Coke outspent Pepsi by a massive margin and protected the impression of Atlanta's Games taking place in Coca-Cola's headquarter city. Some have suggested that Coca-Cola's massive activation program also limited attention to sponsors in other categories. Nike, on the other hand, not only outspent Reebok (the official sponsor) but it also out-executed Reebok with local promotions designed to catch the eye of spectators and visiting media.

AMBUSH AND BEER

The beer category, like beverages and apparel, is also a place where ambush marketing is very common. For example, at one time, Miller Lite was the official beer of the NFL and every year hoped to showcase its investment in the NFL by presenting a trophy for community service to a deserving NFL player. But A-B, a major competitor, upped the stakes, without the benefit of an official sponsorship of the NFL (or its Super Bowl championship event), by creating a distinctive television campaign called the Bud Bowl where bottles of Budweiser played a game of football against bottles of Bud Light.

The imagery of *talking bottles* was ludicrous at a certain level . . . but when Budweiser bought an exclusive position on the Super Bowl telecast (ensuring that every beer ad was a Bud, Bud Light, or Michelob commercial), it did not take Miller executives long to realize that what people were seeing during the big game easily overpowered exclusive category rights that had been purchased with the NFL. It is perhaps no surprise that in Canada, similar battles have traditionally happened between Molson's and Labatt's over Canada's most prized ongoing winter programming: Hockey Night in Canada. In Australia, the famous battles have often featured telecommunications giants such as Telstra, Vodafone, Optus, Virgin, Orange, and 3.

SUMMARY

An Olympic marketing executive or scholar might conclude this chapter with the following points:

- A marketing person working for a sport organization that sells sponsorships to generate incremental revenue for the good of a league, team, or event should advise existing sponsors and new sponsors to expect the likelihood of ambush efforts by parties not officially affiliated with the sponsor-selling property. To avoid talking about ambush marketing is to abdicate responsibility. That said, the sports property must also plan how it will help its sponsor face an ambush attack.

- Since an ambush, by its very nature, can take place at any point during the shared journey of sponsorship, sponsor-selling properties must be constantly vigilant as to efforts taken by nonsponsors. This requires familiarity with local, state, and federal laws as well as knowledge of ways to fight illegal usage of trademarked or protected copyrights or intellectual property.

- Sponsors that seek positions as official sponsors need to activate their sponsorships aggressively or run the risk of having a competitor confuse a given population as to who the official sponsor is. If the sponsor with the official rights is not proactive and comprehensive, it is likely they will be "flanked" or "face guerilla" warfare efforts by their competitors.

- If a party is not an official sponsor and recognizes in advance that a competitor is going to invest heavily in a sponsorship (such as one involving the Olympics), that party needs to be adept at measuring the cost-effectiveness of that official sponsorship and stand ready to redirect marketing funds to an area where the official sponsor may not be looking. Said another way, if an official sponsor is completely consumed with its efforts associated with something like the London 2012 Games, it may leave itself vulnerable in other parts of the world.

- Lastly, in the modern Olympic world, where misbehavior or "unfair" practices can be remembered for a long time, companies choosing to ambush an official sponsor or major sports property should expect negative media, a damaged reputation in future sponsorship negotiations, and the future challenges if they ever seek to become an official sponsor of the sports property they ambushed.

Key Chapter Questions

1. Consider the seven types of ambush marketing. Find an example of one of these types of ambush from a recent Olympics or World Cup. How successful was the ambush?

2. Provide an example of a marketing ambush that you would not consider illegal. Why?

3. Return to the Anheuser-Busch example. What do you think are the roles and responsibilities of marketers who use an athlete's sexuality or promote other characteristics that are counter to Olympic values?

4. How have USOC national sponsors been ambushing TOP sponsors?

Key Chapter Takeaways

1. Marketers must advise sponsors about the likelihood of and responses to ambush marketing by nonsponsors.

2. If an official sponsor is not proactive in facing the guerilla warfare efforts of its competitors, then it runs the risk of having its market confused about who own the official sponsorship.

3. Nonofficial sponsors must recognizes when a competitor is going to invest heavily in a sponsorship (e.g., an Olympic Games) so that they can evaluate other opportunities and redirect marketing efforts to other markets where the competitor might leave itself vulnerable.

4. Ambush marketing around global events can bring negative media attention.

18

Ambush Marketing Case Studies

The first 17 chapters of the book have outlined the marketing and legal aspects of the Olympic Games, global sport, and ambush. The first chapters of Part III of this book have provided an in-depth review of ambush marketing, including many insider views, frameworks, strategies, and tactics, as well as views from both the ambusher and the ambushee. This chapter shares case studies—really mini-case studies—to illustrate and provide deeper illustrations of the various concepts shared to date. These are all case studies of ambush marketing at the global sport level. There are seven cases:

1. Free Beats for Olympic Athletes
2. Nikė and London 2012
3. FIFA 2010 and the Bavaria Babes
4. Kulula: The Unofficial National Carrier
5. 2011 Rugby World Cup and The Mermaid Club
6. Show Your Colors Now: Scotiabank and Vancouver 2010
7. Durex Condoms and the 2012 Olympic Games: Official Supplier and Ambusher at Same Time

Case Study 18.1

Free Beats for Olympic Athletes

The London Organizing Committee of the Olympic and Paralympic Games (LOCOG) was the organization responsible for overseeing the planning, development, and presentation of the 2012 Summer Olympic and Paralympic Games. After the 2012 Games were awarded to London, England, in 2005, the LOCOG was established in order to perform the roles required to mandate support and promote the development of the planning and construction of new venues and infrastructure (IOC, n.d.).

The 2012 Olympic sponsors, partners, and supporters collaboratively spent billions of dollars (or pounds) to have their brands and products associated with the London Games. If a nonsponsor attempted to ambush the Games, they would face hefty fines—up to 20,000 pounds (Peachey, 2012), as established by LOCOG and the IOC (Peachey, 2012). There were only two ways that corporations could be legally associated with the London 2012 Games: as a TOP sponsor or as a LOCOG sponsor (Addley, 2012).

In 2005, when London was named the host for the 2012 Games, the British government passed a new law, the London Olympic Games and Paralympic Games Act 2006 (the Act), to amend the existing UK laws relating to intellectual property. Along with the Olympic Symbol (Protection) Act of 1995, these laws protect the sponsors and partners from unauthorized advertising or ambush marketing (Addley, 2012).

There are many reasons the IOC and LOCOG take ambush marketing so seriously. According to a 61-page document outlining the Act, there are certain rights given to companies who invest millions of pounds to help support the planning, staging, and organization of the 2012 Games officially (Addley, 2012). Nonsponsors who seek the same benefits for free, without investing in the Games are considered to be engaging in ambush marketing (Chadwick & Burton, 2010).

Beats Electronics

Beats Electronics is a producer of audio products and equipment that was founded by rapper and hip-hop producer Andre "Dr. Dre" Young and Interscope-Geffen-A&M Records chairman Jimmy Iovine in 2006 (Beats, n.d.). It debuted its first products, Beats by Dr. Dre Studios headphones, in late 2008 and in its original product line was comprised of the Beats by Dr. Dre headphones (Beats, n.d.). In promotional materials, Dr. Dre outlined the product advantages by alleging that listeners were not able to hear all of the music with most headphones, and that Beats would allow to hear music the way artists hear it (Beats, n.d.).

Although, Beats is not an official sponsor of any sporting events, in 2012 they were

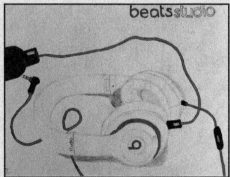

listed as a partner of the (.RED) campaign with the mission of preventing the transmission of the HIV virus from mother to child by 2015 (Beats, n.d.).

(Continued on next page)

Case Study 18.1 *(continued)*

Marketing Controversy at Olympics with Free Beats Headphones for Athletes

With the strict rules in place to protect official Olympic sponsors, Dr. Dre and his Beats headphones were at the center of a marketing controversy as a nonsponsor of the 2012 London Games (Billboard Staff, 2012). As a nonsponsor, Beats headphones were not allowed to associate with athletes at the Summer Games (Billboard Staff, 2012). For any nonsponsor, such as Beat, the IOC issued regulations before the Games, stating that athletes are not allowed to promote any brand, product or services within a blog, tweet, Facebook, or any other social media platforms and websites (Billboard Staff, 2012).

This Olympic bylaw was known as Rule 40, which clearly articulates that "Except as permitted by the IOC Executive Board, no competitor, coach, trainer or official who participates in the Olympic Games may allow his person, name, picture or sports performances to be used for advertising purposes during the Olympic Games" (Vinjamuri, 2012). Dr. Dre's company sent some special decorative versions of headphones with the Union Jack flag to high-profile members of the British Olympic team, which included tennis player Laura Robson, diver Tom Daley, and soccer player Jack Butland, who all tweeted about the headphones (Billboard Staff, 2012). According to Chadwick and Burton (2010), this form of ambush marketing is known a *coattail ambushing*. Where there is an attempt by a brand to directly associate itself with an event by using an authentic link other than becoming an official sponsor of the event (Chadwick & Burton, 2010).

Although many Olympic athletes tweeted about the Beats headphones and were seen wearing them on big screens before their competitions, Beats stated that the company developed relationships with athletes year-round and that the IOC took no action (Billboard Staff, 2012). However, this was not the first time Beats had tried this approach of ambush marketing. For instance, in 2008 when the US basketball team was caught sporting Beats's products in Beijing, generating international TV exposure and appreciative tweets from several well-followed athletes, it caught the attention of the USOC as they had received all that attention without paying a price to be an official sponsor of the Olympics (Billboard Staff, 2012).

Case Questions

1. In your view, does Rule 40 have any positive and/or negative impact on the right for freedom of expression for athletes during the Olympic Games?

2. In light of Rule 40, does an athlete's use of the media to cover a practice where the athlete is seen using a specific product create an ambushing of the IOC?

3. Many agree that it is reasonable that the IOC wants to control advertising inside Olympic venues and offer *clean venues*. However, is going beyond that to try and control what athletes say on Twitter and Facebook about the sponsors who have allowed them to compete, crossing the line? In the end, in your view will this help or hurt the Olympic Games?

4. What are your thoughts on the punishments that should be given out to athletes for infringements on social media rules?

5. Research recent developments post-case on the IOC rules about athletes and social media. Summarize recent developments and provide your view on whether these are positive or negative in nature.

6. In your opinion, do athletes need social media coaches?

Case Study 18.2

Nike and London 2012

The London Organizing Committee of the Olympic Games

The London Organizing Committee of the Olympic and Paralympic Games (LOCOG) was the organization responsible for overseeing the planning and development of the 2012 Summer Olympic and Paralympic Games. After the 2012 games was awarded to London, England, in 2005, the LOCOG was established in order to perform the roles required to mandate support and promote the development of the planning and construction of new venues and infrastructure (IOC, n.d.).

The 2012 Olympic sponsors, partners, and supporters collaboratively spent billions of dollars (or pounds) to have their brands and products associated with the London Games. If a nonsponsor attempted to ambush the Games, they would face hefty fines—up to 20,000 pounds (Peachy, 2012), as established by LOCOG and the IOC (Peachy, 2012). There were only two ways that corporations could be legally associated with the London 2012 Games: as a TOP sponsor or as a LOCOG sponsor (Addley, 2012).

In 2005, when London was named the host for the 2012 Games, the British government passed a new law, the London Olympic Games and Paralympic Games Act 2006 (the act), to append the existing laws relating to intellectual property in the UK. Along with the Olympic Symbol (Protection) Act of 1995, these laws protect the sponsors and partners from unauthorized advertising or ambush marketing (Addley, 2012). There are many reasons the IOC and LOCOG take ambush marketing so seriously. According to a 61-page document outlining the Act, there are certain rights given to companies who invest millions of pounds to help support the planning, staging, and organization of the 2012 Games officially (Addley, 2012). Thus, those nonsponsors who seek the same benefits for free without investing in the Games are considered to be engaging in ambush marketing (Chadwick and Burton, 2010).

Nike

Nike and its competitors have a history of aggressive marketing versus one another as both sponsors and nonsponsors of major events around the globe. Nike, a leading sport apparel company, first made headlines with ambush marketing at the 1992 Barcelona Olympics when they sponsored the press conference for the US basketball team despite Reebok being the Games official sponsor of the USOC, following which Michael Jordan accepted his gold medal for basketball, while covering up the Reebok logo on his kit (Sauer, n.d.). Not long after, Nike's successful ambushing of many sporting events is well documented, including the 1998 World Cup, 2000 Sydney Olympics, and the 2002 Boston Marathon (Sauer, n.d.).

Like many nonsponsors who successfully ambush their competitors' official sponsorship status, Nike is crafty and creative and does not cross the legal lines put in place (Sauer, n.d.). Following the legal argument, ambush—as well documented—is ques-

© Lenuraidi | Dreamstime.com—Sports Shoes Photo

(Continued on next page)

Case Study 18.2 *(continued)*

Nike *(continued)*

tioned ethically. Is ambush marketing an ethical business practice? Is it parasite marketing or is it intelligent business practice? For some, it may be the only way to compete with major brands strategically avoiding sponsoring events and instead sponsoring teams or individuals (Sauer, n.d.).

Nonetheless, whether legal, ethical, or strategic, ambush marketing has become a part of the reality of mega-sporting-events. Importantly, brands that spend their time discussing the unfairness of ambush marketing tend to attract very little audience sympathy (Sauer, n.d.).

Nike's 2012 Olympic Gold Medal Ambush(es)

The official sponsor of the 2012 London Games was Adidas. Nike launched a series of promotions to ambush that sponsorship. Most believed that they pushed the limits on ambush marketing when they launched their global TV campaign featuring everyday athletes competing in places around the world named London (Sweney, 2012). Nike later launched its "Find Your Greatness" campaign in 25 countries that aired during the same time period as the Opening Ceremony of the Games. Locations for the TV ad included East London in South Africa, Little London in Jamaica, London, Ohio, in the US, and a health club called London Gym (Sweney, 2012). Based on these tactics, it appears reasonable to assume that Nike's campaign was strategically designed to ambush Adidas, which paid tens of millions of pounds to be the official London 2012 global sponsor (Sweney, 2012). However, according to Nike, their ideas are to "simply inspire and energize everyday athletes everywhere and celebrate their achievements" (Sweney, 2012). View an example ad at www.youtube.com/watch?v=KYtMkhfQfa4.

Nike's ambush of the 2012 Games was not finished with the "Find Your Greatness" campaign. In previous Olympic competitions, Nike matched the color of athletes' shoes to their nation's colors, but the London Games marked the first time that Nike provided shoes in the same shade of yellow neon green named "Volt" (Young, 2013). These eye-catching shoes made their debut on the feet of 400 Olympic athletes, mostly in the track and field events (Young, 2013).

According to Nike's global creative director for the Olympics, painting Nike's Flyknit shoe Volt created a "Team Nike" (Young, 2013). It is reported that Nike undertook focus groups consisting of amateur, college, and professional athletes, showing them the Volt shoes in different colors, finding that, across each athlete group, everyone loved the Volts—not unexpected since it has been scientifically proven that yellow-green neon is the most visible color to the human eye (Young, 2013).

© Miluxian | Dreamstime.com—London 2012 Olympic Marathon Photo

In turn, based on this three-stage strategy, many have suggested that Nike's ambush at the 2012 London Olympics is the most effective ambush to date (Young, 2013).

(Continued on next page)

Case Study 18.2 *(continued)*

Nike's 2012 Olympic Gold Medal Ambush(es) *(continued)*

According to research by BrandWatch, roughly one in ten (7.7 %) internet conversations about the 2012 Olympics were associated with Nike, whereas Adidas was only part of 0.49 percent of conversations (Druce, 2012).

Nike's campaign landed first on *Ad Age's* Viral Chart with 4.5 million views with Adidas third with 2.9 million views. Throughout the Games, Nike generated three times more online chatter than Adidas (Druce, 2012). *Ad Age* also reported—based on an online survey by Toluma GlobalOmnibus-Survey—that of 1,034 US consumers, 37% identified Nike as the Olympic sponsor compared to 24% for real sponsor Adidas (Druce, 2012). This ambush clearly worked.

Following London 2012, Adidas has not yet renewed its contract for the 2016 Games and rumors existed that Nike might take over that role (Hamilton, 2012).

Case Questions

1. Exclusive sponsorships create legal challenges, however, nonsponsors may find ways to circumvent them with a clever strategy. Nike's idea to put the majority of athletes in the same colored shoes and focus on competitions in towns called London elsewhere around the world are perfect examples of them appearing to be an official sponsor.
   a. In your view, is it possible for the IOC and the OCOGs to stop ambush marketing entirely?
   b. Are laws and legislations to stop ambush marketing creating more problems or are they helping to solve them?
2. Social media and online video has evidently leveled the playing field, as so many people search for videos, events, and news online using social tools like Facebook, YouTube, and Twitter. In response, nonsponsors are taking advantage of these tools and bypassing sponsorship bans.
   a. What future steps need to happen to for the IOC to avoid or at least limit social media ambush marketing?
   b. Is it at all possible to stop social media ambush?
3. If Nike—a leader in ambush marketing—become an official sponsor of the 2016 Olympics, will there be less ambush marketing at those Games or would Adidas return the favor? (Note: Nike has previously been an official sponsor (e.g., Sydney 2000 Games).
4. As technology continues to advance, what other areas, aside from social media, may be predicted as possible ambush marketing concerns for the Olympics in the future?

Case Study 18.3

FIFA 2010 and the Bavaria Babes

Background

The Federation Internationale de Football Association (FIFA) is the international governing body of football. FIFA, founded in 1904, is based in Zurich, Switzerland and is responsible for the organization and governance of football's major international tournaments, with the FIFA World Cup being the most distinguished. Since 1930, FIFA has held 20 editions of the World Cup, with the next editions currently set for Russia in 2018 and Qatar in 2022. FIFA presently has 208 member associations (three more than the IOC-recognized NOCs) and its mission is to constantly improve the game of football (FIFA, n.d.).

FIFA World Cup Sponsorship

Shortly after the 2006 FIFA World Cup in Germany, FIFA publicly revealed its new commercial strategy, consisting of a new, three-tier sponsorship structure. The primary tier is composed of the FIFA Partners, the second tier of FIFA World Cup Sponsors, and the third tier of the National Supporters of each FIFA event. Currently, there are six FIFA Partners (Adidas, Coca-Cola, Hyundai/Kia, Emirates, Sony, and Visa) who (i) have the highest level of association with FIFA and all FIFA events, and (ii) play a considerable role in supporting the development of football all around the world, from grassroots right to the top level at the FIFA World Cup. The purpose of the primary tier follows from the IOC's TOP sponsorship model to limit the number of partners and add greater value to the engagement for both sides. In the second tier, FIFA World Cup Sponsors (Budweiser, Castrol, McDonald's) have rights to the FIFA Confederations Cup and the FIFA World Cup on a global basis. The main rights for a second tier sponsor are brand association, such as the use of selected marketing assets, media exposure, and ticketing/ hospitality offers for events. Third tier sponsorships allow companies with roots in the host country of each FIFA event to promote an affiliation in the domestic market.

The major objective of the new FIFA sponsorship strategy is to have a wide but exclusive product category that is supported to Commercial Affiliates, allowing each brand to distinguish themselves from competing brands in their product category (FIFA, n.d.). The three-tier sponsorship structure for 2014 FIFA World Cup Brazil can be found at http://2014fifaworldcupup date.blogspot.com/2014/04/fifa-world-cup-bra zil-2014-logo-mascot.html.

Bavaria Babes Ambush

At any FIFA World Cup, a sea of orange Dutch national team supporters swarms the streets of the host country and its cities in support of their national team. In 2010 in South Africa, the scene was no different, and FIFA, the local hosts, and fans everywhere always welcome such displays of national pride. However, at the 2010 FIFA World Cup, one sponsor tried to use an approach based on this national pride to ambush the event's title sponsor.

Bavaria, a family-owned beer brand originating from the south of Holland, has a history of competing for market share with archrival Heineken and FIFA 2010 sponsor Budweiser. Heineken and Budweiser, which both sponsor many football properties, are often in marketing battles with Bavaria in the Netherlands. In the past, Bavaria has had some reported ambush marketing success from handing out large quantities of

(Continued on next page)

Case Study 18.3 *(continued)*

Bavaria Babes Ambush *(continued)*

orange giveaways outside national football matches sponsored by Heineken. At the 2010 FIFA World Cup, Bavaria sought to replicate these previous successes by launching a campaign around the color orange. First, Bavaria created an orange mini dress that subtly displayed a very small Bavaria brand reference: a compass on the back of the garment, which is only recognizable to avid followers of the brand. Second, after launching the orange dress in the Netherlands, Bavaria ran a media campaign in the Netherlands to drive aware-

near the front, grabbing TV camera attention, Bavaria successfully gained attention by having beautiful women dressed in orange mini dresses, grouped together, cheering vigorously. However, midway through the second half in Johannesburg, stewards abruptly ejected all 36 women. A Bavaria representative expressed that FIFA's reaction was absurd, stating "FIFA does not have the monopoly on orange and people have the freedom to wear what they want" (Guardian UK, 2010).

FIFA's official beer sponsor is Budweiser,

© Stylephotographs | Dreamstime.com—Friends Celebrating With Beer Photo

ness of the orange dress. Finally, Bavaria sent a group of 36 women wearing the orange dresses to cheer the Dutch during their match against Denmark at the 2010 World Cup (Armour, 2010).

According to Simon Chadwick, an expert in sports marketing, this form of ambush marketing performed by Bavaria is known as *distractive ambushing*—one of several types of indirect ambushing. Companies, like Bavaria, use distractive ambushing to have a promotional existence at an event, but without making specific reference to the event itself. The purpose of this strategy is to disturb the public's consciousness and increase awareness from the event's audience (Chadwick & Burton, 2010). With seats

which pays millions of dollars to be a sponsor. With the significant revenues coming from sponsorship, FIFA pursues any ambusher. As a result, police questioned all 36 women, with two being charged under the South African SA Merchandise Marks Act. Since Bavaria is not an official World Cup sponsor, they are not allowed to promote its brand in relation to the tournament and FIFA wanted to make it clear to everyone that ambush marketing would not be tolerated (Stal, 2010). However, many in the Netherlands, including high-profile politicians, came to the aid of Bavaria and all charges against the 36 women were dismissed.

Consequently, one could argue that all of the uproar against Bavaria only served to

(Continued on next page)

Case Study 18.3 *(continued)*

Bavaria Babes Ambush *(continued)*

drive awareness, build positive associations, and limit Heineken's presence. Thus, although FIFA's strategy was intended to end Bavaria's World Cup presence and control ambush marketing, in the end, it only created more public attention, as many people sympathized for the brewery and women involved (Stal, 2010).

Case Questions

1. In your view, did FIFA and law enforcement agencies act appropriately? Why?
2. In your opinion, was it fair for FIFA to kick out all 36 women wearing the orange dresses (with a miniature logo) that was only noticeable to a small population?
3. Should FIFA incorporate more restrictions regarding spectators' clothing attire? Is it feasible for FIFA to regulate these restrictions?
4. Did FIFA go too far with not "tolerating" ambush marketing from Bavaria, when teams such as Brazil, Netherlands, Portugal, USA, South Korea, Australia, New Zealand, Serbia, and Slovenia were all outfitted by Nike when the official World Cup sponsor is Adidas?
5. What can FIFA do to prevent nonofficial World Cup brands like Nike and Bavaria from marketing their products?
6. Despite the many legal charges directed towards Bavaria, in the end, their marketing scheme created more positive public attention. To avoid rewarding the *bad guys*, what could have FIFA done differently with handling Bavaria stunts?
7. Could the IOC's leadership team learn anything from this situation?

Case Study 18.4

Kulula: The Unofficial National Carrier

Kulula Air

Kulula Air is a South African low-fare airline that was established in July 2001. It is a wholly owned low-cost subsidiary of British Airways franchise Comair. Kulula Air operates on major domestic routes out of Tambo International Airport outside Johannesburg, plus limited international flights to Namibia, Mauritius, Zambia, and Zimbabwe. As a fun-loving and professional airline, passengers are assured that safety precautions are taken before every flight, and aside from booking cheap flights, today passengers are offered affordable hotel accommodations and other means of travel in South Africa.

In addition to being known as a low-fare airline, Kulula has built a reputation for its distinctive, brightly colored, and often humorous aircraft livery, as well as for airline attendants and pilots injecting a sense of humor during flights. For example, one attendant was reported to say during a safety briefing that "There may be 50 ways to leave your lover, but there are only 4 ways out of this airplane," and another noted after landing, "Ladies and gentlemen, we have landed in Cape Town. Please take all your possessions. Anything left behind will be shared equally between staff. Please note we do not accept unwanted mothers-in-law or children" (Kulula, n.d.a).

© Ratmandude | Dreamstime.com—Boeing 737-8K2 (WL)—Takeoff—Lanseria Airport Photo

Kulula Air Sponsorship

Kulula Air is reported to be an avid supporter of charities that make a difference in people's lives. For instance, Kulula Air donates to the South African Police Services and sponsors "Movember," a cause that helps to raise awareness and funds for men's health, specifically prostate and testicular cancer. The Kulula staff and even their planes have participated in raising significant funds for these charities (Kulula, n.d.b). The airline shows their visual support for the cause by painting a mustache on their already quirky planes.

For example, the staff and loyal customers of Kulula were able to help raise over R430,000 for the Community Crisis Center in Reiger Park, which is east of Johannesburg. This NGO offers a feeding arrangement for orphans and vulnerable children, community-based care and HIV/AIDS programs. In addition, the much-

needed funds help with the expansion of infrastructure and life skills training programs for caregivers, auxiliary social workers, and center management.

Kulula supports Casual Day, a fundraising project that raises awareness about people with disabilities. Their efforts raised R97,000 in 2013. Kulula is also in a partnership with Food & Trees for Africa, where indigenous trees and grass are planted at schools in rural communities throughout South Africa, with the goal to provide the opportunity for disadvantage kids to play in a healthy environment. As part of this partnership, Kulula is helping to (i) increase biodiversity and the conservation of the natural ecosystem, (ii) expand working opportunities by offering tree planting jobs, and (iii) provide related small business opportunities, such as for nursery growers to supply saplings (Kulula, n.d.b).

(Continued on next page)

Case Study 18.4 *(continued)*

2010 FIFA World Cup

In the months prior to the 2010 FIFA World Cup (February 2010 to be precise), Kulula took out a full-page ad in the South Africa's *Sunday Times* that did not go unnoticed. The ad offered attractive offers for summer fares, but it was designed with hand-drawn images of soccer balls and a stadium with the note "Unofficial National Carrier of the 'You-Know-What.'" Although the ad made no specific reference to the World Cup, which was set to begin in June 2010, the association was evident to most. Known academically as indirect ambush marketing (intentional association through suggestion or indirect reference), this tactic is popularly known as *associative ambushing*, and involves a nonofficial sponsor using imagery or terminology in order to create an illusion that its organization is associated with a sporting event (Chadwick & Burton, 2010).

As a result of this ad, FIFA announced publicly that it was not pleased that Kulula's ad made a clear reference to the World Cup tournament, suggesting that it infringed South African legislation against ambush. In particular, FIFA implied that Kulula's ad broke the national ambush-marketing law that was introduced in 2003 for the Cricket World Cup, hosted by South Africa. This law provided FIFA, based on the previous legis- lation from the Cricket World Cup, with control over ad space in host cities, with new additional bylaws implemented specifically for the 2010 FIFA World Cup prohibiting all promotional and marketing activity in a one- kilometer radius around South Africa's host stadiums.

Kulula's responded, via their spokes- woman, by stating that many people across South Africa were against FIFA's actions, noting that FIFA does not own South Afri- ca's soccer stadiums, soccer balls, and vu- vuzelas (South African plastic trumpet used by football fans) (Moerdyk, 2010).

The outcome was application of the law and sanctions against a relatively small na- tional sponsor (as compared to global FIFA sponsors such as Sony, Visa, and Coca- Cola). FIFA, as it should, responded quickly against Kulula, where the repercussions were entirely adjudicated by civil officers, judges, and lawyers (BBC News, 2010). Al- though sanctions were levied against Kul- ula, many argue that the South African air- line achieved its return on investment, since it benefited greatly from the attention gar- nered, perhaps encouraging other organi- zations to attempt similar ambush tactics, where the results could be the same (Mo- erdyk, 2010).

Case Questions

1. Do you think local ambushers (such as Kulula) should be treated differently than large, global ones (such as Nike)?
2. What do you think of Kulula's response to articulate that they were surprised by FIFA's complaint?
3. Do some online research and determine if this particular incident led to the introduc- tion of an increase in the number of busi- ness seeking to take advantage of using adverts to promote unofficial products.
4. It's been acknowledged that FIFA's reac- tion to Kulula's ambushing resulted in far more publicity than their single-page ad would have. For future World Cups, what changes or improvements does FIFA need to make in order to prevent ambush- ers from reaping benefits in this area?
5. Does Kulula's involvement with the com- munity (charitable donations and fund- raising), bring less negative attention against them when they infringe upon FIFA's rules and regulations?

Case Study 18.5

2011 Rugby World Cup and The Mermaid Club

IRB Rugby World Cup

After the Olympic Games, the FIFA World Cup and the IAAF World Championships, the Rugby World Cup is arguably the most important sporting event globally. The Rugby World Cup is an international rugby union competition organized by the International Rugby Board (IRB) and has been held every four years since 1987. The current layout of the tournament features twenty nations competing over a month in the host country with two stages—group and knock out. Nations are divided into four pools, A through D, with five in each. After round-robin pool play, the winner and runner up of each pool enter the knockout stage, consisting of quarter- and semi-finals and the final (World Rugby, n.d). Although not as widely contested and followed as the FIFA World Cup, the Rugby World Cup attracts considerable attention around the globe.

Major Events Management Act (MEMA)

The Major Events Management Act (MEMA) was passed in 2007 in New Zealand to provide protection for organizers and sponsors of major international events hosted domestically. Chosen to host the 2011 World Cup, it was expected that the Rugby World Cup 2011 would be the largest event ever hosted in New Zealand. This was an important reason why the MEMA was included to prevent ambush marketing by protecting the use of key event symbols, images, and words, as well as providing *clean zones* and *clean transport routes* around stadiums forbidding unauthorized advertising and street trading.

New Zealand was the first country in the world to have nonevent-specific ambush marketing legislation, which is believed to be a significant advantage towards bringing major events to New Zealand in the future. Specific to the Rugby World Cup 2011 (RWC 2011), the legislation ensured that exclusive rights of association was granted to RWC 2011, protecting sponsors, thus encouraging sponsors to establish or renew rights in relation to future tournaments, which in the end goes back into funding the game of rugby globally (Ministry of Business, Innovation & Employment, 2007).

Wellington's The Mermaid Club Strip Bar

Despite city council officers helping police the MEMA legislation and the implementation of proactive ambush marketing preventive strategies with local business, it was not long after the RWC 2011 began that Wellington's The Mermaid Club ("Mermaids"), a strip bar, was threatened with enforcement action following its ambush activities. Warnings were issued to Mermaids, threatening that it could face NZ$150,000 in fines. It was the first official case of RWC 2011 ambush marketing (Nicholas, 2011).

The tactic put in place by Mermaids was to hire scantily attired young women in stilettos and "All Blacks" uniforms to hand out two-for-one flyers (two dances for the price of one) to male rugby fans after Wellington's first tournament match on September 11, 2011. The flyers were dispersed around the Wellington Regional Stadium

(Continued on next page)

Case Study 18.5 *(continued)*

Wellington's The Mermaid Club Strip Bar *(continued)*

passageway and at the Wellington railway station, both well-established *clean zone* areas meant to protect official tournament sponsors (Nicholas, 2011). Most viewed this effort as ambush marketing, specifically as *associative ambushing*—which involves an organization using imagery or terminology affiliated with an event to create an indirect reference that it has links to the sporting event. In the case of Mermaids, since the young women were wearing "All Blacks" uniforms, it was seen to demonstrate that they did in fact have some level of affiliation with the RWC 2011 tournament.

Others also suggested that Mermaids' activities could be a form of *distractive ambushing*, where an organization creates a promotional presence at or near an event without making specific reference to the event itself. It was felt that this could be the case here since, even though the young women were wearing rugby jerseys, Mermaids still made a promotional appearance at and near one of the World Cup venues, which resulted in influencing the public (Chadwick & Burton, 2010).

Police, Wellington City Council, and the Economic Development Ministry contacted Mermaids, advising that prosecution action would be considered if further advertising or promotional activities took place inside or visible from the Wellington Regional Stadium clean zones (Brandchannel, 2011). Although those associated with Mermaids expressed that the warnings were an overreaction and that they were being treated unfairly by authorities, they instructed staff to stop handing out flyers in the clean zones (although they continued to do so in the main public streets of Wellington). However, despite this response, reports are that a very positive business result happened for the bar with visiting fans crowding the strip bar after the match and spending a significant amount of money (Nicholas, 2011).

Case Questions

1. Do you believe that officials reacted too harshly towards Mermaids? Why or why not?

2. Should anti-ambush legislation include inner-city areas as *clean zones* to prevent small business like Mermaids from promoting by false affiliations?

3. If the scarcely attired young women were not dressed in "All-Black" shirts, would this still be ambush marketing?

4. Should officials be more or less stringent towards their initial penalties to small local businesses? Why or why not?

Case Study 18.6

Show Your Colors Now: Scotiabank and Vancouver 2010

Vancouver Olympic Committee (VANOC)

VANOC was a nonprofit organization responsible for planning, developing, organizing, financing, and orchestrating the 2010 Winter Olympic and Paralympics. After the 2010 games were rewarded to Vancouver, British Columbia, in 2003, VANOC was established in order to perform roles required to mandate support and promote the development of sport in Canada (VANOC, 2010).

VANOC Sponsorship

VANOC (The Vancouver Olympic Committee) presented three tiers of national sponsorship to Canadian companies. Tier one consisted of airlines, banking, brewery, telecommunications, and petroleum categories. Tier two represented clothing, cruise lines, hospitality, postal service and courier, computer hardware, internet, home improvement, telecom hardware (nonwireless), insurance, resources, office products, and retail companies sectors. Tier three included airport, catering, consulting services, consumer goods, department store, food products, freight forwarding and customs brokering, market research, lumber, hotels, health services, greeting cards, furniture, mining, network equipment, packaged goods, personal care products, rail services, heating, ventilation and air conditioning, snowmaking, and grooming equipment, ticketing, temporary power, recruitment and staffing, and security equipment.

As VANOC sponsors, companies had exclusive rights to Olympic logos and the opportunity to develop an inclusive marketing platform around the Olympic Rings. In addition, sponsors had the advantage of market share exclusivity, cross-selling, in-store marketing, and fundraising programs, as well as benefiting from the *halo-effect* provided by the Olympics; the ability to be affiliated with Olympic core values (Bradish, 2010).

To protect its sponsors, VANOC spent roughly $40 million to buy every square inch of outdoor advertising space in Vancouver and surrounding mainland areas, extending from billboards to transit buses during the Olympic Games. The space purchased by VANOC was re-sold to top Olympic supporters, giving them the opportunity to use prime visibility for advertising and preventing corporate rivals from ambush marketing (Canada 2010, 2010).

Scotiabank

Originally founded as the Bank of Nova Scotia, Scotiabank is the third largest bank in Canada, with a growing international presence. Offering a variety of financial products and services such as personal, commercial, corporate, and investment banking, Scotiabank offers services (as of 2010) to nearly 19 million customers in more than 55 countries around the world. For the decade leading up to the 2010 Olympic Games, Scotiabank had become actively involved with sponsorship and branding, particularly in sports. As of 2010, Scotiabank was the title sponsor of Guadalajara's Scotiabank Aquatics Center, Calgary's Scotiabank Saddledome, Ottawa's Scotiabank Place, and supported several running events including the Vancouver Half-Marathon, the Toronto Waterfront Marathon, and the Scotiabank Calgary Marathon. In 2007, Scotiabank became a sponsor of CBC Television's Hockey Night in Canada and, as of 2010, was the official bank of the National Hockey League and National Hockey League Players Association. Within the NHL, Scotiabank—as of 2010—maintains partnerships with the Montreal Canadiens, the Ottawa Senators, Calgary Flames, Jarome Iginla, Tessa Bonhomme, and Cassie Campbell (Scotia Bank, n.d.).

(Continued on next page)

Case Study 18.6 *(continued)*

Scotiabank Accused of Ambush Marketing

Just a few weeks before the Vancouver Olympic Games officially kicked off, VANOC had to respond to accusations that Scotiabank's "Show Your Colours" contest—led by ex-Olympian gold medalist and well-known hockey commentator Cassie Campbell—was ambush marketing. The contest encourages fans to show their national pride.

What it means and feels to be a proud Canadian is something truly unique and special for every one of us. Show Your Colours is a call to action for Canadians to show their pride and encourages them to think about how they can show the world what makes Canada a truly amazing nation—from its environment to its citizens, coast to coast.

The "Show Your Colours," campaign took place in Vancouver and asked Canadians to express their national pride through personal stories and photographs. This form of ambush marketing is known as *values ambushing*, where the use of an event's (such as the Olympics) cardinal values or themes are indicated by a nonofficial sponsor to form an association with the event to allure the consumers that they are associated with the event. In this case, Scotiabank is argued to be trying to reap the benefits of the *halo effect* (created by the Olympics),

by using key values of pride, togetherness, support, and excitement in their campaign. Furthermore, with the help of ex-Olympian star Cassie Campbell, the use of *coattail ambushing* also took place, involving Scotiabank directly associating itself with the Olympics by using an accredited former Olympic athlete and gold medalist (Hinka, 2010; Chadwick & Burton, 2010).

Although some view campaigns like this as harmless and about national pride, rights holders and official sponsors think otherwise and know that they can confuse consumers. In this case, Scotiabank's, according to VANOC, was not harmless and it hurt the official sponsor, the Royal Bank, and undermined its contribution to athletes and the Games. In 2005, the Royal Bank signed an eight-year deal worth US $110 million to be the official sponsor of the Games. For this reason, VANOC advised Scotiabank to postpone the campaign because it undermined the value of RBC's sponsorship (Hinka, 2010). Although Scotiabank, following a reportedly respectful discussion with VANOC, agreed to postpone the Show Your Colours contest, the campaign was still found on the Scotiabank's website several days after VANOC's allegations (Hinka, 2010).

(Continued on next page)

© Urmoments | Dreamstime.com—IIHF Women\'s Ice Hockey World Championship—Gold Medal Match—Canada V USA Photo

Case Study 18.6 *(continued)*

Case Questions

1. Why would some view Scotiabank's campaign as harmless?
2. In what capacity does Scotiabank's campaign undermine the value of Royal Bank's sponsorship?
3. Does Scotiabank's Show Your Colour campaign exhibit motive to use the influence of preconceived beliefs (halo effect) affiliated with the Olympics?
4. VANOC negotiated a mutual agreement to postpone the Show Your Colours campaign, yet afterwards, the contest was still found on the website. Did VANOC act as you think they should have? If you were the Royal Bank, would this be adequate?
5. Should there have been better preventative measures from VANOC to prevent competing nonofficial sponsors from ambushing so closely to the Olympics?
6. Should there be stronger regulations and laws to avoid the use of current and former Olympic athletes in nonofficial sponsors' ambushing campaigns before and after the Olympics?

Case Study 18.7

Durex Condoms and the 2012 Olympic Games: Official Supplier and Ambusher at Same Time

The five-ring logo of the IOC has enormous value and has been used in a variety of marketing activities—legal and illegal, moral and immoral, effective and ineffective—for decades. Although they were not the first industry to pick up on the value of the rings, condom companies have recently received considerable attention due to the high level of condom use by athletes in the Olympic village during the Games. Durex, a leading manufacturer and official supplier to the London 2012 Games, distributed 150,000 condoms during the two weeks of the Games. However, from an ambush marketing perspective, it wasn't this usage that attracted attention but the advertising campaign that Durex launched alongside its supplier status that got the attention of TOP sponsor Proctor and Gamble, also a manufacturer of condoms, whose brand competes with Durex.

This case provides a good example of the challenges facing sponsors and rights-holders around sponsorship and ambush.

Durex and London 2012

Durex is the largest manufacturer of condoms in the world. Its parent company, Reckitt Benckiser, is a major competitor of Proctor and Gamble (P&G) who is a TOP sponsor of the IOC. Both companies offer an extensive variety of household products. Durex was the official supplier (not sponsor) of the London 2012 Games local organizing committee (LOCOG).

Although publicly admitting that "[w]e're restricted by the Olympics' organizing committee guidelines on what we can and can't say" (Boyle, 2012). Durex still launched an advertising campaign alongside its supplier role that many have suggested is award-worthy. It featured Durex colored condomns in the iconic shape of the Olympic rings with the tagline, "Usain—not every man wants to be the fastest in the world."

When first tweeted, this ad was retweeted more than 1,700 times in the first 48 hours (Yahoo! Sports, 2012). A similar graphic with five colored condoms in the shape of the five rings was also used in promotions.

19

Concluding Thoughts and Future Trends

As you come to the end of the book, just like the end of any Olympic event, it becomes time to sort out what has been learned, what has been accomplished, and really, who gets the gold, the silver, and the bronze. Less politically correct but equally important and relevant to this book, who cheated or simply skimmed the material because reading is hard for them or the specifics of the Olympics is not their "thing"?

The Olympic Games—or any mega-sporting-event for that matter, are all about levels of performance, outcome, and global relevance.

We, as the writers—or the creators of the book, if you will—set out to provide a facilitated book that encompasses a course that seeks to build your knowledge and understanding of global marketing, Olympic marketing, and ambush marketing. Although highly interrelated, each of these concepts has its own distinct elements. So, we hope they are your gold, silver, and bronze "learning medals" and that your ability to understand, work with, or share has significantly increased. And, although they are not medals per se, we threw in a dose of leadership, the law, sales, and ethics just to round out the learning!

All four are vital aspects for any sport marketer.

From the onset, with a team of authors with both academic and professional experiences was thought to be appropriate, given the lack of a strong conceptual (or traditional) framework in these areas, as well as their intensely applied—not to mention off the record—nature. Many books can be written by a single person but the nature of this, we felt, required a variety of perspectives and experiences.

So, given the three medals of gold (global marketing), silver (Olympic marketing), and bronze (ambush) marketing, the hope is that learning of each has occurred in each area, with a summary of each provided here.

SUMMARY: GLOBAL MARKETING

Much has been written in many places about marketing on a global scale. Whether called *international marketing*, *global marketing*, or *worldwide marketing*, the concepts and content are very similar. The objective here was not to rewrite or reconceptualize global marketing. Indeed, in the ten chapters of Part I of the book we sought, first, to, outline the core concepts and, second, to apply them to the contexts of global sport, sport law, and the Olympic Games. This second objective is very important and, as such, a chapter was devoted to outline the global sport system, one to leadership, two to the legal aspects, and a chapter to the role of the Olympic Games in the global sport market.

At this stage, the goal was to provide for a clear understanding of the core concepts of global marketing, including understanding of differences by culture and language, the importance of segmentation, global brands, international pricing, and sponsorship sales—with a much deeper knowledge of the central aspects of these chapters. Really, there are seven key things about global marketing with which you should—at this stage—be very comfortable. First, although it is not necessary to have all of their names committed to memory, you should have a handle on the organizations and structure of global sport. You should be highly aware of the distinction between the Olympic movement and the professional sport industry, who the main players are, who holds the resources, how each is typically structured, and which organizations make the important decisions.

Second, you should know that leaders are vital to the success of organizations in global sport. More specifically, you should have an idea of what type of leader fits with different situations, as well as an understanding of what it takes to become a leader or at least exhibit leadership qualities. Names like Nelson Mandela, Juan Antonio Samaranch, David Stern, and others should come to mind easily, with the related pros and cons of their leadership styles. Third, in combining the global system and leadership, you should have an idea of what type of individual would make an appropriate leader for what type of organization. For example, should a state/provincial level sport organization in a relatively minor sport hire a former athlete with no marketing background to lead its marketing? Here, you should also be well aware of the sales function in sponsorship, how challenging it is, where you find those skills, and when sales are even possible.

Fourth, although you are not expected to be a lawyer, you are expected to have a grasp of the principal legal concepts in the global sphere (i.e., the role of the law, legal differences country by country) and an understanding of the law and the Olympic Games (i.e., the legal structure of the Olympic Games, the Olympic Charter, legal aspects of ambush marketing). Fifth, you should know the role of the Court for Arbitration for Sport and the procedures it follows, as well as the legal issues related to the fight against doping for sport as led by the World Anti-Doping Agency (WADA).

Sixth, thanks to the inside views of authors Richard Pound—a former Vice-President of the IOC, Chairman of its Marketing Commission and President of WADA—and Rick Burton—a former Chief Marketing Officer of the world's largest National Olympic Committee—you were able to obtain an inside view on sponsorship in both organizations. Burton, specifically, provided you with a view on the day-to-day operations of a National Olympic Committee organization, an articulation of the key issues such a person and organization face, and an understanding of what you need to do if you ever want to work in such a position—easier said than done, mind you! Finally, the section—

led by Richard Pound—IOC member and renowned lawyer—brings together sport marketing and the law. This chapter, as the capstone of Part I, converges the key legal concepts into global sport marketing, providing key insights into marks on goods, regulations, unfair practices, trademarks, consumer protection, product liability, trade names, copyrights, patents, and many more important legal concepts into the reality of the global sport marketer.

SUMMARY: OLYMPIC MARKETING AND SPONSORSHIP

If one was to summarize Part II of this book, one might conclude that while the Olympics are good and certainly one of the greatest concepts ever established, not only for sport but also for efforts promoting world peace (not to mention other important benefits like harmony, globalization, and competition), the Olympics can also be messy. And, from a marketing perspective, they are particularly messy and therefore risky. But they are also full of extraordinary value. In the particular case of sponsorship, this risk and *messiness* is enhanced further as sponsors, nonsponsors, and the IOC endeavor to maximize their respective benefits. Sponsors seek to justify their investments and use the Games to reach customers and build brand. Nonsponsors—and we provided many examples and cases in this respect—seek ways as ambushers to reduce the benefits that their competition (official Olympic sponsors) may enjoy. The IOC puts in place massive efforts to protect the exclusivity of its sponsors and to work in collaboration with them to continue to generate the revenues that enable investment throughout the Olympic movement. These efforts, including the particular strategies and tactics available—are well described in the book.

Part II of the book, which builds to Olympic Sponsorship, also includes chapters on sponsorship and sponsorship sales, two vital—obviously—conceptual areas within Olympic sponsorship (not to mention, global marketing generally). The sponsorship chapter kicks off this part of the book by articulating that sponsorship has earned its place in the marketing mix of organizations around the world. It has become a legitimate and effective tool in the promotional artillery of organizations, one that differs from advertising by its ability to transfer images via the associations that sponsorship provides. For the sponsorship sales chapter, we asked an external sales expert—Professor Pat Ryan—to join the writing team to provide a vision of the reality and issues related to sales of sponsorship in very large organizations, such as the Olympic Games. Specific tactics, strategies, and sales tools are provided. The final two chapters of Part II describe Olympic sponsorship, with a historical reflection on the TOP program and the details of Olympic sponsorship.

When discussing the Olympic Games and sponsorship, it is hard not to recognize their global uniqueness. Indeed, there is no other entity in the world, not even the United Nations, that deals with as many countries or the nuanced politics of sport as it relates to performance, visibility, and power. To that end, the hope is that you have read this book with an eye toward thinking about whether you would ever want to work in the Olympic sports world. If so, this book has offered numerous ways to think about leadership, strategizing solutions, and enhancing your articulation of the big issues.

As was explored throughout the first part of the book, there are literally thousands of organizations and tens of thousands of jobs, if you are interested! Now, clearly, no athlete jumps from local competition to the Olympic stage and no sport administrator (manager, marketer, sponsor, broadcaster, etc.) jumps from local sports to the next Rio de Janeiro (2016), PyeongChang (2018), or Tokyo (2020). For both of those groups, the process takes thousands of hours of hard work and a commitment to becoming the best at something that can be seen. The Olympics will always need the next generation of administrators to help the athletes thrill us from the world's stage. The authors of this book sincerely hope that these chapters and sentiments will give you a clearer understanding of the skills you will need to master and the kinds of challenges you might well face.

The Olympics prove time and time again that amazing stories await. Indeed, for each Games, media reports are filled with concerns, politics, and issues in the days prior to the Opening Ceremonies, only to be (usually) forgotten and replaced with stories of athletes, countries, host cities, and competition in the two weeks of each Games. Miracles take place on ice, asphalt, on running tracks, trampolines, bike seats, sand, in/on water, on snow, and on stunning grass fields. But they also take place in board rooms, cramped offices, and thousands of other settings where humans work harder than you might imagine to support a concept, the Olympic motto, that is as simple as *Citius, Altius, Fortius.* Faster, Higher, Stronger.

If you want to wear the five rings, if you want to work with these particular Games, you will have to adopt that same orientation to achievement. You will need to master faster technology. You will need to think higher-level thoughts to overcome the gravity of mediocre concepts. And you will need to be stronger than ever in your mental acuity and communications.

SUMMARY: AMBUSH MARKETING

No discussion about the sponsorship of major, global events with billions of followers is complete without some attention being given to ambush marketing. Although not always referred to specifically as *ambush* anymore (sometimes *parasite* and sometimes just *marketing*), this type of competitive (or reactionary) marketing is a reality facing sponsors of mega-events, but even more so of major sports properties (such as the IOC, FIFA, or the NFL) tasked with protecting their brands from the competitors of their sponsors to ensure the revenues associated with their sponsorship sales remain and continue to grow both in size and in returns provided to their partners.

The five-chapter sequence in Part III of the book digs deeply into ambush marketing in a way not yet published (to our knowledge). This series of chapters begins with an introduction of ambush marketing, followed by a chapter and exploration of the world of ambush marketing, one about responding to ambush marketing, then presenting a chapter to examine the role of ambush specific to the Olympic Games (an area of expertise of the authors), with a final chapter that presents a series of case examples. The early chapters go in-depth to share the reality of ambush marketing, how both official sponsors and ambushers (or nonsponsors) do not view it as negative but as "let the best marketer win" and that ambush really can work and really is a threat.

Chapter 16 takes the side of the nonsponsor or the ambusher marketer. This is a perspective rarely thought about or often ignored. Perhaps it is taboo. But, for the purposes of this book, it is a view that is vital to understand, particularly for those working in Olympic marketing and sponsorship. Chapters 17 and 18 provide context specific to ambushing at the Olympic Games and includes a battery of case examples of ambush marketing to learn from. Specifically, in Chapter 18, seven case studies are provided of clearly implemented ambush marketing efforts at a variety of mega-sporting-events to illustrate different types of ambush, different outcomes, different roles, and the variety of main concepts related to the topic. Examples from the Olympic Games, the FIFA World Cup, and the Rugby World Cup are all included.

FRAMEWORK FOR THE FUTURE OF OLYMPIC MARKETING

Ancient stadia reveal the importance of sport in our society, and the Olympic movement is the oldest and longest standing representation of sport in the world. To that end, one might expect that sport will be with us 2,790 years from now . . . just as sport, in the form of the Olympics, was with us 2,790 years ago in Olympia when the Games were first held in 776 BC. Then, in the looming shadow of the Temple of Zeus (one of the Seven Ancient Wonders of the World), athletes competed for a series of values that we still recognize today. The legacy of past Olympics is still with us, the energy still in the air as we walk through former host cities and venues, imagining the athletes and the cheers.

The 2014 Winter Games in Sochi currently bear the legacy of being one of the least leveraged for corporate sponsors (IEG, 2014). With Volkswagen as the sole global marketing powerhouse on the Sochi Organizing Committee (compared to multiple major international sponsors aligned with the 2012 London Organizing Committee), stories of corruption and terrorism, and the international attention that was paid to Russia's antihomosexuality laws, the national and worldwide sponsors had the arduous task of activating the sponsorship without allowing their message to be tainted by the Sochi controversies (IEG, 2014).

On the other hand, the mixed reviews over the *missing* Olympic ring in the Sochi logo (which was replaced by a small sun), prompted Audi fans to create a bogus tongue-in-cheek online advertisement with a picture of the rear of two Audi's showing their four-ring brand logo and an accompanying slogan "when four rings is all you need." Audi was not the first to make the most of a bad situation, joining Oreo who tweeted, "you can still dunk in the dark" with a simple picture of an Oreo cookie over a black background after the infamous Super Bowl XLVII power outage. It was a simple cookie ad that generated an impressive 20,000 "Likes" on Facebook, and over 15,000 retweets on Twitter in the few days around Super Bowl, leading Watercutter (2013) to deem it the winner of the *Marketing Super Bowl*. There was also the "erectile dysfunction" in Vancouver where one of the large pillars did not come out of the ground as planned leaving one of the torchbearers unable to light that pillar and leading organizers to change the closing ceremonies to include a humorous set-up—involving a clown mime, the same torchbearer (Olympian Catriona Le May Doan) sparks, feathers, and fake chickens—that made fun of the incident.

During the 2012 London Olympic Games, sponsors, including Adidas and Nike, began social media ads that exploited the awkward timing of the London Tube strike, encouraging audiences to run into work (in Adidas shoes or with a Nike Fuelband), while Pizza Express and Cadbury, among others, presented their products with special discounts and contests, as ways to beat the stress of the transportation delays (Joseph, 2014). More recently, during the 2014 FIFA World Cup, Nike created numerous long-form communiques ("Risk Everything") that were provided almost exclusively for devices where the curious individual could click on a link or enter a website address. In fact, the "Winner Stays" creative was most visible on the company's microsite, where it quickly approached 100 million views (Fidelman, 2014). There are lessons for the future of Olympic marketing: We must respond to the buzz, quickly and with some wit, and then let social media drive the campaign.

In the year 4805, a time that is very hard to imagine, we believe (and hope) athletes will still compete and that variables of what we have presented in this text (books may long be gone by then) may still hold. Winners will be celebrated. The locations of sporting events will matter. The venues, officials, and media will probably all still have roles to play. So we hope this book has helped you better understand the importance of the Olympics, its marketing, and many of the numerous moving parts that play a role in supporting a global tradition of peace, unity, and athletic excellence.

Sponsorship, ambush marketing, the law, licensing, merchandising, sales, leadership, hospitality, and so many other components are real parts of the Games—and they have traveled with us through the centuries. The modern word *sponsorship* comes from the Greek word *horigos* which roughly translated means "I lead the dance." In ancient Greece, citizens of wealth were prevailed upon to help fund the civic activities that served the authorities or the masses. To lead the dance meant that the respective donors were able to wear the ceremonial color purple, lay wreaths or signage at the foot of important statues, and to receive prioritized access to the participants (be they athletes, gladiators, dancers, or performers). The dance, or parade, signaled the arrival of the event. These historic events galvanized the known world and it is not surprising that Roman poet Juvenal, writing in Latin, suggested in approximately A.D. 100 that "everything, now restrains itself and anxiously hopes for just two things: bread and the circus games."

That may be our interpretation and we might infer that Juvenal, who was also a satirist, was mocking the Roman culture that handed out wheat and entertainment to keep the peace or to control political power. But perhaps we should not be surprised. At the Beijing (2008) and London (2012) Olympics, more countries marched into the Opening Ceremonies than there are countries in the United Nations. The world's people do, in fact, desire food, shelter, peace, and sporting competition that allows the world, if only briefly, to wear its finest colors. We can only imagine what we will see in Rio 2016 or Tokyo 2020 but we predict the future of the Olympics will be bright and the marketing, sponsorship, and ambushing will be colorful.

FINAL WORD

Simply stated, we hope this text has given you that impetus. We know athletes never cease to push themselves toward the greatest possible achievement in their area of competition. We think modern students must push themselves in similar ways. Those who rest upon yesterday's laurels are soon surpassed by younger, hungrier achievers. We hope this book has given you some fuel to win your own gold medals.

With all best regards,

Norm, Dick, Benoit, Rick, and Michelle

Endnotes

CHAPTER 1

1. This case study was written one year before the Women's World Cup.

CHAPTER 4

1. At the time of publication SportAccord was undergoing some organizational challenges with members threatening to leave and the leadership likely to change. Since this issue was ongoing at the time of publication, it was not included in this section.

CHAPTER 7

1. This chapter was written using the authors' professional experience and knowledge. The following works, while not cited in the chapter, served as general references for the authors while writing this chapter:

Abeza, G., Baka, R., Burton, R., O'Reilly, N., & Seguin, B. (2013). National Olympic hospitality houses: Objectives, variations, and mini-cases. In Baka, R., & Hess R. (Eds.), *On the Periphery: New Perspectives on the Olympic Movement* (pp. 33-40). Sydney, NSW, Australia: Walla Walla Press.

Burton, R. (2013). Investigating Olympic sponsorship: A contemporary review of selected activation and achievement. In Frawley, S., & Adair, D. (Eds.), *Managing the Olympics* (pp. 165-181). London, England: Palgrave Macmillan.

Burton, R., O'Reilly, N., & Sequin, B. (2012). Stakeholder perceptions of short term marketing tactics during the Olympics. In Maennig, W., & Zimbalist, A. (Eds.), *International Handbook on the Economics of Sporting Mega Events* (pp. 140-161). London, England: Edward Elgar.

Wikipedia (2008). *Summer Olympics*. Retrieved from http://en.wikipedia.org/wiki/2008_Summer_Olympics

CHAPTER 8

1. 1929 UKPC 86.
2. "CAS Mediation Rules" (1 September 2013), online: CAS http://www.tas-cas.org/d2wfiles/document/307/5048/0/Mediation20Rules20201320_clean20final_ggr.pdf

3. CAS establishes an *ad hoc* Division of the Court at the Olympic Games (as well as other major games and world championships). Arbitrators are appointed for the purpose and disputes are to be heard and decided within 24 hours from the time the appeal is filed.
4. This addition is an adaptation from a speech given by book author Richard W. Pound on March 13th, 2014, at the University of Windsor Law School Windsor, Ontario Canada.

CHAPTER 9

1. See Intellectual Property Law of Canada, Stikeman Elliott, 1.02(1).
2. *Inland Revenue Commissioners v. Miller & Co.'s Margarine Ltd.* 217 A.C. 223–224. (1901)
3. (1842), 6 Beav. 66, 49 E.R. 749.
4. *Ibid.*, p. 752.
5. *Erven Warnink B.V. v. J. Townend & Sons (Hull) Ltd.*, [1980] R.P.C. 31, per Lord Diplock.
6. R.S.C., 1985, c. T-13.
7. In the particular constitutional context in Canada section 7(e) has been held to be unconstitutional as impinging on property and civil rights, matters within the legislative competence of the provinces. *MacDonald v. Vapor Canada Ltd.*, [1977] 2 S.C.R. 134.
8. *Consumers Distributing Co. v. Seiko Time Canada Ltd.*, 1 C.P.R. (3d) 1 at 19 (1984)
9. R.S.C., 1985, c. F-27.
10. *The Vegetable, Fruit and Honey Sales Act*. Retrieved from http://www.qp.gov.sk.ca/documents/English/Statutes/Repealed/V2.pdf
11. R.S.C., 1985, c. 20 (4th Supp.).
12. R.S.C., 1985, c. G-10.
13. R.S.C., 1985, c. F-9.
14. R.S.C., 1985, c. F-10.
15. R.S.C., 1985, c. F-12.
16. R.S.C. 1990, c. L-20.
17. R.S.C., 1985, c. S-8.
18. R.S.C., 1985, c. B-6.
19. R.S.C., 2001, c. 26.
20. R.S.C., 1985, c. 32 (4th Supp.).
21. R.S.C., 1985, c. E-14.
22. R.S.C., 1985, c. R-10.
23. Patent Act (R.S.C., 1985, c. P-4), at section 2.
24. One example of this is the trade-mark of "Shredded Wheat." See: *Canadian Shredded*

Wheat Co. Ltd. V. Kellogg Co. of Canada Ltd., (1939) 55 R.P.C. 125.

25. *Compo Company Ltd. V. Blue Crest Music Inc.*, [1980] 1 S.C.R. 357 at 372.

26. See IOC, *History of Olympic Marketing*, 2013, p. 30. Also Barney, Wenn and Martyn, *Selling the Five Rings: the International Olympic Committee and the Rise of Commercialism*, Salt Lake City, The University of Utah Press, 2004, pp. 31–49.

27. Ibid.

28. Ibid.

29. *Act to Incorporate the United States Olympic Association* (http://www.gpo.gov/fdsys/pkg/STATUTE-78/pdf/STATUTE-78-Pg383.pdf)

30. Ibid.

31. *Olympic and Amateur Sports Act* (http://www.gpo.gov/fdsys/pkg/CRPT-105srpt325/pdf/CRPT-105srpt325.pdf)

CHAPTER 12

1. See Olympic Charter at Article 7 and especially Article 7.2.

2. See, generally, Olympic Charter and, in particular, Articles 1, 2, 7, 15, 24, 32–44, 45, 46, 48, 50, and 51–56.

3. Olympic Charter, Articles 25 and 26.

4. Olympic Charter, Article 27.

5. Olympic Charter, Articles 27 and 28 (and bylaws).

6. Olympic Charter, Article 27, 27.4 and bylaws to Rules 7–14, especially 4.3, 4.9, 4.10.1.

7. Olympic Charter, Article 28.3.

8. Olympic Charter, bylaws to Rules 7–14, bye-law 4.7.

9. The IOC had established an Emblems Commission in 1967, whose mandate was to supervise the use of the Olympic rings. Membership was not restricted to IOC members and included, inter alia, representatives of NOCs. There were obvious tensions where NOCs had their own marketing programs, since they did not want the IOC to be carrying on marketing activities in their territories that might be competitive with their own and they argued for a rule that would prevent the IOC from entering their territories at all, or at least without their permission.

10. See discussion below.

11. The analogy of sport as war was introduced and described in detail in Chapter 4.

12. At one stage, the situation had been so serious

that a city in Japan was named Usa, so that goods could be marked as "Made in USA."

13. The USOC reasoning on that point was somewhat specious: the assertion was that any amount paid by a broadcast sponsor to the broadcaster would, had it not been paid to the broadcaster, have been paid to the USOC.

14. One notable example that illustrates the point was the decision of the Los Angeles Olympic Organizing Committee to award sponsorship (in the predigital photography days) rights in the film category to Fuji Film. Kodak responded actively, including sponsorship of USA Track and Field. There was considerable market confusion as to which corporation had which marketing rights.

CHAPTER 13

1. http://www.michaelrpayne.com/downloadables/Michael%20Payne%20Gold%20story.pdf

2. This is something of an overstatement (convenient as it may be when dealing with the private sector), since the US government had protected the Olympic rings and the word *Olympic* for the benefit of the USOC by special statute and provided tax relief in respect of donations to the USOC, but it was true that there was no direct government funding directed at the USOC.

3. This has not stopped OCOGs from regular complaints that they could have gotten *more* from TOP categories on a stand-alone basis.

4. The IOC has agreed to a standstill agreement with the USOC on this allocation issue (and others) until 2013, which effectively means that there will be no change in the allocations until sometime after the 2020 Games, awarded in September 2013, to Tokyo, Japan. Some have suggested that this factor, along with the share of US television rights that accrues to the U.S. Olympic Committee (no other NOC has such an arrangement) played a role in the stunning first round elimination of Chicago in the competition to host the 2016 Olympic Games.

CHAPTER 14

1. Olympic Charter, Bye-law to Rules 27 and 28, page 62.

2. This exercise formally includes the Paralympic Games, but for convenience, references will be to the Olympic Winter Games only.

3. Whistler is formally the Resort Municipality of Whistler (RMOW).

Index

Author Biographies

Norm O'Reilly

Norm is chair of the world-ranked Department of Sports Administration in the College of Business at Ohio University. He also holds the Richard P. & Joan S. Fox Professor of Business at Ohio. In 2013, he was recognized as one of the "Five to Watch" in sport business in Canada by *The Globe and Mail*. Previously a faculty member at the University of Ottawa, Syracuse University, Laurentian University, and Ryerson University, Norm has also held visiting positions at Stanford University (two occasions) and the University of New South Wales in Australia. Norm is an active consultant and expert legal witness. Prior to joining academia, Norm held professional positions with Sport Canada, Triathlon Canada, and the 2008 Toronto Olympic Bid. He has been a member of the 2004, 2008, and 2010 Mission Staff for the Canadian Olympic Committee at the Olympic Games. A former varsity level swimmer and Nordic skier, Norm is an active triathlete who has completed six Ironmans and represented Canada in his age-group at five World Long Distance Triathlon Championships.

Richard W. Pound

Richard is a lawyer and CPA and is Counsel in the Canadian law firm, Stikeman Elliott LLP. He has been a member of the International Olympic Committee (IOC) since 1978 and for some twenty years was responsible for all television and marketing activities of the IOC. He is past president of the Canadian Olympic Committee and was a double Olympic finalist in swimming and a 1962 Commonwealth Games champion. Pound was the inaugural president of the World Anti-Doping Agency and is the current chairman of Olympic Broadcasting Services. He is Chancellor Emeritus of McGill University. He has written extensively on Olympic and other subjects.

Rick Burton

Rick is the award-winning David B. Falk Distinguished Professor of Sport Management in Syracuse University's David B. Falk College of Sport and Human Dynamics. He served as the chief marketing officer for the U.S. Olympic Committee at the Beijing 2008 Summer Olympics, where he directed the USOC's partnerships for IOC and USOC sponsorship activation at the world's largest sporting event. Rick was the Commissioner of the Sydney-based National Basketball League (a two-continent league with teams in Australia, New Zealand, and Singapore). During the last

20 years, his scholarly research and commentary has appeared in multiple peer-reviewed journals. Rick has written for the *New York Times, Wall Street Journal, Ad Age, Sports Business Journal, SI.com, Sport Business International, Stadia* and hosted his own sports business television show in Portland, Oregon.

Benoît Séguin

Benoît is an associate professor of sport management, specializing in sport marketing at the University of Ottawa. His research on sponsorship, ambush marketing, and Olympic Marketing has been published in a variety of international journals and co-authored *Olympic Marketing (Routledge)*. Benoît has extensive professional experience having held leadership positions with Diving Canada, Synchro Canada, Aquatic Federation of Canada and as Assistant Chef de Mission for Canada's team at the 2003 Pan American Games. He is a supervising professor at the International Olympic Academy (Olympic marketing and sponsoring), at the Russian International Olympic University (business of sport and the Olympics) and a lecturer for the Executive Masters in Sport Organizations Management (MEMOS), an international program supported by Olympic Solidarity.

Michelle K. Brunette

Michelle is a PhD candidate at Nipissing University with a focus on the intersection of sport, culture and education. She teaches international health in the School of Human Kinetics and directs institutional planning at Laurentian University. She co-authored *Public Private Partnerships in Physical Activity and Sport (Human Kinetics publishing)* with Norm O'Reilly. Michelle is an executive member of the Sudbury Rocks Race, Run, or Walk for Diabetes, a founding board executive for the Young Professionals Association, and the former athlete representative for Ringette Ontario. She is an avid athlete participating in ringette, soccer, and competitive distance running.

Contributor Biographies

Amanda Fowler

Amanda is a graduate of the J.D. program at the University of Windsor. She obtained her Bachelor of Arts (Honors) in Political Studies and History from Queen's University. Amanda was actively involved in her law school community where she was the Vice President of the Sports and Entertainment Law Society, Co-Chair of the UWin Sports Conference, and an NHL Arbitration Competition competitor. While studying abroad in Australia, Amanda represented the Bond University Soccer Club. In a recent project, Amanda conducted research for a Doping Appeal to the Sport Dispute Resolution Centre of Canada. Amanda is currently working at a law firm in downtown Toronto.

Pat Ryan

Pat Ryan is a senior instructor at Syracuse University delivering courses on the principles of sport, sport organization, management, and the Olympic experience. He led a student engagement program for campus internships and has led the annual Syracuse University Abroad Olympic Odyssey program to provide students firsthand exposure to the Olympic legacies in London, Paris, Lausanne, Greece, and Lake Placid. In sport he has been professionally involved with organizations such as Syracuse University Athletics, NY State ORDA, the Baseball Hall of Fame, and the Syracuse Chiefs.

References

Aaker, D. A. (1991). *Managing brand equity: Capitalizing on the value of a brand name.* New York, NY: The Free Press.

Addley, E. (2012). *Olympics 2012: branding 'police' to protect sponsors exclusive rights.* The Guardian, Sports. Retrieved July 15, 2013, from http://www.theguardian.com/sport/2012/apr/13/olympics-2012-branding-police-sponsors

Ad wars. (2009). Retrieved July 17, 2014, from http://www.ahmedabadmirror.com/index.aspx?page=article&sectid=44&contentid=2009082920090829021656312df81c137

AMA (2013). Definition of Marketing. Retrieved from https://www.ama.org/AboutAMA/Pages/DefinitionofMarketing.aspx.

AMA Pro Racing. (2013). Retrieved October 19, 2013, from http://www.amaproracing.com

Andrews, J. (2014). The ambush marketing vs. sponsorship debate. Retrieved February 10, 2014, from http://www.sponsorship.com/About-IEG/Sponsorship-Blogs/Jim-Andrews/February-2014/The-Ambush-Marketing-vs--Sponsorship-Debate-Spring.aspx

Armour, Nancy. (2010). Mini-dressed fans questions at World Cup. Retrieved September 23, 2011, from http://www.msnbc.msn.com/id/37712281/ns/business-world_business/t/mini-dressed-fans-questioned-world-cup/#.TxWuwGDgLR1

Armstrong, K. (1999). A quest for a market: A profile of the consumers of a professional women's basketball team and the marketing implications. *Women's Sport and Physical Activity Journal, 8*(2), 103–12.

Arshad, S. (2014). 10 most valuable sports brands 2014. *TSM Plug.* Retrieved from http://www.tsmplug.com/richlist/valuable-sports-brands

Arthur, B. (2012, August 9). London 2012 Olympics: Canada's women's soccer team may have won bronze on Thursday, but it's unlikely a medal could shine more brightly. *O Canada!* Retrieved from: http://o.canada.com /sports/london-2012-olympics-canadas-womens-soccer-team-may-have-won-bronze-on-thursday/

The Association of IOC Recognized International Sports Federation (ARISF). (2013). Members. Retrieved October 11, 2013, from http://www.arisf.org/members#Air%20Sports

Athletic Management. (2014). Hooters sponsorship sparks debate. Retrieved May 20, 2014, from http://www.momentummedia.com/articles/am/am1602/hooters.htm

ATP World Tour Tennis. (2013). Calendar. grand slams. Retrieved October 19, 2013, from http://www.atpworldtour.com/Tournaments/Event-Calendar.aspx

Australian Baseball League. (n.d.). Retrieved October 15, 2013, from http://web.theabl.com.au/index.jsp

Australian Football League. (2013). Retrieved October 18, 2013, from http://www.afl.com.au

Badminton World Federation. (2012). Organization. Retrieved October 9, 2013, from http://www.bwfbadminton.org/page.aspx?id=15367

Bailey, R. (2005). Evaluating the relationship between physical education, sport and social inclusion. *Educational Review, 57,* 71–90.

Battista, S. (2014, January/February). Will power, *The Hub Magazine,* 22–26.

BBC News. (2010). FIFA order South Africa airline to drop 'ambush.' Retrieved November 20, 2011, from http://news.bbc.co.uk/2/hi/8576220.stm

Beats by Dre. (n.d.). *Headphones. Powerful Sound and Audio Technology.* Retrieved June 22, 2013, from http://ca.beatsbydre.com

Becker-Olsen, K. (1998). *Corporate sponsorship: A look at the moderating effects of fit and reach on image and purchase intentions.* (Doctoral dissertation, Lehigh University).

Bell (2013). Bell Canada 2012 corporate responsibility report. Retrieved June 14, 2014, from http://www.bce.ca/assets/widgets/Responsibility/CR-report-2012/EN/2012_CR_report_en.pdf

Berkes, H. (Narrator) (2009, October 1). *Morning edition.* [Radio broadcast]. Washington, DC. National Public Radio. Retrieved January 30, 2014, from http://www.npr.org/templates/story/story.php?storyId=113351145

Berrett, T., & Slack, T. (1999). An analysis of the

influence of competitive and institutional pressures on corporate sponsorship decisions. *Journal of Sport Management, 13*, 114–38.

BEVNET (2014). Retrieved November 11, 2014, from http://www.bevnet.com/news/2014/red-bull-to-pay-13-million-for-false-advertising-settlement

Billboard Staff. (2012). *Beats by Dre Causes Marketing Controversy at Olympics with Free Headphones for Athletes.* BillboardBiz. Retrieved June 30, 2013, from http://www.billboard.com/biz/articles/news/branding/1084395/beats-by-dre-causes-marketing-controversy-at-olympics-with-free

Blaikie, H. (February 2006). Let the Games begin? Under pressure, Esso replaces its Olympic trip prize. *Canadian Marketing and Advertising Law Update.* Retrieved from www.heenanblaikie.com/fr/publications/item?id=901

Boone, T. (2004). Is sports nutrition for sale? *Professionalization of Exercise Physiology, 7*(7). Retrieved February 20, 2014, from http://faculty.css.edu/tboone2/asep/ IsSportsNutritionForSale.html

The Boston Globe. (2014). Olympics notes: Doping test costs Sweden. Retrieved February 24, 2014, from http://www.bostonglobe.com/sports/2014/02/24/sweden-backstrom-denied-from-playing-gold-medal-game-because-failed-doping-test/rIecbrIw1td2jvk1m4r7CO/story.html

Boyle, M. (2012, March 1). *Top secret: Durex's Olympic Condoms.* Retrieved from http://www.businessweek.com/articles/2012-03-01/top-secret-durexs-olympic-condoms

Bradish, C. (2010): Vancouver 2010: An examination of community and corporate investment. *Brock University, Department of Sport Management.* Retrieved October 11, 2011, from www.omero.unito.it/?download=Symposium_ppt_Bradish.pdf

Brandchannel. (2011). Rugby World Cup goes after strip bar for ambush marketing. Retrieved October 29, 2011, from http://www.brandchannel.com/home/post/2011/10/05/Rugby-World-Cup-Strip-Bar-Ambush-Marketing.aspx

British Baseball Federation (n.d.). Retrieved October 15, 2013, from http://www.britishbaseball.org/

British Waterpolo League. (2013). Retrieved October 19, 2013, from http://www.bwpl.org

Brokaw, A .J. (2000). An explanation of attendance in division II college football. *Cyber Journal of Sport Marketing, 4*(2–3). Retrieved from pandora.nld.gov/tcp/10007

Brunette, M. K., Lariviere, M., Schinke, R. J.,

XiaoYan, X., & Pickard, P. (2011). Fit to belong: activity and acculturation of Chinese students. *Journal of Sport Behavior, 34*(3), 207–227.

Bryant, C., Lindenberger, J., Brown, C., Kent, E., Schreiber, J. M., Bustillo, M., & Canright, M. W. (2001). A social marketing approach to increasing enrollment in a public health program: A case study of the Texas WIC program. *Human Organization, 60*(3), 234–246.

Burton, R. (2001, July 8). The yea and nay of Beijing's Olympic bid: China makes good business sense. *New York Times*, Y29.

Burton, R. (2011, January 2). Looking back for sports' first female pitchman. *New York Times*, S10.

Burton, R. (2012, June 9). For disgraced athletes, the wrath of Zeus. *Wall Street Journal*, p. C2.

Burton, R., & O'Reilly, N. (2014a). Bach's history a signal that his leadership will be proactive. *Sports Business Journal, 16*(41), 25.

Burton, R., & O'Reilly, N. (2014b). How will Olympic sponsors respond to future host sites? *Sports Business Journal, 16*(45), 11.

Busbee, J. (2014). The most-attended sporting event in the country? Races baby. Retrieved February 20, 2013, from https://ca.sports.yahoo.com/nascar/blog/from_the_marbles/post/The-most-attended-sporting-events-in-the-country?urn=nascar,243650

Butterworth, T. (2011). ABC News attacks scientist who exposed bias in obesity research. *Forbes.* Retrieved February 20, 2014, from http://www.forbes.com/sites/trevorbutterworth/2011/06/22/abc-news-attacks-scientist-who-exposed-bias-in-obesity-research/

Cairns, D. J. A. (1988). *The remedies for trademark infringement.* Toronto, CAN: Carswell.

Canada 2010. (2010). 2010 business opportunities. VANOC sponsorship. Retrieved October 10, 2011, from www.canada2010.gc.ca/business_affaires/1-eng.cfm

Canadian Broadcasting Corporation. (2010). A record 5.816 million Canadians watch FIFA World Cup final. *Canadian Broadcasting Corporation.* Retrieved from http://www.cbc.ca/revenuegroup/mobile/touch/a-record-5816-million-canadians-watch-fifa-world-cup-final.html

Canadian Intellectual Property Office (CIPO). (2014a). A guide to industrial design. *Industry Canada.* Retrieved from http://www.cipo.ic.gc.ca/eic/site/cipointernet-internetopic.nsf/eng/wr03636.html

Canadian Intellectual Property Office (CIPO). (2014b). Trade-marks examination manual. *In-*

dustry Canada. Retrieved from http://www.cipo .ic.gc.ca/eic/site/cipointernet-internetopic.nsf/eng /wr03636.html

Canadian Paralympic Committee. (2013a). About us. Retrieved September 15, 2013, from http:// www.paralympic.ca/about-us

Canadian Paralympic Committee. (2013b). What is parasport? Retrieved October 5, 2013, http:// www.paralympic.ca/what-parasport

Canadian Paralympic Committee. (2013c). Our history. Retrieved October 5, 2013, from http:// www.paralympic.ca/our-history

Canadian Paralympic Committee. (2013d). Paralympic sport. Retrieved October 5, 2013, from http://www.paralympic.ca/paralympic-sport

Canadian Paralympic Committee. (2013e). Different disabilities. Retrieved October 5, 2013, from http://www.paralympic.ca/different-disabilities

Canadian Paralympic Committee. (2013f). Partners & sponsors. Retrieved October 15, 2013, from http://www.paralympic.ca/partners-sponsors

Canadian Paralympic Committee. (2014). Canadian Paralympic Committee 2013–2014 annual report. Retrieved from http://paralympic.ca/sites /default/files/uploads/ContentImages/About/an nual_repport_2013-2014-en-low-v2.pdf

Canadian Soccer Association. (2014). Annual report—capturing the moment. Retrieved from http:// www.canadasoccer.com

CBCNews. (2013). Russian anti-gay bill passes, protestors detained. Retrieved June 11, 2013, from http://www.cbsnews.com/news/russian-anti-gay -bill-passes-protesters-detained/

CBCNews British Columbia. (2009). Lululemon scolded for linking clothing to the Olympics. Retrieved January 2, 2012, from http://www.cbc .ca/news/canada/british-columbia/story/2009/12 /16/consumer-lululemon-olympics.html

Cooper, B. (2010, March 21). One body of marketing rights and countless stakeholders wanting to use it: How do you keep them all satisfied? Presentation at the Canadian Sponsorship Forum, Toronto, CAN.

CFL. (n.d.) Retrieved October 18, 2013, from http://www.cfl.ca

Chadwick, S, and Burton, N. (2010). Ambushed! Retrieved December 22, 2011, from http://on line.wsj.com/article/SB100014240529702047 31804574391102699362862.html

Chinese Professional Baseball League (Taiwan). (n.d). Retrieved October 15, 2013, from http:// www.cpbl.com.tw

Cialdini, R. B., Borden, R. J., Thorne, A., Walker, M. R., Freeman, S., & Sloan, L. R. (1976). Basking in reflected glory: Three (football) field studies. Journal of Personality and Social Psychology, 34, 366–375.

CNN. (2013). Video sequence. Retrieved August 18, 2014, from http://edition.cnn.com/video/? /video/world/2013/08/03/pkg-dougherty-russia -anti-gay-law.cnn&video_referrer=http%3A%2 F%2Fedition.cnn.com%2F2013%2F10%2F1 4%2Fworld%2F2014-sochi-winter-olympics -fast-facts%2F

The Coca-Cola Company. (2010). Coca-Cola Great Britain FAQs. Retrieved November 1, 2013, from http://www.coca-cola.co.uk/faq/olympic -games/how-long-has-coca-cola-been-associated -with-the-olympic-movement.html

The Coca-Cola Company. (2013). Coca-Cola celebrates more than 80 years of Olympic partnership with largest-ever activation. Retrieved November 1, 2013, from http://www.coca-colacom pany.com/press-center/press-releases/coca-cola-cele brates-more-than-80-years-of-olympic-partner ship-with-largest-ever-activation

Cofaigh, E. O. (2011). Motor sport in France: Testing-ground for the world. International Journal of the History of Sport, 28(2), 191–204.

Columbian Professional Baseball League. (2013). October 15, 2013, from http://lcbp.co

Commonwealth Games Federation. (2013). The story of the Commonwealth Games. Retrieved October 7, 2013, from http://www.thecgf.com /games/story.asp

Cooper, B. (2008). Journal of Sponsorship. 2(1).

Cooper, B. (2010, March 21). One body of marketing rights and countless stakeholders wanting to use it: How do you keep them all satisfied? Presentation at the Canadian Sponsorship Forum, Toronto, CAN.

Cornwell, T. B., Roy, D. P., & Steinard II, E. A. (2001) Exploring managers' perceptions of the impact of sponsorship on brand equity. Journal of Advertising, 30(2), 41–51.

Court of Arbitration for Sport. (2014a). 20 questions about the CAS. Retrieved September 5, 2014, from http://www.tas-cas.org/en/20ques tions.asp/4-3-218-1010-13-0-0/

Court of Arbitration for Sport. (2014b). CAS arbitration No CAS OG 14/01. Retrieved from http://www.tas-cas.org/fileadmin/user_upload /Award2014-0120_FINAL_.pdf

Court of Arbitration for Sport. (2014c). CAS mediation rules. Retrieved September 1, 2013, from http://www.tas-cas.org/d2wfiles/document/307 /5048/0/mediation20rules20201320_clean20fi nal_ggr.pdf

Court of Arbitration for Sport. (2014d). Costs. Retrieved August 18, 2014, from http://www.tas-cas.org/arbitration-costs

Court of Arbitration for Sport. (2014e). History. Retrieved August 10, 2014, from http://www.tas-cas.org

Court of Arbitration for Sport. (2014f). Men's ski cross media release. Retrieved February 23, 2014, from http://www.tas-cas.org/d2wfiles/document/7381/5048/0/media20release20CAS20sochi206.pdf

Court of Arbitration for Sport. (2014g). Origins. Retrieved August 9, 2014, from http://www.tas-cas.org/history

Court of Arbitration for Sport. (2014h). The decentralized CAS offices and the ad hoc divisions. Retrieved August 10, 2014, from http://www.tas-cas.org/en/infogenerales.asp/4-3-240-1011-4-1-1/

Craig, C. L., Tudor-Locke, C., & Bauman, A. (2007). Twelve-month effects of Canada on the move: A population-wide campaign to promote pedometer use and walking. *Health Education Research, 22,* 406–413.

Crary, D. (2014). Human rights pledge urged for future Olympic hosts. Retrieved February 22, 2014, from http://www.deseretnews.com/article/765648301/Human-rights-pledge-urged-for-future-Olympic-hosts.html

Crimmins, J., & Horn, M. (1996) Sponsorship: From management ego trip to marketing success. *Journal of Advertising Research, 36*(4), 11–21.

Crompton, J. L. (2004). Sponsorship ambushing in sport. *Managing Leisure, 9,* 1–12.

Crowley, M. G. (1991) Prioritizing the sponsorship audience. *European Journal of Marketing, 25,* 11–21.

Dalakas, V., & Levin, A. (2005). The balance theory domino: How sponsorships may elicit negative consumer attitudes. In G. Menon & A. R. Rao (Eds.), *Advances in consumer research* (pp. 91–97). Duluth, MN: PUB.

Dalakas, V., & Rose, G. (2004). The impact of fan identification on customer response to sponsorship. In B. Pitts (Ed.), Sharing best practices in sports marketing: The Sports Marketing Association's inaugural book of papers (pp. 57–69). Morgantown, WV: Fitness Information Technology.

Davis, J. (2008). *The Olympic games effect: How strong marketing builds strong brands.* Singapore: John Wiley & Sons.

DePauw, K., & Gavron, S. (2005). *Disability sport* (2nd ed.). Champaign, IL: Human Kinetics.

Dharod, J. M., Drewette-Card, R., & Crawford, D. (2011). Development of the Oxford Hills healthy moms project using a social marketing process: A community-based physical activity and nutrition intervention for low-socioeconomic-status mothers in a rural area in Maine. *Health Promotion Practice, 12,* 312–321.

Dime. (2011). The top 5 basketball leagues outside of the United States. Retrieved October 15, 2013, from http://dimemag.com/2011/07/the-top-5-basketball-leagues-outside-the-united-states/

Dominican Professional Baseball League. (n.d.) Retrieved October 15, 2013, from http://www.lidom.com/home/

Druce, S. (2012). Adidas vs Nike- Battle of the brands. *Mars London.* Retrieved August 8, 2013, from http://marslondonblog.co.uk/2012/08/17/adidas-vs-nike-battle-of-the-brands/

Dutch Baseball League. (n.d.). Retrieved October 15, 2013, from http://www.baseballnetherlands.com

Eastern Ontario District Soccer Association. (2013). *Club directory.* Retrieved from http://www.eodsa.on.ca/DisplayPage.aspx?ID=2073

Edmonds, S. (2013, June 26). One down, three to go as CFL season ushers in new stadium boom. *The Globe and Mail.* Retrieved from http://www.theglobeandmail.com/sports/football/one-down-three-to-go-as-cfl-season-ushers-in-new-stadium-boom/article12821574/

The Eight Inning Stretch. Leagues around the world. Retrieved October 15, 2013, from http://eighthinningstretch.com/leagues-around-the-world/

Ellis, D. (2013). *Theorizing ambush marketing in the Olympic Games* (Unpublished doctoral dissertation). University of Ottawa, Ottawa, Ontario, Canada.

Ellis, D., Scassa, T., & Séguin, B. (2011b). Framing ambush marketing as legal issue. *Sport Management Review, 14*(3), 297–308.

Elliot, S. (2010, February 11). Subway takes ambush marketing complaints in stride. *New York Times,* February 11. Retrieved March 1, 2014, from http://mediadecoder.blogs.nytimes.com/2010/02/11/subway-takes-ambush-marketing-complaints-in-stride

ESPNcricinfo20. (2013). Retrieved October 20, 2013, from http://www.espncricinfo.com/ci/content/series/592761.html

Eurohandball. (n.d.) Retrieved October 19, 2013, from http://www.eurohandball.com

EuroHockey. (2013). Leagues, teams, countries. Retrieved October 18, 2013, from http://www.eurohockey.org

Fahy, J., Farrelly, F., & Quester, P. (2004). Competitive advantage through sponsorship: A conceptual model and research propositions. *European Journal of Marketing, 38*, 1013–1030.

Falk, D. (2010). *The bald truth*. New York, NY: Pocket Books.

Federation international d'Escrime. (2013). About FEI. Retrieved October 10, 2013, http://www.fie.ch/InBrief/Fencing.aspx

Federation Internationale de Gymnastic. (2013). Retrieved October 10, 2013, from http://www.fig-gymnastics.com/vsite/vtrial/page/home/0,11065,5187-187975-205197-45048-285446-custom-item,00.html

Federation Internationale de Natation. (2011). Retrieved Oct 10, 2013, from http://www.fina.org/H2O/index.php?option=com_content&view=section&layout=blog&id=37&Itemid=357

Federation International de Volleyball FIVB. (2013). Retrieved October 10, 2013, from http://www.fivb.org

FEI. (2013). About FEI. Retrieved October 10, 2013, from http://www.fei.org/fei/about-fei

Feldman, J. (2014). Protecting Olympic sponsorship from ambush marketers. Retrieved February 5, 2014, from http://www.enlightresearch.com/insights/2014/2/5/protecting-olympic-sponsorship-from-ambush-marketers.html

Ferrand, A., Chappelet, J-L., & Séguin, B. (2012). *Olympic Marketing*. London UK: Routledge.

Ferreira, M., & Armstrong, K. L. (2004). An exploratory examination of attributes influencing students' decisions to attend college sport events. *Sport Marketing Quarterly, 13*, 194–208.

FIBA. (2013). Organization. Retrieved October 9, 2013, from http://www.fiba.com/pages/eng/fc/FIBA/fibaStru/p/openNodeIDs/963/selNodeID/963/fibaCentBoar.html

Fidelman, M. (2014, July 1). Nike is dominating the World Cup – here's why. *Forbes*, Retrieved from http://www.forbes.com/sites/markfidelman/2014/07/01/nike-is-dominating-the-world-cup-heres-why/

FIFA. (n.d.). *The Organization- Sponsorship Strategy*. Retrieved September 22, 2011, from http://www.fifa.com/aboutfifa/organisation/marketing/sponsorship/strategy.html

FIFA. (2013a). FIFA Women's World Cup Canada 2015™ match schedule unveiled. Retrieved from http://www.fifa.com/womensworldcup/organisation/media/newsid=2035770/

FIFA. (2013b). FIFA Women's World Cup Qualifiers. *FIFA.com*. Retrieved December 16, 2013, from http://www.fifa.com/womensworldcup/qualifiers/index.html.

Forbes. (2014). The world's highest-paid tennis players. Retrieved from http://www.forbes.com/pictures/mli45jdmh/1-roger-federer-2/

Freedhoff, Y., & Hébert, P. (2011). Partnerships between health organizations and the food industry risk derailing public health nutrition. *Canadian Medical Association Journal, 183*(3), 291–292.

Funk, D. C., Mahony, D. F., Nakazawa, M., & Hirakawa, S. (2001). Development of the sport interest inventory (SII): Implications for measuring unique consumer motives at team sporting events. *International Journal of Sports Marketing and Sponsorship, 3*, 291–312.

Funk, D. C., Mahony, D. C., & Ridinger, L. L. (2002). Characterizing consumer motivation as individual difference factors: Augmenting the sport interest inventory (SII) to level of spectator support. *Sport Marketing Quarterly, 11*, 33–43.

Funk, D. C., Ridinger, L., & Moorman, A. (2004). Exploring the origins of involvement: Understand the relationship between consumer motives and involvement with professional sport teams. *Leisure Sciences, 2*, 35–61.

Georgetown Law. (2014, February). Olympics and international sports law research guide. Retrieved February 22, 2014, from http://www.law.georgetown.edu/library/research/guides/lawolympics.cfm

German Bundesliga. (2013). Retrieved October 15, 2013, from http://www.baseballgermany.com

Gibson, O. (2012). London 2012 Olympics will cost a total of £8.921bn, says minister. *The Guardian*. Retrieved February 23, 2014, from http://www.theguardian.com/sport/2012/oct/23/london-2012-olympics-cost-total

Givemesport. (2013). Top 20: Best leagues in world football. Retrieved October 18, 2013, from http://www.givemesport.com/342964-top-20-best-leagues-in-world-football

Giving USA Foundation. (2013). Annual state of giving report. Retrieved February 23, 2014, from http://www.givingusareports.org/

Green, B. C., & Chalip, L. (1998). Sport tourism as the celebration of subculture. *Annals of Tourism Research, 25*, 275–291.

Green, B. C. (2001). Leveraging subculture and identity to promote sport events. *Sport Management Review, 4*, 1–19.

Grier, S., & Bryant C. A. (2005). Social marketing in public health *Annual Review of Public Health, 26*, 319–339.

Griggs, G. (2012). Why have alternative sports

grown in popularity in the UK? *Annals of Leisure Research, 15*(2), 180–187.

The Guardian UK. World Cup 2010: (2010). Women arrested over 'ambush marketing' freed on bail. Retrieved September 23, 2011, from http://www.guardian.co.uk/football/2010/jun/16/fifa-world-cup-ambush-marketing

Gwinner, K. (1997). A model of image creation and image transfer in event sponsorship. *International Marketing Review, 14*(3), 145–58.

Hall, J., O'Mahony, B., & Vieceli, J. (2010). An empirical model of attendance factors at major sporting events. *International Journal of Hospitality Management, 29*, 328–334.

Hamilton, I. (2012). It's gotta be the shoes: Nike's ambush marketing plan. *Sports Business Now.* Retrieved August 11, 2013, from http://sportsbusinessnow.com/its-gotta-be-the-shoes-nikes-ambush-marketing-plan/

Harnden, T. (2008). Barack Obama picks 'best cabinet basketball team in history.' The Telegraph. Retrieved December 16, 2014, from http://www.telegraph.co.uk/news/worldnews/barackobama/3796397/Barack-Obama-picks-best-cabinet-basketball-team-in-history.html

Harper, S. (2014). *A great game: The forgotten leafs and the rise of professional hockey.* Toronto, CAN: Simon & Schuster.

Hershey's (2014). Participants landing page. Retrieved June 14, 2014, from https://www.hersheystrackandfield.com/participants.aspx

Hinka, M. (2010). Is Scotiabank's promotion an ambush or a gold-medal performance? Retrieved January 4, 2011, from http://www.cbc.ca/news/blogs/business/moneytalks/2010/01/michael-hlinka-is-scotiabanks-promotion-an-ambush-or-a-gold-medal-performance.html

HockeyDB. (n.d.) Leagues. Retrieved October 19, 2013, from http://www.hockeydb.com/ihdb/stats/leagues.html

Hoek, J., & Gendall, D. (2002a). Ambush marketing: More than just a commercial irritant. *Entertainment Law, 1*(2), 72–91.

Hoek, J., & Gendall, P. (2002b). When do ex-sponsors become ambush marketers? *International Journal of Sports Marketing & Sponsorship, 3*(4), 383–402.

Houpt, S. (2011). In sunny Riviera, storm clouds gather. *The Globe and Mail,* June 24.

Howard, D. R., & Crompton, J. L. (1995). *Financing sport.* Morgantown, WV: Fitness Information Technology.

Hughes, V. (2013, August 15). Personal interview.

iballunited. (2013). Top 25 men's International Basketball League rankings. Retrieved October 15, 2013, from http://iballunited.blogspot.ca/2013/01/iball-uniteds-2013-top-25-mens.html

IBF. (2013). About IBF. Retrieved October 9, 2013, from http://www.ibf-usba-boxing.com

ICF-Planet Canoe. (2012). About ICF. Retrieved October 10, 2013, from http://www.canoeicf.com/icf/

IEG. (2004). Sochi Sponsor Profile: Omega. Retrieved from http://www.sponsorship.com/Sponsorship-Consulting/Sochi-2014-Olympic-Sponsorship-Insights/Omega.aspx

IEG. (2011). Leading property practices: Eight ways to add value to sponsorship offers. Retrieved October 30, 2013, from http://www.sponsorship.com/iegsr/2011/05/09/Leading-Property-Practices--Eight-Ways-To-Add-Valu.aspx

IEG Sponsorship Report. (2011). 2011 Sponsorship spending. *IEG Sponsorship Report.* Downloaded March 4, 2012, from www.sponsorship.com.

IEG. (2014). Sochi's sponsorship picture. Retrieved February 24, 2014, from www.sponsorship.com

IGF. International Golf Federation. (2013). About IGF. Retrieved October 10, 2013, from http://www.igfgolf.org/about-igf/

Inside Hoops. (2013). Basketball leagues. Retrieved October 15, 2013, from http://www.insidehoops.com/basketball-leagues.shtml

Intel. (2014). Intel involved volunteers. Retrieved June 14, 2014, from http://www.intel.com/content/www/us/en/corporate-responsibility/intel-involved.html

International Biathlon Union. (2013). Basics. Retrieved October 10, 2013, from http://www.biathlonworld.com/en/basics.html

International Bobsleigh & Skeleton Federation. (2013). About & events. Retrieved October 10, 2013, from http://www.fibt.com/fibt-federation/organization.html

International Event Group. (2013). Winning with sports. Retrieved November 1, 2013, from http://www.sponsorship.com/Resources/Winning-with-Sports.aspx?utm_source=homeSlider&utm_medium=site&utm_content=sliderWinningWithSports&utm_campaign=sliderWinningWithSports

International Federation of Association Wrestling Styles. (2013). Retrieved October 10, 2013, from http://www.fila-official.com/index.php?lang=en

International Handball Federation. (2010). IHF profile. Retrieved October 10, 2013, from http://www.ihf.info/TheIHF/Profile/tabid/74/Default.aspx

International Ice Hockey Federation. (2013a). The IIHF. Retrieved October 10, 2013, from http://www.iihf.com/iihf-home/the-iihf.html

International Hockey Federation. (2013b). HIST IHF. Retrieved October 10, 2013, from http://www.fih.ch/en/fih/history

International Judo Association. (2007). Main IJA. Retrieved October 10, 2013, from http://www.intjudo.eu/main.php

International Luge Federation. (2013). Events. Retrieved October 10, 2013, from http://www.fil-luge.org/index.php?id=461

International Paralympic Committee. (2013g). History of the paralympic movement. Retrieved October 5, 2013, from http://www.paralympic.org/TheIPC/HWA/HistoryoftheMovement

International Paralympic Committee. (2013h). The IPC—who we are. Retrieved October 5, 2013, from http://www.paralympic.org/TheIPC/HWA/AboutUs

International Rugby Board. (2013). History & events. Retrieved October 10, 2013, from http://www.irb.com/history/index.html

International Sailing Federation. Events. Retrieved October 10, 2013, from http://www.sailing.org/news/isaf_events_news.php

International Shooting Sport Federation (ISSF). (2013). Retrieved October 10, 2013, from http://www.issf-sports.org

International Skating Union. (2013). Retrieved October 10, 2013, from http://www.isu.org/vsite/vtrial/page/home/0,11065,4844-128590-129898-19296-68634-custom-item,00.html

International Ski Federation. (2013). Retrieved October 11, 2013, from http://www.fis-ski.com

International Table Tennis Federation (ITTF). (2013). Retrieved October 10, 2013, from http://www.ittf.com

International Tennis Federation ITF. (2013). Organization. Retrieved October 10, 2013, from http://www.itftennis.com/about/organisation/role.aspx

International Triathlon Union ITU. (2013). About & events. Retrieved October 10, 2013, from http://www.triathlon.org/about

Irwin, R., & Sutton, W. (1994). Sport sponsorship objectives: An analysis of their relative importance for major corporate sponsors. *European Journal of Sport Management*, 1(2), 93–101.

Italian Baseball League. (n.d.) Retrieved October 15, 2013, from http://www.fibs.it/it-it/news-in-english.aspx

IOC. (n.d.). *The IOC Sponsorship.* Retrieved July 22, 2013, http://www.olympic.org/sponsorship

IOC. (2008). *Survey: All countries.* Lausanne, CH. International Olympic Committee.

IOC. (2011). *The IOC.* Retrieved December 22, 2011, from http://www.olympic.org/

IOC. (2012). IOC marketing: Media guide London 2012.

IOC. (2013a). International sports federations. Retrieved November 11, 2013, from http://www.olympic.org/content/the-ioc/governance/international-federations/

IOC. (2013b). Olympic charter. Retrieved September 9, 2013, from http://www.olympic.org/documents/olympic_charter_en.pdf

IOC. (2013c). The organization. Retrieved November 11, 2013, from http://www.olympic.org/about-ioc-institution

IOC. (2014). *Olympic marketing fact file.* Lausanne, CH. International Olympic Committee.

ISM. (2005). Institute for Sport Marketing Case Studies. Laurentian University 2003–2005.

Joseph, S. (2014, February 6). Adidas, Nike, Pizza Express exploit tube strike buzz. *Marketing Week.* Retrieved February 25, 2014, from http://www.marketingweek.co.uk/sectors/media/news/adidas-nike-and-pizza-express-exploit-tube-strike-buzz/4009408.article

The Judicial Committee of the Privy Council Decisions. Retrieved October 1, 2014, from http://www.bailii.org/uk/cases/UKPC/1929/1929_86.html

Kahle, L. R., & Riley, C. (2004). *Sports marketing and the psychology of marketing communication.* (Chapter 14). Mahwah, NJ: Lawrence Erlbaum Associates Inc.

Keller, K. L. (2003). *Strategic brand management: Building, measuring, and managing brand equity* (2nd ed.). Upper Saddle River, NJ: Prentice Hall.

Kelly, M. (2010). World Cup TV ratings show huge rise. *CBC.* Retrieved from http://www.cbc.ca/sports/soccer/world-cup-tv-ratings-show-huge-rise-1.948992

Kent, M. (2009). The Relationships between the Olympic Movement and its Stakeholders. The Structure of the Olympic Movement, p. 1. Retrieved October 4, 2014, from http://www.olympic.org/Assets/XIII%20OLYMPIC%20CONGRESS/PDF/ACTES_3.3/MUHTAR_KENT_ENG.pdf

Kim, N., & L. Chalip. (2004). Why travel to the FIFA World Cup? Effects of motives, background, interest, and constraints. *Tourism Management, 25*, 695–707.

Kinney, L., & McDaniel, S. R. (1996). Strategic implications of attitude-toward-the-ad in leveraging event sponsorships. *Journal of Sport Management, 10*(3), 250–261.

Koenigstorfer, J., & Groeppel-Klein, A. (2012). Implicit and explicit attitudes to sponsors and ambushers. *European Sport Management Quarterly, 12*, 477–499.

Korean Baseball Organization. (n.d). Retrieved October 15, 2013, from http://www.koreabaseball.com/Default.aspx

Kotler, P., & Andreasan, A. (1995). In D. R. Howard & J. L. Crompton (Eds.), *Financing sport.* Morgantown, WV: Fitness Information Technology.

Kotler, P., & Keller. K. (2011). *Marketing management.* Upper Saddle River, NJ: Pearson Hall.

Kotler, P., & Singh, R. (1984). Marketing strategy and the science of warfare. In R. B. Lamb (Ed.) *Competitive strategic anagement* (pp. 94–133). New York, NY: Prentice Hall.

Kover, A. J. (2001). Editorial: The sponsorship issue. *Journal of Advertising Research, 41*, 5.

Krashinsky, S. (2014). Nike starts playing Russia card in lead-up to Olympics. *Globe and Mail.* Retrieved January 28, 2014, from http://www.theglobeandmail.com/report-on-business/industry-news/marketing/nike-starts-playing-the-russia-card-in-lead-up-to-olympics/article16373912/

Kulula. (n.d.a). Kulula Airlines. Retrieved November 20, 2011, from https://www.kulula.com/

Kulula. (n.d.b). Kulula Sponsorship. Retrieved November 20, 2011, from https://www.kulula.com/info/oursponsorships.aspx

LawInSport. (2014). Homepage. Retrieved June 6, 2014, from http://www.lawinsport.com/about-us

Lettner, M., & Burton, R. (2014). Marketing and destination branding. In J. Beech, S. Kaiser & R. Kaspar (Eds.). *The business of events management.* New York, NY: Pearson Education Limited.

Lipovetsky, G. (2011, July 27). Ten inexpensive ways to reach your target market. *The Globe and Mail.* Retrieved February 28, 2014, at http://www.theglobeandmail.com/report-on-business/small-business/sb-tools/ten-inexpensive-ways-to-reach-your-target-market/article584372/

Liga de Beisbol Profesional Roberto Clemente (Puerto Rico). (n.d) Retrieved October 15, 2013, from http://www.ligapr.com

Lyberger, M. R., & McCarthy, L. (2001). An assessment of consumer knowledge of, interest in and perceptions of ambushing marketing strategies. *Sport Marketing Quarterly, 10*(2), 130–137.

MacIntosh, E., Nadeau, J., Séguin, B., O'Reilly, N., Bradish, C., & Legg, D. (2012). The role of mega-sports event interest in sponsorship and ambush marketing attitudes. *Sport Marketing Quarterly, 21*, 43–52.

Maher, A., Wilson, N., Signal, L., & Thomson, G. (2006). Patterns of sport sponsorship by gambling, alcohol and food companies: an Internet survey. *BMC Public Health, 6*, 95–99.

Mailonline. (2012). Sport: The 2013 golden ticket: Which sporting event are you looking forward to most next year? Retrieved October 14, 2013, from http://www.dailymail.co.uk/sport/article-2255245/2013-golden-ticket-The-main-sporting-events-year.html

Major League Baseball League. (n.d.) Retrieved October 15, 2013, from http://mlb.mlb.com/home

Major League Roller Hockey. (n.d). Retrieved October 19, 2013, from http://www.mlrh.com

Mangold, W. G., & Faulds, D. J. (2009). Social media: The new "hybrid" element of the promotion mix. *Business Horizons, 52*, 357–366.

Martyn, S. G. (1996). *Toward an impasse: An examination of the negotiations behind the inclusion of the United States Olympic Committee in the Olympic programme.* Centre for Olympic Studies, University of Western Ontario.

Mazodier, M., & Quester, P. (2010). Ambush marketing disclosure: Impact on attitudes toward the ambushers brand. *Recherche et Applications en Marketing, 25*(2), 52–67.

McCarville, R. E., & Copeland, R. P. (1994). Understanding sport sponsorship through exchange theory. *Journal of Sport Management, 8*, 102–14.

McLeary, N. (2007). Windsurfing: The application of common gym exercises to alternative sports. *Sportex Dynamics, 13*, 15–18.

Meenaghan, T. (1994). Point of view: Ambush marketing: Immoral or imaginative practice? *Journal of Advertising Research, 34*(5), 77–88.

Meenaghan, T. (1996). Ambush marketing: A threat to corporate sponsorship? *Sloan Management Review, 38*, 103–13.

Meenaghan, T. (2013). Measuring sponsorship performance: Challenge and direction. *Psychology and Marketing, 30*(5), 385–393.

Melanson, A. (2011). *The ABCs of RBC's philanthropic focus.* Bloom for nonprofits. Retrieved September 5, 2011, from http://bloomfornonprofits.com/2011/02/the-abcs-of-rbc%E2%80%99s-philanthropic-focus/

The Mexican League. (2013). Retrieved October 15, 2013, from http://www.milb.com/index.jsp?sid=l125%C2%A0

Meyer, M. (2009, August 3). One world, one dream, one year later. *Sports Illustrated*, 66–72.

Mickle, T., & Lefton, T. (2011, January 24). Subway signs fresh face Ohno. *SportsBusiness Journal*, *13*(36), 5.

Microsoft. (2014). Corporate citizenship. Retrieved June 18, 2014, from http://www.microsoft.com/about/corporatecitizenship/en-us/serving-communities/employee-giving/

Ministry of Business, Innovation & Employment. (2007). *A Guide to the Major Events Management Act 2007*. Retrieved October 28, 2011, from http://www.med.govt.nz/majorevents/pdf-library/resource-bank/guide-to-the-major-events-management-act-2007

Moerdyk, C. (2010). Kulula is outwitting FIFA at every turn. Retrieved November 20, 2011, from http://www.bizcommunity.com/Article/196/147/45942.html

Moorman, A. M., & Greenwell, T. C. (2005). Consumer attitudes of deception and the legality of ambush marketing practices. *Journal of the Legal Aspects of Sport*, *15*, 183–211.

Mullin, B., Hardy, S., & Sutton, W. (2000). *Sport marketing* (2nd ed.). Champaign, IL: Human Kinetics.

Mullin, B., Hardy, S., & Sutton, W. (2007). *Sport marketing* (3rd ed.). Champaign, IL: Human Kinetics.

National Lacrosse League. (2013). Retrieved October 19, 2013, from http://www.nll.com

National Pro Fast Pitch. (2013). Retrieved October 19, 2013, from http://www.profastpitch.com

NFL. (n.d.) Retrieved October 18, 2013, from http://www.nfl.com

Nicholas, L. (2011). Naked ambition: Strip bar threatened with fines for ambush marketing. The Sydney Morning Herald. Retrieved October 28, 2011, from http://www.smh.com.au/rugby-union/rugby-world-cup/naked-ambition-strip-bar-threatened-with-fines-for-ambush-marketing-20110930-1l0md.html

Nichols, L. (2011). A skate park in the Pentagon's likeness: Militarism, hegemony, and skateboarding on the web. *International Journal of Sport & Society*, *2*, 17–28.

Nicholls, J., Roslow, S., & Dublish, S. (1999). Brand recall and brand preference at sponsored golf and tennis tournaments. *European Journal of Marketing*, *33*(3/4), 365–387. Otker, T. (1988). Exploi-

tation: The key to sponsorship success. *Marketing and Research Today*, *16*(2), 77–86.

Nike. (2012, July 15). Nike launches find your greatness campaign. Retrieved Dec 10, 2013, from http://nikeinc.com/news/nike-launches-find-your-greatness-campaign-celebrating-inspiration-for-the-everyday-athlete

Nippon (Japan) Professional Baseball League. (n.d). Retrieved October 15, 2013, fromhttp://www.npb.or.jp/eng/

Official Website of the Olympic Movement, "The Organization" (2013a). Retrieved from Olympic.org http://www.olympic.org/about-ioc-institution

Official Website of the Olympic Movement, "International Sports Federations" (2013b). Retrieved from Olympic.org http://www.olympic.org/content/the-ioc/governance/international-federations/

O'Reilly, N., & Brunette, M. K. (2013). *Public private partnerships in physical activity and sport*. Champaign, IL: Human Kinetics.

O'Reilly, N., Gibbs, C., & Brunette, M. K. (2014). Professional team sport and Twitter: Gratifications sought and obtained by followers. *International Journal of Sport Communication*, *7*, 188–213.

O'Reilly, N., Nadeau, J., & Kaplan, A. (2011). Do fans want their team to be competitive in the short-term (the next game) or the long-term (the full season), and does the answer affect management decisions? *European Sport Management Quarterly*, *11*, 73–86.

O'Reilly, N., & Madill, J. (2012). The development of a process for evaluating marketing sponsorships, *Canadian Journal of Administrative Sciences*, *29*, 50–66.

O'Reilly, N., & Séguin, B. (2011). *Sport marketing: A Canadian perspective*. Toronto, CAN: Nelson Education.

O'Reilly, N., & Séguin, B. (2013). *Sport marketing: A Canadian perspective* (2nd ed.). Toronto, ON: Nelson Education Ltd.

OSEG. (2013). Lansdowne. Retrieved from http://www.oseg.ca/lansdowne/

Park, M., Yoh, T., Choi, Y., & Olson, M. (2011). Consumer attitudes toward the Paralympic Games and purchase intentions toward corporate sponsors of the Paralympic Games: Market segmentation strategy. *Journal of Venue & Event Management*, *3*, 1–15.

Payne, M. (1998). Ambush marketing: The undeserved advantage. *Psychology and Marketing*, *15*(4), 323–331.

Peachey, Kevin. (2012). *Olympics: Tackling ambush marketing at London 2012*. BBC News Business.

Retrieved July 25, 2013, from http://www.bbc.com/news/business-18628635

P&G. (2012, April 17). Procter & Gamble launches global thank you, Mom campaign. Retrieved October 25, 2013, from http://news.pg.com/blog/thank-you-mom/procter-gamble-launches-global-thank-you-mom-campaign

Pegoraro, A. L., Ayer, S. M., & O'Reilly, N. J. (2010). Consumer consumption and advertising through sport. *American Behavioral Scientist, 53*, 1454–1475.

Pointstreak. (n.d) Lacrosse. Retrieved October 19, 2013, from http://www.pointstreak.com/lacrosse/lacrosse-list.html

Portlock, A., & Rose, S. (2009). Effects of ambush marketing: UK consumer brand recall and attitudes to official sponsors and non-sponsors associated with the FIFA World Cup 2006. *International Journal of Sports Marketing and Sponsorship, 10*, 271–286.

Pound, D. (2004). *Inside the Olympics: A behind-the-scenes look at the politics, scandals, and the glory of the Games.* Canada: John C. Wiley and Sons Canada Ltd.

Pound, R. W. (1996). The importance of commercialism for the Olympic movement. International Olympic committee: Olympic message sources of financing sports, *3*, 10–13.

Pound, R. (2006) *Inside the Olympics.* Toronto: John Wiley and Sons Canada.

Pound, R. W. (2008). The rule of law at an Olympic moment, *Journal of Parliamentary and Political Law,* 2 JPARPL 1 at 1.

Professional Auto Racing. (n.d.). In *Wikipedia.* Retrieved October 15, 2013, from http://en.wikipedia.org/wiki/Auto_racing

The Professional Hockey Leagues of North America. (n.d.) Retrieved October 19, 2013, from http://www.dickestel.com/hockeyleagues.htm

The Richest (2014). Retrieved Nov 10, 2014, from http://www.therichest.com/sports/the-top-10-highest-paid-boxers-of-all-time/

Rifon, N. J., Choi, S. M., Trimble, C. S., & Li, H. (2004). Congruence effects in sponsorship: The mediating role of sponsor credibility and consumer attributions of sponsor motive. *Journal of Advertising, 33*, 29–42.

Robertson, D., & Pope, N. (1999). Product bundling and causes of attendance and non-attendance in live professional sport: A case study of the Brisbane Broncos and the Brisbane Lions. *Cyber Journal of Sport Marketing, 3*(1). Retrieved from pandora.nla.gov/tcp/10007

Sandler, D. M., & Shani, D. (1993). Sponsorship and the Olympic Games: The consumer perspective. *Sport Marketing Quarterly, 2*(3), 38–43.

Sauer, Abram (n.d.). Ambush marketing: Steals the show. Brand Channel. Retrieved June 28, 2013, from http://www.brandchannel.com/features_effect.asp?pf_id=98

Scassa, T. (2011). Ambush marketing and the right of association: Clamping down on the reference to that big event with all the athletes in a couple of years. *Journal of Sport Management, 25*, 354–370.

Scotia Bank. (n.d.). Sponsorships. Retrieved January 4, 2012, from http://www.scotiabank.com/ca/en/0,,2469,00.html

Séguin, B., Lyberger, M., O'Reilly, N., & McCarthy, L. (2005). Internationalizing ambush marketing: The Olympic brand and country of origin. *International Journal of Sport Sponsorship and Marketing, 6*(4).

Séguin, B., & O'Reilly, N. (2007). Sponsorship in the trenches: Case study evidence of its legitimate place in the promotional mix. *The Sport Journal, 10.* Retrieved from http://www.the sport journal.org/article/sponsorship-in-the-trenches-case-study-evidence-of-its-legitimate-place-in-the-promotional-mix

Séguin, B., & O'Reilly, N. (2008). The Olympic brand, ambush marketing, and clutter. *International Journal of Sport Management and Marketing, 4*, 62–84.

Sibley, A. (2012, July 12). 8 of the biggest marketing faux pas of all time. *Inbound Marketing.* Retrieved February 27, 2014, from http://blog.hubspot.com/blog/tabid/6307/bid/33396/8-of-the-Biggest-Marketing-Faux-Pas-of-All-Time.aspx

Shani, D., & Sandler, D.M. (1998). Ambush marketing: Is confusion to blame for the flickering of the flame? *Psychology & Marketing, 15*, 367–383.

Shaw, H. (2010). Olympic ambush. *The Montreal Gazette.* Retrieved January 3, 2012, from http://www.montrealgazette.com/business/money/Olympic+ambush/2529181/story.html

Sleight, S. (1989). *Sponsorship: What it is and how to use it.* London: McGraw-Hill.

SportAccord. (2012). List of International Sports Federations. Retrieved October 11, 2013, from http://www.sportaccord.com/en/members/index.php?idContent=644

Statistic Brain (2014). Retrieved July 3, 2014, from http://www.statisticbrain.com/nascar-racing-statistics/

Statistics Canada. (2012). *Focus on geography series, 2011 census.* Statistics Canada catalogue no. 98-310-XWE2011004. Ottawa, Ontario. Analytical products, 2011 Census. Last updated October 24, 2012. Retrieved from http://www12.statcan .gc.ca/census-recensement/2011/as-sa/fogs-spg /Facts-cma-eng.cfm?LANG=Eng&GK=CMA& GC=505

Statistics Canada. (2013). Median total income, by family type, by census metropolitan area. CAN SIM, table 111-0009. Retrieved from http:// www.statcan.gc.ca/tables-tableaux/sum-som/l01 /cst01/famil107a-eng.htm

Stikeman Elliot. (n.d.). Intellectual property law of Canada (pp. 2–11). Retrieved from http://www .stikeman.com/cps/rde/xchg/se-en/hs.xsl/1313 .htm

Stal, Patrick. (2010). FIFA's persistence builds perception of Bavaria brand in Netherlands. Retrieved September 24, 2011, from http://www .interbrand.com/en/knowledge/blog/post/2010 -06-23/FIFA-s-persistance-builds-perception-of -Bavaria-brand-in-Netherlands.aspx

Stotlar, D. K. (1993). Sponsorship and the Olympic winter games. *Sport Marketing Quarterly*, 2, 35–43.

Strasser, J. B., & Becklund, L. (1991, 1993). Swoosh: The unauthorized story of Nike and the men who played there. New York, NY: Harcourt Brace Jovanovich.

Sweney, M. (2012). Olympics 2012: Nike plots ambush ad campaign. *The Guardian.* Retrieved January 21, 2014, from http://www.theguardian.com /media/2012/jul/25/olympics-2012-nike-am bush-ad

Tapscott, D. (2009). Grown up digital. New York, NY: McGraw Hill.

Topendsports. (2013). Major world sporting event calendar. Retrieved October 13, 2013, from http:// www.topendsports.com/events/calendar.htm

TORONTO 2015 Pan American/Parapan American Games. (2013). About the Toronto 2015 Parapan Am Games. Retrieved October 7, 2013, from http://www.toronto2015.org/lang/en/the -games/about-the-toronto-2015-parapan-am -games.html

Tripodi, J. (2001). Sponsorship—A confirmed weapon in the promotional armoury. *International Journal of Sports Marketing and Sponsorship*, 3(1), March/April, 1–20.

UCI World Tour. (2013). UCI World Tour calendar 2013. Retrieved October 18, 2013, from http://www.uciprotour.com/templates/BUILTIN

-NOFRAMES/Template3/layout.asp?MenuId =MTY2NzU&LangId=1

Ueberroth, P. (1985). *Made in America.* New York, NY: William Morrow and Company.

Ultimate Fighting Championship (UFC). (2013). Retrieved October 19, 2013, from http://www .ufc.ca

Union Cycliste Internationale. (2013). Mission statement. Retrieved October 10, 2013, from.http:// www.uci.ch/templates/UCI/UCI3/layout.asp? MenuId=MTY4MzM&LangId=1

Union de Pentathlon Moderne (UIPM). (2013). Retrieved October 10, 2013, from http://www .pentathlon.org

Valtat. A. (2013, March 8). Playing with our senses: Unveiling neuromarketing techniques [blog]. Retrieved February 28, 2014, at http://aurelievaltat .eu/playing-with-our-senses-unveiling-neuromar keting-techniques/

Vail, S. (2007). Community development and sport participation. *Journal of Sport Management*, 21, 571–596.

Valtat. A. (2013, March 8). Playing with our senses: Unveiling neuromarketing techniques [blog]. Retrieved February 28, 2014, at http://aurielieval tat.eu/playing-with-our-senses-unveiling-neuro marketing-techniques/

VANOC. (2008). *Real 2010: Protecting the brand.* Vancouver, BC: Vancouver Organizing Committee for the Olympic Games.

VANOC. (2010). *The Vancouver Organizing Committee for 2010 Olympic and Paralympic Winter Games.* Retrieved October 10, 2011, from http:// www.canada2010.gc.ca/prtnrs/covanoc/050101 -eng.cfm

Vinjamuri, D. (2012). U.S. Athletes Are Right About Twitter: Rule 40 Exposes the Flaw in Olympic Thinking. Forbes. Retrieved June 23, 2013, from http://www.forbes.com/sites/david vinjamuri/2012/08/01/the-athletes-are-right-about -twitter-rule-40-exposes-the-paradox-at-the-core -of-the-olympic-games/

Visa. (2011). Visa You and 10 Super Bowl sweepstakes & Visa NFL integrated marketing campaign. Retrieved October 25, 2013, from http:// corporate.visa.com/_media/visa-nfl-campaign.pdf

Volleywood. (2013). Professional League Champions. Retrieved October 19, 2013, from http:// www.volleywood.net/leagues/spain/various-pro fessional-leagues-global/

Watercutter, A. (2013). How Oreo won the marketing Super Bowl with a timely blackout ad on Twitter. *Globe and Mail.* Retrieved February 25,

2014, from http://www.wired.com/underwire/2013/02/oreo-twitter-super-bowl/

Water Polo Australia. (2013). Retrieved October 19, 2013, from http://www.australianwaterpolo.com.au

Weeks, C. (2014, February). Olympic athletes urged to cut ties with sponsors like McDonald's and Coke. *The Globe and Mail.* Retrieved February 21, 2014, from www.globeandmail.com.

Wei, W. (2012). Nike's fantastic find your greatness ad campaign was the most pirated ad this month. Business Insider. Retrieved December 16, 2013, from http://www.businessinsider.com/the-10-most-viral-ads-of-august-2012-8

West, G. (2013). Nike inspires a winter sport with "play Russian" just do it campaign. Retrieved January 25, 2014, from http://www.thedrum.com/news/2013/11/29/nike-inspires-winter-sport-play-russian-just-do-it-campaign-designed-russian-market

Wilkinson, D. G. (1993). *Sponsorship Marketing: A Practical Reference Guide for Corporations in the 1990's.* Toronto, CAN: The Wilkinson Group, (p. 287).

Williams, S. (2014). Sochi 2014: Sweden hockey star Nicklas Baskstrom sixth doping case of Games. *The Sydney Morning Herald.* Retrieved February 24, 2014, from http://www.smh.com.au/sport/winter-olympics/sochi-2014-swedish-hockey-star-nicklas-backstrom-sixth-doping-case-of-games-20140224-33b25.html

Winkler, L. (2008). Rich history of U.S. presidents and sports. Pipe Dream, November 4. Retrieved November 4, 2014, from http://www.bupipedream.com/archive/5718/rich-history-of-us-presidents-and-sports/

World Anti-Doping Agency. (2009). Constitutive Instrument of Foundation. Retrieved from http://www.wada-ama.org/Documents/About_WADA_Statutes_2009_EN.pdf

World Anti-Doping Agency. (2014a). About WADA. Retrieved June 20, 2014, from http://www.wada-ama.org/en/About-WADA/

World Anti-Doping Agency. (2014b). Governance. Retrieved June 20, 2014, from http://www.wada-ama.org/en/About-WADA/Governance/

World Anti-Doping Agency. (2014c). Strategic plan. Retrieved June 20, 2014, from http://www.wada-ama.org/en/About-WADA/History-Mission-Priorities-and-Strategic-Plan/Strategic-Plan/

World Archery. (2013). History of world archery. Retrieved October 10, 2013, from http://www.worldarchery.org/en-us/home/history/historyofworldarchery.aspx

World Boxing Association. (2013). Events. Retrieved October 16, 2013, from http://wbanews.com

World Curling Federation. (2013). About & events. Retrieved October 10, 2013, from http://www.worldcurling.org/about-the-wcf

World Rowing. (2013). Retrieved October 10, 2013, from http://www.worldrowing.com/fisa

World Rugby. (n.d). About the Rugby World Cup. Retrieved October 28, 2011, from http://www.rugbyworldcup.com/

World Taekwondo Federation. (2013). Retrieved October 10, 2013, from http://www.tkd-itf.org/pagina.php?idpag=1120&web=47&lng=3

World Wrestling Entertainment. (2013). Retrieved October 19, 2013, from http://www.wwe.com

Yahoo! Sports. (2012). Clever billboard from Durex wins gold medal for Olympics advertising. Retrieved December 4, 2013, from http://blog.sfgate.com/olympics/2012/07/31/clever-billboard-from-durex-wins-gold-medal-for-olympics-advertising/

Yan, A. (2013). 2014 Winter Olympic games in Sochi, Russia: Most expensive Olympic games ever—estimated cost, $50 billion, so far. *Travelers Today.* Retrieved June 24, 2014, from http://www.travelerstoday.com/articles/4523/20130204/2014-winter-olympic-games-sochi-russia-expensive-50-billion-50-london-ice-dome.htm

Young, N. (2012). How Nike pulled off brilliant ambush marketing in the Olympics. *The Drum.* Retrieved July 18, 2013, from http://www.thedrum.com/news/2012/08/22/how-nike-pulled-brilliant-ambush-marketing-olympics